*ACHILLES AND THE TORTOISE*

# Mark Twain's Fictions

"Achilles will never be able to overtake the Tortoise. He must first reach the point from which the Tortoise started. By that time the Tortoise will have got someway ahead. Achilles must make that up, and again the Tortoise will be ahead. He is always coming nearer, but he never makes up to it."

—the paradox of Zeno of Elea,
as recorded by Aristotle in *Physics*

"By the terms of the Law of Periodical Repetition nothing whatever can happen a single time only; everything happens again, and again, and yet again, and still again—monotonously. Nature has no originality—I mean, no large ability in the matter of inventing new things, new ideas, new stage effects. She has a superb and amazing and infinitely varied equipment of old ones, but she never adds to them. She repeats—repeats—repeats—repeats."

—the "Mad Philosopher" as quoted in
Mark Twain's "Papers of the Adam Family"

# ACHILLES
## AND THE TORTOISE
# Mark Twain's Fictions

## Clark Griffith

The University of Alabama Press
Tuscaloosa and London

Copyright © 1998
The University of Alabama Press
Tuscaloosa, Alabama 35487-0380
All rights reserved
Manufactured in the United States of America
First Paperback Edition 2000
1 2 3 4 5 • 04 03 02 01 00
∞

The paper on which this book is printed meets the minimum requirements of
the American National Standard for Information Science-Permanence of Paper
for Printed Library Materials, ANSI Z39.48-1984.

Library of Congress Cataloging-in-Publication Data

Griffith, Clark, 1924–
    Achilles and the tortoise : Mark Twain's fictions / Clark
Griffith.
       p. cm.
    Includes bibliographical references (p.) and index.
    ISBN 0-8173-1039-8 (alk. paper)
       1.  Twain, Mark, 1835–1910—Criticism and interpretation.
    2.  Humorous stories, American—History and criticism.  I.  Title.
    PS1338.G75   1998
    818'.409—dc21                                            97-33330


British Library Cataloguing-in-Publication data available

*For Audrey and Abby*
*For Brad, Sam and Carl*

# CONTENTS

# Acknowledgments

It has occurred to me that among the handful of colleagues whom I both admired and liked during thirty-five years in the academy, three were Mark Twain experts. The late Walter Blair did me a good many kindnesses over the years. John C. Gerber was my first graduate teacher of any real value, and later a colleague and friend. Though I have not seen him for a quarter of a century, Paul Baender remains something more than a pleasant memory. I suppose I have produced a Mark Twain who, in some respects, would (will) be a mysterious stranger to all three. But I have written with their dedication to craft and scholarship constantly in mind.

The first draft of the manuscript was read by Messrs. Michael Stamm and Michael Snell. Mr. Paul Wotipka read the second. Their criticisms, often severe, always kept me aware that the book had some potential if only I was willing to work at it. Professor Louis J. Budd proved a generous and particularly helpful reader of the final draft. By drawing attention to how I needed to distinguish between "Humor" as used in Jonson's comedies (and as I believe in the work of both Mark Twain and Melville) and the current, common usage, as in the title of the journal *Studies in American Humor,* Professor Budd forced me to revise for the last time, and made my presentation much clearer.

I am grateful to the staff at the Knight Library of the University of Oregon for putting in my hands early on a photocopy of the Reverend George Sumner Weaver's *Lectures on Mental Science According to the Philosophy of Phrenology,* a pamphlet on morality and the "humors" that Sam Clemens read and heavily annotated in 1855. As it turned out, all the essential information was present and of course much more accessible in an excellent essay by Professor Allen Gribben—but there was no way of knowing this at the time.

Finally, I need to acknowledge several graduate students at Oregon who, in seminars in Mark Twain or Melville or in lecture courses combining Mark Twain with Melville, were patient with my ideas, and both challenged and refined them through their papers and comments. They include, more or less chronologically, Mr. James Lyndon Johnson and Mr. James Caron, whose dissertations I presently directed and who have gone on to make their own significant contributions to the study of Mark Twain and of American humor; Mr. Victor Bobb; Mr. Michael Powell; Ms. Angela Estes; Mr. Wotipka; Mr. Snell; and Ms. Perrin Kerns, whose casual observation that Bakhtin might shed some light on the end of *Huckleberry Finn* persuaded me that when it does not dissolve into jargon (or, more especially, encourage the jargon of its English Department acolytes) the shock of the new can be a very useful context for better understanding the old.

I seem to remember William Empson saying somewhere that while he delighted in the play of ideas that caused him to see things in a new way and hence made revisions a pleasure, he had little taste for revising in terms of style sheets and academic manuals. I thank my editor at The University of Alabama Press, Mr. Curtis Clark, for respecting my preference for Empson over the world's nit-pickers.

A dozen or so sentences in the third essay are taken from my paper, "Merlin's Grin: From 'Tom' to 'Huck' in *A Connecticut Yankee*," *New England Quarterly* 48 (March 1975), 26–48; half again that many in the essay on *Pudd'nhead Wilson* appeared first in my paper, "*Pudd'nhead Wilson* As Dark Comedy," *Journal of English Literary History* 62 (Spring 1976), 209–28. Reviewing both papers, I have found them not wrong, but inadequate in their "rightness"; this book seeks among other things to amend their shortcomings. I am grateful to the editors for permission to reuse a little of the old material here. I have the permission of Little, Brown to quote from *The Collected Poems of Emily Dickinson*, #125, "For each ecstatic instant." I have the permission of Harcourt Brace to quote nine lines from Richard Wilbur's translation of Molière's *Tartuffe*.

*ACHILLES AND THE TORTOISE*
# Mark Twain's Fictions

# The Essays: Form and Content

What eludes [us] . . . in his gaze?
                    —Wright Morris of *Pudd'nhead Wilson*[1]

Science has found a treatment which inhibits one form of cancer, while it simultaneously induces the growth of another.
                    —a recent issue of *Time Magazine*

## I

These essays attempt to show how Mark Twain organized his fictions and, in turn, was himself reorganized in the process of creating them. Seeking an answer to Wright Morris's question (what were those sad, cold eyes looking at?), the essays arrive ineluctably at the conclusion that, over and over, they were focused upon the bitter realization, the vision of a complete moral and social futility, which is embodied in *Time*'s sardonic commentary upon one example of modern medical research. In demonstration, issues are raised about the narratives, and much indebted to criticism that has gone before, I try to supply resolutions that will seem both fresh and plausible. Some of the issues are old hat: what were Simon Wheeler's motives? how do we explain the melancholy— and more to the point, the oddly parallel—endings of *Huckleberry Finn* and *A Connecticut Yankee in King Arthur's Court*? Others take a more original tack: why is the ultimate accolade paid to Horace Bixby ("'he's a lightning pilot'") accompanied with the sobering thought that he is this by virtue of being "'the Shadow of Death'"?; in "A Recent Carnival of Crime in Connecticut," where someone dies and someone else survives, which is which?; why must Injun Joe die so needlessly and absurdly in McDougal's Cave?; while he was agreeing to foreshorten the manuscript, why at almost the last minute did Mark Twain add two and a half new chapters to *The Adventures of Huckleberry Finn*?; what is the true relationship between the Italian twins and the outcome of *Pudd'nhead Wilson*?; who is the stranger who "corrupts" Hadleyburg (and what, in context, does "corrupt" signify)?; why, professing to despise everything Poe wrote, was

Mark Twain drawn steadily toward Poe's gothic effects, so that in virtually the last thing he wrote, he constructs a haunted castle, and in the manner of "House of Usher" discerns the crack that will presently bring it down in ruins? Underlying all the questions, whether conventional, or ones that seem to have dropped through the cracks of prior analysis, are two yet more fundamental matters, invariably posed by students of Mark Twain, yet often forgotten along the way so that they are not so invariably answered. Why is he funny? How is it that, focusing upon the bitter and the meaningless, he can consistently cause us to laugh at this spectacle?

Strictly speaking they are essays, not chapters in a book. Each develops its own argument, is self-contained, and can be read independently of the others. It may as well be added that the material proved somewhat less tractable when I sought to reshape it as chapters, under a more informative and engaging title. Yet quite as if they were chapters, the essays are meant to be taken in consecutively, and hence seen as stepping stones or building blocks toward the development of a sustained and coherent thesis. The terms of the thesis are fourfold: I shall call them The Comic Impulse; The Creation of Caricatures; The Twin Faces of Reality; and Philosophical Speculations about Reality. My methods as an essayist will be clarified, I think, if I list the four in tabular form, undertake a brief definition of each, and suggest in a very preliminary way complications that can arise from assembling them as they were regularly assembled in Mark Twain's imagination.

*The Comic Impulse.* Mark Twain yearned to regard life, and the literature he based on life, comically. The pattern he would gladly have brought to his work is that of Shakespeare in the romantic comedies (particularly *Much Ado About Nothing* and *A Comedy of Errors*), of Dickens in *David Copperfield,* and, still closer at hand, the one Howells utilized for *The Rise of Silas Lapham.* Outrageous things occur; life seems all but overwhelmed by the sudden intrusion of dark and complex vicissitudes; the identity and other precious and personal entitlements are lost or stolen. But because the outrages happen, major figures work through them, or are moved through them, or both work and are moved toward the achievement of a comic resolution. Mark Twain had little taste for the wedding vows which seal and sanctify the happy ending in Shakespeare and Dickens (neither, for that matter, did Howells). Rather, together with Howells, he associated the comic ending with the drama of an initiation story. Having borne up under hardship, having vanquished temptation, the comically transfigured self would come to (be granted) a new understanding of the meaning of selfhood and of one self's obligations and responsibilities to other selves in the human community. Although Mark Twain would hardly have used the term, the successful *rite de passage* is beyond doubt one of the matters he had in mind when he spoke of the moral seriousness, the necessity for "preaching" and "teaching," which lay at the core of his humor.[2]

*The Creation of Caricatures.* In our mind's eye we persist in figuring Mark Twain as the creator of what writing manuals like to call the "well-rounded," "fully realized" human character. The fact is, however, that the bent of his genius lay in a very different direction. From first to last he was the inventor of freaks, grotesques, human deformities: the inveterate creator, in a word, of caricatures. As a technique of the cartoonist, caricature consists of squeezing the complete personality into one all-defining physical detail (the Nixon nose, the Neanderthal brow of Ronald Reagan, the rubber features of Bill Clinton, etc.). In the fiction of Mark Twain, this same technique results in personalities who seem rooted morally and emotionally to one spot, who are constrained to do and to say the same things as if by rote; whose lives are dominated by the repetitive and the unalterable, by obsessive patterns of behavior. From these highly specialized selves, and not out of variety or "well-roundedness," Mark Twain generates laughter. Well before the point was formulated in 1900, he perfectly exemplified the central insight of Henri Bergson's theory of laughter. He understood, with Bergson, that we laugh at the *thing* trying to be a human being, at the encrustation of the mechanical on to the living.[3]

*Comedy vs. Caricature.* Clearly the two are incompatible, perhaps even adversarial in their relationship. David Copperfield is ideally well suited to be the comic hero. He can change, develop, throw off the crippling obsessions—the compulsion to be loved; the equally compulsive need to protect and serve others—which were imposed upon him by an unhappy childhood. By contrast, and however unlike they are in other respects, Steerforth and Mr. Micawber share the fate of having no comic future. As the one must trick, deceive, betray, and deceive and betray again, until he is finally eliminated by the book, so the other is constrained to speak only of prodigious hopes and groundless expectations—and would no doubt be speaking of them still were we to locate him in the Australian outback to which, having exhausted his possibilities for laughter, the book eventually banishes him. Eschewing the presentation of David Copperfield types (his one attempt at emulation resulted in the very different *Adventures of Tom Sawyer*) Mark Twain avoided Dickens's mawkishness, what passes for his "moral sublime," but is actually the unbridled sentimentality of many episodes and of the closing pages of the book. But exceeding Dickens in the art of caricature, he is left with Steerforths and Micawbers who cut him off from Dickens's initiation motifs. The conflict between a desired action, and actors who cannot possibly encompass and perform it, begets a frustration which is indispensable to any understanding of how and what Mark Twain wrote.

*Reality—Its Two Guises.* Like Howells, whom he deeply admired, but also like George Eliot who "just tire[d] [him] to death,"[4] Mark Twain was a realistic writer, in the great tradition of nineteenth-century literary realism. As such, he had no difficulty with definitions which have proved ambiguous and troublesome to a more recent sensibility. Reality, for him, was readily apprehended as the complex events and circumstances that take place in the world out there. Physically, the real was likely to be River, village, villagers, and the villagers' interrelationships; as a preoccupation with history took over, the locus of reality was merely shifted to the villages and villagers of other times and places. Aesthetically and morally, the real consisted of "real grasshoppers" in opposition to "artificial" ones, as Howells put it in a famous passage; it was the dreary, ugly, yet quite unavoidable accumulation of details which George Eliot assembles in Chapter 17 of *Adam Bede.*[5] But if the shape and texture of the real gave Mark Twain no trouble, his sense of how reality operates to affect human lives led him into a contradiction of truly fascinating proportions.

In one sense life lived fully and deeply in the real is an absolute prerequisite to any drama of comic fulfillment and moral initiation. Two kinds of people weave their ways through Mark Twain's narrative world. There are fantasizers who seek to take the real world into their heads, to subdue it with language, to spice up the dreary, ugly and familiar with images and conceptions of their own devising. Such figures are foolish, foolhardy, and without necessarily meaning to be the creators of dark mischief for themselves and others; above all they are fixated—locked always in place by the sheer demands of ego. Then, there are the realists. More respectful of what is out there, realists are by virtue of this knowledge truer and richer personalities; figures endowed with greater adaptability; not necessarily happier in the real world, but far more attuned to the world as an existent fact, to who and where they are with regard to reality, and to the obligations they bear to others in human society. They deserve initiation therefore—except that by a strange paradox they are prevented from attaining it by the nature of reality itself.

To grasp the paradox, we must again distinguish between what we think of Mark Twain and how Mark Twain actually thought. In the stereotype he is the creator of people whose itchy feet and yen to be forever on the go are the equivalent of his own. They may travel far: to Arkansas or Camelot. They may simply circulate up and down the byways of a more limited environment. At all events they strike us as perpetually in motion. And yet, and yet. No aspect of his work can be more curious—or more persistent—than Mark Twain's certainty that nothing and nobody ever really moves at all. The world and its occupants stand stone still, as though life were congealed and petrified. Yesterday and today; the time and place of departure, the place and time of arrival; the first step and the last step of any journey: these are not different points in time and space. They are a single, unparticled and undifferentiated point, made to seem different only by being labeled with different names. The discrepancy between the appearance of motion and the actual underlying stasis of all things is nothing less than Mark Twain's standard joke.

In telling and retelling the joke, he anticipates what amounts to an unresolved contradiction in Bergson's *Laughter*. For Bergson, nature, a source of grace, flexibility and suppleness, is the desideratum for human behavior, while at the same time from "heartless, witless" nature come the traps—the instinctual drives and other tics—that mechanize human life. Aware of the contradiction, Bergson chooses to slip quietly past it, as seems often the way with romantic philosophers. But as a writer of realism Mark Twain was forced to meet head on the twin guises of reality. On the one hand, people are rendered into caricatures by withdrawing from the real into the mechanics and rituals of some private fantasy. On the other hand, the fixed and frozen features of reality are imposed upon people—to turn them into caricatures. Starting out with opposite premises, "fantasizers" and "realists" are seen to end up in the role of collaborators, even as co-conspirators. They constitute a unified, monolithic personality, one which is made to seem various only because of the fiat of nomenclature, which calls one a "fantasizer," terms the other a "realist."

*Philosophizings.* The idea that movement is illusory both predates and postdates Mark Twain's curious insight. It was the central tenet of pre-Socratic philosophy from whence it emerges most famously as Zeno's paradoxical account of the Tortoise and Achilles, eternally engaged in their fixated, running-in-place race to nowhere:

> Achilles will never be able to overtake the Tortoise. He must first reach the point from which the Tortoise started. By that time the Tortoise will have got someway ahead. Achilles must make that up, and again the Tortoise will be ahead. He is always coming nearer, but he never makes up to it.[6]

More modernly, an identical sense of stasis launches the absurd world of Camus's *Myth of Sisyphus*:

> Rising, streetcar, four hours in the office or the factory, meal, streetcar, four hours of work, meal, sleep, and Monday Tuesday Wednesday Thursday Friday and Saturday according to the same rhythm.[7]

—and produces in Sisyphus a figure forever completing the same action, forever recognizing that the action is left incomplete and meaningless. Where the alleged truth of experience is so utterly foreign to everyday perception, the images to express the disparity would seem to require the intensely strange tinged with the air of a certain kookiness.

A commonplace has held that philosophizing was not good for Mark Twain, that his development as a writer was impeded when he moved from dramatizing toward abstract speculation, or that his humor turned to philosophic propositions fated him to become dry, sterile and humorless.[8] The fact remains, nevertheless, that appreciating the playfulness of his imagination, we must accept in the bargain the philosophical origins from which the play sprang. That the world stood stone still was self-evident to Sam Clemens as early as 1855, when he recorded the fact mockingly in the first of his notebooks. Between 1865 and 1910, the question (and consequences) of why it does so gave rise to some of the funniest, as well as most poignant passages in Mark Twain's art. What is man?, in other words, could be the cream of the jest long before Mark Twain may have spoiled the fun by commencing to take and ask the question seriously.

The resistances, the response of *yes, but,* which I hope have been evoked by these generalizations will (I also hope) in some measure be countered by the seven ensuing essays. Through copious illustration the first three attempt to make more specific the essentials of Mark Twain's art. They take for subjects the failure of the comic structure, the jokes and laughter that were left to Mark Twain in the wake of each new failure, and the Janus-face of reality that liberates one in order to leave one enslaved. I call them "polemical" essays, not because they present an extreme case, but in terms of the extremities that were necessary to Mark Twain in his presentation of the caricatures of a caricature-making world. In Part II, the three essays take a somewhat different look at what James Cox and others have called the trilogy of the Mississippi River. Emphasis falls not simply upon typologies of scene, situation, and character types in *Tom Sawyer, Huckleberry Finn,* and *Pudd'nhead Wilson;* the concern is also with continuity of theme. The argument is that in the first and most trivial of the three books, Mark Twain came close to realizing a comic ending, only to watch it slip from his grasp in the concluding episodes. The next two books, whatever else they do, investigate the full consequences of this disappearance.

The last and longest essay needs special explanation. Because he tended to scorn the "dead" writers and their "dead" literature as dull and tiresome and full of pompous truths which were in reality barefaced lies, Mark Twain encourages the perception that his own writing sprang *sui generis* from low brow American humor, and until near the end at least was more nearly addressed to "belly" and "members" than to thought or ideas. Probably one side of him—the tough-guy/showman/entrepreneurial side—would have rejoiced in the view that, working the vein of conventional nineteenth-century fiction, he was but a "jackleg novelist."[9] But my objectives are unabashedly literary and philosophical. In ways that I feel are true to the deeper and more sophisticated Mark Twain, I want to relate his work to such "highbrow" contexts as a theory of comedy, to other aspects of critical theory and to traditional metaphysics. I want to view his work through the eyes of writers whom he actively mocked or no doubt would have ridiculed had he ever known about them. Melville fulfills this purpose in part, though he does so with a special warrant.

Repeatedly as I encountered the mock doleful tones of getting nowhere in Mark Twain, I heard the tones echoed by the brooding, yet chipper voice of Ishmael in *Moby-Dick*. Putting together the two writers who seem never to have met or read from one another is not a wholly new idea. There are cross references to *Moby-Dick* and *Huckleberry Finn* in Daniel Hoffman's study of the American fable; Richard B. Hauck's "cheerful nihilism" is seen to provide an atmosphere for both *The Confidence Man* and *Life on the Mississippi*; and Kenneth S. Lynn, trying to prophesy Huck's probable fate in the "territory," has invoked images of the *Pequod*, "not so much bound to any haven ahead as rushing from all havens astern."[10] Gradually, though, I came to believe that, no matter how different were their means of expressing what they saw, Melville and Mark Twain looked at reality and the human being's impossible relations with the real world in exactly the same way. In my last two-part essay I shall portray them first as writers who discerned at the core of human experience what Ishmael calls "a vast practical joke": a joke which both fascinated and victimized, a joke which neither writer always appreciated, though each was constrained to tell and repeat it endlessly. And finally I shall couple them as two old men, writing with no thought of immediate publication, but writing in search of the meaning of the joke—twins at last in *Billy Budd* and *The Mysterious Stranger Manuscripts*, if only because their representation of the cosmic jest has always involved them in an elaborate theory of twinship and in the practice, throughout all their work, of the fine art of twinning. I will argue that, contrary to all our presuppositions, this obsession with doubles doubled the great realist and the primary exemplar (in fiction) of the American Renaissance into secret sharers, purveyors of essentially the same dark vision.

## II

"You're a difficult problem," said K, comparing them as he had already done several times; "how am I to know one of you from the other? The only difference between you is your names; otherwise you're as like as—" He stopped and then went on voluntarily: "You're as like as two snakes."
—Kafka in *The Castle*

There have been two key influences, one overt and constant, the other more nearly an occasional partner, on the form of my essays. W. H. Auden has supplied (or has confirmed for me) not just the definitions of such crucial terms as "comic," "laughter," "jokes," "practical jokers," and "sick jokes"; I have freely appropriated the combination of exposition with outline which is a characteristic of Auden's prose pieces. The outline form seems beautifully adapted to the way Mark Twain himself organizes: to both the episodic nature of his fictions, and his habit of setting up some clear and distinct position and then doubling it into its opposite in order to render it ambiguous before demolishing its effectiveness entirely. Outlining also accords with his tendency to treat narratives, short and long, as the debates or colloquies conducted between adversaries, who as it turns out are strangely linked. It is a tendency which has called to mind a second influence upon my approach to Mark Twain.

Although direct references to Mikhail Bakhtin do not appear until well along in the book, and then are chiefly restricted to two sections of the essay on *Huckleberry Finn*, I have been conscious throughout of the degree to which Bakhtin's sense of a "destructive monologism" describes Mark Twain's structures, the simple, straightforward confrontation of "Recent Carnival of Crime in Connecticut," which is a dialogue spoken by two confirmed monologists, as well as the far subtler and more complex divisions of *Tom Sawyer* and *Pudd'nhead Wilson*, where all the apparent look of community is lost in a babble of monologistic voices, each one speaking to and for and of itself. Conversely the most life-affirming moments in Mark Twain—Huck and Jim on the raft; Hank Morgan's delivery of Camelot from the world Arthur botched into a "happy, prosperous kingdom"—would seem to reflect Bakhtin's "dialogic imagination," with its meeting at the boundary of selfhood of different individuals, who while retaining their unique identities are yet able to *"look into the eyes of one another or with the eyes of another."*[11] But of course the joyous moments never last in Mark Twain; they are merely the illusions of a fixed and rigidified world, where nothing ever moves or changes. And, again, in Bakhtin's terminology lies an apt description of their failures. One way of thinking about the last fifth of *Huckleberry Finn* is to call it a "carnival" lapsing back into the darkness and chaos of the "saturnalia"—or better yet, perhaps, as an example of carnival atmosphere cruelly disguising the saturnalian.

I am aware that a collection of essays allows one the kind of latitude that is not necessarily positive or productive. For example, I have been able to deal at length with "Old Times on the Mississippi" and the ending of *Huckleberry Finn* in two different places and in two considerably different ways, a practice that the more straitened form of a group of chapters would probably discourage.

Again, since each essay works out of a special focus and has its own closure, I may have left to the reader the need for establishing more transitions than even a well-disposed reader will care to make. The results will perhaps seem needless repetition, lack of continuity, redundancy intermingled with a certain choppiness. Yet I like to think that in repeating and foregrounding and calling for connections that at times remain only implied, I as critic and explicator have to some extent written in imitation of Mark Twain's own practice, as over the course of fifty years he ventured from fiction to fiction.

Early in the twentieth century he left unpublished a sketch which, in later times, Albert Bigelow Paine would appropriately entitle "The Victims." The sketch is about picnicking, a pot-luck supper for the young of some nameless, hypothetical village. Accordingly, it is about relations between the children who set forth and doting mothers who see to it that each takes along to potluck a suitable contribution.[12]

First, the village and picnic atmospheres are established when little Johnny Microbe begs to attend, saying "all the nicest creatures [in town] were going to be there." After invoking protection for him from the Great Spirit, Mama Microbe equips him in style by looking up Little Willie Molecule, also on *his* way to the picnic, and biting off Willie's head. Thereafter we mount swiftly up what Romantics, humanists, and Charles Darwin would call the organic and well-organized Great Chain of Being. As Microbe kills Molecule, so (I omit certain steps) Johnny Microbe is killed by Mama Anthrax; Peter Anthrax is killed by Mama Germ; Germ is killed by Spider which is killed by Bird which is killed by Weasel which is killed by Fox which is killed by Wildcat which is killed by Lion which is killed by Tiger which is killed by an apparently prehistoric Elephantus Ichtyosaraus Magatherium—until by a fine logic we arrive at the very summit of the scale, Jimmy Gem-of-the-Creation Man. Now, interestingly, the gender of parenthood changes. It is Papa Gem-of-the-Creation who accommodates his son's needs, and thereby (such is ever the way with the conscious designs of humanity) bestows largess not just upon a potluck supper, but all the rest of creation. On the prowl for anything that moves Papa

> hid behind a wall . . . shot little Jumbo . . . traded [his tusks] for a cargo of black
> men and women . . . sold them to a good Christian planter . . . and said "By cracky
> this is the way to extend our noble civilization."

But from the greatest of victims great and small, the sketch comes full circle back to the smallest again. Our position in the end is with the first of the many grieving survivors, as in the cool of the evening we hear the woes of Mother Molecule:

her heart broke and she gave it up, weeping and saying The good spirit has deserted my Willie, who trusted him, and he is dead and will come no more.

It is all here, we think to ourselves: the fury of Mark Twain's old age, the well-developed sense he has come to have of life as a process of universal cannibalism, one more letter from the earth wherein predator and prey do their one thing without ceasing, under the eyes of an approving God. And we are right to think so, of course—provided our rightness does not blind us to the craft of the sketch. For one thing there is the marvelous medleying of proper names and voice tones, as Johnny Microbe's wheedling gives way to the chirping insistence of Little Dora Sparrow, the sensuous, almost flirtatious begging of Sissy Bengal Tiger, the lumbering and single-minded wish to be present of Jumbo Jackson Elephantus. More to the point, we need to be ever mindful of the fine art of committing murder. These creatures do not simply kill; they do so with zest, ardor, a total dedication, so that Mama Sparrow, having "harpooned Spider with her beak," will now send forth Little Dora to be done in by the "joined teeth" of Mama Weasel, while Mama Tiger "caved in the west side of Cabel Lion with a pat of her paw," and will presently discover that Little Sissy Tiger is "fetched" with a "wipe and rap" of the 19-foot trunk of Mama Elephantus, who "observing that [Sissy] did not respond but seemed satisfied with things as they were, carried her home [to Jumbo Jackson], cradled on a pair of 22-foot tusks." A kind of infectious glee takes over: theirs in doing it; Mark Twain's in recording the doing of it; ours in watching it done. In the midst of appalling circumstances, the festive atmosphere, the excitement and anticipation of attending a village social are never wholly lost.

Twenty-five or thirty years earlier, certainly no later than 1875, Mark Twain had written essentially the same story. Divided into three brief parts, it is entitled "Some Fables for Good Old Boys and Girls." It appears for the first time in that frequently neglected treasure trove *Sketches New and Old*, later to become Volume XIV of *Mark Twain's Works*.[13]

This time the prevailing mood is one of unrelieved buffoonery. On a Spring day all the small creatures of the forest go forth on an expedition into the clearing, where they "will verify the truth of the matters already taught in their schools and colleges and also . . . make discoveries." Non sequitur soon follows nonsense, as they come upon a long row of telegraph wires and presume them to be the webs of still larger insects; as, in a frenzy of logic, they deduce "the parallels of latitude" from nearby railroad tracks, or identify the passing of the "Vernal Equinox" with a train that goes whizzing past them. In Part II they enter a ruined town where the only remaining signs of habitation are ancient and disfigured billboards ("'Billiards,'" "'For Sale Cheap,'" "'Telegraph

Office,'" "'No Smoking'") which, lacking a Rosetta Stone, Professor Grasshopper mistranslates "with considerable plausibility, though not to the perfect satisfaction of all the scholars." Pausing before a decayed museum, once the property of one Varnum (read P. T. Barnum), the insects take it for catacombs of the human dead, and investigating the well-stuffed effigies of a "Captain Kidd" and "Queen Victoria" conclude that human life survived on straw which, "eaten so many years gone by," still remains undigested, "even in its legs." With the onset of Fall in Part III, they throng back to their lairs and nests, to ponder, pontificate, and lay plans for next year's pilgrimage. The lone dissenter, all the while, has been an industrious Tumble Bug, too busy trundling along his tiny ball of excrement, to be much moved by scientific speculations. ("Fable," 157, 164–65, 188.)

Once again, we think, it is all here. This is carefree, untroubled Mark Twain, not quite at the top of his form probably, but writing with a kind of easy zaniness, a willingness to set up the structure of the fable, just to see what crazy things might happen. And, as before, we are not wrong—always provided we take into account one significant omission. Never, during their peregrinations, do the creatures of the forest encounter a living human being. There is much talk of a species, now long extinct, which once went about uttering sounds like "'haw haw,'" "'haw, haw,'" "'dam good,'" "'dam good,'" while individual members blew smoke into one another's faces. ("Fable," 179.) There are the forlorn and deserted town, the devastated museum, the train and telegraph wires that seem to rise up out of nowhere and disappear into nothingness. But of man's actual, immediate and physical presence there is no evidence. It is as if the "good old boys and girls" of the title had (like the lads and girls of *Cymbeline*) all returned to dust—as if the fable were written from the perspective of some post-historical future, when humanity has all gone away, leaving to the surviving animals and insects the task of interpreting human history as best they can. Thus the roles of tumble bug and his excrement turn out to have a more than incidental importance. They make death and dung the subjects of this story, as more than a quarter of a century later death and dung will be deeply embedded into "The Victims."

For the two stories are related. The jocularity of "Fables" no more hides (but rather underscores) a certain covert despair than the despair of "Victims" conceals (but rather highlights) a covert jocularity. They are akin to K's mysterious companions in *The Castle*, in the sense that when the narratives are viewed side-by-side, the undoubted demonism of the second loops back over three decades to disclose the "serpentine" qualities of the first. They become, in a term that will much resonate throughout Mark Twain, identical twins. And from their doublings, the internal doublings of tone that each story displays, the external doublings of attitude that make for a common effect in both stories, I believe two inferences might be drawn.

The first has to do with narrative structure, or in the old fashioned term with "plot." I shall try to show that like other writers of a quirky and highly specialized genius—like Melville in the nineteenth century, Flannery O'Connor, Nathanael West or Saul Bellow in the twentieth—Mark Twain had but one story, one plot-line, to present. He told it so artfully that finesse of manner may readily be mistaken for change and variety. All the same, it was *the* story, following a single direction and a single set of narrative rhythms to the achievement of one dead-end conclusion. As all the world knows, Mark Twain's last twenty years were beset with an almost unending succession of personal crises. So deeply are the misfortunes supposed to have affected the man and his work that it has become possible to speak of a "late Mark Twain" as, for wholly different reasons, we distinguish and set apart the late Henry James. But the concepts "early" and "late," with their implication of profound changes in manner and outlook, seem to me inapplicable to Mark Twain. He did not so much develop as return to and re-enact, augment and complicate the one "given" which seems forever to have lain in wait for his imagination.[14] If his work and life are aptly defined by Van Wyck Brooks's early phrase "the ordeal of Mark Twain" (and I think this is very much the case), the ordeal was already functioning in the 1860s, when it produced merriment tinged with bitterness, and continued to be operative in 1908, when two years before Mark Twain's death it was still busily producing much bitterness, invariably underlain with merriment. In a very real sense the shape of one of his narratives is synonymous with the shape of Mark Twain's career.

The second inference has to do with tone: with what we hear in literature, and with the relationship of what is heard to the author's personality. In *Was Huck Black?* bold new claims are staked for Mark Twain's "political correctness." Through impeccable research and a series of fascinating if occasionally debatable connections, Shelley Fisher Fishkin is concerned not simply with how Black voices and Black folkways were bonded into the character of Huck and so made Huck's story the first truly multi-cultural book in American literature; her broader aim is to show that, having begun as an avowed racist, S. L. Clemens, around the time he was turning himself into Mark Twain, began to question racial hierarchies, and gradually "subverted and . . . deconstructed blackness and whiteness in fresh and surprising ways."[15] She thus claims him for one of ours, we being possessors of the postmodernist sensibility at its tolerant, equable and radical best. And yet for all the originality of her presentation, Professor Fishkin actually confirms an older and more traditional view of

Mark Twain. Often suspecting there must be more to it than this, we still cherish the jovial, twinkly-eyed humorist, the notion of one who could write bitterly yet always with a certain tolerance of human failings, the idea of an Horatian satirist constrained to show us our queernesses and quirkinesses, but always for our own good and in the hope of our moral improvement. In *Was Huck Black?* Mark Twain simply steps forth as more genial and twinkly-eyed, more humane and folksy, more generously inclined toward us than we had hitherto suspected.

No matter how marvelously appealing, both the image and the premise seem to me fundamentally mistaken. A far truer picture emerges from Justin Kaplan's seminal biography. Here, Mr. Clemens and Mark Twain coalesce into a kind of perpetual agitation, capable of spontaneous and not always timely combustions which are as fearsome to watch as they are fascinating to watch. He is seen as the doting father who yet psychologically terrorized his three daughters; as a gregarious man of the world who cultivated many friendships, yet could at a moment's notice subject his friends and neighbors to practical jokes which were tasteless and tactless at best and at their worst hurtful and humiliating; as a loyal brother who spent a lifetime belittling and exploiting his admittedly addle-pated older brother, Orion Clemens—and letting Orion know about it; as a great hater (at times without much provocation) in public and in private a good deal of a snide backbiter; in short, as the supreme egotist whose tireless apologies for self-indulgence, always predicated upon the certainty of being forgiven, were themselves but another form of egotism. Perhaps in all these matters he was also, as we say, only human, though in fairness the behavior often seems more extreme than typical. But the point is that the images revealed by Kaplan do not add up to a twinkly eyed humorist, much less to a political correctness that has as its aims never to offend (never to patronize the other) and never to be offended (never to be put off by the other's lifestyle, however outrageous or distasteful it may seem). Rather, the images fairly vibrate with offense: the self-styled martinet, the aggressive will to power, the joker who victimizes and then adds insolence to injury by rubbing the victim's nose in it.[16] There was an "imp of the perverse restless in Mark Twain," observes James Lyndon Johnson, echoing Poe but following Justin Kaplan's lead. And while this is not the primary concern of *Mark Twain and the Limits of Power,* Professor Johnson almost alone among the critics has had the courage to relate what the man wrote to a streak of meanness he discerns in the man.[17]

Following Johnson's lead I wish to reconsider from one last angle the sketches which were introduced several paragraphs ago. Early and late, the sketches, to be sure, do remove barriers, erase distinctions. But whether genial or brutal, they perform the erasure to no happy, multicultural ending. The clear intent of both is to show that while life is, surely enough, equalized, the equalizing force is not love and not tolerance and not respect or good feelings—but a pervasive corruption achieved through the exercise of ego. Moreover, a close look will discover that one distinction has not been removed. If "The Victims" descends at last from the triumphant huzzahs of a slave trader to Mama Microbe weeping in the twilight, the implication is that in the smallest, most death-giving form of life we find a sensitivity not vouchsafed to the greatest and most fully developed form. And while the insects and animals of "Fables" are anthropomorphized, still we will not miss the point that they and their foolishness live on, while their models have long since become straw-stuffed figures in a museum, the relics of some distant anthropological and archaeological past. Both sketches are profoundly anti-humanistic. Their subject is the doubly damned human race: damned in the expletive sense of being no goddamned good; damned in the metaphysical sense of being God damned through all eternity to be no goddamned good. Their shared tone suggests that the world is (or would be) a better place if humanity was dispensed with, if human life were long ago dead and forgotten.[18]

Comedy and satire are invaluable tools of the liberal, humanistic imagination. Each in its own way, both look to correct the present state of things through appeals to reason and conscience. As the one redeems by trying to wrest at least some modicum of light out of darkness, so the other tempers excess, and consoles with the hope of a more moderate, better ordered world to come. As I indicated at the beginning, however, Mark Twain, though he might yearn for the comic and the satiric, was cut off from both. He holds reason and conscience to be responsible for things as they are. His occasional forays into conventional comedy result in the sort of appalling sentimentality, which betrays a complete lack of conviction about the comic outcome. Essaying satire, he floundered on the hard fact that he had no ideal to substitute for reality. His pen "warmed up in hell" might, to be sure, savage lynchings, berate warmongering and imperialism, tick off each and every morbidity of the "persons sitting in darkness." Yet the pen was finally merely enraged and rather noisy; short of exterminating the brutes, it could inscribe no means of curbing the brutishness, much less for curing it. His humor was different. What it was the essays to come will try to say. For the moment, I am content to relate the difference to what eludes us in his gaze. It is told of James Joyce that in his old age he confessed his eyes were weary because he had been looking at the world a long time and found it a "perfect nullity." I shall argue that the sad, chill eyes of Mark Twain reflect the fact that when he looked at reality he found a perfect fixity and futility, and reflect as well that in the frozen features of the real world he found the perfect sources for creating laughter.

A great deal has been left out of my essays. Except for the double emphasis upon "Old Times on the Mississippi" and a sentence or two about *Roughing It*, I have found no place for the travel narratives. For the reasons just specified, I feel little bound by chronology or by any sense of Mark Twain's genetic growth as a writer. Nor, finally, am I much concerned with the causes, the personal or cultural origins for a world view which strikes me as bizarre, cranky and eccentric to the point of perversity—but (for exactly these same reasons) unfailingly funny. To paraphrase Lawrence, I want to read the tale closely, and not, except on relatively rare occasions and then rather perfunctorily, the mind of the teller. Despite these limitations, however, the essays constantly seek for a particular kind of comprehensiveness. I am in search of an understanding of Mark Twain's "poetics." Having already alleged that he has nothing less (or more) than a standard joke to share with us, I hope to explore the joke in such a way that it and the habitual retelling of it will illuminate nothing less than his total oeuvre.

## NOTES

1. Morris's brilliant foreword is to the Signet Edition of *Pudd'nhead Wilson* (New York: New American Library, 1964), vii–xvii, xvi.

2. From *Mark Twain in Eruption*, ed. Bernard DeVoto (New York: Harper, 1940), 202–03.

3. Henri Bergson, *Laughter*, tr. Fred Rothwell, repr. in *Comedy*, ed. Robert W. Corrigan (San Francisco: Chandler Publishing Co., 1965), 477. Also in Wiley Sypher, ed., *An Essay on Comedy* (Baltimore: Johns Hopkins University Press, 1956).

4. From *Mark Twain's Letters*, ed. Albert Bigelow Paine (New York: Harpers, 1911), 454–55. Mark Twain addresses the comment to Howells, who had his own well-known reservations about the fictional technique of George Eliot, though with respect to the "morality of realism" and what the objective world can teach the individual, all three writers seem in substantial agreement.

5. Howells, *Criticism and Fiction*, repr. in *Documents of Modern Literary Realism*, ed. George J. Becker (Princeton: Princeton University Press, 1963), 134; George Eliot, *Adam Bede* in the Modern Library Edition of *Best Known Novels of George Eliot* (New York, n.d.), 129–30. The details Eliot specifies in this chapter, combining theory with practice, are not unlike those which turn up in Mark Twain: the awkward, the broad-faced, the elderly and middle-aged, with very "irregular noses and lips . . . , but with an

expression of unmistakable contentment." If Mark Twain is rarely quite so graphic, this (as I shall try to show in the essay on *Huckleberry Finn*) is because he depends more on experiences heard than seen: more on the aural than the photographic representation.

6. The paradox of Zeno of Elea, as recorded by Aristotle in *Physics*. The fictions of Jorge Luis Borges often turn, in one way or another, on Zeno's paradox, and Borges's "pairings" with Mark Twain have recently been explored by Robert Kiely in *Reverse Tradition* (Cambridge: Harvard University Press, 1993). But I have found still more relevant the experimental fictions of Robert Coover, and I would particularly cite, at this point, Coover's "In a Train Station," *Pricksongs and Descants* (New York: New American Library, 1969), 98–104. Mark Twain's path crossings with postmodernists of a dark persuasion (Coover, Vonnegut, John Hawkes, Flannery O'Connor) will be a subdued but persistent refrain of my essays.

7. Albert Camus, *Myth of Sisyphus*, repr. in *Ten Modern Short Novels*, ed. Leo Hamalian and Edmond L. Volpe (New York: G. P. Putnam's, 1958), 643.

8. My mild rejoinder here to Henry Nash Smith, *Mark Twain: The Development of a Writer* (Cambridge: Harvard University Press, 1962), and James M. Cox, *Mark Twain: The Fate of Humor* (Princeton: Princeton University Press, 1966), in no way detracts from my admiration for these books. I am much indebted to both; both would surely appear on any hypothetical list of the ten best single-American-author studies written in our century. It is simply that both take the view that Mark Twain cannot be funny when he is broaching philosophical or metaphysical subjects. This, I think, is a view that shortchanges him.

And, interestingly enough, the inevitable reaction has set in. Three recent books, the brilliant (if somewhat dogged) *In Bad Faith: The Dynamics of Deception in Mark Twain's America* of Forrest G. Robinson (Cambridge: Harvard University Press, 1988); Susan Gillman's *Dark Twins: Imposture and Identity in Mark Twain's America* (Chicago: University of Chicago Press, 1989); and Shelley Fisher Fishkin's *Was Huck Black? Mark Twain and African American Voices* (New York and Oxford: Oxford University Press, 1993), have been so diligent in their search for Mark Twain's ideas and ideology as to seem at times to forget that Mark Twain is funny. Again, this does not mean that I have failed to profit from these works, the account of Professor Robinson because I so often agree, those of Professors Gillman and Fishkin because in disagreement with many of the ideas, I have found them a useful foil to my own.

A work which strikes a nice balance between the philosophic and the funny is James Lyndon Johnson's *Mark Twain and the Limits of Power: Emerson's God in Ruins* (Knoxville: University of Tennessee Press, 1982). But the closest approximation to my wish to put a few laughs back into Mark Twain comes in two books which, with a certain trepidation, I read while undertaking a last rewriting: Don Florence, *Persona and Humor in Mark Twain's Early Writings* (Columbia, Mo.: University of Missouri Press, 1995), and Bruce Michelson *Mark Twain on the Loose: The Comic Writer and the Ameri-*

*can Self* (Amherst: University of Massachusetts Press, 1994). Though instructed, and particularly with reference to Professor Michelson, much entertained, I believe it fair to say that because of our differing scopes and emphases, the trepidation was largely unwarranted.

9. The phrase is Mark Twain's, worked by Robert Wiggins into the title of a not very good book, *Mark Twain, Jackleg Novelist* (Seattle: University of Washington Press, 1964).

10. See Daniel G. Hoffman, *Form and Fable in American Fiction* (New York: Oxford University Press, 1961); Richard B. Hauck, *A Cheerful Nihilism* (Bloomington: Indiana University Press, 1971); and Kenneth S. Lynn, *Mark Twain and Southwestern Humor* (Boston: Little, Brown, 1959), 319.

11. Bakhtin, *Problems of Dostoevsky's Poetics,* tr. and ed. Caryl Emerson (Minneapolis: University of Minnesota Press, 1987), 292–93.

12. "The Victims" was printed for the first time in *Mark Twain's Fables of Man,* ed. John S. Tuckey (Berkeley: University of California Press, 1972), 135–40. All references are to these five pages, and I have not clogged the text with page numbers. Though Professor Tuckey's introductory comments are insightful, I would vigorously disagree with his premise that we are given only an outline, a "skeletal draft," of a story which remains to be completed. "The Victims," for all its odd appearance on the printed page, is one of the most finished of Mark Twain's short narratives. It is a sketch, but not sketchy. Nothing could readily be taken away—nothing needs to be added.

13. We know that "Fable" was written prior to 1875, because of the dating of Mark Twain's prefatory note to *Sketches New and Old.* My references are to the *Collected Works,* Hillcrest Edition (New York: Harper, 1903), where the "Fable" runs from page 156 to page 189.

14. My point is anticipated in a narrower and more specific way when Forrest Robinson observes that Mark Twain's "town is strangely . . . like a set, with houses and fences set in a row along a single street. In fact, with appropriate adjustments, the scene served Mark Twain as a kind of stage prop, a permanent fixture. . . . " *In Bad Faith,* 140. I would want to add that it is not just setting, but also character and event and situation, which exert this "strangely" magnetic hold over Mark Twain's creativity.

15. Shelley Fisher Fishkin, *Was Huck Black? Mark Twain and African American Voices* (New York and London: Oxford University Press, 1993), 80.

16. Justin Kaplan, *Mr. Clemens and Mark Twain* (New York: Simon and Schuster, 1966). For what can only be termed Mark Twain's psychological abuse of his daughters, see pp. 307–10. For his practical jokes, particularly one on the stuffy but unoffending Thomas Bailey Aldriches (they were the Clemens's houseguests at the time), see Chapter 9. The whole of Chapter 14 is a running account of the behavior of a venomous and vindictive man. And while the chapter is set in the late 1880s, when Mark Twain was under considerable stress induced by ill health, financial and family woes, and the im-

minent failure of the Paige typesetting machine, still in Chapters 1 and 2, having located him in New York and on the *Quaker City*, Kaplan makes it clear that he was a walking bundle of hostilities, perfectly prepared to badmouth in private an assortment of friends who seemed intent upon doing him good.

The truth is that the figure presented by Kaplan is not so much the last of the nineteenth century's gentleman authors as (together with Stephen Crane) the first of the moderns. Sexual peccadilloes aside, he bears a curious resemblance to the troubled and turbulent subjects of Jeffrey Meyers's recent biographies: Hemingway, Fitzgerald, Edmund Wilson, most recently Frost.

17. Johnson, *Mark Twain and the Limits of Power,* 140.

18. *Was Huck Black?* quotes at some length from Mark Twain's chance encounter with George Griffin, who had formerly been his butler in Hartford. As Mark Twain tells the story, he invited Griffin to accompany him to the offices of *Century Magazine,* whereupon

> the array of clerks in the counting room glanced up with curiosity—a *"white man"* & *a negro* walking together was a new spectacle to them. The glances embarrassed George, but not me, for the companionship was proper . . . & besides deep down in my interior, I knew that the difference between those poor transient things called human beings . . . was but microscopic, trivial, a mere difference between worms. (124.)

Ever eager to put his best foot forward, Professor Fishkin would emphasize the good will and easy air of acceptance in the passage. Frankly, what interests me is the reductionism.

But both views are there. And from their coexistence, a certain strategy emerges. First, differences are recognized, and bridged with the thought that the companionship is proper. Next, differences disappear, bridging becomes unnecessary, for the "white man" and "negro" are (like all human beings) mere worms.

Readers, particularly readers distressed by the endings of *Huckleberry Finn* and *A Connecticut Yankee*, would do well to keep this strategy in mind.

# PART I
# THREE POLEMICAL ESSAYS

# Mark Twain and the "Infernal Twoness": An Essay on the Comic

Put in something about the Supernal Oneness. Don't say a syllable
about the Infernal Twoness.
                —Poe in "How to Write a Blackwood's Article"

Of course my title juxtaposes the great funny man's pen name with a phrase
from the great writer of horror fiction. As it happens, Poe used the phrase in
one of those places where he was trying to be egregiously funny. It likewise
turns out that the funny man was led by the implications of the phrase to perceive life as a horror story. There is a certain disingenuousness to my syntax
of course. I am trying to create an atmosphere, an air of wry ironies—the sort
of odd and unexpected couplings which often occurred to the funny man
when, looking attentively at experience, he observed (or remarked) twain and,
having looked, picked up his pen to record (or mark down) twain. But the
syntactic duplications are also meant to imply a sequel. They suggest individu-
alities related so intimately—so absolutely interchangeable each with each—
that once the twain have been remarked and marked, one looks again and finds
a convergence of the twain into unity. With all due apologies to the horror
man, then, the topic of my first essay is actually Mark Twain and the Infernal
Oneness.

## I

Which twin has the Toni?
                —TV commercial

I knew a man so unpopular he was an only twin.
                —Nightclub joke

Chang and Eng to begin with. They were born in Siam of Chinese parentage in
1811. Linked chest to stomach by a thick and flexible band of flesh they were

for some years exhibited in the sideshows of Europe and the United States. Following their retirement from the circuit around 1855 they settled near Mt. Airy, North Carolina, married farm girl sisters, traveled to-and-fro on a monthly basis between adjacent dwellings, and by the time of their death in 1874 had fathered (respectively) twelve and ten children. The Siamese twins were thus his fellow countrymen and still very much names in the news when, as he remembered it, Mark Twain portrayed them for the first time in the mid-1860s.[1]

He begins by playing with the undoubted fact of their proximity in space. When they were lost as children, their mother looked for only one of her sons and invariably found them both. But if the twins march physically in tandem, each is attuned to the beat of his own special morality. Eng is Baptist; and Chang, a devout Roman Catholic, consents to the total immersion of their totalized body "on the grounds that it should not 'count.'" During the Civil War Chang fought for the Confederacy while Eng was a Union partisan. They took each other prisoner at the battle of Seven Oaks, and a military tribunal finally decided the case by agreeing to consider both spoils of war "and then exchanging them." Though the court had to cope with a collective presence, it is very much the individual difference which intrigues Mark Twain. Eng has a taste for strong drink, but Chang belongs to the Good Templars and is a "hard working, enthusiastic supporter of all temperance reforms." And then comes the "snapper" in the form of the tie that binds utterly. On days when the Templars parade, Eng celebrates by getting drunk—and Chang, soon intoxicated by their common bloodstream, has no choice except to jeer as riotously as his brother and to join waggish Eng in throwing "rocks and mud" at the passing parade.

Obviously other emphases were possible. With no loss of the absurdity of the situation we might have been shown the frustrating consequences for Eng of Chang's sobriety. Or Eng's bad manners would have struck us as more appealing had his antics been directed toward a dour group of spoilsports. The Templars, however, seem quite pathetic in their bewilderment: unsupported by the legalisms of the court, how are they to explain the treachery, the act of desertion which is entailed when two actors become one action? And so, by portraying the twins as he does, Mark Twain insinuates into an adversary relationship a strangely conspiratorial air. Beneath the skin they share the Siamese twins differ in the most fundamental respects. They are as unalike as Catholic from Protestant, as slaveholder from abolitionist, as tippler from teetotaler. Yet should their mother come looking for them now, she would still find both: Chang *and* Eng, drunk as lords, one because he drinks, the other because he steadfastly does not; Eng *and* Chang, engaged in a disruption of the civil order, one because it suits him to be disorderly, the other because he is borne helplessly along in despite of his best wishes and intentions.

We are told that among primitive peoples the birth of twins can occasion two widely divergent responses. In some quarters twins are seen as a mark of the gods' favor, as bearers of fertility and abundance, who are themselves either deified ultimately or elevated at once to the status of tribal elders. Elsewhere twins are regarded as monstrosities, a tell-tale sign of their mother's adultery, a horror to be shrunk from or put to death since it violates the natural order of life. I believe a point is not being pushed immoderately if we find in Mark Twain's life-long love affair with twins and twin relationships exactly this same ambivalence.

Positively, the notion of doubles and doublenesses so liberated his imagination that it is never far from the finest of his streaks of fine madness. To cite but a handful from among the great wealth of later instances: one sees the sheer grotesqueness of Chang and Eng repeated in Miss Wagner's eyeballs (one natural and sky blue; the other glass, borrowed and yellow) as they rotate fiercely (but not always synchronically) in "Jim Blaine and his Grandfather's Old Ram" . . . or notes it in Huck's marvelous (if fleeting) image of "Old Baldy Shepherdson" riding out to feud with his mane of thick white hair streaming down from behind . . . or hears it in the oxymoron of Eve when she announces in "Papers of the Adam Family" that after a few years in Eden she and Adam have "nine children, now—half boys and half girls" . . . or, above all, detects it hovering over those three pairs of arms which protrude outrageously from a single torso in Emmeline Grangerford's self-portrait. But negatively the creation of his first *folie à deux* was likewise an ill omen for Mark Twain. Already twins were embodying the "infernal twoness" which passes over into an "*infernal oneness*"— the sense of a world that has been absurdly cut into two parts, and then perversely assembled again—upon which he would presently come close to floundering, and from which, as three further examples will suggest, he may well have derived some considerable anxiety even at the outset.

## II

> It did well now, except that always at ten minutes to ten the hands would shut together like a pair of scissors, and from that time forth they would travel together.
> —Mark Twain in "My Watch"

The out-of-date television commercial in Part I, as well as the nightclub joke which was outdated before it ever got told, were not chosen idly. In each of my examples, the commercial's problematics (which is which?) are gradually replaced by the certainty of the joke (both are one):

*The Bad Boy and the Good Boy.* They are protagonists in separate stories which Mark Twain also ascribes to the later 1860s. Brought face to face (or rather set down in adjoining texts) they demonstrate how perfect strangers, with no biological connections whatever, can be identical twins—that is, the mirror or reversed images of one another. As their careers develop, furthermore, each manages to elicit from the reader some striking reversals of attitude.

Jim, at first glance, exemplifies Mark Twain's cute and endearing little scamp. Or if the term "vernacular" is to be thought of as determining lifestyles as well as stylistics, he is among the earliest of Mark Twain's vernacular heroes, being the sort of character who prefers practice to theory and does not so much plan life as will it to exist for him from moment to exciting moment. And the technique of *carpe diem* serves him wonderfully well. Through a series of instant gratifications coupled with surprisingly negative consequences, Jim steals apples and is not paddled (or for that matter even detected) by Farmer Acorn; breaks the Sabbath by going boating, but does not perceive God's wrath descending from a lightning bolt; repeatedly strikes his sister in anger, and never once watches her "linger in pain through long summer days, and die with sweet words upon her lips that redoubled the anguish of his broken heart." But petty larceny is clearly not quite the moral equivalent to battering one's sister into insensibility. And within a few years (only five pages of text) the "charmed life" of a small boy has come to seem the somewhat more sinister magic of a dirty old blackguard. Though "universally respected" to the end, Jim now is prized as the "wickedest, infernalest scoundrel in his native village," and eventually he goes to the Legislature as a reward for having axe murdered his wife and children.

Jacob Blivens is the prototype of the plodding and conventional dullard in Mark Twain's fiction. He structures life—and capitalizes concepts—according to the Word, the word coming in his case out of innumerable Sunday School manuals which plot the careers of Good Boys from their first Heroic Feats through their Death Bed Speeches and on to their entry into the Kingdom of Heaven. Yet our sense of Jacob as hopeless prig has to be somewhat modified when, rushing to aid a blind man whom bad boys "have pushed over in the mud," he is cursed and thrashed by his confused beneficiary. And in the end, when he discovers finally and forever why it is not healthy to be good, we hardly know whether to laugh or shudder. Sitting on an empty nitroglycerine can, so that bad boys will not tie it to the tail of a dog they are tormenting, Jacob is mistaken by a village alderman for one of the miscreants. The resulting whack to the seat of his dynamite-stained pants splatters Jacob, alderman and "fourteen or fifteen dogs" over the space of four townships. So scattered are the good boy and his environment that "five inquests" are required to discover how (or if) anyone died.

Colloquial Jim and Scriptural Jacob well illustrate the dictum of Kurt Vonnegut that since reality seems what each of us imagines it to be, each had better be careful about what is imagined. Starting with radically opposed images of life—and coming from extreme opposite ends of a moral continuum—they pursue goodness and badness to the performance of a single destructive action. Devoid of the look-alike, stagger-alike, jeer-alike relationship of Chang and Eng, they nonetheless retain Chang and Eng's remarkable facility for doing alike. It is small wonder that when William Dean Howells read their biographies in the early 1870s, he found in Jim and Jacob stuff too strong for readers of the *Atlantic Monthly*.[2] By focusing doubly on doubles Mark Twain had made it all too clear that society can afford neither the luxury of the left hand which entertains it by spurning its basic decencies, nor the good offices of the right hand which blows up the social order while trying to correct some of its very real faults.

"*Mark Twain*" and "*Green Face*." Snug in the study of his Hartford mansion, a fictive "Mark Twain" undergoes a *doppleganger* experience which reads like a parodic version of Poe's "William Wilson" or, better yet, of the visitations that came induced to Dr. Jekyll and unbidden to the elder Henry James. Across the threshold walks a figure who seems a stranger initially, though his shambling gait and drawling manner of speech soon confirm him to be an old familiar. The caller is "Mark Twain's" double, his other and presumably better self—in a word his "conscience," incongruously personified as a monster who particularly repulses his host because he is "covered all over with a fuzzy, greenish mould, such as one sometimes sees upon mildewed bread."[3] Although the term nowhere appears in the story, such is the stress on the physiognomy of conscience—his "sharp little eyes" and "foxlike cunning" of expression; his leerings and grimaces—that it seems legitimate, as well as dramatically effective, to call him "Green Face." ("CC," 136.)

But if "Green Face" is a double, there is an astonishing singleness of purpose about the effects he produces. The year is 1876, a time of economic panics which have sent countless tramps beating a path to the back door of "Mark Twain." Last week he turned one of the beggars away with a churlish excuse, and "Green Face" rebuked him for behaving ungenerously. Just yesterday, therefore, tactics were reversed. Yet when "Mark Twain" fed and clothed a beggar, he heard from "Green Face" that this was an example of his excessive leniency. *Is there any way*, cries one half of a morally tormented personality to his morally exacerbating adversary, "is there any way of satisfying that malignant invention called conscience?" To which the other half replies, *none whatsoever:* "my business—and my joy—[are] to make you repent of everything you do." ("CC," 144.)

In these straits, exorcism would appear to be the only possible solution. And we may well feel that the encounter between them could properly have ended with "Mark Twain's" killing of "Green Face" who, far from constituting a better self, must now seem to us as demonic and dehumanizing as he is implacable. Instead of ending there, however, the story goes on through four additional paragraphs to describe an orgy. Free at length to do whatever he likes, the narrator explodes Connecticut into a bloody carnival of crime. Without guilt or fear of recrimination he indulges himself to behave like the Bad Little Boy grown up. He swindles a poor widow, violently settles outstanding scores against old enemies—and caps it all by murdering all the tramps in the neighborhood, stacking their bodies like pieces of firewood, and transporting them for future use to the wood bin in his cellar.

From a serene study to mayhem in the cellar, via invasion at the back door. Suddenly we recognize that a decade before Stevenson tidied things up in his conclusion, Mark Twain has devised a plausible, perhaps *the* most plausible, ending for the "Strange Adventures of Dr. Jekyll and Mr. Hyde." For the functions of "Green Face" are actually two-fold: first to suggest monstrous patterns of behavior; next to harry and flagellate that part of the total self which tries to avoid the actions or (at worst) engages in them pusillanimously. And as Chang was able to act decisively only after being assimilated into Eng's drunkenness (or Eng's wish for baptism) so in a subtler and more knowing way the weaker side of an identity has been submerged and exterminated in "The Facts Concerning the Recent Carnival of Crime in Connecticut." In a sly subversion of what the facts say ostensibly, it is not "Green Face" with his foxy countenance and mad, malicious eyes who lies dead at the end. Rather, the facts are as they are because fretful, well-intentioned, shilly-shallying "Mark Twain" dies— whereupon the narrator is reborn to be the Green Monster *in toto.*[4]

*Village and River.* Between them in 1875, when they play a first major role in Mark Twain's autobiographical fiction, lie a great many clear-cut differences. Though drenched in sunlight (and though one can readily imagine how its flurry of activities might seem picturesque and dramatic to the weary, way-worn eye of a steamboat traveler) the village has for the boy who narrates the material the drawback of being sluggish and monotonous most of the time, a place destitute of more than momentary interest because he has long since come to know it too familiarly. On the other hand the river speaks to him of constant and purposed motion; its boats and their crews are models of pure epic poetry and power; and capable of arousing even the sleepy village twice daily, river life hints of the truly exotic places and the continuous excitement to which, if he proves good and diligent, it may one day carry the narrator. At its simplest the ploy in "Old Times on the Mississippi" is that of rescuing the boy from dullness and giving him his fling in the promised world ahead.

Underlying his odyssey, however, is a second and graver issue which reaches out to embrace "you"—the reader—whom Mark Twain self-consciously addresses throughout. "You" have to agree with the boy that Hannibal is no country for young men. The days he spends there are "dead" and "empty"; in short order they would reduce him to another of the town loafers who sit among the pigs and decaying watermelon rinds on Water Street, "chins on breasts, hats slouched over their eyes, asleep." ("OT," 64.)[5] Hoping to avoid moral stultification, the boy needs to be challenged in horizons broader and more demanding than Hannibal's. Thus "you" watch with approval while consciously in search of adventure, Mark Twain's young novice-from-the-backwaters is drawn along unconsciously into what seems the classic pattern of an initiation story.

His quest for pure adventure leads predictably enough to a series of disenchantments. Gradually it is discovered that steamboats operate all night as well as in the daytime; that chugging upstream they must leave the current and cling to the difficult banks of the river; that on board at all times is a fair quota of fragrant drunks and other human riffraff. As these revelations take hold, the narrator has what amounts to a *déjà vu* experience. Having watched the village subside and become "dead again" ten minutes after each of the two-a-day steamboats departed, he now finds beneath the glamour and hectic flow of river life a similar death's head. The analogy through which he expresses his ultimate disillusionment could apply equally well to the aesthetic structure of *both* Hannibal and the Mississippi:

> No, the romance and poetry were gone from the river. All the value any feature of it had for me now was the amount of usefulness it could furnish toward the safe piloting of a steamboat. Since those days I have pitied doctors from my heart. What does the lovely flush in a beauty's cheek mean to a doctor but a "break" that ripples above some deadly disease? Are not all her visible charms sown thick with what are to him the signs and symbols of hidden decay? ("OT," 93.)

But where "hidden decay" was the essence of the village, the recognition of the skull below the surface of the river seems a valuable part of the narrator's growth toward maturity. The insight measures his ability to put aside grandiose notions about travel, and to establish himself as a full-fledged member of the river's family by mastering 1300 miles of the river's mystery. So, the question becomes: does his stress on "usefulness" and "safe piloting" ("OT," 93) mean that the river provides a moral education? There can be no other way of answering the question than to look, *through the eyes of Mark Twain,* at those whom the river has educated.

A bit of an ambiguity accompanies Horace Bixby's "daring deed" in Chapter 7. True, Bixby cuts a grand and flamboyant figure—is quite literally a demi-god in the boy's view—as he guides his steamboat at nightfall through the snags, reefs, and sunken wreck off Hat Island. Yet the truth is that Bixby succeeds less as the wise, prudent "guru" we have come to expect than as a show-off, performing this daring deed for no better reason than to excite adulation from his colleagues in the pilothouse. With their echoes of something out of Fenimore Cooper, the very style and title of Chapter 7 imply the inflated, the needlessly grandiose, the larger-than-life scaled up to an absurdity. And as if in confirmation that there is more to Bixby's achievement than meets the naive eye of the cub, Mark Twain ends the chapter by invoking a voice which is at once admiring and admonitory. Bixby is a "'lightning pilot,'" says the voice—but he is so by virtue of his intimacy with "'the Shadow of Death.'" ("OT," 82.)

And there is more. Hardly is the somewhat equivocal episode off Hat Island finished before Bixby reappears in a pique, so incensed this time at a trifling breach of pilothouse etiquette that he declines to share with his relief the steamboat's position in a "particularly wide and blind part of the river, where there was no shape or substance to anything." ("OT," 85–86.) Next in quick succession enter Bixby's professional peers: Mr. X, the pilot as somnambulist (*vide* those who sleep on Water Street!) . . . George Ealer, slipping away from the wheel where he belongs for a snack in the dining room . . . Mr. Brown, he of the indefatigable memory, but also as we learn from *Life on the Mississippi* of the deafness and irascibility which make him impervious to the simplest instructions . . . profligate Stephen, using his steamboat as the weapon in a constant war of nerves he conducts with various employers. These are figures who not only render debatable the pious insistence that "your true pilot cares nothing about anything on earth but the river." ("OT," 78.) (*No,* one wants to say, in Mark Twain's version of him *your true pilot cares for nothing except his own ego*); they point inexorably toward the finale with which in the early 1880s Mark Twain chose to round off "Old Times." When George Ealer calls for more steam, bursts the boilers of the *Pennsylvania,* and with the maimed and dying scattered all around him proceeds to look for the lost pieces of his chess set, he in no way departs from the great tradition of piloting. It is simply that for him the "charmed life" of the pilot runs out, with the result that shades of a Good (or is it Bad?) boy grown up, he strews over the river and along the banks the bodies of several hundred passengers and crew members, including Mark Twain's brother, Henry Clemens.[6]

The implications seem unmistakable. Ennui and a good measure of ineptitude are everywhere. And just as having come to know it intimately "you" would not wish to drowse away a lifetime in the village, just so a closer acquaintance with the dark mischief practiced in the pilothouse might make "you" wary of entrusting "you" or "yours" to the river either. But what, then, happens to "Old Times" as an account of a moral education? Of course the theme of initiation must have exerted a powerful temptation for Samuel L. Clemens, to whom the Mississippi had taught a profession, a subject matter, a vocabulary, a style, a pen name, a way of looking at experience, etc. etc. River life also bequeathed him a recurring nightmare about coming to disaster off Hat Island, however—[7] which may explain why, with respect to the narrator inside the text, Mark Twain uses what Sam Clemens had learned about seeing the world to shape conclusions which are quite antipathetical to an initiation story. For difference, which is the essential ingredient of any initiation motif, he substitutes resemblance shading off into outright similitude. He shows us Town and River betwinned.

Not, to be sure, that one dissolves into the other, in the manner of Chang's disappearance into Eng's drunkenness, or the total displacement of "Mark Twain" by his alter ego, "Green Face." Each retains its own identity. But as with "Bad Boy"/"Good Boy" both labor under a hovering fatality which first locates Town and River at sharply opposed ends of an aesthetic-moral continuum, and then gradually converges them into a single setting designated by two different names. Mark Twain begins with a joke. When seen from the perspective of River, Town presents just that same illusion of colorful, meaningful activity which will presently characterize the disenchanted cub's sense of River life. Both places are fraudulent and in an identical way. The joke is repeated when Mark Twain brings the boy out of childish daydreams into the real, adult world, only to make adult reality itself a place for enacting the vain and sometimes destructive fantasies of bored, childlike little pilots. Both places are dangerous and in an identical way. But the most somber version of the joke is reserved for the conclusion. Having become aware that death-by-sloth is a likely consequence of remaining in Water Street, we are left by no means assured that the narrator—or "you"—will survive longer or with any greater dignity among the reckless energies expended on the River. Both places are destructive and in an identical way.

And so, perhaps in defiance of what Clemens had intended at the outset, Mark Twain can finally do no better than bracket his narrator's apprenticeship between the rotten watermelon rinds of the opening chapter and the decaying corpses on the river and in Memphis hospitals which bring the narrative to a close. In the end the two settings of "Old Times" have assumed if not Chang-and-Eng's single fixed posture at least the single, fixed pattern of behavior exhibited by Jim and Jacob. Town and River suggest that if moral development was the goal set for him, the cub has as little to hope for in the pilothouses he came to as from the decaying village environment he left behind.


## III

*Qui pense, rit.*
>                          —old French proverb

Life is a comedy to those who think.
>                          —made wordier in English

Comedy . . . 1. A play, motion picture, or other work that is humorous in its treatment of theme and character and has a happy ending.
>                          —*American Heritage Dictionary*

If the two proverbs speak accurately, they mean that Mark Twain is accorded less than his rightful due. Deeming him a practitioner without peer of the fine art of evoking laughter, we cite this preeminence as proof that he was not, not even when he wished or purported to be, much of a thinker. The inevitable voice from the back row of a classroom but echoes Leslie Fiedler's strictures:

> his serious ideas eventuate in the sophomoric cynicism of "What Is Man"?, his serious aesthetics in the sentimental banalities of *Joan of Arc,* his serious bawdry in the pseudo-archaic smutty jokes of *1601.* . . . His wisest books [were] those he wrote dreaming not thinking.[8]

For impatient undergraduate and sophisticated critic alike the key to Mark Twain is that, without plan or pretention, he just wrote it down and made it funny. Both sophomore and savant would resist finding in his humor anything that has been worked out reflectively (anything bordering on ideas of depth or substance) because (shucks! and golly gee!) he just wanted—that is, he was only competent—to tell a rousing good story.

Nevertheless the proverbial point seems not irrelevant to the five stories we have been examining. With growing complexity these narratives have moved from high jinx to personal history; from a generalized absurdity to the specific difficulties of a narrator in an absurd world; from Jim and Jacob, each free to do his thing, both fated to do one thing, to the moral and geographical paradoxes of the Mississippi valley, which leave the boy free to go, yet fate him to arrive at last in much the same death-giving atmosphere from which he set forth. As they move, then, just writing it out humorously has yielded up an overview of experience, one that is structured, coherent, consistently developed—and, in the hands of some other writer (a Melville say) might even pass for being as profound (and rather sad) as it is witty (and both devious and deconstructive). And in the first and no doubt zaniest of the five, Mark Twain makes explicit the connection between having fun and meditating over funny implications. There is, says his narrator, something of an "instructive nature" to be gleaned from watching as conjoined Chang and Eng get roaring drunk and pelt the Good Templars: "Let us heed it; let us profit from it."

Suppose we took his invitation seriously? What might be learned from the Siamese twins and the other twinships of personality and place that come after them? Two things, I suggest—both matters that strike to the very heart of Mark Twain's art. First, we would become conscious of a pattern, or a rhythm of presentation, which are sometimes reflective of the Western tall tale, though they are not always this (however "tall" it may be, there is nothing remotely "western" about "Crime in Connecticut"); sometimes suggestive of the conflict between "conventional" and "vernacular" values, though again not always (the pairing of conventional and vernacular has little if anything to do with the pair who appear in "Personal Habits of the Siamese Twins"); sometimes flavored by the oral qualities of native American humor (though only a few scenes from "Old Times" would seem well suited to the stage, while the full effect of Good Boy/Bad Boy would probably come from reading their adventures side-by-side, rather than hearing them in sequence)—but which do seem invariably rooted in any dictionary definition of comedy. The narratives cause us to laugh by showing us humorous characters and situations, as the dictionary says comedy should do. They thus remind us that whatever other distinctive qualities his work possesses, Mark Twain was first and foremost a worker in the long tradition of literary comedy. Secondly, however, we would become aware of a hitch in the rhythm, a jarring of the pattern, which while by no means unprecedented, and hence not really unique to Mark Twain, does draw attention to itself through the repetitiveness with which he uses it. The repetitions undercut what dictionaries say about the "happy endings" of comedy. They thus remind us that in order better to appreciate Mark Twain's particular effects, we need to understand how he altered and modified certain of the assumptions which define the great comic tradition.

(1) *Traditional comedy.* It has been called the completion of a tragedy, a literary form which, having first explored the dark cave, succeeds (however provisionally or temporarily) in transferring darkness up and out into the world of the sunlight. Another, less metaphoric and perhaps slightly more earthbound definition finds that comedy "signifies a coming together of black and white and of wisdom and folly, a fusing of forces . . . , a settlement, a subsiding, a silence. . . ."[9] From both definitions, with their common stress on twosomes (cave/sunlight; wisdom/folly) and a fusing of two, I believe a third formulation becomes possible. Comedy does not simply thrive upon the portrayal of double

qualities, or of twins; it is inherently a process which dramatizes the act of twinning. Consider the following illustrations, most of them acknowledged as grand moments in the comic tradition:

Aristophanes's women conspire to declare war on the masculine community as a means of preventing man made conspiracies, which have resulted in declarations of warfare.

The virtue of Shakespeare's Hero is taken from her by Don John's plot, and then denied her a second time by a senseless society that prefers sensory evidence to reason. But through the nonsense of Dogberry and company, all is set to rights again. And in the end Hero enjoys the rational pleasures of exoneration, apologies and a wedding.

Credulous Orgon is readily taken in by Tartuffe because Orgon believes in everything. When knowledge of the world's wickedness is finally thrust upon him, he does a complete turnabout, supposing that never again will belief in anything be possible:

> Enough, by God! I'm through with pious men
> Henceforth I'll hate the whole false brotherhood
> And persecute them worse than Satan could.

But wise Cleante says no; the good life requires a healthy balance of doubt sometimes and faith on other occasions:

> Ah, there you go—extravagant as ever!
> Why can you not be rational? You never
> Manage to take the middle course, it seems,
> But jump instead between absurd extremes.[10]

After finding the natural world "friz to her axes" during a Kentucky blizzard, Davy Crockett takes from bountiful nature a ton or two of hot bear oil, greases the globe back into motion, and strides homeward carrying a "piece of sunrise in [his] pocket."[11]

Shamed by his birthright, and also by the sexual inadequacies he feels, Mel Brooks's young Frankenstein has assumed the name "Fränken/steen/" and settled for teaching general science at a small college on the American prairies. When circumstance draws him back to Transylvania, the temptation proves irresistible, so that like his grandfather before him he creates a monster. This time, however, a second surgery is performed during which Dr. Victor Frankenstein III reassumes his rightful name, shares his intellect with the monster, and receives in return a share of the monster's sexual potency.

For all their many obvious and very specific differences (their vast range of chronology, style, and thematic emphasis), *Lysistrata, Much Ado About Nothing,*

*Tartuffe,* "Sunrise in His Pocket," and *Young Frankenstein* are linked through their display of a common dynamic, a shared structure. All bring into the foreground the "negative occasion" (Professor Frye's "potential tragedy," Walter Kerr's blackness and folly) which sets things going. But then, by a tactic of not so much eliminating this disruption as of absorbing its impact—and hence of utilizing the intrusion—all make the "negative occasion" the basis for arriving at a "positive outcome." I call the two of them, "negative occasion"/"positive outcome," twins. They are literally inverted images, as different as light from dark, hollow from swell, lefthandedness from righthandedness. All the same, they partake of each other in the sense that each is vitally and equally necessary to the total, the organic drama. As with biological twins, the substance of the negative flows into and then through the substance, the very bone and blood, of the positive. Though Don John "certainly means nothing but harm," as W. H. Auden observes, "yet it is thanks to him that Claudio obtains insight into his own shortcomings and becomes, what previously he was not, a fit husband for Hero."[12] And Auden's observation about *Much Ado* applies fully as well to the other illustrations. Without the threat of war, no need for an ingenious peace plan; without a frozen natural world all around him, no occasion for the legendary Crockett to use nature in the form of bear grease, and no conquest by Crockett over nature; were it not for Tartuffe and the monster, no redeeming self-knowledge could come to either Orgon or Young Frankenstein.

Traditional comedy thus proceeds dialectically; it exploits the built-in or the intrinsic doubleness of experience, in order to push forward, to affirm, to "get somewhere." The question of exactly how negative is assimilated into positive, as well as the issue of whether the direction of their synthesis might not be reversed, are matters to return to in two later sections of this essay. For now, the point is that the five examples have medleyed opposites into a new and life-affirming wisdom, an at least momentary triumph of Fortune over Fate which, whether it is earned from within or bestowed *deus ex machina,* is the norm of the comic structure.

(2) *Mark Twain's comedy.* There is surely no need to demonstrate its basis in doubleness. Twins abound, springing up as if in consequence of a compulsion to see two everywhere, to write out of the certain knowledge that everywhere there are two. What does bear emphasizing, though, is how instead of being interrelated serially—one preparing for hence leading to the other—the twins are now interrelated to become interchangeable. The common destructiveness of Jim and Jacob (of Chang and Eng) leaves both parties in each pairing, as well as the two pairings themselves, quite indistinguishable. But more is involved than simply interchangeableness. A process of transference, and hence of absolute coalescence, also takes place. For all practical purposes, benevolent Chang and well-intentioned "Mark Twain" lose their proper identities as they

are absorbed into Eng and "Green Face." And if, in context, both these meta-morphoses are more frivolous than earth shaking (the "autobiographical" un-dertones of the second do lend it a certain mock-seriousness), the same ex-change of features has taken a graver and more pensive turn in "Old Times on the Mississippi." Here the town, which in terms of value ought to be fully set apart from the river, nonetheless has all its shabbiest features duplicated on the river, so that the bleak denouement of river life (a proliferation of corpses) had already been anticipated by the living dead who dwell in town. Separate places, they are likewise the same place—except of course for the names they bear.

Accordingly, the twins Mark Twain imagines greatly resemble the hands of an extraordinarily endowed pocket watch about which, in another neglected piece from *Sketches New and Old,* he wrote in the early 1870s. The twins are destined to meet at some theoretic ten-minutes-until-ten (to meet by fate, yet likewise fortuitously, one notes; the connotations would be very different if the time were midnight or high noon). Thereafter, round and round go the twins, their circular journey-in-tandem inviting two possible interpretations. In one, a disappearing act occurs. Big hand runs atop and hence, blotting it from sight, seems to absorb little hand, just as Chang's quest for a "model life" disappears into the riotous bloodstream he shares with Eng, or just as "Mark Twain's" dis-appearance into "Green Face" becomes a signal for the carnival to begin. The key to the second scenario is a kind of helpless submission. Though one is displayed and the other hidden, each hand is there and maintains its separate identity, but as if magnetized by some superior force (drawn together by some defect of the watch's total mechanism) both hands are conjoined to point to one end, as the different motivations and patterns of behavior of Jim and Jacob result in a single calamitous action, or as Town and River point in lock step to false expectations, disillusionment and death without dignity. But whatever the interpretation, it is never accurate to say of the hands on the face of the watch that they register nothing. Singly or collectively they record the true sameness amidst seeming variety—the mimicry of motion surrounded by actual stasis—which are everywhere the hallmarks of Mark Twain's work. The irony is that apparently giving the correct time for only two minutes out of every twenty-four hours, they are actually telling the right time all the time. The twinned hands have replaced an emphasis upon "getting somewhere" with the drama of "getting nowhere."*

I suggest that moving and moving to go nowhere is the spectacle at which

---

* One can hardly doubt that Mark Twain wrote in response to Paley's famous analogy. Well and good that the watch's existence should point back to a Creator. But suppose the timepiece is deformed—forever, as we say, out of whack!

we laugh in the early short stories of Mark Twain and, most especially (since there it is presented most elaborately), in "Old Times on the Mississippi." It is funny to find that Hannibal seen from the standpoint of a steamboat possesses exactly the same illusion of high drama as the steamboat seen from the perspective of Hannibal, for this makes town and river identical twins. And it is funny to discover that the boy's derring-do fantasies before he leaves home correspond exactly to the fantasies of full grown pilots who are bored by the monotony of their vocation in the pilothouse, for this makes youth and age (novice and expertise; naiveté and wisdom) identical twins. On the other hand twinning of this sort will hardly proceed from the negative occasion to a positive outcome—will hardly signify "settlement" and "subsiding" (in Walter Kerr's terms) or bring radiance forth from the dark cave (in the images of Professor Frye). It must result, rather, in repetition, fixity, a sense of standing stock-still—and perhaps, underlying them all, feelings of entrapment and frustration. These are qualities noted by a contemporary critic of Mark Twain, who wrote of *Roughing It* shortly after the book appeared in 1871. Beneath the high spirits and steady flow of adventure, the critic implied, lay a feeling that for all that really came of the experience, one "might as well have stayed at home." Tragedy is what William Dean Howells chose to call it—an "extravagant joke" that forever skirted the "nether-side of tragedy."[13]

## IV

"The novelists might be the greatest possible help to us if they painted life as it is, and human feelings in their true proportion and relation. . . . "
—Mr. Sewell in *The Rise of Silas Lapham*

It was from out of the rind of one apple tasted, that the knowledge of good and evil, as two twins cleaving together, leaped into the world. And perhaps this is the doom which Adam fell into of knowing good and evil; that is to say, of knowing good by evil.
—Milton in "Areopagitica"

Perspective determines what a writer sees, the shape and focus the writer imposes on the created world. But particularly when shape and focus seem slightly (yet noticeably) askew, another question is raised. What determines perspective? In other words it is not enough to invoke traditional patterns of comedy in order to show how the conventions were at once exploited and varied by Mark Twain. The more complicated problem is *why*. Why starting from the same perception of twinship that preoccupied Shakespeare and Mel Brooks did Mark Twain totalize his opposites not into the comic affirmation, but rather the stasis and futility of running in place? I hope to propose an answer by next locating his version of the comic in a context supplied by the traditional comic novel of the nineteenth century.

Dickens seems an obvious choice for such a comparison—and it is surprising that criticism and literary history have not done more to bring together these funny fellows and master showmen.[14] The better choice, however, is William Dean Howells. Vis-à-vis Mark Twain, Howells does not always receive a particularly favorable press. He is seen as a timid and censorious reader, busily nitpicking the "coarsenesses" out of *Tom Sawyer* and *Huckleberry Finn*. It has been duly noted that his attitude can become patronizing, so that the title of his late memoir, *My Mark Twain,* has about it something of the same proprietary gush that characterized "the divine Jane," his pet name for Ms. Austen. Yet whether as friend working patiently with manuscripts or professional reviewer commenting on the finished product, Howells read attentively, with an interest that never flagged (as it did for example seem to wane with respect to the later Henry James), and with an appreciation not just of the humor but also of the way Mark Twain intermingled the humorous with a realistic sense of the darker underside of human experience. Now I wish to return the favor. I want to read *The Rise of Silas Lapham* very much as I think it might have been read by Mark Twain in 1884–85. My aim of course is not to supply another explication of *Lapham,* though, in truth, a reading with Mark Twain always over one's shoulder does seem to turn up narrative emphases and complications that have not invariably been caught by Howells's devotees. Rather, the concern is to understand Mark Twain's "perspective" by detecting in *Lapham* practices which Mark Twain might have regarded as similar to his own—and also practices and attitudes which he might have admired, but could not emulate.

The book (or first magazine installment in the *Century*) which Mark Twain opened in 1884 or 1885 itself opens with the presentation of a dialectic, the development of a set of twins whose names are "nature" and "commodity." The paint, as it seeps one morning from the soil of the Lapham farm in Vermont, has utterly no value in or of itself. In fact, it might well be regarded as a great misfortune since it soon sprawls across land that has hitherto been used for farming. Within the paint, of course, lies the potential for becoming useful and, after further refinement, even decorative. But before raw nature can be transformed to a valuable product, two actions have to intervene. Silas's intelligence must supply him with an idea about how to cope with the mess. The diligence of Silas must allow him to act on his idea, until through a combination of ambition, hard work and business acumen, chaos is recast into orderly rows of "The Persis Brand."[15] Though participating in both members of the original dialectic, intelligence and diligence are obviously of a different order from either. Neither "nature" nor "commodity" they are instances of what I want to call a "third condition." It is the function of the "third condition" to combine and mediate, to touch on something in such a way that, though retaining its original features, the something is changed to something else, and something better. Paint-as-slovenly-nature bridged to paint-as-disciplined-commodity is the particular achievement of the third condition here. From the incident, however, we may move to another generalization about the comic structure. In comedy, this same "third condition" is what is required to draw "positive outcomes" out of "negative occasions."[16] The third condition, in a word, is the great assimilator—the great synthesizer—which makes comedy possible.

The first dialectic in *Lapham* gives rise to the much more complicated twinning that occupies the foreground of the novel. On one side is life "western-style": Laphams, roots in rural Vermont, execrable taste and crudities of behavior that at times border on boorishness—but also the energy, openness and goodheartedness that bespeak a close proximity to nature. Life "eastern style" comprises the other side: Coreys, traditions of Harvard and patrician Boston, patronizing airs, artificiality and an excessive sense of social distinction—but likewise the wit, charm and impeccable taste that come in consequence of being urbane and cultured. Fine ironist that he is, Howells can discern amusing connections between the two sides; the pairing of Paint King with dilettante painter has often been observed. And as a confirmed moralist he is never behind hand about emphatically separating "stalwart achievement" from "sterile elegance." (*RSL*, 128.) At his best, however, he addresses the situation through the eyes of a Balzacian realist. His narrative is concerned to show that despite their individual strengths both ways of life are deeply flawed and that contact between them often brings out the worst in each. Seeking to ape high society, Silas forgoes common sense and commits a number of unpardonable acts, not the least of which is trying to manipulate Irene into marriage with Tom Corey. Conversely, the presence of the Laphams serves to underscore the vast emptiness of the Coreys' days, and it evokes the finickiness and catty snobbery of which the Coreys are all too capable.

Without doing so obtrusively, therefore, Laphams and Coreys add up to a total civilization which, in the hundredth year of the American republic (the events take place in 1876) is sorely in need of regeneration. More than a medleying of opposites is called for this time. If resolution and redemption are to occur, the negatives of each group will have to be shown as possessing a potential for positive behavior; then, perhaps, recognizing their latent compatibility, both groups can join into the positive outcome of an initiation story or a successful social comedy. This is the complex strategy which Howells undertakes to work out in *Lapham*. The novel becomes his secular version of Milton's

Fortunate Fall. Significantly, the strategy is launched by an event that takes place in Chapter 14 at the Coreys' dinner, where on the face of it relations between the two groups reach a low point, and the prospects for harmonizing eastern with western—hosts and their guests—have never seemed dimmer.

Desultory table talk drifts to the subject of the "'deserving poor'" in a nearby slum. For a moment or two, it is suggested that the mansions of Beacon Street, left empty through the summer by vacationing owners, ought to be thrown open to "'poor creatures stifling in their holes and dens . . . the little children, dying for some wholesome shelter.'" Of course the moment and the mood soon languish (what of the furniture? asks Anna Corey). And it is noteworthy that from having proposed sacrifice, the diners pass next to a discussion of the contemporary novel *Tears Idle Tears* (they retitle it *Slop Silly Slop*) which allows them to snicker at the possibility of sacrificial conduct. (*RSL*, 171–75.) Nevertheless, the aim of this episode is not just satirical. The diners truly feel a sense of guilt, really desire to take some sort of responsibility for the unfortunate. If only they knew how, the Coreys and their circle—none of them bad people— would like to do more with their lives than smoke cigarettes aesthetically like Bromfield, or tread a dreary social routine in the manner of the Corey women and Miss Kingsbury.

At the time, uncouth Silas "had wanted to speak up," but was too muddled with wine and self-importance to do so. Presently, however, he demonstrates that he understood what the Coreys were saying, and he shows them how to bring to fruition their own best impulses. The prospective buyers of his lands in Iowa are wholly unknown to Silas; living somewhere off in England, they are less his familiars by far than the Boston slum dwellers. Yet when in Chapter 25 he discovers the lands to be worthless, he does on behalf of these faceless and anonymous people a remarkable thing. Putting aside self and family, he chooses bankruptcy in preference to selling. If this seems an extreme gesture, it likewise amounts to a full realization of what the diners could merely talk of doing. Lapham has succored and sheltered the complete stranger.

The impressive movement of *Lapham* is thus at once circular and upward. First, natural and overly aggressive Silas takes from well-meaning but effete culture an idea that is noble: a restatement of the Golden Rule, an affirmation that one *is* one's brother's keeper. Next, he energizes the idea, thereby curbing his aggressive tendencies, and turns it back to its donors as an accomplished fact. The third stage completes a synthesis of the best of nature with the best of culture, and uses the fact that they can now minister to one another to explain the title of the book. In the end the gentry of Beacon Street cannot really accept Silas as socially one of theirs. They behave awkwardly with respect to the marriage of Pen and Tom, which, however, is so de-emphasized by the conclusion that it seems less a test of anyone than a kind of narrative sop. For the important thing is that the gentry do honor and admire Silas. Without fully comprehending his sacrifice, or quite grasping how the idea for acting sacrificially originated with them, they are still exalted and uplifted by the force of the example it presents. As the comments of the Reverend Mr. Sewell make evident, in the personal rise of Silas the whole of a social scene has been revitalized and left morally superior to what it was before.

If shrewdness and hard work were the meliorating forces which transmuted nature into commodity, what makes possible the far less predictable convergence of Lapham and Corey? Upon what, in other words, does Howells predicate a "third condition" for the initiation story? Two matters are involved, I think, the first being definable as *pluck*.

Even when they strike us as least attractive the major characters of *Lapham* are actuated by the wish to change and renew themselves; they are creatures of reason and conscience, who share the nineteenth-century conviction that it is proper (and always possible) to rise to "better things" on the "stepping stones" of dead and discarded identities. The only exception of consequence would be Silas's once and present business partner, the somewhat mysterious Milton K. Rogers. Again and again, Rogers is portrayed through a single set of descriptive terms, emphasizing his woodenness and deadness; over and over, he turns up to express the same obsessions, which are greed and a need for business conniving. He seems less character than caricature. But he is this because he has no inner life, no desire to change and grow and be morally otherwise—in a word no pluck. Typifying the worst of east (like Bromfield Corey he is well spoken, but a poseur) and the worst of west (as his dealings with Silas make manifest), Rogers is incapable of drawing moral sustenance from either way of life. The reconciliation of Laphams with Coreys stems from the slow and tentative way in which members of each group can come to imagine being members of the other. Rogers is prepared to imagine being only himself, Milton K. Rogers. Notably, the act of reconciliation leaves him ruined completely, a robot still, as from his initial appearance in Chapter 3 his "dust colored face" and "dead . . . air" and voice "like two pieces of wood clapped together" had made him seem more a mechanical man than a human being with human potential. (*RSL*, 40.)

The second, and no less essential matter, is definable as *luck*. It is not by chance that, opening in the Spring, *Lapham* proceeds in straight-line fashion through all four seasons of the year 1875. The passage from Spring to Winter registers the downward trajectory of Silas, as he moves from the birth of social and financial delusions to the time when a "'cold wave'" strikes his business and fires at the paint mine are banked "for the first time in memory." (*RSL*,

287.) But it likewise supplies the general atmosphere of blight and morbidity that envelopes everyone else in the novel—and every action, ranging from Rogers's reappearance to the hysteria of Irene and Pen to the disaster of the dinner party. Modern life itself seems to be dying down into a cold wave. Yet if Spring prepares for Winter, Winter can give promise of the rebirth of Spring. In the Spring of 1876, Silas arises Phoenix-like from the uninsured ashes of his mansion. He casts off Rogers's influence. He makes his great moral choice. Brought down, he is also brought back to the green world of Vermont. And as he goes, the Boston world he left behind has, with him and through him, been restored to some semblance of health and sanity. Straight-line turns to cycle, as the rotating seasons that thrust a social scene down toward blight and darkness have all the while been working to return the scene back into the world of the sunlight.

*Pluck,* then, is the inner drive—the intelligence, the human resourcefulness—that allows negative occasions to be meliorated into positive outcomes. *Luck* is an underlying principle of benevolence that absorbs negative into positive, as a testament to the essential fitness of experience. Portrayed by *Lapham* as forces that join, the two are also themselves joined in the book, as seems invariably to be the case in traditional comedy. In fact, from the way pluck and luck both merge and are merged, it becomes possible to treat *Lapham* as one more example of the traditional comic formulation—and then to complicate the formula a bit. It seems legitimate to say that although the twins east and west (culture and nature) much need each other, they are shown in the book to travel in fundamentally reversed directions, with the ironic result that while moving apart they likewise repeat one another's mistakes. Yet were it not for this adversarial relationship, and the tensions and antagonisms it begets, there would be no basis for plucky Lapham to take from the Coreys an idea which both smooths his rough edges and also brings out the best in them, as the Coreys rise up to honor him for his moral heroism. That is the familiar pattern of comedy. Now, the complication. What ultimately synthesizes the twins is— and it is equally in all the other examples of traditional comedy I have cited—a rhythm or momentum that does not come exclusively from either twin. They are united by the third condition, consisting partly of their pluck. But it is pluck acting in conjunction with luck: it is the concerted force of *pluck-luck* that saves them—earns for them the comic ending.[17]

Often irascible with respect to the fictions of his contemporaries, Mark Twain may have begun reading Howells as a matter of courtesy, after the two became fast friends in the mid-1870s. But I like to suppose that by 1884 doing the merely polite thing had been supplanted by a genuine interest in what Howells wrote, and the way Howells worked through various problems of nar-

rative as he assembled a good story. There is much in the dialectical presentation of *Lapham* which had to be appealing to Mark Twain, whose own works
stressed doublenesses and the ironic and humorous links which the doubles
share. Like most contemporary readers, Mark Twain probably saw the Corey
dinner party as the dramatic high (and low) point of the novel. And his enjoyment would surely have been enhanced through the recognition that in portraying two sets of characters who speak the same language, yet speak it so
differently as to be virtually unintelligible to one another, Howells was using a
technique he himself had employed in the early sketches and in *Roughing It*.
Finally, unlike certain modern readers, Mark Twain would not have been put
off by anything "transcendental" or excessive in Lapham's determination not to
commit fraud. Cynically (and secretly), he might have noted that no good deed
goes unpunished, since Silas's self-impoverishment must also result in the im-
poverishment of decent, uninvolved workers who tend the paint mine in Vermont. On the other hand, in 1884 Mark Twain had just created a character who
willingly risks Hell in order to maintain an impractical, socially unconven-
tional commitment to a Black companion. And four years later, toward the end
of *A Connecticut Yankee in King Arthur's Court,* he would show that the cost
of Hank Morgan's wish to reform Arthurian society was the renunciation of
Hank's privileges and prerogatives as "The Boss." The private action that goes
well beyond the bounds of self-serving practicality was by no means unfamiliar
in his writing.

All the same, admiration does not necessarily result in the capacity, or even
the wish, to emulate. Among the characters and character relationships formed
in *Lapham,* Mark Twain no doubt made all the correct moral responses. The
fact remains, however, that aesthetically speaking he could feel fully at home
with only one of Howells's characters—and this, by all odds, the least attractive
one. He might soften the villainy by turning it into a feckless, tunnel-visioned
disregard for the welfare of others, as he does with Horace Bixby and George
Ealer in "Old Times on the Mississippi." Alternatively, he might maintain the
villainy, yet take the sting out of it by treating it as a humorous stereotype
which can do no real harm, as is the case with both the Good Boy and the Bad
Boy. But Mark Twain was utterly devoid of Howells's faith in the "third condition," that mediating principle which lets darkness and blight descend, yet
wrests from the descent a return of light. His sense of the damned human race
allowed for no pluck-luck formulation, whereby driven or partial selves are
made whole though self-sacrifice or good fortune or a combination of self-
sacrifice and good fortune. Accordingly, wherever he begins and however he
proceeds, he must come around at last to the figure of Howells's moral-social
cipher. That is, he must ultimately represent for us some version or other

of Milton K. Rogers, and present us with some version or other of Milton K. Rogers's ultimate triumph.

And the wonder is he makes the spectacle seem funny. For though shunted aside in Howelis's version, Milton K. Rogers clearly belongs to what in Mark Twain is the indestructible company of Eng and old "Green Face." Like them, he demonstrates that Falls are pratfalls—hence never Fortunate, though always laughable.


## V

Darwin abolished special creations . . . and hitched all life together in one unbroken procession of Siamese twins.
            —Mark Twain in "The Secret History of Eddypus"

He said a body had got to perpetuate [the bad God] in all kinds of ways. Tom allowed he said propitiate, but I heard him as well as Tom, and he said perpetuate.
            —Huck in *Huck and Tom Among the Indians*

In the beginning, says the Manichee of the 6th century A.D., the universe was not void or without form. Rather, prior to the beginning the twins Light and Dark had always coexisted as equal but separate entities. Their collision, really as a kind of comic inadvertence at the beginning (they simply looked up and noticed each other for the first time) was at once of the profoundest significance and ludicrous. It results in a classic instance of eschatology worked up into the terms of scatological narrative. Having devoured the Sons of Light, the Archons of Dark were compelled, through a ruse of Light, to disgorge and excrete their feedings. Passing voluptuously before Darkness, the Daughters of Light secured a further release of entrapped goodness when they caused the evil Archons to ejaculate. Out of this mess of soilings and spendings—this by-now thoroughly mixed substance of good and evil—emerged the beginning as human life knows it. First came the formation of the material universe; then the creation of Adam and Eve; next human history; and finally the purpose of history. For, half cosmology, half tall-tale (withal a wonderfully solemn and grotesque account of the discovery and settlement of a brave new universe) Manicheanism is also deeply preoccupied with the meaning of things to come. In the unfolding of history is discerned a constant process of converting negative occasions into positive outcomes. "The King of Light ordered the present world built out of mixed particles," writes an early disciple of Mani, "so that through time the light particles might be separated out of the dark particles."[18]

I hold the structure of traditional literary comedy to be instinctively, inveterately (and no doubt far, far more often than not) subliminally Manichean. Of course when it starts off by exploring the dark cave, the comic text is simply in search of those complications and conflicts which are the stuff of life in any piece of interesting literature. Again, when it delivers darkness into the sunlight, comedy may be dependent upon any number of strategies for the happy ending, ranging from Professor Frye's Christian transcendence to "sweet are the uses of adversity" to "making the best of a bad lot." But what distinguishes the great moments of comedy is not so much point of departure or place of arrival as it is the sheer drama of moving between these two radically opposite poles. It is the vital continuity of extracting light out of the mixed particles of experience which counts for the most. Whether seen chiefly as a matter of willed effort or of underlying benevolence or of both in an exact balance (truly *pluck-luck*) it is the impulse behind the continuity, the energy that sets the progression in motion and keeps it going, which is made to seem most impressive. And in stressing process, as well as in equating process with progress, comedy reveals its origins in the Manichean world view. The house that Mani built can as readily accommodate Victor Frankenstein's joyous use of the monster as Silas's somber realization that he had to clamber out of a "'dark hole'" before recovering green Vermont—and still have space left for Hero and Claudio, who do not so much earn a triumph over Don John as have their nuptials bestowed upon them in demonstration of the fact that life *does* eventually turn out well. These figures, and many more besides, are but attuned to the edict of the King of Light which says what comedy says: that while there is no extinguishing darkness, the dark acts do generate a journey, and the journey gets somewhere.

Manicheanism is an efficient way of structuring experience. Simply and straightforwardly, it demystifies everything we call process, ranging from phases of the moon (a receptacle forever gathering, transferring and reabsorbing liberated Light) to the comic outcome. Probably there are more Manichees on earth than conventional theology has dreamt of. But, precisely by virtue of remaining so neat and comprehensive, it is also open to a vastly different interpretation. Suppose, for example, the present world had been blueprinted by an edict from the King of Dark? If transitions from cave to sunlight no longer seem likely, still the dualities persist, with the promise, not to say the necessity, of one thing being assimilated by—transformed into—something else. How might a creative imagination respond to this prospect? What might be the look of narrative under this new dispensation? Let us try to answer by constructing hypothetically (though not, I expect, implausibly) the case of a confirmed moral dualist who, at the age of thirty or thereabouts, might resist certain of the labels we will apply to him, but not, I suspect, the habit of mind which the terms designate.

Without the promise up ahead of Augustine's Christianity, he has begun to sense with Augustine that when life is apportioned too nicely between Light and Dark, "one can make out no progress in it."[19] As a matter of fact, though never able to muster the cool detachment of a Voltaire (whom he knows and respects by now) or of a Pierre Bayle, he is already susceptible to believing that a world where Light is gained through the test of Dark is really the world of battered Candide—or Bayle's world, in which legs are gratuitously broken to demonstrate the prowess of a Divine Bonesetter. And so, with no knowledge of Captain Ahab and with (as yet) none of Ahab's clenched-fist rage, he is nonetheless borne along on Ahab's journey toward "'the darker half . . . , a prouder, if darker faith!'"[20] It will be seen that the attitudes taking possession of this figure are by no means a rarity among writers of the American nineteenth century. He shares perspectives with Melville and Emily Dickinson, with Stephen Crane and Henry Adams—confirmed moral dualists all, each nagged by the suspicion that the pairings on the mottled surface of experience are so tipped toward the dark side as to be shaped and linked by some sort of underlying monism. But our figure, as he well knows, is one singled out to "excite the *laughter* of God's creatures."[21] And this means that his earliest intimations of inequity, disequilibrium, and the Infernal Oneness will come when he adds a "snapper" to the "snapper" which had previously been added to a "snapper." As peace-loving Chang is drawn ineluctably under Eng's drunken and disorderly influence, and while readers are told there is much to ponder in the spectacle, it occurs to the narrator that

> having forgotten to mention it sooner, I will remark in conclusion, that the ages of the Siamese twins are respectively fifty-one and fifty-three years. ("Siamese Twins," 280.)

Examining them from the standpoint of a total career, Henry Nash Smith and more recently Susan Gillman have detected in Mark Twain's presentation of twins a mystery of identity. "Were the twins one person or two?" Professor Smith asked rhetorically. "If two, could either be considered truly his own master?"[22] Out of like questions Professor Gillman develops her narrower and far more specialized analysis of Mark Twain. He was, she argues, fatally at a loss to draw with firmness and clarity any of the boundaries that normally distinguish one person, or state, or condition from another. The amorphous relationship—a failure to tell twins apart, a corresponding inability to put twins together meaningfully—thus shapes a body of writing which early on had to forsake "literal, literary conventions of external, consciously controlled identity," which presently "became entangled with a social convention that treats identity as culturally controlled," but which ended up portraying an "imposture that is . . . internal, confusing and therefore uncontrollable: a psychologi-

cal as opposed to a social condition." And the climax (if not precisely the cul-
mination) of this movement occurs with Mark Twain's choice of the title for a
late, typically murky, typically "decentered" narrative. The title was *Which Was
It?*—"it" being seen by Professor Gillman to incorporate uncertainties of dress,
gender, race, the law; of dream vs. waking, freedom vs. captivity, appearance
vs. reality; of the many-faceted personality and the muddled state of society
generally.[23]

But I propose a very different mapping of Mark Twain's reliance on twins—
and hence a very different view of his work. When doubles recur in his fictions,
they are never borrowed from Plautus or *A Comedy of Errors*, where the ambiguity of which-is-which is central. Nor is the tone of the presentation ever really provisional, problematic, or, in any meaningful sense, interrogatory. Nor,
consequently can *Which Was It?* be other than ironic, the wry mockery of an
author who asks, having already perfectly grasped the answer and grasped, as
well, that "murkiness" and "decenteredness" (both synonymous with "imbal-
anced") are products of the answer rather than the question.[24] From the moment the "personal habits" of twins first crossed his mind, Mark Twain knew
to a certainty which-was-which. He understood that far from muddying relationships in the real world, the doubles defined reality and, what is more,
pointed to the fixed-as-fate inevitability which reality brings to pass in human
affairs. His knowledge was of two oppositional identities who are fused infer-
nally through the transforming authority—the "third condition"—of primogeniture.

This is the perception which explains why (who will doubt it?) 53-year-old
Eng does not so much lead Chang astray as assimilate the "younger" twin into
an "older" twin's prerogative for mischief. Eng has seniority. It explains why
warring tendencies in a narrator's mind are resolved only when, like little hand
below big hand, effete and decorous "Mark Twain" who only wanted to do the
right thing is overridden by "Green Face," and thereupon liberated by "the
right thing" to the commitment of a mass murder. "Mark Twain" has succumbed
to the underside of personality, which is more energetic because primal—more
primitive.[25] But there is more. The reign of darkness is our key to why the good
boy and the bad boy, each after his own fashion a "plucky" boy, have to end up
as one boy, climaxing *his* career with a single destructive action. Most particularly, it elucidates for us why at the end of a long journey, which was supposed
to lead outward and upward to personal enlightenment, Mark Twain (never
having heard of him either) must ponder Ishmael's question, "But whereto does
all this circumnavigation conduct"—and conclude with Ishmael "only through
numberless perils to the very point whence we started." (*Moby-Dick*, 1846.)
For as if thrusting back to a world view even more primordial than that of
Manicheanism, Mark Twain, whether by design or intuitively, arrives at the de-

termination of the progenitors of Mani himself. Twins are his means of dramatizing the recognition that the underlying principle of *luck* is what it is, and
hence the luck-shaped outcomes of the present world are what they are, because first in the order of creation came the twin Ahriham, who was dark, corrupting and disruptive, and not until afterward (two years? six months? merely
as a kind of negligent afterthought?) was born the gentle, giving and benign
brother, Ohrmad.[26]

A world with one immutable outcome is not just devoid of improvement,
progress, or any ultimate purpose; it is a world without movement. Only give
him time, therefore, and Mark Twain will add most wonderfully to the absurd
and grotesque spectacle of getting nowhere, which is the substance of his early
fictions. He will render inviolate the sunlit world of Tom Sawyer by dropping
over half of it (the deeper, darker, realistic half) a curtain. But an inviolate
world is a world without motion. Dissatisfied with this result, he will lift the
curtain, bring Huck Finn out of the thoroughly flawed world it discloses to the
high comic resolve of Chapter 31 in Huck's adventures; and then take pains to
raise the curtain on a Huck who, having fallen under Tom's spell, is going home
to Tom's world as one wholly indistinguishable from Tom Sawyer. As before,
nothing moves. Mark Twain will locate Hank Morgan in the text of a medieval
romance, which being fixed, frozen and Platonized rules out any possibility for
motion, and relocate him after a while in the flow of human history, which is
equally fixed, frozen, immobilized—and hence antipathetical to change. He
will write a detective story in which, having solved a crime of 23-years standing, the detective reveals the world to be exactly as it was on the day the crime
was committed. He will give us theories of civilization in which everything
"moves" and "evolves"—and then, in a striking parallel with Nietzsche's "eternal recurrence," he will contradict the usual meaning of movement and evolution by arguing that everything is really being repeated, so that the wonders of
today are nothing more than a reenactment of yesterday's follies. He will compose a Nietzschean rite de passage wherein Theodor Fischer seems elevated
from human ignorance to knowledge of the gods—only to show how ignorance, knowledge, the gods and Theodor (now renamed August Feldner) are
all aspects of one vast and presumably unmoving nothingness. And in the end,
with Vonnegut's sardonic gesture of "so it goes"—with Moses Herzog's " 'We're
lost! Fucked!' " on his mind if not his lips—he will consign the whole business
to wander forever through a limbo he styles "the Great Dark." But, since it is
limbo, wandering there must of course consist of one unceasing, hence station-
ary voyage through a single drop of water.

Oh, there is no end to the illusion of motion in Mark Twain. The world that
rotates and rotates to stand stone still, that changes and changes to deny every

and any possibility of change, is Mark Twain's *sine que non:* his standard joke. And what is his, and our, response to the joke meant to be? Why, insistently we are urged to share in a sound that is much heard in Mark Twain's early stories, and will (if somewhat more helpless and hopeless) continue unabated into the late ones as well. In one sense we are encouraged to join Eng's guffaw at Chang's discomfiture, to ally ourselves with the belly-laugh sneer that Jim proffers on his way to the Governor's Mansion, to become one with the mad chuckle of Jacob Blivens as he wreaks devastation from a humane act. In a larger and deeper sense, though, our snickers reenact those of Creative Mar-plots as they survey the unequal, out-of-balance handiwork which they have brought to pass in Connecticut and the Mississippi Valley: handiwork which is what it is, because (and once more a paraphrase of the horror-man is in order) Light has dwindled down and "Darkness . . . [holds] illimitable dominion over all."[27]

For where the Manichean twins Dark and Light are hitched together by the twins *pluck and luck,* all acting in concert, the motions of John the Bastard may one day merge with those of Dogberry and Verges to produce Hero and Claudio at the head of a grand comic processional. Then, though we will certainly have laughed at mistakes made and stupidities revealed along the way, the final pleasure we take will not quite be expressed through laughter. But the circuit of comedy is altered when the tune called for two is invariably the prerogative of a dark and leering first-born. Now, fated villainy prances center stage, trailed always by good intentions that can come to nothing. Now, each "positive pos-sibility" will only loop back to duplicate its "negative occasion." We are denied the comic resolution, and left instead with an example of that well-turned ca-per we call "the joke." To amend Oscar Wilde a little,[28] it would take a leaden sensibility not to laugh at the successful gull of prim, obtuse Hero and her gul-lible compatriots. Yet while the impact of the joke may be more immediate— more side-splitting to watch than the moral outcomes of comedy—still the joke risks unsettling our sense of the fitness of things. Indeed, in the presence of the joke, laughter, which is our only adequate response, may also be a re-sponse that is more than slightly unnerving. In the word Tom used, the laugh may have to "propitiate" the bad god. Or, in the word Huck understood, it may have to function as a tool for the bad god's "perpetuation."[29]

## NOTES

1. Mark Twain supplies dates for "The Personal Habits of the Siamese Twins," "Story of the Bad Boy," "Story of the Good Boy," and "My Watch" in Volume XIX ("Sketches New and Old") of *Works,* Hillcrest Edition (New York: Harper, 1903). Refer-

ences to the four stories I will be emphasizing are from this volume: "Personal Habits of the Siamese Twins," 273–80; "Bad Boy," 54–60; "Good Boy," 60–68; "My Watch—An Instructive Little Tale," 11–16. Since the stories are very short, I have not clogged the text with page numbers.

2. *Selected Mark Twain–Howells Letters, 1872–1910*, ed. Fredrick Anderson, William M. Gibson, and Henry Nash Smith (Cambridge: Harvard University Press, 1967), 21.

3. References to "Recent Carnival of Crime" (hereafter "CC") are from *Selected Shorter Writings of Mark Twain*, ed. Walter Blair (Boston: Houghton Mifflin, 1962), 135–50.

4. Mark Twain's reactions to "Jekyll and Hyde" (1886) are well known. It was, he acknowledged, a work of "genius and power"; yet the story erred in allowing the "dual persons in one body . . . to step into the other person *at will*." Though he goes on in the same passage to belittle "Carnival" as (in comparison to Stevenson) a "crude attempt to work out the duality idea," it must be emphasized that his text does *not* enact Stevenson's "error." True authority has always lain with "Green Face," so that at the end one partner has displaced—replaced—the other, without regard to the other's wishes or will. Also, of course, Mark Twain offers us no sententious lawyer (named Utterson!), to neaten up the deranged world and restore it to normal with a few well-uttered platitudes, as happens in Stevenson. See *Mark Twain Notebook*, ed. Albert Bigelow Paine (New York: Harper, 1936), 348–50.

Of the interpretations which read "Carnival of Crime" as well-wrought fiction (instead of mere autobiography) the one which comes closest to mine is offered by Gregg Camfield. "By story's end," he writes, "the narrator is just as 'devilish' [as his conscience]. One of the implicit answers to Clemens's conundrum, then, is that the conscience reflects all of a human being's 'malignant' traits . . . in order to balance them in action." But my view is that "Mark Twain" becomes as devilish as "Green Face" precisely because he becomes "Green Face," who sets all his "malignant traits," hitherto repressed, into full motion. See *Sentimental Twain: Samuel Clemens in the Maze of Moral Philosophy* (Philadelphia: University of Pennsylvania Press, 1994), 119.

5. All references are to "Old Times on the Mississippi" ("OT") in Walter Blair's *Selected Shorter Writings of Mark Twain*, 64–130.

6. The catastrophe appears in Chapter 20 of *Life on the Mississippi*, in effect the next-to-last chapter of "Old Times." I have used the Signet Edition of *Life* (New York: New American Library, 1961). The transitional chapters—15–21—run from 99 to 139.

7. *Mark Twain's Notebooks and Journals*, ed. Frederick Anderson and others (Berkeley: University of California Press, 1975), Vol. II, 449–50.

8. Leslie Fiedler, *Love and Death in the American Novel* (Cleveland: Dell, 1966), 560, 565.

9. The first definition is of course that of Northrop Frye, "The Argument of Com-

edy," *English Institute Essays* (New York: Columbia University Press, 1949), 61. My sense of "traditional comedy" is also much affected by Professor Frye's chapter "The Mythos of Spring: Comedy" in *Anatomy of Criticism* (Princeton: Princeton University Press, 1957), 163–86, and by Susanne Langer, "The Comic Rhythm," *Feeling and Forms* (New York: Scribners, 1953), 326–50. The second, "earlier" definition is from Walter Kerr, *Tragedy and Comedy* (New York: Simon and Schuster, 1967), 64.

10. Molière, *Tartuffe*, tr. Richard Wilbur (New York: Harcourt Brace and World, 1965). The exchange takes place in Act V, scene i, 301.

11. "Sunrise in His Pocket," *Native American Humor,* ed. Walter Blair (San Francisco: Chandler, 1960), 285–86.

12. Auden, "The Prince's Dog," in *The Dyer's Hand* (New York: Random House, 1948), 205.

13. Howells's review appeared in the *Atlantic,* June 1872. It is reprinted in his *My Mark Twain* (New York: Harper, 1911), 113–16.

14. The fullest accounts of which I am aware are W. H. Auden's brief (and slightly disappointing) note "Huck and Oliver," repr. in Henry Nash Smith, ed., *Mark Twain: A Collection of Critical Essays* (Englewood Cliffs, N.J.: Prentice-Hall, 1963), 112–17, and the excellent essay of J. Hillis Miller, "Three Problems of Fictional Form: First-Person Narration in *David Copperfield* and *Huckleberry Finn*" in *Experience in the Novel: Selected Papers from the English Institute* (New York: Columbia University Press, 1968), 35–60. A parallel study would, I suspect, begin with contrast: *Oliver Twist* or *David Copperfield* vs. *Tom Sawyer* or *Huckleberry Finn*, as Professor Miller demonstrates and as I have argued in the Introduction. But it would end in similarity. With what Chapter 12 of *Bleak House* calls "the perpetual stoppage," Dickens has come upon a world weighed down (bogged down) by weariness and lassitude, an essentially unmoving and unmovable world. He has, in other words, developed or had thrust upon him essentially the same view of experience which Mark Twain knew intuitively from the outset. The darkness of later Dickens has been much studied, though probably never better than in two early pieces of criticism: Lionel Stevenson, "Dickens's Dark Novels: 1851–57," *Sewanee Review* (Summer 1947), and Edgar Johnson, *Charles Dickens: His Tragedy and Triumph* (London: V. Gollancz, 1952.)

15. All references to *The Rise of Silas Lapham* are to the Norton Critical Edition, ed. Don L. Cook (New York: Norton, 1982). Hereafter, the title will be abbreviated *RSL*.

16. Perhaps quite knowingly, Howells has drawn upon Emerson's *Nature*, published in 1836. There, in the second chapter called "Commodity," details from the physical world ("fire, water, stones, corn, etc.") are turned into "useful arts" through the agency of the third condition, named "wit of man." It might also be noted that *Nature* itself is a kind of comedy—a Divine Comedy, with "Inferno" left out. In "Purgatory" (the lower world, the world as it is) wit, perspective, love of knowledge serve to link the "not me" to the "me," while, properly tested (or "disciplined") by the lower, the human spirit and

the human will-to-know act as third conditions which presently link "lower world" to the Paradise of Spirit which is envisioned in the last section of Emerson's little book.

17. Though both *pluck* and *luck* enter into the third or transforming condition of comedy, they may of course be present in different proportions. Thus, *Much Ado About Nothing* would seem to present *LUCK/pluck*, *Lysistrata* is more nearly a matter of *PLUCK/luck*. I shall return to these distinctions, and make more of them, in the essay on *Pudd'nhead Wilson*. For now it seems worth adding that one of the marks of Howells's skill is how deftly he maintains the balance in *Lapham*.

18. Hans Jonas, *The Gnostic Religion* (Boston: Beacon Press, 1958), 224. Though it necessarily makes but a single appearance in this study of Mark Twain, words are not adequate to express my indebtedness to this book.

19. Peter Brown, *Augustine of Hippo* (Berkeley: University of California Press, 1969), 46–48.

20. *Moby-Dick*, ed. G. Thomas Tanselle (New York: New American Library, 1983), 1080.

21. Sam Clemens to Orion and Mollie Clemens, dated 19 October 1865. Reprinted in *My Dear Bro: A Letter from Samuel Clemens to his Brother Orion*, ed. Frederick Anderson (Berkeley: University of California Press, 1961), 6–8.

22. Smith, *Mark Twain: The Development of a Writer*, 174.

23. Gillman, *Dark Twins: Imposture and Identity in Mark Twain's America*, 8, 172–79.

24. "The Man that Corrupted Hadleyburg" and *Which Was It?*, narratives in which boundaries are said by Professor Gillman to collapse into chaos, will be examined from quite another standpoint in my last essay.

Now seems a good time to note some curious affinities between *Dark Twins* and *Was Huck Black?* The same refusal (or inability) to work within established categories is said by one book to be the measure of Mark Twain's confusions, by the other to characterize his tolerance. I suggest that the first view short changes his work by making it more helplessly confused than is ever the case; that the second imputes to his work attitudes which we would like to find but which (alas) are not really present to the significant degree upon which *Was Huck Black?* insists.

25. Again, a cross reference to R. L. Stevenson seems in order. Pretty clearly Jekyll/Hyde, "Mark Twain"/"Green Face" conform to what in a later time we have come to think of as Superego and Id. But where Stevenson's smooth, lucid lawyer who explains the story incarnates the Ego, Mark Twain has no Ego to offer us. The concept of the well adjusted personality (so central to traditional comedy) will forever elude him as a comic ending, will forever lie beyond his creative grasp. He may very well crave both; but both are denied him by his curious view of how reality works.

26. Jonas, *The Gnostic Religion*, 217.

27. I have slightly amended the last three sentences of Poe's "Masque of the Red

Death"; in the original they read: "And the life of the ebony clock went out with that of the last of the gay. And the flames of the tripods expired. And Darkness and Decay and the Red Death held illimitable dominion over all." It might be amusing to ponder some connections between Poe's "ebony clock" and Mark Twain's pocketwatch.

28. At the death of little Nell. One might add that it would also take a hard heart not to laugh at the confusions of Silas, though the heart is of course meant to be gladdened when he overcomes them. But with all moral inhibitions gone (as they must be in a world governed by darkness) the heart is free to laugh freely at the antics of John the Bastard—or at manipulations and maneuverings emitted, like so many splinters, from the wooden lips of that Bastard, Milton K. Rogers.

29. The emphasis here, as I said in the "Introduction," is on the tale rather than the teller, whom I leave to the fine insights of Justin Kaplan. Yet having used Mr. Kaplan, in the introduction, to spell out a trace of meanness in Mark Twain, I feel obligated to gloss *Mr. Clemens and Mark Twain* for some evidence of why the teller's attitudes developed as they did.

So, concisely: He was born into a family of moderate means and some social distinction, both of which were suddenly taken from him during early adolescence when his father died. He achieved quick eminence on the River, only to have his career stripped from beneath him with the outbreak of the Civil War. He sat out the war in Nevada Territory, safely, but technically as a deserter, and (who will question it?) with the guilty sense of how others, of his age and station, were fighting, suffering and dying back East. He had next to no formal education, preferring instead travel and adventure, and spent much of his mature life consorting with those who would remind him of his rough edges. Like Gatsby he pursued the grail and, unlike Gatsby, won her, though not until the distressed Langdons had made it clear to him that they were checking out his every reference. He had a Midas touch, which betrayed him into bankruptcy; a plebeian's craving for social eminence, underlain by the plebeian's suspicion that when he did dine with kings and millionaires he was present as their funny man; a compelling need for love, together with the sense that loved ones failed him (Susy and Livy died, Clara was "difficult," the epilepsy of Jean brought disgrace to the Clemenses).

Small wonder then if the tale kept veering toward darkness and lodged there. Examined long-range, events in the teller's life habitually followed the same pattern. If it was hardly his style, Mark Twain would have well understood the Emily Dickinson poem which begins

For each ecstatic instant
We must an anguish pay
In keen and quivering ratio
To the ecstasy.

And he would have grasped as well (not all Dickinsonians do) how "ratio" does not signify equal or tit-for-tat:

> Bitter contested farthings—
> And Coffers heaped with tears!

Tragic for Dickinson, the imbalance is the stuff of Mark Twain's comedy.

# Mark Twain and the Sick Joke: An Essay on Laughter

*Sudden Glory* is the passion which maketh those Grimaces
called LAUGHTER; and is caused by either some act of their own,
that pleaseth them; or by the apprehension of some deformed
thing in another, in comparison whereof they suddenly
applaud themselves.

—Hobbes in Book I of *The Leviathan*

## I

With or without Mark Twain bestriding it like a colossus, an essay on laughter
must begin with obligatory references to the instinctive life of nature in contrast to human life which is both instinctive and self-conscious. Here in this
nexus (this often uneasy but always inescapable meeting ground between
partly nature's, partly ours) is, say many experts, the place where the experience of laughter originates. Instead of citing the experts directly, however, I
shall first consign them to a footnote and, much indebted to their wisdom, undertake some examples of my own.[1]

(1) During a flood animals band together instinctively or reflexively and
seek the security of higher ground. If the flood recurs next year those who survived this time will do the same thing again . . . and yet again. Theirs is the
mechanical will to escape danger.

Human beings take to the hills too of course, and go perhaps as the result
of having been first alerted by the animals. But because they can remember,
plan, predict, and compile weather forecasts, even the least technologically sophisticated of human beings are likely to do one thing more. Sooner or later,
they will build earth walls, dikes, dams in order to control the flooding. Theirs
is the conscious need to prevent danger.

(2) Among mammals in nature mating occurs at certain biologically deter-

mined periods of the year and has for its purpose the propagation of the species. Any female in season can arouse any healthy male. As human breeders learn to their sorrow, the pedigreed female and the male cur from the garbage dumps will fulfill nature's injunction to increase and multiply quite as well as any other pair.

Among human mammals the same biological process involves selection, choice, an act of discrimination. The urge is identical for both groups. But the second enacts the urge in ways that are more deliberate and consciously creative.

Elementary. But next I add two complications, the first one farfetched though by no means inconceivable in the modern world, the other a commonplace:

(3) A society goes on a dam-building binge. In the name of "safety," "progress," "vision" or whatever, it erects concrete barriers everywhere, including places where none is needed or appropriate. Such a society would clearly be psychopathic, and, by the way, not wholly unlike the one that made a fetish of backyard bomb shelters a few years back. But if we could observe it rather than share in its madness, we might want to say of it that is a laughable society, in no way amusing to itself, yet made ridiculous to us by the intense (and quite mechanical) fear that "*The floods are coming, the floods are coming.*"

(4) In literature as in life we encounter the figure of the relentless rake. He is a seducer by rote, to whom any and every woman regardless of age, size, shape or appeal is automatically a challenge. Clinical psychology recognizes the type; and medicine, feminism, sexual harassment statutes, and tragedy can portray him as dangerous to himself and others. But seen from a different perspective—viewed as Sir John Falstaff or Faulkner's Januarius Jones, the satyr of *Soldier's Pay*—he is also one to be laughed at. He is the victim less of an unmanageable Oedipus complex than of the laughable truth that "*Seduction means to do and say / The same tired things in the same set way.*"

By way of these examples and complications, it is now possible to rejoin the experts. We can see, as they do, how the laughable consists of an unexpected submergence of the conscious into the mechanical, or (working it the other way around) of an intrusion of the purely mechanical performance into what we expected would be a consciously controlled situation. We may say with them, furthermore, that the experience of laughter—strictly a spectator sport—occurs when, to a spectator's astonishment *who* becomes *which*. Then the human being who ought to behave with ease, grace, flexibility, adaptability, discrimination etc. is actually seen to behave with the rigidity and tireless regularity of the thing, the machine in human form. And at this spectacle we laugh.

Thus, in an example supplied by W. H. Auden:

We laugh *at* the man who walks obliviously along and slips on a banana peel. The joke is that as the most self aware creature on earth he should have watched where he was going, and as the most flexible and adaptable of creatures he should have exercised his knowledge and his freedom to step aside. (Ultimately, of course, we may also laugh *with* him. Suppose he jumps up, brushes himself off and says "Clumsy of me, but I was hurrying along to the bathroom!" Then he will have demonstrated the subjection of consciousness to insistent natural processes not once, but twice over.) But there would be no joke and (says Auden, arguably perhaps) we would not laugh, or not in the same way anyhow, at the man whose self awareness could not have spared him when he slipped and fell on an icy sidewalk.

Again, in an instance of Bergson's "rigidity":

We laugh *at* (and although for different reasons we may well laugh *with*) a giggling, repetitious drunk. The joke is that seeking freedom from mundane cares, he has actually become a slave to the mundane, a classic case of the "mechanical encrusted on to the living." But this encrustation would have gone too far, and our laughter would turn to anxiety if that of the drunk's became hysterical; or amusement would turn to outright disgust if the drunk vomited and collapsed in a public place.

Or to come to the joke that is written down, and hence prepare the way for Mark Twain:

In George Washington Harris's "Rare Ripe Garden Seed," when Sut's friend, Wat, confronts his bride of four-and-a-half months and her fullterm baby, we, Sut and George laugh at Wat's dogged demonstration of the self-evident: "'Aprile, May, June, July an' mos' haf ove August . . . haint enuf, is hit, Mammy?" But if Wat were too much the clod to suspect his cuckoldry, there would be no need for the ciphering and so nothing to laugh at. And were he suddenly to burst into tears, presumably all of us would stop laughing, seeing a nearly exact parallel between Wat's situation and that of Roger Chillingworth, whom Hawthorne does his best to keep totally unfunny.[2]

The qualifications about when to laugh and when to stop are important—at least to most of the experts. Believing that there is more to laughter than a "sudden glory"—as no doubt they would affirm there is more to life than Hobbes's characterization of it as "nasty and brutish and short"—they wish to place rather severe limits on the funny spectacle. Accordingly, they would argue that the transformation of conscious into mechanical patterns of behavior ceases to be laughable if it proceeds to the point of inflicting actual pain on a victim, or of causing us as we watch to feel that our own sense of well-being is in jeopardy. Yet there is something to be said for Hobbes's refusal to equivocate. Even in a world of jokes the victims *are* victimized. And it seems to me noteworthy that as in my two complications those who evoked laughter (the dam builders and the seducers) were simultaneously in need of diagnosis, so in the three illustrations we are shown to laugh at someone's physical discomfiture (the man on the ground may well have sustained a broken back and become paraplegic); at the helplessness of someone (however much it is self-induced by the drunk); and at someone's grave moral dilemma (Wat does genuinely suffer—until Mary assures him she swallowed by accident "rare, ripe garden seed," which can bring corn, tomatoes *and* babies to fruition in only half the usual time). If the laughable are at once funny and morbid, the experience of laughter would appear to be as potentially cruel as it is liberating.

Let us, therefore, put a case anatomically. Rolling up from the human belly, the deepest and richest of laughs will just possibly find their progress impeded, their explosion into pure, pleasurable sound blocked, unless along the way the occasions which beget laughter have acted upon another part of the body. This action involves what, in a somber moment, Bergson termed an "anesthetizing of the human heart."[3]

## II

> I *have* had a "call" to literature . . . to seriously scribbling to excite the *laughter* of God's creatures.
> —Mark Twain to Orion Clemens in 1865[4]

> About once in two minutes his right arm swung to its resting-place on his back again—just the action of a machine, and suggestive of one; regular, recurrent, prompt, exact.
> —Mark Twain writing of Petroleum V. Nasby in *Autobiography* I, 71

No more than George Washington Harris, whose work he did admire, would Mark Twain consciously have patterned getting laughs upon a sophisticated and highly intellectual theory. And the argument for fitting the theory to Harris—whose jokes, as Edmund Wilson once (arguably) observed, are almost unfailingly cruel and brutal—would seem far less applicable to Mark Twain. Despite his affinity for the Sut Luvingood stories, we would reject it partly on the grounds of Mark Twain's genius (others abide our philosophizings, thou art funny), and partly for reasons having to do with the "warmth," spontaneousness," and, even during his darkest days, the "moral fervor" which are widely (if perhaps not quite universally) taken for granted as the staples of his humor.

Yet from his comments on Petroleum V. Nasby's[5] stage manner, it is clear that Mark Twain keenly understood the kinship between laughter and the mechanized life. Moreover, the same understanding is displayed several years later when, in the essay "How to Tell a Story," he wrote what has been called the fullest theoretical account of his own humorous practice. There, seeking to explain why an audience "have laughed until they are exhausted, and the tears running down their face," he chooses for illustration "a dull witted old farmer who has just heard [a funny story] for the first time . . . and is trying to repeat it to a neighbor.

> But he can't remember it; so he gets all mixed up and wanders helplessly round and round, putting in tedious details that don't belong in the tale and only retard it; taking them out conscientiously and putting in others that are just as useless; making minor mistakes now and then and stopping to correct them and explain how he came to make them; remembering things which he forgot to put in their proper place and going back to put them in . . . —and so on, and so on, and so on.[6]

Thus, in both instances, laughter is evoked by a freak, a deformity, a grotesque figure: the one because Nasby adopts the role, the other because the old farmer is made (condemned to be?) all this in the nature of things. And in terms of this double emphasis—this stress upon made-up helplessness and a helplessness that is genuine—I want to consider whether those who laugh *in* or *at* or both *in-and-at* Mark Twain's jokes are ever quite so pure in heart or life-affirming as at first glance they may appear to be. The controlling word is "ever," since my intent is to begin at the beginning—that is, with the story which probably occasioned Mark Twain's "Dear Bro" letter to his brother, and certainly launched his entry into the public domain of American humor.

In all American literature, there is probably no set of circumstances better known. A stranger from back east rides up to a deserted mining camp in northern California. He has brought along a commission from a friend at home to locate the whereabouts of a Reverend Leonidas J. Smiley. When he puts his question to a "garrulous and goodnatured" old miner, Simon Wheeler responds with the story of Jim Smiley and his notorious jumping frog. Interrupted briefly by a voice that calls to him from outside the "decaying tavern," the storyteller pauses for breath, and is about to pass on to an account of Jim Smiley and his one-eyed cow when the narrator breaks free and rides off in confusion and frustration.[7] He leaves behind, however, a question. Why did we laugh? If the narrator who presents the circumstances found nothing to amuse him while listening to Simon, why should we be amused? Why should *I* laugh?

These are not issues for the reader of G. W. Harris's "Rare Ripe Garden Seed." There, clearly, Mammy and Mary have taken advantage of Wat's natural limitations and mechanized him completely, in order to laugh up their sleeves a bit, even as they save their skins from his possible wrath. Nor would they be issues for the spectator who finds in Petroleum V. Nasby's pendulum-like gyrations and metronome-like delivery aspects of a stage performance. Finally no problem exists with respect to the old farmer, since (however pathetic he may seem) a wealth of exposition (he is old, forgetful, "dull-witted," a rube, one who craves attention, etc.) explains the vagaries and eccentricities of his narration. But in "Jumping Frog" who is playing with whom—or is it play, and (if so) what motivates the game, and why is play a necessity? The story troubles like "a rat in the wainscot," to invoke Rebecca West's phrase for another, quite different narrative which both urged her in and shut her out.* Granted it is vintage Mark Twain, what is the point to "Jumping Frog"? Why am I supposed to be amused? Perhaps, I conclude, the answer lies in drawing a distinction which seems not to have been made very much of previously. It is a matter of determining whether to laugh *at* or laugh *with*.

(1) *Laughing at.* According to the account he wrote much later, Mark Twain first heard the story of the gambler and the frog at Angel's Camp east of Sacramento, where it was told by a miner who had no idea of saying anything funny.[8] The possibility arises, then, that "Jumping Frog" means for us to laugh *at* Simon: at his monotone, his methodical and unvarying pace as he goes "drifting along through such a queer yarn without ever smiling." Yet if the joke is on Simon, we ought to be mindful that our laughter is evoked by qualities that are far more complex than the man's humorlessness. Behind his monotone there apparently lies the photographic memory of Simon. He is the victim of a flawless—but mechanically flawless—total-recall, which allows him to summon up every last detail out of the past, not excepting long stretches of bygone conversation repeated verbatim, while at the same time he is left wholly unable to cope with even the simplest request in the present. Mark Twain has thus mechanized Simon, fated him to be humorless, but also fated him to a number of other, rather more unpleasant conditions. Furthermore, he has mechanized him in a particular way.

It is of real interest, I think, to compare Simon's powers of recollection with those that Mark Twain will presently create (or re-create) in other places. When, considerably excited by strong drink, Jim Blaine tries to tell the story of an old ram, or when in "Old Times on the Mississippi" the marvelously equipped Mr. Brown attempts to relate any story, or when the old farmer goes bumbling along in "How to Tell a Story," all are soon caused to flounder in what, with respect to Brown, Mark Twain calls "a great misfortune." ("OT," 112.) Such are

---

* Ms. West was writing of Henry James's *The Sacred Fount*—which, regarded in certain lights, would be a fine example of a joke, maybe even a joke that is very sick.

their retentive capacities that *this* reminds Blaine, Brown, and the farmer of *that;* they interject, digress, roam and wander, stray so far down all manner of labyrinthine ways away from the point that the point itself is never reached. Simon, by contrast, seems lodged inescapably on the point. It is as though the very name *Smiley* were a sort of pull-cord, extending from a wind-up toy: a Captain Kangaroo doll. The cord gets pulled when someone mentions the magical name. Thereafter, the mouth flies open as though on battery-operated signal, and without relevance or sense of purpose, with neither emphasis nor inflection, out it all rolls, one memory of Smiley (one anecdote about Smiley) after another. If we laugh, while the narrator refrains, perhaps on second thought we might want to consider whether his sympathies and sense of courtesy are not greater than ours. We take our pleasure from watching one who runs interminably on, never ever runs down, yet demonstrates the phenomenon of running in chains. In the disparity between excessive means ("he backed me into a corner," says the narrator, "blockaded me there with his chair") and the *non sequiturs* that go nowhere, Mark Twain has turned one "great misfortune" into another that is still greater. He has made us see Simon as grotesque, perhaps peevish and senescent, certainly as addled, fixated and, all in all, a rather pitiful fellow.

(2) *Laughing with.* Understandably, therefore, criticism has much preferred to believe we laugh *with* Simon. His, we are often told, is deadpan humor. He is actually the highly conscious storyteller who chooses on this particular occasion to make his material as mechanical, as repetitious and pointless as possible. This is the measure of a harmless, perhaps even well-intentioned prank, through which western man in the open air, knowing perfectly well what he is about, has a bit of good-natured, perhaps purposeful sport with the slicker from back east. Suppose, then, feeling a story so artful can hardly have been assembled by a wind-up doll (a dummy to its own ventriloquist), we elect to see through the prank and to laugh with it? Then, as we ally ourselves with Simon's game and share in the pleasure he takes from playing it, I suggest our laughter might well be edged with a certain bafflement, not to say a tinge of nervousness. We are brought face to face with the intriguing question of Simon's motives.

To teach, it has been alleged; to tease the outsider in order to present to him an "object lesson in democracy."[9] But what, exactly, indicates that the outsider is in need of learning anything? Granted his behavior is stiff and formal, that he speaks in the phrases of sedate Boston or cultivated St. Louis; still he presents himself civilly enough, bringing along none of the brag or patronizing that had characterized another visitor to the west in S. L. Clemens's earlier sketch on "The Dandy and the Squatter."[10] Can manner alone, or manner in conjunction with polite language, be deemed sufficient explanations for the elaborate expenditure of energy that comes when Simon backs his visitor into a corner, traps him behind a chair, imposes upon him the tireless monologue-in-monotone? The aim seems less to instruct playfully than to befuddle, take-in, put-down: to use play as an instrument for humiliation. And the vast deal of hard work seems neither prankish nor sportive. It smacks, rather, of the deviousness, and also of the strange and mystifyingly impersonal will to power, which are qualities better associated with the actions of a confirmed practical joker.

If, as the mellifluous stranger, I sell you discounted shares in a gold mine, knowing the certificates bear as much relation to real gold as does the back room printing press on which I prepared them—in such circumstances you will no doubt feel abused and taken advantage of, yet not in ways you ought to find altogether incomprehensible. Consider my actions, though, if as a visitor in town you appeal to me for directions to the bus station and, having supplied detailed and kindly instructions, I know that by following them faithfully you will arrive at the extreme opposite end of town from where the station is actually located. The first trick may do more measurable harm. But you can take consolation from knowing that it evolved out of a greed which is identical to your own. By the second, you are brought into the presence of the wholly unaccountable. Why so much time and effort expended on a victim whom the trickster has never seen before, and will in all likelihood never meet again in this world or the next? I have given you a brush with the impersonal other, which yet delights to turn you into its puppet. At the very least, as you nurse your sore and aching feet, you are likely to have the sense of being backed into a corner, your every means of understanding blocked off—and all for no ostensible purpose.

"The practical joker," writes W. H. Auden, "must not only deceive but also, when he has succeeded, somehow unmask and reveal the truth to his victim."[11] Looking back on our street corner encounter, you may want, as best you can, to recover my facial expression, my tone of voice as I spoke so helpfully and generously to you about the way to the bus station. In "Jumping Frog" does Mark Twain supply any evidence which might unmask and reveal a practical joke? Much has been made of the simplicity and charm of Simon's story, its splendid Homeric epithets, its tone of wonder and revery, its lyric grace, its easy, unthreatening manner. Regarded from one perspective, however, the story hangs together by virtue of presenting these quite congruent details: two maniacal gamblers; the gratuitous cruelty perpetrated by one of them at the expense of an old Parson Walker; such assorted freaks and oddities as a dog with no hindlegs, an asthmatic horse, a tail-less and one-eyed cow; a fantastically described race-to-the-death, the outcome determined when one frog has had its mouth cruelly pried open and been brutally stuffed with buckshot. Through the texts they invent, the constituent images they thrive on, the inventors become known to us. Not only does Simon waylay the unoffending visitor; he gives some inkling of why, by regaling the visitor with a series of aggressive, hostile, life-hating and life-denying details and anecdotes. Well and good that we should join with the critical establishment and laugh *with* Simon. But if we do, there are ample grounds to suspect that we are laughing with a peculiar and perhaps rather frightening fellow, the creator of a landscape that is altogether as mean, ugly and distorted as are the surreal backgrounds of John Hawkes and Flannery O'Connor.

Now surely I commit heresy. To suspect that "genial garrulous" open-faced old Simon Wheeler might be more than slightly demented . . . to allege that if this is not the case, the alternative is to see him as a tease, with the tease's covert malice, who belongs in the company of Brockden Brown's Carwin, Poe's Diddler or the sweet-voiced stranger in Melville's *Confidence Man*. Such speculations seem well designed to head nowhere. If not unAmerican or symptomatic of a failed sense of humor, at least it is a matter of wondering in terms of motivations about which the story itself keeps perfectly silent, and so it frets and stews in a way that serves to complicate what (for Heaven's sake!) was only meant as "a good joke." And to the truth of the next-to-last charge anyhow, I eagerly plead guilty. Let it be emphasized that although I (in company with many other readers) have inferred them aplenty, there are no discernible motives anywhere in "Jumping Frog."

None is specified because our angle of vision, the narrator, displays some interesting inflexibilities of his own. The man is profoundly—unbelievably—incurious. Fully aware that he seems to be the object of somebody's laughter, he limits his explanation to the practical joke which, he believes, originated back east. He has been bored and exasperated because "a friend of mine, who wrote me from the east" sent him on a fool's errand to "old Wheeler." But he does not raise the question of *why* he was sent (*what* Mr. Anonymous, back east, knows about Simon would obviously come as fascinating news to the reader). Nor does he seek to understand why, or if, old Wheeler fooled him.

The result is a presentation so wholly objective as to border on proto-expressionism. Two voices loom up and take over. One speaks with non-stop vehemence, the other in tones that betray confusion and a certain understandable anxiety. But just as behind the first voice there is no particularizing detail—no hint of the background, or personal history, or inner life—that would explain so much sheer volubility, so by its obliviousness the second voice is made to shy away from explanations. It is as though while writing out the joke in 1865,

Mark Twain had been concerned only with getting it down on paper, with presenting it as a pure verbal construct, an exercise in the fine art of telling. He seems to have forgotten that even if it is only in a comic routine, when two voices (apparently egged on by a third) clamor for our attention we need to have some notion of why they speak, and speak to one another, as they do.

But then, suddenly, one recognizes how opaqueness is actually the cream of Mark Twain's "good joke." His method of presenting the experience has rendered moot any valid distinction between laughing *at* or laughing *with*. Either way, laughter is generated by the same spectacle of being fated and helpless. For whether Simon is demented or perverse—or perhaps perverse because demented—the portrayal of him causes us to see Simon as a pawn, a series of mechanical gestures in thrall to something larger than himself—in short, as a human robot, whose behavior becomes accountable solely in terms of the way the robot behaves. And just so with the narrator. Representation causes us to see him as the eternal fool, forever alert to do another's bidding, forever victimized, and not simply by Simon's volubility, but more especially by the trap of his own credulous good will. Simon and narrator thus look forward to the humor of Mark Twain's so-called growing pessimism. The ambiguous teller of the story leaves us not far removed from "Baker's Blue Jay Yarn" where, sharing Baker's laughable euphoria, we must share as well in the madness and single-track misanthropy that make him funny. The straight man, as he listens in a good-natured daze, points ahead to *Pudd'nhead Wilson*, in one sense the story of a joke first told, then acted out, both times with disastrous consequences, by one without a shred of humor, whom Mark Twain will describe as a "piece of machinery—a button, crank, or lever."

"Jumping Frog" does much more, however, than anticipate two specific episodes. What is adumbrated in the sketch that first won him a national reputation is nothing less than the general drift of Mark Twain's aesthetics. Although emphases vary from narrative to narrative, the aesthetics involve laughing at (and/or with) meanness of spirit that readily passes over into the practice of a thoughtless cruelty, which is all the more terrible for being thoughtless; laughter which therefore betrays and puts on display latent hostilities, rather than dissipating them; laughable situations so outrageous as either to be wholly anti-social or else to unite society in some violation of everything that is implied by civic virtue. Without hesitation, I call them the aesthetics of the sick joke. For a while the joke was tempered by Mark Twain's ability to keep it carefully distanced from his audience—perhaps by his reluctance to deal openly with forms of behavior which one side of his creativity found repugnant. But eventually distance and reluctance were supplanted by proximity and necessity. Mark Twain fell to repeating the sick joke because he found it everywhere enacted in the real world, and, as an artist who prized honesty, he had to retell it. And to all this the miner (intoxicated to obliviousness by legends of Jim Smiley) and the narrator (intoxicated by the vanity of good will to the point of fatuity) serve as prelude. It is not by chance that at the end of this essay where the joke has become at least distressing, and again on the concluding pages of my last essay when joking has assumed truly volcanic proportions, I shall want to remind readers of Simon and Stranger, conjoined like twins and catering to one another in the mutual helplessness they share.

## III

Humorous. Having or characterized by humor; funny; laughable; comical . . . witty; droll . . .
—*American Heritage Dictionary*

Any room can present a tragic front; any room can be comic.
—Crane, "The Blue Hotel"

I do not laugh easily.
—Mark Twain in the *Autobiography* II, 153

For an illustration, I need a joke extreme enough to offend good taste, while it also remains printable. To be on the safe side, I shall take an example, though not the reading or application of it, from Auden's essay "Notes on the Comic," as high minded as it is indisputably brilliant:

A MOTHER (*to her blind child*): Now, dear, shut your eyes and count twenty. Then open them, and you'll find that you can see.

CHILD (*after counting twenty*): But, Mummy, I still can't see.

MOTHER: April Fool![12]

Had Mr. Anonymous, that murky figure back east, told the story, "Jumping Frog" might well have ended "April Fool"; a covert version of the line would work nicely if we think of Simon in the role of confidence man. (Is it suppos- able that he might have exchanged a long, knowing wink with somebody dur- ing the interval when he was called outside the tavern: his p'ints don't hold a candle to my p'ints?) Noting all this, however, we will of course hasten to add that mother-child goes leagues beyond any of the most sinister implications of Simon-stranger. But consider:

(1) A bad boy named Jim Blake sets out to do all manner of minor mis- chief, and regularly gladdens our hearts when he is not caught stealing

apples, punished for violating the Sabbath, etc. But mischief has a built-in momentum, so that Jim is a shade less endearing—though equally as invulnerable—when he next molests animals at the circus or cuffs his sister into insensibility. Finally he grows up to axe-murder his wife and children, and an appreciative community elects him to the legislature.

(2) Meanwhile Jacob Blivens, a good boy, must seem something other than just a prude when he runs to help a blind man whom "bad boys have pushed over in the mud"—and he verges toward outright poignancy when his confused and frightened beneficiary thrashes him for taking the trouble. Still failing to comprehend how it is "not healthy to be good," Jacob next sits on an empty nitroglycerine can which bad boys are about to tie to the tail of a dog they are tormenting. A village alderman mistakes him for one of the miscreants. And the whack to the seat of his dynamite-stained trousers scatters Jacob, alderman, and fourteen dogs (but not of course the bad boys who run away) across four townships.

(3) Or not to be sexist about it: in the next town over, three girls (Mary, Hope, Cecilia) have obtained such a degree of piety and perfection that it is granted them to pray and have the prayers instantly answered. They beseech rain in order to end a local drouth—and the torrents come down for many days until "the countryside is flooded, the whole region well-nigh afloat." They invoke cold weather for the benefit of an old woman perishing of fever—and although it is midsummer the destruction of crops by frost and snow is soon complete. They pray an exemplary youth back from the tomb—and within weeks he forsakes his blameless ways, robs and murders, breaks the hearts of his family, and is executed for a capital offense. At last the village decrees that while "Ask and ye shall receive" is excellent theory, those who practice it shall suffer death. When the Holy Children pray anyhow, they are hunted down by "a maddened populace, and shot."[13]

These narratives, written by Mark Twain during the later 1860s or early 1870s, are if more genteel, because more general or more typal, hardly healthier or less violent than mother-child. The sick jokes of a just slightly tenderer (or perhaps a more heavily censored) age, we might call them. Furthermore, they are linked to mother-child through a common pattern of development.

The thing to observe about all four is how each one derives laughter from a character who has made the self-conscious determination to behave *naturally*. Jim: he simply wishes to be free of the artificial rules and Sunday school imposed regulations of organized society. Jim wants to play as nature's child. Jacob: his morality rests on the presumption that since animals and the afflicted are beloved of nature, a good boy who protects dogs and cripples will be acting in full accord with nature's benevolence. Jacob wants to live according to the rules of the beloved and loving Old Mother. Cecilia and company: they take for granted the efficacy of simple and natural innocence. The Holy Children are steadfast in the belief that sound hearts and "right" natural feelings will lead, in an instant, to direct encounters between this world and the Higher World. And finally Mother, as the key to the rest: I think it is probably wrong to conclude that this monster shocks us into appalled and incredulous laughter as a result of departing from what we like to call the natural proclivities of motherhood. The plain truth is that heartless, witless nature can be very callous where matters of parents and their young are concerned. An English bulldog of my acquaintance, who wailed piteously through a long night for three stillborn pups, was yet moved to reject absolutely one of the survivors who, as it turned out, had been whelped with a congenital (and fatal) lung disorder. From a realistic standpoint, therefore, it seems proper to say of the mother that she has allied herself with Old Mother Nature's great law of the extermination of the weak through a selection of the fittest. Perhaps her "April Fool"—other equally obscene punch-lines ("Gotcha!"; "Look again, dummy") are possible—indicates how conscious she is of playing on her child the trick of the natural cycle, which creates, maims, shuns and destroys its progeny. April, as the poet tells us, is the cruellest month.

But what are the consequences when a human being tries to live solely with reference to nature's design? Jim, who would be spontaneous as the wind; Jacob, intent upon being liberated to practice the mindless benevolence of puppy dogs; the Holy Children through their primitive faith; the mother, with her knowing use of a response which is appropriate only to the world of instinct, are not liberated by their choices. Quite the contrary. They are dehumanized, made as mechanically heartless and witless as nature is. They are rendered unfit for society. And by virtue of this fact, they are also rendered, in the dictionary's definition of the term, humorous. Not that the automata find themselves "comical" or "droll," to be sure; not that they ever laugh. In their busyness—their total dedication to being natural—they have no time for laughter. But we are made to see them as funny in a grotesque way, because for all their commitment to freedom they must end up performing one bad (one good, one pious and destructive, or one outrageous) action over and over again. Each has obvious affinities with a society which, as if modeling itself on beavers and earthworms, builds one dam after another—or with a rake who, as if taking his cue from bulls, roosters, and billy goats, is frozen to the single posture of making himself sexually available to woman after woman. And a raconteur who, for whatever reason, is driven to present life as an unending series of freaks— who invents or remembers one monstrosity after another—seems to share some fascinating affinities with them.

Laughter at the sick joke, then, is our response to a fundamentally "naturalistic" presentation. We watch while humanistic, or socially oriented, norms of behavior are thrust downward into the norms of mechanized, unpitying nature almost, though not quite, far enough to make this descent become actively discomforting to us. The effect, in fact, can be rather wickedly delicious. And it is never more so than when the butts of the joke (stranger, child, Jim's family, Cecilia's fellow citizens) give way to the victims we "know":

> *Reporter (satisfying what is, after all, an instinctive curiosity—and also oblivious to everything except a professional duty to ask questions):* And did you enjoy the rest of your evening at Ford's Theater, Mrs. Lincoln?

or:

> [*in an updated version:* But did you enjoy the rest of your ride through beautiful downtown Dallas, Mrs. Kennedy?]

or:

> *Mark Twain (doing only what he was invited there to do: being funny):* Mr. Emerson came and looked on a while, and then he takes me by the buttonhole and says—

> > Give me agates for my meat;
> > Give me cantharides to eat;
> > From air and ocean bring me foods,
> > From all zones and altitudes.

> Says I, "Mr. Emerson, if you'll excuse me, this ain't no hotel."[14]

Mark Twain was pilloried in the newspapers for failing to be a gentleman, and (at times, anyhow) he professed himself covered with embarrassment. Officially of course we would want to call "reporter" a cad and brute, and hope his editor would sack him at the earliest opportunity. Perhaps, though, the true consequence for "us"—us as eavesdroppers on "reporter" or members of the audience at the Whittier birthday dinner—is better set forth in "Wakefield," Hawthorne's proto-naturalistic portrayal of a sick joke. We gasp and laugh with horror because "we know that none of us would perpetrate such a folly." On the other hand, we also gasp and laugh with secret delight because our aggressions are released by the knowledge that "some other might"—and, as a matter of fact, has!

So, though teetering on the brink of something monstrous, sick jokes can yet safely be drawn back, and even regarded as socially useful to us. They are instances of Freud's liberating "wit." They bespeak the comfort we take from snickering harmlessly behind our hands at the pain of the high and mighty; the relief we feel when denizens of cloud-cuckoo-land, whom we honor (but whose serenity and fame are perhaps a bit obnoxious to us) have been brought down a peg or two; the discharging of our guilts and anxieties through laughter at the ridiculous spectacle of a mother who clearly is burdened by neither. Nevertheless, the threshold to the truly monstrous *is* there. And from literary naturalism come some particularly interesting examples of how readily the sick joke may cross over it.

Thus Zola's moments of greatest human depravity (Gervayse and Coupeau necking among the filthy linens of *L'Assommoir*) are but the reworking of episodes which in some other place (compare *The Merry Wives of Windsor*) would be hilariously funny. Or Stephen Crane's "Blue Hotel," apparently much indebted for scenery and characters to Mark Twain's *Roughing It*, might also be thought of as working through to all the darkest potentialities of "Jumping Frog." Once again, in a western setting, a voice without discoverable motive takes over: a voice so tireless, fixated and obsessed—withal so frozen to a single point—that it appears hopelessly cut off from the point of anything real or meaningful. As before, consequently, the response must consist of incredulity, mingled with a half-amused sense of wonder. "'Man, man . . . have you gone daffy?'" cries Scully to the Swede early on. And for many pages this continues as the collective question of all of them, Scully, Cowboy, and Easterner. *Can such things be? Is it possible for this Swede to go plunging along through such an absurd reconstruction of Ft. Romper, Nebraska, without ever once smiling?* But if the presence of a cranky, deadpan game is everywhere suspected, this time there can be no final remission through anyone's laughter. Literary naturalism, with its acute sensitivity to encroachments of the natural upon the human, is constrained to treat the sick joke not as a temporary aberration, or momentary escape from the real, but rather as the essential and defining characteristic of reality. The voice that mysteriously arises to dominate "The Blue Hotel" not only becomes its own executioner; by the sheer mechanical pertinacity it practices, it likewise cuts through a thin veneer of blue paint, and raises the question of whether all of life is not a sick joke: "a whirling, fire-smitten, ice-locked, disease-stricken, space-lost bulb."[15]

But let us not probe further at dark extremes where humorous behavior possibly ceases to be humorous. At this point the need is to retreat backward into the warm, cheery, sunny side of laughter; into "Mark Twain country," as some might call it. And yet, upon reflection, the retreat may not be easy. Having led us across the threshold Mark Twain has a way of blocking our way back again.

For as we have seen, the means through which the sick joke evokes laughter may differ in degree, yet they do not really differ in kind, from the underlying principles of all laughter. To a greater or lesser extent all jokes and all the laughter they occasion come in consequence of submerging consciousness into the mechanical. This is so whether Simon chooses to masquerade as a bump-kin or has been created to be genuinely addled; whether "reporter" and Mark Twain have done their gaffes and *shtick* thoughtlessly or with malice afore-thought. And it is likewise the case whether we, in our spectator's role, laugh *at* the unfortunate Simon or, confident that he can mean no real harm, indulge ourselves to laugh *with* Simon at the bewildered stranger. But such a submer-gence represents the triumph of heartless, witless nature over distinctively hu-man—distinctively social—values. It is, by definition, anti-social in character. It does not so much lead, after a while, to a mother playing tricks on her blind child as it presents this same trick, endlessly varied, over and over wherever we look. Ergo: the sick joke makes explicit the fact that all jokes are sick, and that no such thing as healthy and humane laughter exists.

No doubt these statements are wildly exaggerated. Certainly (excepting Hobbes) they surpass any of even the sternest, bleakest views of laughter de-veloped by the experts on whom I relied at the beginning. I am also aware that they contradict a general consensus about the therapeutic or redemptive value of human play that is central to accounts of the ancient carnival, to theories of the evolution of culture, to psychoanalytic theory, to modern self-help books, and perhaps simply to common sense. The business of this essay, however, is with the preeminent funny man, Mark Twain. And for him, I am convinced, the statements were profoundly true. Unless laughter could lead to something beyond itself, the laugh remained a shocking affront to the warmth, the dis-crimination, the sense of proportion that ought to make, and keep, us human. Left to itself, the laugh commented negatively upon both those who do it and those who cause it to be done. And so, inevitably, anxieties rose in his mind concerning the principal source of laughter. Any number of literary terms might be applied, or actually have been adapted, to those sudden, deflating moments when human relationships go awry in Mark Twain's work. One thinks of tragedy, pathos, irony, satire, farce, even gothic melodrama. Chief among the terms, though, would be "the joke," that alteration of tone and situation which clears the air of all apparent progress toward a "positive outcome," and reveals instead that nothing positive has happened, or ever can happen.

Consequently, it is not by accident that the funny man could conceive of creativity as a "dry tank," being mysteriously filled from the outside. Nor is it a matter to be passed over lightly that in the same letter where he spoke so glowingly to Orion about his capacity to create laughter he went on to liken this talent to a "mighty engine," driven by "pistons & cylinders & shafts."[16] Mark Twain illustrates classically the writer at war with his own genius. From the outset he seems to have intuited that his fictions would be patterned by helplessness in combination with great energy, the lassitude of getting nowhere, but also a furious running in place which preceded the dead ends. He seems to have grasped that the fictions would be portraying "cranks" and "levers" because his own creative powers were thoroughly mechanized. And he seems to have surmised, most crucially, that so little would the results please him, he would often wish to disclaim all responsibility for what his genius produced. The perception of this state of affairs made him no less a humorist (always provided we understand the historical roots of his humor), though over the course of time it doubtlessly exacted a considerable toll on his good humor.

## IV

"All I know is, it suits Tom Sawyer."
—Tom in his *Adventures*

Human beings *can* be awful cruel to one another.
—Huck in his *Adventures*

Surely it is not for want of specific examples that one might hesitate to call Mark Twain the creator of sick humor. The evidence accumulates, from destructive boys (and girls), who are stereotypes, to the more fleshed-out chicaneries of Duke and King; from "Cannibalism in the Cars" to the various cannibalistic rites practiced at places like Bricksville, Camelot, Hadleyburg, and Eseldorf. These narratives are accounts of perverse games as fundamentally sick people play them, sometimes in the name of profit or vengeance, but chiefly for fun and meanness, and for the pure, unalloyed joys of one-up personship. Furthermore, they are accounts of how in the process of diddling others, the diddlers are themselves diddled—caught in the snares, the single frozen stance, of one long, unvarying practical joke which the narrating voice in Mark Twain's work plays on diddlers and non-diddlers alike.

It is not practice, then, which negates or, as it may be, softens and mellows the fatality of laughter in Mark Twain. Rather, it is a matter of theory. We are reluctant to think of Mark Twain as habitually a sick humorist because of the awkwardness of adjusting the naturalistic bias of sick jokes to what we think we know of Mark Twain's morality. If any one point seems certain to us, it is that throughout his fiction the human life spent in close proximity to nature enjoys certain moral advantages—a freedom and freshness, a dignity, a capacity for wise human involvements—which are not so readily available to those human beings who dwell too much, or too exclusively, within the social community. Quite clearly this is the view which shapes the more sanguine readings of "Jumping Frog," readings wherein Simon, as a kind of "tutelary deity," is seen to educate the stranger concerning what one critic calls "the superiority of vernacular brotherhood over the competitive individualism which animates genteel attitudes."[17] (Though we are shown nothing whatsoever of Simon's motives, we know him to be simple and natural and countrified; hence by a leap of inference he also becomes wise of heart.) In a more general way the view has at once confirmed, and been confirmed by, Henry Nash Smith's seminal account of the "conventional" and "vernacular" styles in Mark Twain's work. Presumably the view explains why, despite a chronology that relates him to the age of literary realism and might well locate him among the first of the literary naturalists, we continue to regard Mark Twain as the last of the great romantic writers (as if the last of the romantics were not quite likely to be the first of the naturalists). But why go on about the ethical imbalance of town to countryside in the world he creates? The dichotomy is as self-evident—its differing values as seemingly inarguable—as are the differing ethics and attitudes of the two major characters in whom Mark Twain has seen fit to make the moral superiority of nature over town dramatically explicit.

Thus, more than slightly repelled by their subject these days, critics of Tom Sawyer present Tom as deeply flawed because altogether too acculturated. He rebels only very tamely against society, say his detractors, and will, in any case, grow up as a politician or general or some other of society's one-horse heroes. Putting the case this flatly, however, blurs an interesting continuity which links Tom to Mark Twain's bad little boy, Jim Blake. If, like Jim, Tom seems destined for social eminence, he also shares with Jim a keen sense that the best way to gratify both himself and society lies in a mastery over nature and in the skillful mimicking of nature's actions. Together with Jim, he would drop out to play naturally, before dropping back in to claim his social rewards in the Legislature.

In an ascending order of value, for example, Tom's ideas of a rousing good time are these: to meow like a tom cat . . . to fool Aunt Polly with the ruse of a rat or a snake behind her . . . to conjure up pirates, Indians, outlaws and assorted bogeys from the woods around St. Petersburg . . . to dig for buried treasure by the light of a particular phase of the moon, or beneath the shadow of an especially shaped tree limb . . . to confront McDougal's Cave with greater native cunning than that of Injun Joe, and hence to succeed the halfbreed as master-of-revels in the dark natural world below the town. At the top of the hierarchy, furthermore, comes an incident which, for all his bogus erudition, endows Tom with nothing less than the powers of a shaman or primitive magician. Among the Sandwich Island papers in Roughing It, Mark Twain had written with mock wonder of the "natives who [are] able to lie down and die whenever they want to, whether there is anything the matter with them or not."[18] It is even so for Tom, when he sets out to gratify his wish to "die temporarily."[19] Resurrected to hear himself eulogized, he has committed serious social offenses, in that his trick grieved Aunt Polly and brought needless trouble and anxiety to the entire village. All the same, his instinct for play emerges triumphant. He has demonstrated to some very awed spectators the power he possesses to "lie down and die [or rise up and be celebrated] whenever he wants to."

Plainly implied throughout his own adventures, Tom's rapport with the world of instinct is reaffirmed in an especially revealing pattern that occurs at both the beginning and end of *The Adventures of Huckleberry Finn*. Assembling a robber band or stealing Jim out of slavery are, to be sure, activities that Tom structures and executes with scrupulous devotion to his literary sources. But as the first culminates in the pursuit of frightened Sunday school children through the forest, so the high point of the second is not attained until Jim has become an animal and Tom can hound him, as if he were a beast of prey, across the swamps and woodlands of southeastern Arkansas. We come to recognize therefore that the hunt—the predatory action; the most ancient and atavistic of nature's rituals—is the organizing principle to which Tom's imagination always responds with a particular fervor. (Even his "funeral" is no exception. What does it signify, if not a hunter's return from the wilderness, bearing on his back, like a trophy to be stuffed and admired, his own marvelously restored identity?) And the peculiar charm of tracking down Jim derives, as Tom sees, from the possibility that the event may be prolonged indefinitely:

> he said . . . we could keep it up all the rest of our lives and leave Jim to our children to get out. . . . He said that in this way it could be strung out as much as eighty years, and would be the best time on record.[20]

The absurdity of the hope, at which we laugh, should not blind us to its appalling consequences. In his relentless quest for sport, Tom fates all experience to be the eternal prey, crouched beneath the leering grins of eternally swooping predators. He thus allies himself in yet a third way with the sick joke of the bad little boy. For although the parallel would be evident to neither of them, both Tom and Jim Blake as they borrow from nature have reduced play, their playmates, *and themselves as players* to the faceless anonymity—the frozen, repetitious, profoundly anti-human postures—of figurines on a farcical or burlesqued version of the Grecian Urn. (Or perhaps it is not a farcical version at all; Tom and Jim Blake have simply brought to the surface the dark inhumanity—the terrible freezing of life into art and artifact—which serious readers have detected in Keats's presentation.)

While Tom, keeping one eye on the romantic text, yet looks to nature for the fullest realization of his fantasies, something surpassingly odd happens to Huck Finn. However reluctantly, nature's child is drawn back from loose-fitting clothes and long nights under the stars to take a stand inside the social community. Hidden in the brush on the night when Injun Joe and his henchman plot their practical joke on the Widow Douglas, Huck wants only to run away and hide. Every instinct for self-preservation urges him to get cracking those mechanical little legs as fast as ever he can. But remembering that she did him a kindness once, he is forced to measure the Widow's vulnerability against automatically fleeing for cover, as the frightened animal would do. His decision to stay and seek help for her is not simply a way through which Mark Twain displays Huck's physical courage. The larger aim is to show how natural inclinations can play tug-of-war with a social obligation—and to reveal how, in fulfilling the second, Huck will deny or repress the first.

His decision thus anticipates, in small, Huck's crisis of conscience in the thirty-first chapter of his own narrative. As before, if it were only instinct that spoke to him, Huck would know perfectly well how to react by doing the easy and natural thing. Through a series of knee-jerk responses he would send his letter posthaste to Miss Watson, mouth the prayer of the just, and thereafter experience the "washed clean" feeling that can come when one has been true to the demand of one's most spontaneous and thoughtless impulses. What prevents the solution that comes naturally is an image that forms and refuses to dissolve in the consciousness of Huck:

> I see Jim before me all the time: in the day and in the nighttime, sometimes moonlight, sometimes storms, and we a-floating along talking and singing and laughing. But somehow I couldn't seem to strike no places to harden me against him, but only the other kind. (*AHF*, 269–70.)

The emphasis upon recollection, reflection, and the relationship between two people is of the utmost importance. It allows Mark Twain to justify Huck's rhetoric, while at the same time he keeps the content consistent with what can plausibly be thought and spoken by a fourteen-year-old boy living in the antebellum American South. Huck is not laying down a challenge to slavery. He has not assumed an abstract concept called "the white man's burden," or inveighed against the ugly injustices of racial prejudice. Least of all does he meditate philosophically over the virtues of freedom or address himself to the topic of human responsibility. All he says is that because I have come to love this man, I intend to stay with him even if the intention condemns me to hell. But if the thought delimits his motives, it likewise humanizes Huck's action—and what is more serves to endow the action with the richest kind of social significance. Feeling himself irreparably cast out of respectable society at this point, Huck has nonetheless engaged in a type of commitment which (so far as we can tell) only the socially oriented, the community oriented, human being is capable of making. Prompted by memory, actuated by the desire for a specific companion, he is lifted beyond the reflexive, undiscriminating life in nature. He makes a deliberate and highly selective choice about when, and how, and upon whom to bestow his affections. To use the full force of Eric Fromm's title, he has set himself free by escaping *from* freedom.

Labels prove slippery, then, in *The Adventures of Tom Sawyer* and *The Adventures of Huckleberry Finn*, Mark Twain's twin portrayals of boyhood on the river. The freedom and spontaneity which Mark Twain is supposed to "privilege" or "valorize" can only create the caricature (surely Tom Sawyer is as trapped and one-dimensional as are his knee-jerk reactions to a single motivation), while the emergence of character is dependent upon a growing acceptance of the social restraints which Mark Twain is supposed to deplore. With respect to the two figures involved, the effect is like watching a criss-cross of identical twins, the behavior of each resulting in a dramatic pattern we were prepared to expect of the other. But of course the last fifth of the second book puts the twins back together again.

No more than a few hours (or ten printed pages) after Huck makes his declaration in Chapter 31, a reunion of two old comrades occurs, and with it the following conversation:

> HUCK (*hearing that Tom will participate in the theft of Jim*): Oh shucks! you're joking.
>
> TOM: I ain't joking either.
>
> HUCK: Well, then, joking or no joking, if you hear anything about a runaway nigger, don't forget to remember that *you* don't know nothing about him, and *I* don't know nothing about him. (*AHF*, 284.)

Needless to say, Tom is mistaken. Though he plays it for "the *adventure*" rather than for laughs (*AHF*, 357), it is a joke he is about to perpetrate. His hoax will combine an instinct for hunting with approximately the same ground rules which had governed burning live dogs to death on the streets of Bricksville.

But what of Huck, right as always, judging correctly that since the plan is Tom's there must be a joke in the offing. Well, Huck never laughs either, of course. Nor, to begin with, will he approve or even fully comprehend Tom's joke, the drift of which strikes him as tedious, impractical and excessively arty-craftsy. Let us, however, not err on the side of supposing Huck to be totally devoid of sportiveness. The boy who once turned aside Tom Sawyer's attempts to pigeonhole him by insisting "I ain't everybody" (*ATS*, 234) has, within a few ensuing months, so multiplied his identity that he dies twice and is twice re-born, changes his sex, acquires at least five specifiable aliases, and lays claim to a veritable plethora of new family trees, not to mention home addresses, alleged destinations, or reasons for traveling. His means of effecting these metamorphoses are noteworthy. Though they spring from motives more disinterested and are put to purposes less mean and frivolous, Huck's tactics are still of a kind with the wiliness, the opportunism and sheer love of incantatory magic which likewise actuate Tom Sawyer (as Tom turned small children to A-rabs, so Huck fetches Sarah Williams and George Jackson out of the void) and, for that matter, the Duke and the King. The plain truth is that Huck enjoys charades. At every bend of the river, fooling old Jim has for a long while been his recurring obsession. It washes him clean of boredom, is the source of an instant gratification, just as the obligation to feel guilty and apologize afterward is something he has to work out consciously, and work up to haltingly. Hence Tom's elaborate strategies soon make a convert—and, moreover, an eager ally—of Huck. Almost at once his language changes. From the bewildered reportorial mode that told us what Tom does in Chapters 35 and 36, style takes on a frankly conspiratorial air and becomes, by the last four paragraphs of Chapter 37, an account of the game we, Tom and I, are playing. But now Huck has no need to feel embarrassed. He has already uttered a formulation through which whatever is heartless or anti-social in the game can easily be disguised as a joyous, natural pastime. All one must do is forget to remember.

A revealing way of dealing with the complex art of the last fifth of *Adventures of Huckleberry Finn* is to contrast it with Faulkner's technique in the short story "Was," the first narrative in *Go Down Moses*. Both are concerned with a mechanical and therefore essentially humorous ceremony. It consists of the ritualistic setting free of a slave, so that white masters can know the pleasure of pursuing, capturing, releasing, and retaking their property over and over. (Though "influence" is certainly not to the point, the paraphernalia of the fox hunt in "Was" is clearly prefigured by Tom's sense of Jim as his quarry in a hunt.) But in two crucial respects the methods of portraying this situation differ. First, Mark Twain is much more explicit about supplying a background for the feelings of the violated slave. Whereas Tom's Turn in "Was" is represented altogether from the outside, the mask dropped from Jim in Chapter 15 of *AHF*. There what seemed an object, which was meant solely for the diversion of its white masters, suddenly stepped forth as a flesh-and-blood personality, who could cry in his anger and anguish *I ain't a plaything and those who fool me are "trash."*

The second achievement of Mark Twain directly contradicts the implications of the first. Where "Was" is careful to keep the hunt funny, yet uses the laughable qualities as an index to the underlying horrors of molestation and rape in a plantation culture, Mark Twain, having laid bare a skull beneath the skin of good humor, goes on to act as if the moment of disclosure had never occurred. No transformation in literature is more decisive—or could be handled with greater seeming obliviousness—than the one through which he modulates Jim's conscious indignation in Chapter 15 into the tireless, reiterative (and immensely funny) voice of old Sister Hotchkiss, summing up a long week's mischief with the pronouncement " 'Says I . . . I b'lieve the nigger was crazy.' " (*AHF*, 345–46.) And Mark Twain's trick, we perceive, lies merely in reversing the order of Huck's oxymoronic verbs. Any cruelty is rendered permissible and laughable at the close of *AHF*, because all of us have been instructed to remember to forget that we are laughing at a man whose nightmare vision of the worst that could happen to him has come true, and therefore is happening in fact.

So, as inexorably as if their presence were foreordained, the dramatis personae of a sick joke have gathered. Two boys, each old enough to know better and one sufficiently involved to be conscious of the treachery, speak to a Black man who hungers for freedom and dignity and most of all for the privilege of being let alone, while both within and outside the story, members of an audience are listening:

> BOYS: Cover your eyes. Count to twenty by fives. When you look again, you'll be out here with us.
>
> MAN (*covers; counts; looks. Speaks [see Chapter 38] through broken teeth*): I still ain't out there, Misto Tom and Huck honey.
>
> BOYS (*in the monotone of identical twins*): April Fool, Jim!
>
> INSIDE AUDIENCE: I b'lieve he's crazy.
>
> OUTSIDE AUDIENCE: Ha-ha-ha and/or ? ? ?

Laughing, we become fully participant in Hobbes's "Sudden Glory." Our laughter is at what ought to be the silent wretchedness of a Black man; at exercises of energy and industriousness that fixate Tom and Huck, leaving them equally as much rooted to one spot as is Jim in his airless room; at adults whose behavior approximates frantic scurryings on an anthill—except (such being the consequence when human drives are translated into the wholly natural) the furor can produce only obliviousness and a kind of benign cruelty. What remained ambiguous twenty years earlier in "Jumping Frog" has now been clarified as the entry into a veritable bargain basement of deformities. Who among those who clatter and cluck, mill and swarm, are cuffed and submit at the Silas Phelps plantation is not a deformity? Thus the degree of our laughter will depend upon the extent to which our hearts are anesthetized.

But perhaps one is to be pardoned for feeling that the most interesting case is the heart of Mark Twain. Which is not to indulge in fruitless speculations about all those other endings he might have written. It is, rather, a matter of trying to understand why he was compelled to write the one he chose, and why, having chosen it, he seems to write it out with such evident pleasure and zest.


## V

Slave. 1. One bound in servitude. . . . 2. One who is submissive or subject to a specified person or influence. 3. A machine or component that is controlled by another machine or component.
                    —*American Heritage Dictionary*

Could anything be more preposterous than to suppose that Achilles (the "swift of foot"), if he gave the tortoise (one of the slowest moving creatures) a slight handicap, could never even tie him in the race?
                    —from an account of Zeno of Elea

It is not worthwhile to try to keep history from repeating itself, for man's character will always make the prevention of the repetitious impossible.
                    —Mark Twain in his *Autobiographical Dictation*

By definition, a slave ought to be just about the funniest figure on earth. No doubt words like "enchained" or (if we pursued them historically) "enthralled" and even "enchanted" are well suited to describe a slave's condition. But remembering the etymology of "humorous" and "humor," we might do best to think of slavery as an "enhumored" state, the slave as exemplifying a thoroughly "enhumored" self. What extreme imbalances of fluids in the body once brought to pass for Robert Burton and other renaissance psychologists, the unmitigated fact of being owned body-mind-and-soul achieves for the slave. Thereby, he or she is wrenched out of the world of conscious choice and human discriminations; is rendered instead a robot, eternally at the disposal of the possessing other who pulls the strings; is, in short, transformed from being who to behaving as which, a "machine or component." A slave—make no mistake about it—is funny; hence "Jim Crow," the minstrel performance, and underlying and sanctifying both, the stereotype of laughing children (including childish adults) in the fields and shanties behind the plantation house.[21]

About the only thing funnier than a slave might be the face to face conjunction of two slaves. Now from stage-right enters volatile and voluble Simon Wheeler, deaf to every sound except the magic sound of Smiley. And now from stage-left comes the sober and decorous stranger, intent only upon asking one civil question about Smiley. Whatever controls them, each is possessed, beside himself, caught helplessly to spin forever in his own narrow orbit—in a word "enhumored." Meeting by chance at center-stage, both the enhumored selves conspire to double the pleasure of laughter. Moreover, the relationship between them looks ahead to the time when Tom Sawyer's amorality will disappear stage-right, leaving the focus solely upon what seem the growth and development of Huck and Jim, only to reappear from stage-left, in demonstration of how Jim and Huck all the while were standing stock-still in the cruel fantasy world of Tom. These pairs, and many others like them, seem created for the joy of telling Mark Twain's favorite joke, which (whether or not Mark Twain knew of the precedent) is but a reworking of the race in Zeno's famous paradox. The twins have been coupled to make manifest existence in an "enhumored" world, a world without meaningful motion. They define life as an "enhumored" process which, from starting blocks to destination, remains fixated and inalterable, and is always engaged in the busy-busy, pointless-pointless, funny-funny activity of getting nowhere.**

If humor, properly understood, can thrive on the presentation of slaves, freeing the slave has been a traditional subject of comedy. This is literally the case in Plautus and in Shakespeare's *Comedy of Errors*, a reworking of Roman

---

** "Enhumored" is a term of my personal coinage, although through the analogies of slavery and enslavement I hope that it speaks, and will continue to speak, for itself. Professor Louis J. Budd, however, has shrewdly observed that in order to make my case emphatically, I need to distinguish between "enhumored selves" and the self who, in a more modern sense, is "humorous."

The contemporary usage of "humorous" seems to derive from the early eighteenth century; the word is flavored with a distinctively Enlightenment optimism. According to Stuart Tave, in *The Amiable Humorist*, it describes a person with a peculiar (a wry-to-antic) disposition which allows for perceiving the ridiculous, the ludicrous, the comic in any situation, and allows as well for effectively giving expression to this perception. Humorous, then, is a deliberate, wholly self-conscious way of remaining open to the world, while protecting oneself against the limitations and affronts which the world imposes. (Voltaire can write humorously amidst the horrors of *Candide;* a century later, and well past the Enlightenment!, Sut Luvingood can still be said to comment humorously, even—contra Edmund Wilson—with a certain red-neck amiability, on the predicament of Wat.) As such, humor in the modern sense is a gentler, a less mordant but, all the same, a kissing cousin of irony.

It appears to me that nothing could be more remote from this relaxed (this detached or, in the parlance of today, this "laid back") attitude than the populace of Mark Twain's fictions. Despite our natural inclination to cast him as the principal ornament of American humor in the nineteenth century, the fact is that his work actually thrusts back to an older time, when humor was treated as the determinant of experience rather than a personally and socially useful way of coping with the world, and (perhaps rather like yesteryear's DNA) served as the absolute master of personality, rather than as a free and easy response which the personality might cultivate and develop. From a twin made drunk by the bloodstream, though he craves sobriety, to a garrulous old miner with but one name on his lips, to a farmer who is funny by virtue of helplessly botching the joke, to two adolescent boys whose compulsion to play eventually blinds them to every other consideration—Mark Twain's robots are humorous simply and solely because they are enhumored: that is, without hope of being anything else. They belong to the party of battered Candide and befuddled Wat, as opposed to that of Candide's narrator or Sut. And it is of some interest that in my third polemical essay, we will find Sam Clemens, on the threshold of maturity, confronting a theory of humors which is meant to explain the world and yet ends up by enslaving—or enhumoring—life.

comedy. But the subject persists long after the formal institutions of slavery cease to be relevant. Thus the rise of Silas Lapham is predicated upon striking from Silas's eyes the blinders of an enslaving delusion (a delusion that has made him bad businessman, bad father and husband, in sum, bad citizen), while Davy Crockett's entrapment by nature is portrayed as the first essential step in his ultimate triumph over nature, the precise meaning of that triumph being implicit in the fact that, at the end, he "walked home"—that is back to the community that has benefited from his victory. Setting-the-slave-free accords exactly with the formulation of traditional comedy, the Manichean pattern of the comic structure: without the negative occasion of captivity (without captured particles of light), no march toward the positive outcome of releasing light from darkness, and hence being at liberty again. The action effectively twins *pluck and luck* into the comic dynamic of getting somewhere.

These situations cluster around the poles of violation and possibility. It is always possible that Simon might have answered as politely as he was asked; that the sisters' pieties might have seemed merely a harmless delusion; that, no matter how frantic, the Good Boy's wish to be heroic might have seemed morally more edifying than the hysterical destructiveness of the Bad Boy—though in these cases of course Mark Twain would have had no story to tell. There would have been stories, however, with the murder of "Green Face" in "Carnival of Crime," or had the apparently zig-zag, up-and-down structure of "Old Times on the Mississippi" not settled finally into a confining circle. Out of possibility there could have come comic accounts of the personality in transition, as "Mark Twain" learns to live both with and without moral conventions (some are useful, some not), or as the cub comes to mediate between dreams and reality, the desire to play and the acceptance of responsibility. But the business of Mark Twain is to make us laugh. And not only are the laughs he creates rooted in a denial of possibility; they involve a violation of personality, a form of reductionism such as is explored by Peter Gay in one of his late commentaries on the role of wit and humor in Freud.

In an essay called "Serious Jests," Professor Gay explicates fully and with great sympathy Freud's well-known dictum that "jokes . . . make possible the satisfaction of a drive (whether lustful or hostile) standing in its way; . . . jokes, then, represent a rebellion against this authority, a liberation from its pressure." But in keeping with his title he adds another side to the matter of joking and joke-telling, a side that Freud left unaddressed. True, jokes may subvert and circumvent the oppressive. Yet they

> may, and often do, aim not at the mighty but at the defenseless. A joke at the expense of a dictator is one thing. A joke at the expense of some relatively impotent

social group—whether blacks or gypsies or Jews—is quite another. Moreover, a joke may reduce the listener's sympathy for victims. By making something unfunny appear funny, a joke can diffuse justified indignation, [so that] a smile or the explosion of laughter can take the place of an action.

It is hardly by accident—indeed, it seems a perfect instance of Freudian determinism—that writing these lines about what Freud left out should remind Professor Gay of Mark Twain and Mark Twain's appeal for Freud. Though the chosen illustration involves one of Mark Twain's spoofs at the expense of his fatuous and pathetic brother, Orion Clemens, the seriousness of "serious jests," or the dark and hostile side to unbridled joking, serve as a fine gloss on all of Mark Twain's endings, including the last 15 chapters of *AHF*.[22]

For whether urging us to laugh with or laugh at, Mark Twain is a past master of down-your-nose laughter at the expense of the helpless and the impotent. Without fail, his characters are or eventually become caricatures: figures seen from above and at a great distance, as they are assembled into a handful of mechanical gestures, or turned to robots through the force from within of an absolutely ruling obsession. The condition of any Mark Twain narrative—short or long, sketch or novel—is that before the curtain falls all must be slaves. And true to the pattern, all are enslaved at the close of *Huckleberry Finn*. As Tom subordinates Jim, Huck, and the Phelpses to his will, so Tom's own will is subordinated to the craving he feels for manipulation and play. And as for Huck, though he endows the book with a particularly rich vein of possibility and both tests and is tested by possibility through many complex chapters—well, Huck too is the product of an imagination which finds in repetition and obliviousness the most reliable means of evoking laughter. Thus he must finally appear as just one more violated personality, a wraith of his former self, plodding without memory or emotion through what seems an interminable nightmare.

If as an author well known for humor I present you with a perfectly impenetrable sketch (a collection of purely performative actions) into which you persist in reading a democratic message and other grave moral complications, you have little to blame except your own academic stuffiness. Knowing yourself to be in the hands of a funny man, you should have been more heedful of how *caveat emptor* applies to reading books as well as to buying them.

The situation is radically changed, though, when a creative writer plucks out of a world of caricatures two figures whose development, through increasingly lyrical prose, seems the point of creativity (and the object of the reader's growing emotional engagement), only to beat a hasty retreat at the last so that Jim is shriveled to a minstrel mush-mouth, while Huck remains as the voice which records, but nothing much more than a recording voice. Now, feeling properly "sold," the reader seems entitled to complain a bit. What motivated Mark Twain? When he grasped the conventions of comedy so clearly and could portray them with such vividness, why at the last did he choose to turn on the conventions, despoil them with ridicule, replace the open world of comedy with the brutalities of a sick joke?

The key, I believe, is not to be found in a failure of nerve, as Leo Marx once famously argued; or in the transcendence of conscience through play, as James Cox rather heartlessly alleged, before he underwent a change of heart; or, though it is intelligently worked out, in Neil Schmitz's allegory of the post-Reconstruction South.[23] The end of *Huckleberry Finn* hews too close to the pattern of all Mark Twain's endings for any of these premises to seem helpful. Nor is it primarily a wish to be entertaining (although, in all candor, Mark Twain craved popularity and brisk sales, and was never unmindful of what the public expected from its funny fellows)—or primarily a matter of Mark Twain's racism (although, again to be candid, the nervousness of school boards and the occasional animosities of liberal and African American readers of *Huckleberry Finn* are not beyond some justification). No, if a taste for minstrel performances and a certain latent racism were involved, Mark Twain's closures rest on a deeper basis, have a more philosophic and aesthetic grounding.

Even in places where the tactic seems totally out of place, he plunged social norms into the mechanics of heartless, witless nature because in his view he was emulating the direction taken by reality itself. The transitions in his work from the character with possibility to the diminished, the demeaned and deeply violated caricature—or, what is essentially the same thing, the hardening of our hearts, so that we may have a bit of sport at the expense of the driven and one-dimensional enhumored (who might otherwise cause us to weep)— are both measures of Mark Twain's steadfast commitment to the principles and practices of literary realism.

## NOTES

1. In alphabetical order: W. H. Auden, "The Joker in the Pack" and "Notes on the Comic," *The Dyer's Hand*, 246–72, 371–85; Eric Bentley, *The Life of Drama* (New York: Atheneum, 1964), especially "Farce," 220–56; Henri Bergson, "Laughter," in *Comedy*, ed. Robert W. Corrigan (San Francisco: Chandler, 1965), and in *An Essay on Comedy*, ed. Wylie Sypher (Baltimore: Johns Hopkins University Press, 1956); Sigmund Freud, *Jokes and Their Relation to the Unconscious*, tr. James Strachey (New York: Norton, 1960); Horace Kallen, "The Aesthetic Principle in Comedy," *American Journal of Psychology* 22 (April 1911), 137–57; Susanne Langer, "The Rhythm of Comedy," *Feeling and Forms*

(New York: Scribners, 1953); Benjamin Lehmann, "Comedy and Laughter," *University of California English Studies* 10 (University of California Press, 1954), 81–101.

2. "Rare Ripe Garden Seed" appears in *Native American Humor,* ed. Walter Blair (San Francisco: Chandler, 1960), 380–88. Wat's refrain-lament is repeated three times on 385.

3. "Laughter," in Corrigan, *Comedy,* 472.

4. *My Dear Bro: A Letter from Samuel Clemens to his Brother Orion,* 6–7.

5. For the benefit of the uninitiated: Petroleum V. Nasby (born David Ross Locke) was one of the "literary comedians" who, like Mark Twain, enjoyed great reputations as public "lecturers" during the 1860s and 1870s. Though their paths may have crossed earlier on the lecture circuit, Mark Twain seems to have been a member of the audience for the first time in Hartford in the mid-1870s. A selection from Nasby's work appears in Walter Blair's *Native American Humor,* 410–12. Alas, the material seems drearily unfunny when read from the printed page. He needed those gestures!

6. Blair, *Selected Shorter Writings of Mark Twain,* 241.

7. All references are to "The Notorious Jumping Frog of Calaveras County" in Blair, *Selected Shorter Writings of Mark Twain,* 13–18. Since the sketch is brief, I have not clogged the text with page numbers.

8. "Private History of 'The Jumping Frog Story,'" first published in *North American Review* in April 1894 and collected in Mark Twain, *How to Tell A Story* (New York: Harper, 1897), 149–63.

9. The extreme case is presented by Paul Schmidt, "The Deadpan on Simon Wheeler," *Southwest Review* 41 (Summer 1956), 270–77. More moderate versions appear in Lynn, *Mark Twain and Southwestern Humor,* 145–47; Cox, *Mark Twain: The Fate of Humor,* 29–32; Smith, *The Development of a Writer,* 11.

10. This sketch, printed in a humor magazine called *The Carpet Bag,* and signed "by S. L. C.," has been attributed to Mark Twain by Walter Blair. See *Selected Shorter Writings,* 1–2.

11. "The Joker in the Pack," 255.

12. "Notes on the Comic," 372. Mr. Auden's comment is worth noting: "This has the same relation to the comic as blasphemy has to belief in God, that is to say, it implies a knowledge of what is truly comic."

13. "The Holy Children," *Mark Twain's Fables of Man,* ed. John S. Tuckey (Berkeley: University of California Press, 1972), 69–77. Since the story is very short, I have not clogged the text with page numbers. James Lyndon Johnson writes revealingly of the sketch and of its relationship to *Huckleberry Finn* in *Mark Twain and the Limits of Power,* 76–79.

14. "Whittier Birthday Speech," Blair, *Selected Shorter Writings,* 152.

15. I conclude that the sick joke constitutes the basic structure of the naturalistic novel. Consider: Marcus's joke on McTeague and the joke on both of them at the end of

*McTeague;* the suicide of the children (for that matter the whole of the relationship between Jude and Sue) in *Jude the Obscure;* Lantier at the Louvre or Lantier in the alcoholics' ward (even Gervayse shakes with laughter) in *L'Assommoir;* the conclusion of *Nana.* And even when the more melodramatic qualities of naturalism drop away, the sick joke remains, as witness the careers of both Hurstwood and Clyde Griffiths.

No doubt we are dealing (via Darwinism) with the rediscovery of the "beast within," an essential perspective of the sick joke. But I suspect it is also a matter (again via Darwinism) of the increasing remoteness or downright disappearance of God, that purveyor of Justice and Mercy, which act as preventives to the sick joke. Thus it is quite right for Auden, good Christian that he was, to speak of sick humor as "blasphemy." ("Notes on the Comic," 372.)

In his old age, when he told sick jokes about God (the ultimate Player), Mark Twain blasphemed directly and consciously. But as I try to demonstrate in the next several pages, he may all along have had the sense that he was blaspheming when he did not wish to do so: the sick joke involved one in an act of blasphemy against the good order of society.

16. See Walter Blair, *Mark Twain and Huck Finn* (Berkeley: University of California Press, 1962), 50–51; *Mark Twain Autobiography,* I, 193; *My Dear Bro.* The first chapters of Susan Gillman's *Dark Twins* develop an interesting account of Mark Twain's beliefs in a kind of "automatic writing" and his frequent insistence upon the impersonal powers of "inspiration."

17. Schmidt, "Deadpan," 276. The term "tutelary deity" is applied by Cox, *Fate of Humor,* 30. I confess to not understanding it, any more than I comprehend why Simon's memory, so limited and transfixed, should be called "astonishingly full," 32. It should be added that for my more somber reading of "Jumping Frog," I am often (though by no means always) indebted to Paul Baender's "'The Jumping Frog' As a Comedian's First Virtue," *Philological Quarterly* 40 (February 1963), 120–29. Professor Baender, I believe, would not wish to label the joke "sick."

18. *Roughing It,* The Signet Edition (New York: New American Library, 1962), 359.

19. All references are to *Adventures of Tom Sawyer,* ed. John C. Gerber, Paul Baender, and Terry Firkins (Berkeley: University of California Press, 1980). Hereafter abbreviated as *ATS.*

20. *The Adventures of Huckleberry Finn,* ed. Walter Blair and Victor Fischer (Berkeley: University of California Press, 1984), 310. All references are to this edition, hereafter *AHF.*

21. See C. Vann Woodward, *The Strange History of Jim Crow,* and, in particular Chapter 2, "The Meaning of Slave Tales" in Lawrence W. Levine, *Black Culture and Black Consciousness* (New York: Oxford University Press, 1977).

22. Peter Gay, *Reading Freud: Explorations and Entertainments* (New Haven: Yale University Press, 1990), 144–46. In another essay from the same collection ("Reading

Freud Through Freud's Reading") Professor Gay reminds us that Mark Twain's *Sketches New and Old* appeared on the list of Freud's ten favorite books. (p. 98).

23.  See Leo Marx, "Mr. Eliot, Mr. Trilling and *Huckleberry Finn*," *American Scholar* 22 (Autumn 1953), 423–40; Cox, *The Fate of Humor,* 181–84; Neil Schmitz, "Twain, *Huckleberry Finn*, and the Reconstruction," *American Studies* 12 (Spring 1971), 125–36.

# Sam Clemens and G. S. Weaver; Hank Morgan and Mark Twain: An Essay on Books and Reality

When Huck complains of not seeing "A-rabs," "jewels," and "elephants" on the St. Petersburg landscape, Tom Sawyer tells him that it is because he did not read the right book. "He said," Huck reports, "if I warn't so ignorant, but had read a book called Don Quixote, I would know without asking. He said it was all done by enchantment."[1] Tom thus sets in motion a recurring theme, what amounts to a kind of *ur*-drama, in Mark Twain's work. Quite improbably, he is allied with the good little boy and that terrible trio the Holy Sisters, all led by slavish devotion to the Book into ornamenting and restructuring the real world. Again, since he patronizes Huck and lets Huck know it, Tom allows a book to rise up and disrupt a normal human relationship. And so he joins the party of Jim Blake who, having repudiated Sunday school manuals as fraudulent, goes on to enact an equally outrageous and anti-social narrative called "The Story of the Bad Little Boy," or of Simon Wheeler, who retreats from a simple and civil request for information into a story and, left to his own devices, would prolong the story into a fifty-foot-shelf collection entitled "The Adventures of Jim Smiley."

But in citing a particular book to justify distortions of reality, Tom likewise distorts the book. Far from validating princesses-in-distress or sheikh-bandits at St. Petersburg, *Don Quixote* would of course treat these matters as chimera, hallucinatory experiences, the phantasms of an errant or insane mind. Wholly misrepresented by Tom, the spirit of Cervantes is much more at home in the sixth paper of "Old Times on the Mississippi," where following many mistakes about himself and his place in the real world the maturing cub comes to see the River as a book, whose alphabet and grammar he may now begin to spell out in useful and productive ways.[2] For Mark Twain, then, the conjoining of books and reality seems to result in two situations, so clear and different that the contrast between them may be spelled out with the precision of formula.

On the one hand, doing it by the book turns characters into caricatures, figures of tunnel-vision, who for all their apparent liveliness of imagination are constrained to imagine—see, do, respond—always in just one way. On the other hand, sensitivity to reality invites treating the real world as a narrative—an objective design of tangible-visible-audible qualities, which makes possible insight and knowledge, true human companionship, the potentiality for change, the fully developed personality. This either/or conjunction, together with its odd outcome (or, rather, given Mark Twain's perspectives, its oddly predictable outcome), is the subject of my third polemical essay.

The essay focuses upon three books, and the importance of each at a particular point in time. In the first section, I deal with a book about the real world which (Mark Twain still undreamt of) Sam Clemens read, annotated, and copiously extracted in 1855, when he was twenty years old. The book and its theories will no doubt seem vacuous and sleazy enough to the modern reader. Yet from young Clemens it evoked the attention, not to say the disciplined concentration, that, years later, Samuel L. Clemens would expend in reading such things as Lecky's *History of European Morals,* Darwin's *Descent of Man,* and Carlyle's *French Revolution.* From this unusually animated response, the presumption has to be that at the time the young reader had located values and attitudes which would affect his future, including anything he might subsequently write. The second part of the essay moves forward thirty-five years to the book Mark Twain wrote between 1885 and 1889. Not only is *A Connecticut Yankee in King Arthur's Court* the most bookish of all Mark Twain's books; in ways that have never been sufficiently recognized, it is a book about waking up inside a book, examining the contents, finding them hopelessly estranged from reality, adjusting them to fit the real world, and ending up letting the world as it is rewrite the book. But of course revision has disastrous consequences. Because (as I believe) he comes to deal in all the right ways with and in the narrative of the real world, Hank Morgan is consigned to the company of the relentlessly destructive Good and Bad Boys and, in addition, to that of "Green Face," stacking up corpses in "Mark Twain's" cellar, and of George Ealer, using his pilot's expertise to scatter the wounded and dying across the face of the Mississippi. It is a mysterious paradox. To reject reality is to have the head filled with nonsense and become a ludicrous figure. To accept reality is to strew catastrophes everywhere and become a ludicrous figure. In the third part of the essay, I hope to clarify the mystery by returning for a second, brief look at "Old Times on the Mississippi."

Chronologically, "Old Times" comes slightly past the half-way point between Sam Clemens's reading in 1855 and Mark Twain's publication of 1889. The papers also have interest for the way they present Mark Twain's reconstruction of "Sam" just after young Clemens's reading experience was completed. My concern, however, is less with historical continuity than with stages in the development of a curiously divided, curiously unified imagination. By juxtaposing the book Sam Clemens read with the book Mark Twain wrote, I undertake one more exegesis of the fine art of standing still: the phenomenon of marking and remarking two, but coming up with one. And through the insertion of "Old Times" I undertake one more explanation for the phenomenon: which is that the same underlying monism that led him to see the Siamese twins as "one" brother (led him to see "Mark Twain" disappearing into Green Face to become one; Good/Bad Boy becoming one through the practice of a single form of behavior) also made facts and fictions—the real world and human fabrications of reality—Mark Twain's Scylla and Charybdis: his unyielding rock; his equally intractable hard place.

## I: CLEMENS AND WEAVER

"My boy, you must get a little memorandum book; and everytime I tell you a thing, put it down right away."
            —Horace Bixby in "Old Times on the Mississippi" (75)

Unfortunately most of the notebooks of his *Wanderjahren,* 1857–61, seem not to have survived. What has long been available to us, however, is the notebook that Sam Clemens kept in 1855, just after he left Hannibal for the first time and two years before he went to the River and Horace Bixby's tutelage. The content of this, the first of his extant journals, suggests tutelage of another sort, for it consists chiefly of Clemens's copying out verbatim the views, or the scientific hypothesis, of a contemporary St. Louis clergyman named George Sumner Weaver. Since much is about to be made here of Weaver's *Lectures on Mental Science,* the parameters of my argument had better be established at the outset. Nowhere will it be implied that reading Weaver constituted a transforming experience, a kind of literary "primal scene" that would figure in turning Sam Clemens into a writer of genius. When in his old age Mark Twain located such a scene, the text he remembered was a fragment from someone's biography of Joan of Arc. (In another place, he used impeccable, madcap logic to trace his eminence back to a case of measles he contracted at the age of 12.)[3] Nor will it be suggested that Weaver's *Lectures* directly furnished any of the subjects about which Mark Twain would later write. Treating Weaver as an early "influence," Alan Gribben has shown that Mark Twain occasionally used concepts and drew from terminologies that parallel those in the *Lectures.* But Professor

Gribben acknowledges that after 1855, Weaver is never again mentioned by Mark Twain, who may very well have read him, cast him aside and forgotten about him entirely.[4] For at least a few weeks in 1855, nevertheless, there was the book; and there are young Clemens's well-documented reactions to what the book conveyed. I propose to deal with the relationship in terms of three questions. First, what was the book about? (In order to understand Clemens's responses, we need to know what he was responding to.) Second, what of special significance to him did Clemens appear to find in the book? Third, what drew him to the book, caused him to keep on reading it, encouraged him to respond to it so fully?[5]

(1) Content. As his title indicates, the Reverend Mr. Weaver is committed to nothing less than an explanation of the mental characteristics that govern all human behavior. Toward the end of the *Lectures* he provides an elaborate map of the world inside the skull, a detailed line-drawing which Sam Clemens would record faithfully on one page of his notebook. On this map, certain qualities that determine temperament and personality—"mental groups" or "organs" is the label given to them—are located with respect to the position which each one occupies within the cranium. Thus "reason" and "perceptive intellect" lie along the forefront of the head, while "selfish propensities" exist just over the ears, "moral sentiments" are placed at the very top of the skull, and at the back of the head the "domestic propensities" are situated. The premise is that these individual groups are made perceptible in knobs or bumps or other protrusions on the surface of the skull, so that through the tactile reading of a head the relative strengths (or weaknesses) of each group may be assessed, and a total character assembled. (*NB*, 32.) This of course is the science known as "phrenology," a popular and highly influential doctrine during much of the nineteenth century in both Europe and the United States. (We might want to remind ourselves that in 1848 or 1849, about six years before Sam Clemens read an account of phrenology, a not very prepossessing New York journalist had his bumps charted by the firm of Fowlers and Wells, the publishers of Weaver's treatise. So flattering was the reading that some have conjectured it helped to turn its subject from obscure Walter Whitman into the poet who published his first edition of *Leaves of Grass* in 1855.)

But Clemens, like Weaver himself, seems less fascinated by mapping the brain than by the development of a second, ancillary key to human conduct. Repeatedly in the *Lectures* emphasis is shifted to a restatement of the theory of the bodily humors. The account offered by Weaver is greatly simplified. He has virtually nothing to say about the fluids (blood, bile, and phlegm) which were so central to the formation and functioning of the humors in medieval and renaissance psychology. Basically, though, his equations follow the four-fold typology of the renaissance: *bilious = coarse black hair, sallow skin, a melancholy disposition; lymphatic = pallor, "inexpressive features," a tendency toward "sluggish" behavior; sanguine = red hair, a ruddy complexion, a mercurial temperament; and nervous (or choleric) = fragile physique, light skin colorations, a restless, undirected energy*. Not only does Sam Clemens copy out all four case histories (each runs to approximately 300 words); at the conclusion of each one he summarizes its most salient features in words of his own. Finally—and amusingly—the *sanguine* temperament, which came third in Weaver's quite neutral listing, is shifted by red-haired, mercurial Sam to first in the order, as if belonging at the top of a hierarchy as the most important humor. (*NB*, 21–29.)

It is not difficult to see why Weaver chooses to combine the two hypotheses. Presumably one cannot help the color of the hair one is born with, or bear responsibility for the particular flow from one's bile ducts: the humors *are* inflexible. On the other hand, according to the *Lectures*, the cranial organs resemble muscles, and hence are susceptible to being constantly and consciously exercised. (*Lectures*, 59–60.) Taken together, then, humors and bumps define the personality, but suggest that what has been defined can also be reshaped, modified, set free to suppress its worst aspects, or to improve and enlarge upon the best ones. But if they work differently, the two theories are clearly rooted in a single, underlying process. Each begins with physical manifestations and proceeds backward into the more nebulous areas of thought, feeling, will, and attitude. The formulation which fits both might well be rendered through the phrase "as out, so in." The visible renders manifest and articulate the invisible.

(2) What of special significance to him did Sam Clemens find in the book? Partly on the basis of the book's message, partly from the marginalia of an interested reader, I hazard two guesses. Both perhaps constitute the supreme fictions, the ultimate tall tales of phrenological and humorous doctrine—although I think this is not how Clemens regarded them in 1855.

Any scientific hypothesis has a way of implying great privileges for those whom it seeks to convert. *Only view me sympathetically*, says the scientific text; *attend to my insights, my reasoned conclusions, my truth*—do this and, *freed of superstitions and all other falsities of perception, you will see yourself and your world as if for the first time*. As a matter of fact, the Reverend Mr. Weaver grants his dispensations with an unusually explicit largess. My work, he writes,

> enables us to read character, to study both ourselves and our fellows, to go in, as it were, into the sanctuary of their souls, and sit in meditation when they know not what we are doing, to examine the actions and states of their minds, and make ourselves acquainted with them as they really are. (*Lectures*, 54.)

If Sam Clemens did not take this sentence down, his marginal comments and addenda indicate that he perfectly understood all that was involved in the promise. To Weaver's definition of the nervous type, for example, Clemens adds in parentheses the name "Orion." Again, in the midst of copying from Weaver, he recalls an encounter he had lately with three young women from the village of Florida, Missouri. One he proceeds to investigate in the light, as well as the syntax, of Weaver's theory, concluding that her pride, vanities, and love of being praised in public are all embodied in the shape of her nose:

> small, turned up, or pug, denotes vanity, susceptibility to flattery, &c. (*NB*, 28, 34–35.)

Might this be mockery, a reductio ad absurdum (spiced up with a little Laurence Sterne) of the high seriousness in Weaver's *Lectures?* I find nothing in the tone or the undoubted energy of the notebook entries to warrant such a conclusion, any more than it seems likely that Clemens was a reader of *Tristram Shandy* in 1855. By understanding the message of Weaver, he has the sense of being in possession of some hidden, yet all-explaining truth about his feckless, will-o'-the-wisp older brother Orion, and about the girl from Florida. Perhaps he even suspects that he is now able to stand unbidden in the very souls of these people and to know them and the springs of their actions far better than they can know themselves.

Even as it promises freedom, science has a way of devising new confinements for the recently liberated. Freudianism emancipates us to recognize and to explore the unconscious, while at the same time, and via the object of our explorations, it reminds us that we are all prisoners of the Family Romance. On the last pages of *The Descent of Man*, Darwin beckons his readership upward "to the very summit of the organic scale." But he does so after having first demonstrated to the readers the undoubted fact of their organic kinship with "a hairy, tailed quadruped, probably arboreal in its habits." And if G. S. Weaver hardly belongs in such illustrious company, he exemplifies the movement from self-to-system in a particularly striking manner. Having found two ways of individualizing the behavior of the self, he proves equally adept at constructing a community of selves, though he does so with great optimism. "Love," he explains, is the "magnetic law" which binds us together:

> Adhesiveness loves friends; Veneration loves God; Self-Esteem loves self; Conscientiousness loves truth, right, holiness; Hope loves a glorious future; Benevolence loves an object of need; Ideality loves beauty; Comparison loves analogies. Causality loves the relations of cause and effect; Acquisitiveness loves money; Construc-

tiveness loves mechanics; Tune loves music; Man's whole active nature is expressed by the word *Love.*

This time, Sam Clemens records the entire passage. (*NB*, 32–33.) Although he does so without comment, I surmise that he finds the statement attractive because, for the moment anyhow, he truly believes it—just as he would wish to believe it again thirty years later when Mark Twain wrote the thirty-first chapter of *The Adventures of Huckleberry Finn.* The youthful reader of Weaver's *Lectures* has not merely been told how experience works; he has been granted an insight into what experience is for—into what *he* is for.

(3) But why did Sam Clemens go to the book in the first place? More to the point why, having gone, did he stay with it, take the trouble of laboriously reproducing substantial portions of it, as if wanting to possess what the book said for his very own? The answer is hardly to be found in style, since the manner of the *Lectures* is tedious, sententious, rarely engrossing and never entertaining. Yet an explanation might very well lie in "stylistics," or in an attitude toward style. If the coupling of *"out-to-in"* is the basic direction of Weaver's presentation, behind that formulation stands another sort of implied premise. The phrases to express this one are *world-before-words . . . life-prior-to-language.*

Let me state a case in what I understand to be the context of some nineteenth-century perspectives. "Out there" in the external world, there are many indisputable differences: different shapes, textures, colorations, habits of mind, modes of behavior. Reality in fact is a veritable teeming clutter of blondes and brunettes; of widely spaced eyes and those that are set narrowly; of aquiline noses and round noses; of ebullient optimisms and pervasive glooms. No more than wet/dry, hot/cold, or night/day (which in their objectivity they resemble) can these differences be said to name themselves. Nor in a secularized world is it any longer supposable that designating labels are imposed upon the shapes and forms from the outside by God, the gods or some metaphysical essence. The vocabularies by which they are called—the grammars and syntaxes through which we sort and arrange them meaningfully—all come welling up out of us as human observers. Nevertheless, the world exists anterior to the words that speak it. By attending to the external differences, we are taught a valuable lesson in style, in the proper use of language. Which is to say we learn to adapt and control our words; to direct them outward toward something definite and precise; to pin down in the realness of the real both the words themselves and the inner life which is their source—in short, we come to use language in practical ways and for the encompassing of useful, enlightening, socially productive ends. For granted that the referents "bear" and "bath" ("poison" and "privy") emerge equally from the thinking-conceptualizing-verbalizing human identity. Still, it is a matter of some moment that the words which denominate the experience (bear) to be run from not be confused with those that designate the experiences to be hastened toward (bath). It will be seen that we are not here pondering the question of whether a thousand monkeys pounding on a thousand typewriters might after a thousand days compose *Hamlet,* or a deconstructionist's reading of *Hamlet.* Our focus is on the more mundane issue of using instruments of culture as the means of survival in a very real and very demanding and resistant "out there."

In literature this is the doctrine of literary realism. Realism stresses the exact correspondence between an ordering of words on the one hand and on the other the external order of things, which the words seek to imitate and hence represent with complete fidelity. In science and philosophy the doctrine is called empiricism. The empirical method stresses that only through contact with experience, especially in sensory engagements with the external world, are knowledge and the expression of knowledge ever possible. A recent account of the pseudo-sciences in nineteenth-century America has drawn attention to their roots in the realistic, empirical method. No doubt they were a folly at the time and certainly they seem freakish and foolish by contemporary standards, write Arthur Wrobel and Robert H. Collyer.[6] Yet phrenology, mesmerism, and the humors represented sincere attempts to deal with the real world in its own given terms, and to find in reality the sole basis we have for understanding how the world around us functions. Judged by nineteenth-century criteria, states Professor Wrobel, "their empiricism was above reproach."[7]

Interspersed among his extracts from Weaver is evidence of Sam Clemens's recent exposure to another, very different world view. Thus Weaver on the "bilious humor" is directly succeeded in the notebook by Clemens's summary, cryptic and without apparent judgment, of a debate (perhaps heard? perhaps read about?) between two other St. Louis clergymen:

> Hopson's notion of hell—between <Heav> the sun and earth—Manford's reply—
> . . . Says "Hell *is* there, for it sprung a leak and . . . the drippings set fire to Sodom and Gomorrah and burnt them up." (*NB,* 25.)

W. H. Hopson speaks the language of Biblical fundamentalism; he would explain the world we inhabit in terms of its cosmological kinship with the other worlds called "Heaven" and "Hell." To his other-worldly orientation, Erasmus Manford (a Universalist minister and colleague of G. S. Weaver) apparently responded with a jest about the burning of the wicked cities. And judgment does come within a few pages when Sam Clemens invokes the reaction to the debate (or the debaters) of his free-thinking and much respected uncle, John F. Quarles:

> U. J. says—"If Mr. Hopson should speak to me, I would just calmly and quietly say to him: 'Now, sir, do you just go home and get down on your knees and pray to God.['"] (NB, 33.)

But I believe the whole notebook is to be construed as a judgment. It records the search for an intellectual position, a way of both viewing and articulating experience that would eliminate all vestiges of Hopson-like orthodoxy. Young Clemens found his position by extracting and assembling the this-worldliness of G. S. Weaver.

His sense of the empirical, the strictly experiential quality of the *Lectures* becomes evident in three emendations that Clemens adds to Weaver's analysis of the "sanguine" personality. In the first, gray-eyed Sam amends Weaver's assertion that the sanguine type has "ruddy skin" and "blue eyes" by quietly adding the qualification "or gray." The second consists of a wry, underscored "(*not always*)" when Weaver associates the sanguine personality with a taste for "out-of-door jollity." The third takes the form of two sentences which have been quietly inserted into Weaver's analysis of the sanguine type:

> It is very sensitive and is first deeply hurt at a slight, the next emotion is violent rage, and in a few moments the cause and result are both forgotten for the time being. It often forgives, but never entirely forgets an injury. (NB, 20–21.)

So close are tone and phrasing to those in the original that one must look at both book and notebook to realize that the sentences came not from the author, Mr. Weaver, but from the author's reader, Mr. Clemens.

It is easy enough to laugh at Weaver for his dogmatism and pretentiousness—and hence easy to wonder whether, in imitating him, Clemens is not likewise having a bit of sport. Once again, however, mimicry seems more nearly a gesture of respect than an attempt to be scornful. According to his best lights as a Universalist minister, Weaver had laid aside metaphysics and subordinated spirituality, in order to emphasize a more exact reading of experience. It is this rigor—this concern with elucidating human conduct by grounding it in the actions and reactions of flesh-and-blood human beings—that Sam Clemens seems to find admirable. If he supplements Weaver's reading of the sanguine type, by appealing to a new set of facts, Clemens is only doing with descriptive language what Weaver had encouraged in the *Lectures*. He lets a "given" (a factual, intimately known presence) name and define itself through the words which it seems to furnish, rather than working the naming-process the other way around.

And having done so (it appears) he moves briskly on. Within eighteen months or so, Sam Clemens will be involved with other influences and a different sort of notebook, as he commences his career on the River. In a shade more than a decade he will have sat out most of the Civil War in Nevada territory, turned into Mark Twain, and achieved something more than local notoriety with the publication of "The Notorious Jumping Frog." Two decades beyond reading and copying from Weaver, he will have traveled internationally, written two best sellers, proved himself as a public entertainer in demand everywhere, married prosperously, and settled in as the squire, the paterfamilias, the famous author-in-residence of a posh mansion in Hartford, Connecticut. On the thirtieth anniversary (1885) he will be hardly less than a celebrity: lately the author of *Huckleberry Finn*; the disgraced (though hardly chastened) center of attention at the Whittier birthday dinner; the triumphant performer, without peer, at the testimonial dinner for General Grant; a good bit of a household word, if you please—and this not solely because hawkers are peddling his books from door-to-door in every corner of the land. And through it all, as the arc sweeps steadily upward bearing along a figure who (in his own words) is empowered with the "Midas touch," one hears from Mark Twain never a backward reference to G. S. Weaver. It is as if after causing a brief flurry of excitement, the *Lectures on Mental Science* had been laid aside and forgotten as one more example of the accumulated and perhaps slightly embarrassing junk which characterized Sam Clemens in his "callow youth." (*NB*, 20.)

I suggest, however, that the young man who was cannot—and from the standpoint of literary analysis, should not—be so readily divorced from the man he becomes. Surely there is a point to be made from this fact: that a fledgling humorist and eminent humorist-to-be was exposed at the age of twenty (when he was no longer quite the callow upstart) to an elaborate theory, wherein humor, instead of being associated with humorous in the modern sense (with the amiable, the quizzical or lighthearted of perspective), is seen to control and categorize human personalities with all the rigorous clinical precision of the genetic structure. Or, to work the emphasis the other way around, surely there is significance in this fact: that a doctrine of this-worldliness—an insistence upon the empirical method, a bent for consulting near-at-hand physical evidence before drawing moral or spiritual conclusions, an emphasis upon language as the effect rather than the cause of experience—was early on (though not too early, after all) shared by the same theory with an author whose work would often be self-consciously autobiographical; who would preface the first venture he made on his own into an extended fiction with the assertion: "Most of the adventures in this book really happened; one or two were experiences of my own, the rest those of boys who were schoolmates of mine"; and of whom it has been said that he soon passed from grade-school grammar to a concern with the underlying "principles of language."[8] As he closes G. S.

Weaver and his own first notebook, the mood of Sam Clemens seems not far from exultant. He has found a workable treatise on personality, and has arrived at self-definition by looking at the treatise and then at himself closely. Nevertheless, there is an obvious logical flaw in Weaver's presentation. Encouraging, on the one hand, the view that freedom and understanding must come from fairly wallowing in reality, the *Lectures* emphasize, on the other, that immersion in the real can only demonstrate how the self is fixed and fated by whatever skin colorations and blood-shaped temperaments—whatever specific humor— the self happens to be born with. The paradox is that the same this-worldliness which purports to tell us all we need to know about ourselves is likewise the basis for a rigid determinism (note Weaver's no-nonsense verbs and flat, bald sentence structures), from which no variation or escape is ever possible. My feeling is that whether or not he remembered the name Weaver after thirty years, or for that matter after only one, Weaver's paradox entered very deeply into the thinking of Mark Twain. No doubt the contradiction was enhanced and complicated by Samuel L. Clemens's later reading from Lecky, Darwin, and other moral philosophers. But in its rudimentary form, as propounded by G. S. Weaver, it is a source not only of the bleakness of Mark Twain's art, his sense of reality as paralyzed by fixity and futility, but also of the art's glory, its capacity for equating paralysis with absurdity, so that (humor being humor) laughter could be coaxed from the paralytics.[9]

## II: Morgan and Mark Twain

"Now, here's the point. If I throw any novel into this cabinet with you, shut the door and tap it three times, you will find yourself projected into that book."
—Persky in Woody Allen's "The Kugelmass Episode"

"You'll find the books full of my kind of grasshopper, and scarcely a trace of yours in any of them."
—Romantic to Realist in Howells's *Criticism and Fiction*

I scanned a leaf particularly and saw that it was a palimpsest. Under the old dim writing of the Yankee historian appeared traces of a penmanship which was older and dimmer still—Latin words and sentence fragments from old monkish legends, evidently.
—A Word of Explanation from *Connecticut Yankee*.[10]

Inelasticity supplies the format of Mark Twain's jokes: the obsessional life affixed irrevocably in one attitude, one mode of behavior; the whole of the wide world lodged at a single point in space and time. The jokes, though, are told by and about figures who, like their creator, are drawn by opportunity and itchy feet into strange and exotic quarters of the frozen world. Their careers conform to a basic pattern of departing, being there, coming back. And above all, they go: from home to the River; west to Nevada Territory, California, the Sandwich Islands; east to New York, Europe, the Holy Land; south to the Silas Phelps plantation; round the globe from Elmira, New York to London; backward in time to Eseldorf, Austria; upward (or is it downward?) through space to the Garden of Eden and a season spent in Heaven. But where does Hank Morgan go, after he has been struck on the head in Hartford, Connecticut? Leaving aside the question of how or whether he returns, what does being there signify for him? He goes to the Court of King Arthur, we say confidently. He awakens in ancient Britain on a glorious June morning in the year 528 A.D. And even as this sort of specificity accumulates, a problem is raised.

Let us suppose the date had been 1492, 1066, 1630 . . . 400 B.C. in Athens. Then from the written records of history Mark Twain might have aroused Hank to ally him with real people engaged in the performance of historically certifiable actions in the real world. But though the birth, copulation, death, and sundry other commonplaces of real people were no doubt the order of the day in Britain of 528 A.D., we know next to nothing of what went on at this time, and writing in the 1880s without the benefit of recent archaeological discoveries (of Michael Woods's In Search of the Dark Ages, for example) Mark Twain would have known even less. Poised between the Roman withdrawal at the beginning of the fifth century and the composition of Beowulf near the close of the seventh, sixth-century Britain is a "bookless age," one of those blanks in time we style an "era without history." Because it was a void, furthermore, the period could become ideally well suited to the imaginative constructions which commenced with the French minstrel poets of the tenth century, returned to England as Geoffrey of Monmouth's Historia Regum Britanniae (1140), and by the close of the fifteenth century had been elaborated yet once more in Mark Twain's principal source, the Morte d'Arthur of Thomas Malory. Chiefly myths and legends—with respect to verisimilitude, never more than collections of well-wrought fables—these fictions, assembled several hundred years after the facts, constitute our only real knowledge of the facts. The window that opens for us (and Mark Twain) on Camelot in June of 528 A.D. is a strictly literary window, generally entitled "The Matter of Britain."

All of which means that after he is knocked unconscious at Hartford, it is not possible for a lost, but retrievable historical past to be Hank Morgan's next destination. A stylish image for his journey would be the cinematic device that has frequently opened movies which are based on novels. The image would show Hank reeling backward from the blow until his fall is arrested when he comes up against a conveniently located bookcase. Thereupon one volume tumbles out and, amidst riffling pages and a dissolved binding, Hank tumbles forward to enter the book: to become part of a story-in-progress. It is much to the point that his first glimpses of Camelot should remind the Yankee of scenes "out of a picture book," and that the first jest he undertakes in his new surroundings should turn on whether Clarence is a "page" or a "paragraph." (*CY,* 9, 15.) The emphasis both times catches what nowadays would be termed the intertextuality of his situation. For Mark Twain is not relocating a character in a literal time and place called sixth-century Britain. Rather, in the manner of Woody Allen's postmodern short story "The Kugelmass Episode" (or as in Mr. Allen's experimental movie "The Purple Rose of Cairo") he has set the character down inside somebody else's narrative—one which, as it happens, tells a fanciful story about Britain in the sixth century.

Actually precedent is to be found in his earlier work. Around 1880 Mark Twain had decided it would be great fun to add a character to the cast of *Hamlet.* Through the turmoil at Elsinore would wander Basil, the itinerant book peddler, muttering (in interesting anticipation of T. S. Eliot's lack of an "objective correlative"), "What's going on here? . . . These people are crazy." Once or twice he would come close enough to the throne to address Claudius as "The Boss." While the ghost gathered on the battlements Basil would appear somewhere below, full of confusion, presumably preparing to track the labyrinth by pulling from his pocket an interminable piece of string.[11] Nothing came of the project except a good many pages, largely given over to speeches from Shakespeare. But the tank of inspiration which soon ran dry in 1880 had, five years later, been replenished by a similar idea. "Dream of being a knight errant in armor in the middle ages," ran the first notation for *Yankee.*[12] And by turning the dream from author's to that of character and making it a dream which envelopes and will not terminate ("'Bridgeport,' said I, pointing. 'Camelot,' said he"), Mark Twain goes on to give fresh definition to the old saw about being curled up with a good book. (*CY,* 9.) At the outset, his aim was to thrust Hank (like Basil, the book peddler) into a prior narrative, then step back and watch what might develop.

(1) *Life in a world of words.* Narrative—any narrative, no matter how remote from the real world—presents certain general aspects of the real world. Narrative comprises settings (an environment); a time-scheme of sorts (even if time stands still or runs backward); characters and character-relationships (hence thoughts, feelings, states of consciousness, emotional involvements—all those attributes we associate with personality and the interpersonal). Narrative is a world of words. The intrusion of a stranger into this made-up world

calls for adjustments on both sides, just as it would in actual experience. Emma Bovary imposes her libidinous will on Professor Kugelmass at New York's Plaza Hotel, until distraught and depleted the professor has no taste for encounters with Lady Chatterly or Sister Carrie, but yearns for projection into an old-fashioned textbook called "Remedial Spanish." The situation of Basil, the book seller, is somewhat different: in their magnificent self-absorption the others never really recognize he is present. And at first, adjusting to the narrative world of 528 A.D. seems a matter of importing into the words already there a brash, irreverent new vocabulary. Less contributor to a palimpsest than the voice-over narrator, Hank Morgan brings to bear on the most sacred values of Camelot a sardonic eye and his uninhibited mouthiness. Eventually he will dominate the Arthurian characters by the simple expedient of drawing their attention to Merlin as bore, by scaling down their Round Table into a grease-laden, wine-stained, rat-infested monstrosity. Very soon, though, it grows clear that in this particular narrative world actions are of far more consequence than an ability to see and say. Those who belong in the book by rights will destroy the talkative outsider, unless he learns to perform more forcefully than they can. And this, as Hank recognizes in his prison cell, means becoming a superior magician.

So, with a photographic memory and the information of a Greenwich astronomer, Hank recalls how an eclipse of the sun is scheduled for the summer solstice of 528 A.D. He plots the timing of the eclipse so that it begins at the very moment when he is about to be torched to death, just as a bit later he fetches from a hitherto cloudless sky the thunderstorm that sets in motion the razing of Merlin's tower. Most wonderfully yet, he spreads across the landscape at Camelot newspapers, electric lights, the telephone, munitions and man factories, without once explaining where the raw materials were obtained or how such notoriously public utilities can be kept hidden from most of the Arthurians. During his first days inside the book, Hank is never just a technologically sophisticated Yankee in a land of intellectual pygmies. His feats are those of one who is magically, even supernaturally, endowed; and they are enacted upon a world that is unbounded by probabilities or any need for realism. Mark Twain has sent his protagonist stumbling by chance into an outrageous and outlandish fiction. Anything can happen there. Anything does.

The trouble is that anything threatens to become one thing. Avoiding engulfment by the language of the original, which had been his problem when he tried to rewrite *Hamlet*, Mark Twain turns to dramatic actions, only to find that he has on his hands the gimmick of two competing magics and a single outcome. Variety is needed if he hopes to expand his material beyond the scope of an amusing short story. By an odd irony, the source of variety is located in a group of characters who have no more legitimate entitlement to appear inside this world of words than does Hank himself.

"In the courtly romance," writes Eric Auerbach, "the functionally, the historically real aspects of social class are passed over. Nothing is said about the practical conditions and circumstances necessary to render knights and their castles both possible and compatible with ordinary experience. . . . For where [courtly romance] depicts reality, it depicts merely the colorful surface, and where it is not superficial, it has other subjects and other ends than those of contemporary reality."[13] Accordingly, there can be no place in the original story for a spectacle which nonetheless greets Hank as he mounts up the hill to King Arthur's castle:

> At intervals we passed a wretched cabin, with a thatched roof, and about it small fields and garden patches in an indifferent state of cultivation. There were people, too; brawny men, with long coarse, uncombed hair that hung down over their faces and made them look like animals. They and the women, as a rule, wore a coarse tow-linen robe that came well below the knee, and a rude sort of sandals, and many wore an iron collar. (CY, 13.)

These figures, their shabby background, and the terrible lives they lead, have been added to the book on the shelf. They exist solely by virtue of having been brought into the narrative by Mark Twain—even as Hank was. But of course the two anachronisms function in very different ways. Coming from Hartford, Connecticut, U.S.A., the Yankee is a true outlander, genuinely a stranger in a strange land. Conversely, the rags and tatters have really been there all along. Logically, somebody had to tend the Castle, till the fields, gird up the loins of the knights-errant, feed and water their horses. It is simply that, as Professor Auerbach observes, no one ever looked for the somebody. The Arthurian workers remained curtained off because romancers from Geoffrey of Monmouth through Tennyson had no interest in them. By raising the curtain, Mark Twain acknowledges common sense. He makes the text more empirical by bringing into it matters which ought to be present, but are not. Thereby, he gains a subject for *Yankee*. More is involved than Hank's parlor tricks, or playing games with certain literary conventions. The subject bears on the moral and aesthetic adequacy of a world of words which, though generally modeled on the real world, yet blithely leaves out the social-economic-political realities of which, in large measure, any real world is constituted.

(2) *The words of a world of words.* When he comes back down the hill from the Castle in Chapter 11, Hank Morgan travels through a world of words that Mark Twain has enlarged and made much truer to life. Introduced casually, yet

very pointedly at the beginning, those who do the despised and degrading chores at Camelot have now stepped forth as major characters to be reckoned with in the book. At every turn of the road, the menials confront Hank, pricking his conscience, reminding him of human ties and obligations that greatly impair the freedom he feels at being Boss. Still, the achievement of his first journey through the kingdom is to turn Hank into neither social reformer (a role he stoutly resists) nor a consistent critic of society. It is, rather, to make him a critic of literature: a student of the relationship between fictions and reality, language and life. All unwittingly the Yankee is drawn into and acts out dramatically a controversy about literature that William Dean Howells had for some time been arguing in the pages of *Harper's* and would present as the showpiece of *Criticism and Fiction* when that book was published in 1892.

The second chapter of *Criticism and Fiction* is organized as a kind of morality play in which two spokespeople for different theories of literary language debate for the soul of a young writer. The romantic theorist finds in the words of literature the power to embellish, to idealize and ennoble what would otherwise remain dreary, ugly reality—in a phrase, to turn real grasshoppers into aesthetically satisfying ideal grasshoppers. All the books, says this figure grandly, are "full of my kind of grasshoppers."[14] Speaking for Howells, the realistic theorist concedes the worst about grasshoppers: that they are coarse and as altogether unlovely as the tobacco juice they are alleged to spit, and that it may seem an act of foolishness to waste words by reproducing in books what nature has already produced so lavishly. Yet in the honest representation, says this figure, lies the only possibility we have for writing honest books, books that can teach. A preference for grasshoppers—real vs. ideal ones—is very much the issue that enters into the first long journey of *Yankee* and keeps it going. Even the dialogic or (since neither party to the dispute much listens) the pseudo-dialogic form of Howells's argument has been anticipated.

On one side is the irrepressible Sandy. She speaks in circumlocutions: since the road winds both east and west, who can say whether the route to the castle lies easterly—or westerly? Another of her favorites is the euphemism which, at a moment's notice, is prepared to turn pigs in their sties to ladies dwelling at the ancestral manor house. When all else fails, she resorts to the stilted, spiritualized phrases of the book, telling and telling again one or another of the episodes of Courtly Love or Chivalric Idealism from Malory. For Hank, on the other side, these are words, words, words; ineffectual attempts to make the time pass; sounds passing through one ear and out the other. The Yankee wants facts and figures. Moreover, he expects them to bristle with the salty, no-nonsense colloquialisms that will specify ("'great guns'") how long it takes to get from here to there, and where exactly it is that "'they hang out.'" (*CY,* 55–56.)

This is a standard confrontation in Mark Twain: two speakers, each talking non-stop in his/her own vocabulary, neither one communicating. We are reminded of Bixby and the cub, of Tom and Huck at several points in the adventures of both, of Scotty Briggs and the minister in *Roughing It*. The only problem about the joke lies in determining how and where to allocate our laughter. As the noise goes on, "with" whom do we laugh? "At" whom do we laugh?

Despite Hank's encouragement to treat her as the butt of the joke, in many ways the honors lie with Sandy. Since her language comes out of the book, and is attuned to the book's logic and values, she is perfectly adapted to the environment which the book provides. Like the sentences she weaves together, Sandy as a character is ever free and ever graceful, able to flit through the world of words in any scattered and random manner that best pleases her. She stands in sharp contrast to Hank who often seems as burdened beneath stuffy and fretful language as he is by the armor he wears. We end up laughing at him because while she meanders and he complains, Sandy is comfortable as Hank no longer is, and is completely at home and at ease in the narrative as he increasingly ceases to be.

But in another sense the language which defines her as free also equates freedom with insouciance. If Sandy is never uncomfortable, never mystified or troubled by reality, this is so for the excellent reason that, safely enclosed by a particular kind of story, she never has to make contact with real circumstances in the real world. As in the fictions she relates, she draws between herself and "out there" a series of narrative structures, some borrowed, some of her own devising, all guaranteed to replace perception with imagination, and hence to keep "out there" populated with only the images and interpretations which Sandy chooses to see and elects to make. And though fiction-making in the fiction may be one measure of her charm, the enactment of this same process elsewhere in the early chapters of *Yankee* takes on more sinister implications. At the dungeons of Morgan le Fay, Hank encounters old men who have been imprisoned all their lives not for any deeds they did, but because of the words—the lies, perjuries, sheer human volubility—that invented the deeds. Among a party of slaves he notes how suffering is recorded on the faces of the anguished in a language that is too terrible to read—yet, for the sake of human compassion, must be read and spoken. In her sublime indifference Sandy can (and does) miss the point to all these incidents—the point being of course that unless words are rooted in actual, visceral experience, all usages of lanaguage lead to the same dreary, distorting end. The chipper obliviousness of Sandy to pain is but the obverse side of Morgan le Fay's programmed creation of the painful. In effect, the two function as twins, the Good Girl/Bad Girl of Camelot.

Mark Twain's interplay of opposites thus deepens into a critique of the styles of narrative. And it is appropriate that the climax to the first journey should be embodied in two different ways of telling what is essentially one story, constructed around a single performative gesture. In the end Hank will humor Sandy's pretense that gentlewomen have been enchanted into hogs and may, after suitable hocus-pocus, be enchanted back to gentlewomen again. He consents, that is, to her reconstructions of reality, even to the point of becoming temporarily one of the characters she makes up. But along the way, the inklings of a substitute plot have begun to emerge. Like Mark Twain, the Yankee will alter the original story through the addition of real grasshoppers. Now the technique of the palimpsest becomes meaningful. Across Sandy's child-like scrawls, overriding Morgan le Fay's utterances of Black Magic, Hank will assemble a story which is also concerned with transformation. It will tell how a sluggish, greedy, swinish culture can gradually be metamorphosed into a society of free and productive human beings.

(3) *A world of words and the real world.* To overwrite the fiction with a realistic plot is to conceive of the fiction as a documentary, an imitation of life, a world wrought out of words that is made to correspond as fully and exactly as possible to the contingencies and the tempo of life as it is actually lived in the real world. Perhaps one of the damned things is enough, as Rebecca West is reputed to have said of imaginative writers who take the real world for their subject matter. But, as critics of a "sociological" bent often maintain, more is at stake than an exercise in imitating and transcribing the given. Most of us blunder through the real world experiencing what is there through a thick haze of clichés, stereotypes, and other verbal and optical dodges. Realistic art becomes our shock of recognition, not so much reminding us of the real as stripping reality to its bare essentials, and hence allowing us to discover the real and all it signifies as for the first time. This is a premise which links such otherwise diverse critics of realistic art as Ruskin, Howells, and Lukacs. It is likewise the premise that emphatically distinguishes Hank's second long journey from the first one in *Yankee.*

Incongruity was the key to his expedition with Sandy, the sudden rise in the roadway that disclosed modern gadgetry and knight-vendors in an ancient setting. Horror was there also. Yet the underworld was held at a safe distance by Sandy's good humor, by the perception of atrocities from the outside (so that the victims tended to remain nameless and faceless), and by Hank's habit of confusing Arthurian brutalities with Arthurian quaintnesses. Now, by contrast, the Yankee travels in a so-called disguise that has the ironic effect of both exposing him and leaving him highly vulnerable. Because he is Boss no longer, he must shed the raiment and perspectives of a traveling aristocrat and participate directly in the horrors along the way. He literally becomes, by turns, the beleaguered and suffering peasant, the potential victim of disease, the fugitive on the run, the slave in manacles, an unjustly imprisoned felon, the felon on the gallows. And the more Hank is flung into the dramatic center of things, the greater is Mark Twain's emphasis upon modifying the place and time of the Yankee's journey. Incongruity gives way to similarity and continuity. For the road Hank now follows increasingly leads him straight out of the book where he awakened, and to another kind of awakening in the nightmare of history.

The shift is evident among the sufferers from smallpox. At this point Camelot recedes from view, and the Yankee finds himself enveloped by the atmosphere (and hence the issues and chronology) of *A Modest Proposal* and the *Journal of the Plague Year.* A similar telescoping is achieved through his disquisition on economics, addressed to an audience with the occupations and oddly plebeian surnames of a Renaissance comedy, and by his ordeals as a slave. First the experiences remind Hank of later centuries; next they appear actually to relocate him in the time of *A Shoemaker's Holiday,* in the last days of Bourbon France, in the antebellum American South, in industrial Europe, in the America of Grover Cleveland. Read in terms of the new strategy, the descriptions of London take on great significance. The aim is not to create another anachronism inside the book, but rather to end their journey by delivering the Yankee and King Arthur into the historical city, the city of Elizabeth and Hogarth, of Blake and Marx and Mayhew—history's ultimate cesspool.

So, a narrative that originated in make-believe now proceeds outward through a succession of real points in space and time. Hank has ceased to wander among bookish images of suffering and corruption. The enhanced realism of the book has prepared the way for conducting him outside the story, and into the presence of real suffering and authentic corruption as these have been the historical conditions of all societies, wherever and whenever human beings have gathered. Straight-line though it appears to be, however, the movement from fiction to fact is also complicated by a profound and (one wants to call it) a circle-forming paradox. Before very long it is brought home to the Yankee that history is fully as much dominated by make-believe as the book had been. He is made aware by the nature of his experiences in reality that if the real world is a combination madhouse and torture chamber, it has been thrust into the postures it everywhere displays by the shaping influence upon it of a world of words.

The cause-and-effect relationship is strikingly illustrated by his new traveling companion. Though Arthur shows no taste for repeating Malory (or even, apparently, for reminiscing about bygone glories at the Round Table), he yet shares with Sandy a belief in the absolute power of words to transfigure facts. In moments of crisis nothing can persuade him that he is no longer "King," as he had been called by the book. No evidence, brought to bear from history or amassed through common sense, will cause him to renounce the regal airs and mannerisms which the book had formerly sanctified. But unlike Sandy's, the fictions of Arthur are not attempts to escape reality—to ascend beyond grubby, everyday existence toward an enactment of life in the realm of the ideal. They are born of the far more insidious notion that reality inheres in the fiction. For Arthur is not simply an invention of Merlin the Magician or, along with Merlin, of romancers from Chrétien de Troyes to Tennyson. He comes cloaked in the long tradition of Christian metaphysics, with its emphasis upon flesh-and-blood being reconstituted and hypostatized through the descent into everyday existence of concepts and a vocabulary out of the World above. The tall tale enacted so grandly by Arthur needs no exposition, and no justification beyond its own unique structure. It moves from the invented, well-elaborated silliness of Courtly Love into a bald, flat, take-it-for-granted assertion of the Divine Right of Kings and Princes.

Such is the nature of art that a world of words can wrest the most fundamental kind of truth out of a presentation that bears no likeness to the world as it is. Conversely the world of words may be modeled precisely upon things as they are, yet lose the truth of things within a labyrinth of platitude, self-deception, and human inertia. From the fantasy of 528 A.D. Hank Morgan, neither historian nor sociologist by trade, commences to learn the meaning of history; cast into the blight of history, he discovers the difficulty of sharing what he knows. Thus his lectures on "political economy" fall on deaf ears, because the audience, at once citizens of Camelot and renaissance yeomen, prefers the "meaningless names" for facts to the facts themselves. Repeatedly he recognizes that the abused and tortured of history are strangely content with their lot because a churchly edict or a pronouncement of kingship—a joint mouthing of Church and State—have made the lot seem both legitimate and unalterable. Whether in never-never land or historical London, there is, it appears, no construct of language which is so farfetched or extravagant that somewhere, somehow, some authority-figure has not invoked it as ideology: as the sole, proper determinant of all human behavior. "It was only just words, words," the Yankee reflects at one point. And he goes on to add despairingly, "Words realize nothing, vivify nothing to you, unless you have [experienced] in your own person the thing the words try to describe." (CY, 187, 161–62.)

Toward the close of Edward Bellamy's Looking Backward, published a year earlier than Yankee in 1888 and normally regarded as more tract than novel, an interesting, quite novelistic tableau is presented. Julian West dreams that he sits at breakfast in Boston of the 1880s, reading a newspaper. All around him lie the visible symptoms of a civilization in its death throes, and each symptom has been duly recorded in the paper he reads from. The news of the day is a compendium of crimes, suicides, starvation in the streets, civil strife, and violence. At the end of the enumeration, however, the editor pauses to pay tribute to a tribute: "Decoration Day addresses. Professor Brown's oration on the moral grandeur of nineteenth century civilization." Still dreaming, West next passes through the meanest slums of Boston to his bank, where amidst cheat, fraud, and business-as-usual he is greeted with a paean: "'It's a poem, sir,' cries the bank manager, 'that's what I call it.'" Herein for Bellamy lay the doom of culture in nineteenth-century America: not simply that signifiers no longer bore any discernible kinship with the signified, but that, turning facts to fictions, the verbal structure—the oration, the poem—had come to be privileged as the Supreme Fact. From this nightmare of preferring words to world, Julian West had to be awakened twice over. Both times he is roused in a utopia where the instruments of communication dominate, and society has revised itself by learning to communicate properly.[15]

Although Mark Twain seems not to have read Bellamy until after *Yankee* was completed (then he would respond with great enthusiasm),[16] he shares Bellamy's sense of the reasons for a crisis in culture. And he portrays something closely akin to Bellamy's resolution when, following the tour through history, Hank is restored to the book. "Consider three years spent," says the Yankee in Chapter 40, back now at Camelot, and inviting us to reflect backward on the world of words as it was when he first stepped into its pages. (*CY*, 228.) What changes have occurred during this interval? In particular, what has been the fate of those other anachronisms, the ones who claimed Hank's attention on the opening pages of his manuscript?

It seems fair to say of these characters that from their lives life-denying tall tales have been removed: not just the droll (if somewhat insensitive) mooniness of Sandy, but more crucially the mythologies and superstitions of Arthur and history which, glorifying caste and heredity (the authorities of Throne and Altar), had made the menials slaves and kept them in bondage. And with the stretchers gone, the ornamentation of life has given way to grubbier, more work-a-day reality—but a reality with some built-in ornaments of its own. No doubt we are struck by the goodly share of platitude and Crystal Palace gimmickry in the various inventions Hank now goes on to itemize:

> Schools everywhere, and several colleges; a number of pretty good newspapers. . . . Slavery was dead and gone; all men were equal before the law; taxation had been equalized. The telegraph, the telephone, the phonograph, the typewriter, the sewing machine, and all the thousand willing and handy servants of steam and electricity were working their way into favor. (*CY*, 228.)

Yet for all the smugness often attributed to him, the Yankee makes no claim to inventing these things. He has changed perspectives that make acceptance of the inventions possible. "Practical," by self-definition, "and nearly barren of sentiment," (CY, 8) he has roused the Arthurians from their language-oriented slumbers, and acquainted them with what, for Mark Twain (the admirer of Howells and Bellamy), would be the objectively real, hence self-evident truths of a democratic society. He has instilled a sense of realism, thus familiarizing Camelot for the first time with those material structures and natural relationships which are essential for personal comfort (as opposed to royal privilege), for technological change (in contrast to the stagnations of State and Church), and—one uses the term advisedly—for commonwealth (in contradistinction to the tyranny of a wealthy, empowered few). Set down in the context of the smallpox hut or of the slave market in London, furthermore, the changes amply justify his assertion that the Hell dispensed by Arthur's botchings and the connivings of human history has been abolished, and in lieu of Hell there has come to pass a "happy and prosperous country."[17]

But in order for this to happen, the Yankee, by his presence, has had to rewrite the book. Or rather, like his author before him, he has had to revise premises that link fictive to factual, the literary edifice to the preexistent edifice of objective reality. And both together—author; character-as-author—have effected their changes along the lines of another book which thirty or so years earlier had excited the attention of young Sam Clemens. As the implied author of Yankee, Mark Twain does not simply thrust a stranger from Connecticut into the narrative-in-progress of Malory and the minstrel poets. Present to greet Hank, from the moment of his arrival, are the slaves and drudges whom the implied author also puts in because Malory and the minstrel poets had absurdly left them out. Their existence in the book is what permits Hank to break free of being a stunt man and to emerge as a character in his own right. By the downtrodden and disinherited, he is motivated to become an author. First he conceives of rewriting the story which Sandy tells; next he returns to Camelot (now thought of as the source of history) in order to revise the sad and bitter story which history relates. Author thus puts to other authors an implicit question which character-as-author raises explicitly of his traveling companions. "Why can't you see and say truthfully?" And collaborating to rewrite the book, author and character are at pains to keep the order of things straight and proper: world before words, life prior to language, the undoubted patterns and kinships of "out there" antecedent to the ways in which "out there" is named, appropriated, parceled out in human thought and language. Then, like Sam Clemens reading from G. S. Weaver, both can use words as the instruments for entering into reality, for grasping how the real works and what it signifies, and for transforming the world at their doorsteps into a more useful and more hospitable place. As collaborators in the top or more recent draft of a palimpsest, they conspire to turn fiction-making in the fiction into the drama of being empiricists in fiction.

(4) *Being rewritten by the words.* As Hank rewrites the book realistically, an inevitable consequence is that he rewrites himself. Finding it easy enough to adjust physically to the burden of armor, he nonetheless discovers during his travels with Sandy that chinks have appeared in the armor of detachment he wears. By this vulnerability he is led from darkening the world (or pretending to) for his own amusement to a concern with illuminating the dark byways of history. Though high jinx and buffoonery certainly mark his return to the book in Chapter 38, the summoning of a bicycle brigade and the roundup of unruly knights are now entering wedges into the plan he has for the moral transformation of humanity. There is no end to how images and actions from his narrative serve to measure changes in the Yankee's priorities, or to modify his self-image, and the image he presents to the reader. By Chapter 40 the modifications with their shifting emphasis have brought Hank to the threshold of a great initiation story. True to the classic pattern, the rite de passage consists of renouncing childish freedoms in order to take up servitude to an intense moral commitment. Once Boss of all he surveyed, Hank has become, twice over, a compassionate, even a somewhat driven and fretful father figure: parent to Hello Central; parent, as well, to the world he would redeem from falsehoods and fictions.

But of course the initiation story dies a-borning. Within the space of thirty pages a character who seemed to record the long way he came from selfishness to altruism (from play to moral realism) has been re-created as the raging and destructive maniac on the Sand Belt. No wonder, then, that nowadays the character receives largely negative notices from his critics. It is not without some warrant that the Yankee is often regarded as a proto-fascist, taking up the white man's burden to satisfy his lust for power, and exterminating the brutes joyously when the mob turns against him. But while, in a way, such a view is a great testament to the realism of *Yankee* (it involves debating Hank's personality as one might investigate the half-hidden flaws of some real person in the real world) perhaps a healthy sense of narrative relations, and also of narrative manner, ought to be maintained.[18] Hank Morgan is only a creation of Mark Twain's. Mark Twain is a funny fellow, the practitioner of wry and sardonic jokes. Hence if the words of the book rewrite the Yankee for the last time, this must be so because Mark Twain wants him rewritten.

And in fact the implied author, generally so dormant during the middle stages of *Yankee*, emerges in the closing chapters as a very industrious presence. His handiwork is evident in the wildly melodramatic illness of Hello Central, and in the perfectly pointless journey, for the sake of "sea air," to France (is not Britain the sole enlightened place on earth? how could convalescence in a "queer old [French] castle" help one whose disease is "membranous croup"?). (*CY*, 230–31.) Much abetted by the interdict, the implied author then brings Hank back to a ruined countryside, reminding us that the world the Yankee is about to lay waste had already been devastated before him. But he also returns him to a ludicrous muddling of Malory's poetry with Sir Lancelot's attempts to corner the stock market. For all the world, it is as though the implied author were making fun of Hank. Lurking in the wings or peering down from over the proscenium arch, he seems intent on flinging into the path of the rite de passage one trifling—or absurd—hindrance after another. Which is, I think, exactly the right way to phrase what happens. The circumstances are contrived by the implied author, because the implied author speaks for reality. Although he shares with the Yankee the keen sense that fictionalizing the real world is ruinous, he is also privy to a dark secret about those who are not fiction-makers. He understands that even as Hank Morgan rewrites the book from romance to realism, reality has all along been rewriting Hank Morgan. It has been enhumoring him.

The Reverend Mr. George Sumner Weaver had followed his empirical studies to two quite different conclusions. To begin with, he had theorized as a strict physical determinist, positing the humorous type (and by extension the enhumored self) that acts as it only can and must, according to the dictates of bodily structure and the special colorations of hair, skin, and eyes. But Weaver softened the determinism, first by presuming that faculties in the brain might be modified through self-willed exercise, and second by affirming that individual patterns of behavior were nicely integrated into the upward, onward, purposeful sweep of the whole. Love was the key to his grand design: "Man's whole active nature is expressed by *Love*." In his writing, Mark Twain was led early on to the empirical truth of enhumored selves. What is Simon Wheeler, if not one governed absolutely by his "bumps" of loquaciousness and memory? What are good and bad boys, except two helpless pawns of some quirk in the brain, some kink of blood or bile, that produces, in each, one good little action—one bad little action—repeated endlessly?

Where empiricism could not lead Mark Twain, however, was on to a compensating belief in freedom, or around to any sense of ultimate purpose in the world. In the 1855 notebook, poised between his disavowal of metaphysics and his enthusiastic response to the physical emphases of Weaver, one finds this somber reflection of Sam Clemens:

> A thousand years from now this race may have passed away, and in its stead, a people sprung up wearing the skins of animals for raiment, and for food eating the

berries that may grow where now stand the prouder buildings of this town. And this people will dig up . . . some memorial of the forgotten race—a steam boiler, perhaps—and gaze with astonishment upon it, and wonder who made it; what they made it for. . . . (NB, 25–26.)

The reflection is clarified when, within the next year and working now as a printer's devil in Cincinnati, Clemens met (or Mark Twain would presently imagine he met) a self-taught intellectual named Macfarlane. Listening to this new acquaintance, Clemens heard (is alleged to have heard) the empiricism of G. S. Weaver inverted into a bitter parody of Weaver's optimism:

> [Macfarlane] said that man's heart was the only bad heart in the animal kingdom; that man was the only animal capable of feeling malice, envy, vindictiveness, revengefulness, hatred, selfishness, the only animal that . . . kills members of its own immediate tribe, the sole animal that steals and enslaves the members of any tribe.[19]

Spoofing such concepts as G. S. Weaver's all-engathering Love thus becomes part, though it strikes me as the lesser, more perfunctory part, of Mark Twain's standard joke. The idea that the motions of humanity might be tending upward or outward toward anything of value is debunked with a merry scorn in the early fictions and with merriment increasingly tinged by bitterness in the later ones. But with the concepts gone, the world according to G. S. Weaver remains intact. The residue consists of the tics and gyrations of pre-programmed robots who, since they no longer gravitate toward any meaningful destination, must now be seen as spinning in the orbit of sameness—that is, moving in such a way as to deny the very principle of movement. This is the essence of what is truly original in Mark Twain's standard joke: that change and difference—the usual antinomies of here/there, then/now, progress/retrogress—are but illusions, the fictions we use to mask from ourselves the fact that reality is static, enhumored, an eternal process (or anti-process) of running in place to get nowhere. With merriment and indignation assembled equally for perhaps the first time, Yankee uses its protagonist as an instrument for stripping away the illusions and exposing the dark fatality they conceal.

We say of Hank Morgan that, moving in and out of the book, he is a figure always in motion, traveling to many different places. The fact is, though, that Camelot, where everyday people suffer and die needlessly; London, where everyday they are abused and killed pointlessly; and Hartford, Connecticut, where the prevailing images are of violence, munitions-making, confinement at a nearby insane asylum, and fifteen-year-old Puss Flanagan, doing child labor for the telephone company, are not different places. It is the same merciless, mean-

ingless place, called by many different names. We say that when he enters and
reenters history at several points in time, the Yankee confronts many horrors
and is afflicted with many indignities. But the fact is that he perceives and experiences only *one* continuous horror. Slavery is the common denominator of
his experiences, whether he sees it on the road with Sandy, endures it personally while traveling with Arthur, rages at it in his tirades against Church, Kings,
"droit de Seigneur," and other human stupidities, remembers it as it existed in
France before the Revolution and in pre–Civil War America—or practices it
benignly himself when he imposes what Mark Twain calls his "good heart &
high intent" on the citizens of Camelot.[20] Past and present, like the geographical distinctions here and there, like the cultural labels ancient and modern, *and
also like the language of selfishness and the language of social reform*, are merely
the designations through which history makes various and multiform what is
actually the single condition of human bondage.

And so, traveler to one place, participant in one kind of dramatic episode,
sojourner in a world so fixed as to seem cast in concrete, the Yankee is borne
inexorably along toward his fated appointment with the cruelest kind of stasis.
We say that he changes, develops, grows mature and insightful as the book
proceeds. Alternatively, we allege that his "good heart & high intent" are corrupted by a will to power, which, when frustrated, reduces him to one all-con-
suming temper tantrum. The fact is, however, that both readings are wrong.
Rewriting Hank, the book sees to it that all his actions are but variations (or
still better, but the duplications) of one central action. What did the Yankee do
on the opening pages of the story, where his dream would not, could not, be
dissipated, but where by the nature of the tall tale that enveloped him he was
vouchsafed magical powers to survive? Well, he darkened the world, brought
down electricity out of a cloudless sky, and managed to conceal his marvelous
technology from most of the Arthurians. And what is his role on the last pages
of the story, which has made him a realist, as he made it realistic? Surely
enough, he is still darkening the world, blasting it into an electrocuted mess,
and concealing his intentions from most of the Arthurians, until, corpse by
rotting corpse, the Arthurians—sheer stinking material mass; the physical wall
unmediated by any thought or feeling; reality at its grossest—rise up around
him to conceal the Yankee from view for thirteen centuries.

Romance and realism are the determining modes of *Yankee*. Arranged pa-
limpsest-like, the lineaments of the second gradually replacing and all but blotting out the first, they seem wholly antipathetical: as opposed as poesy to commonplaces; the fictitious to the historical; Morgan le Fay to Hank Morgan;
ancient superstitions to modern enlightenment—a heart of darkness that
Arthur and the minstrel poets devised to a clean, well-lighted place that Hank

creates. The difficulty is that, located at extreme ends of an aesthetic and moral continuum, the two persist in commingling to converge. Where the one goes foolishly along denying reality, the other confronts the real, yet is powerless to control or change it, and eventually uses it as the means of mass destruction. In the end "romance" and "realism" differentiate neither literary modes nor the world views which are presumed to shape the world of narrative. The joke is that they are merely different designations for the same story, a story about warping characters into caricatures, and thus annihilating all distinctively human values.[21]

(5) *Humorous words.* But the fault is not Hank's. And neither can blame be laid at the door of the interdict, or any of history's other superstitions, or of a modern reworking of Malory's Götterdämmerung. No, the joke is on Hank. His downfall was foreordained from the beginning, in a joke told long before he showed any interest in social reform—and then confirmed in an unseemly joke which he tells at just the point where his commitment to reform burns most fiercely. The passage, intruding into the sixth paragraph of Chapter 40, reads as follows:

> Even authorship was taking a start; Sir Dinadan the humorist was first in the field, with a volume of gray-headed jokes which I had been familiar with for thirteen centuries. If he had left out that old rancid one about the lecturer I wouldn't have said anything; but I couldn't stand that one. I suppressed the book and hanged the author. (*CY,* 228)

It is unseemly and intrusive not because the content is brash and a bit callous: Hank has often displayed brashness bordering on small streaks of cruelty and been most amusing while he does so. Rather, the passage jars because it is bracketed by examples of the Yankee's better, more humane side. We proceed too quickly from talk about "schools" and "colleges" and "good newspapers" into the hanging of Sir Dinadan. From the hanging we proceed too abruptly back into lofty generalizations about the end of slavery and the equality of all men and the taxes they pay. The break in tone is too much, a jarring descent into burlesque at a place where making jokes seems inappropriate. One's temptation is to omit the aside, as several pages ago I was careful to elide it.

To omit, however, is to leave out the subject of the passage and hence drop from view a figure who is an oddly major player in the book. Uniquely among the Knights, whether borrowed from Malory or invented by Mark Twain, Sir Dinadan the Humorist is important enough to have a whole chapter named for him.[22] This is Chapter 4 where, first to awaken after Merlin's monologue, the eponymous Sir Dinadan ties empty "beer mugs" to the tail of a dog, then tells about his exploit ("about how the immortal idea came to him") over and over again, until having exhausted the topic, he falls to stringing together "played out . . . worm-eaten jokes" that were "worse than the minstrels, worse than the clowns in the circus." Clearly the chapter belongs to the din of Dinadan. Furthermore, by a certain strict logic of narrative, it can be shown that with his second appearance in Chapter 9 Sir Dinadan becomes the determinant of everything else that happens in *Yankee*. As before, he assails Hank with anecdotes that were old "before the dawn of history," which causes Hank to expostulate . . . which is misinterpreted by Sir Sagramore as an affront to him . . . which provokes Sir Sagramore's challenge . . . which leads the King to remind Hank presently that "he ought to be starting out to seek adventures and get up a reputation of a size to make [him] worthy of breaking a lance with Sir Sagramore" . . . which motivates the Yankee to travel . . . which draws his attention to the true state of affairs in Camelot . . . which turns him into the dreamer of a new world order . . . which (finally) brings him full-circle back to his "Fight with the Knights" in Chapter 39. And as if in confirmation of this pattern of causality—this sense that in *Yankee* all roads lead out of one set of stale jokes—in Chapter 21 as he hastens along to shore up the Holy Fountain (but also to transform a praying monk into a shirt-making dynamo) Hank has one more, indirect encounter with Sir Dinadan. He is joined by a pilgrim with a "fat good humored face" who "began eagerly and awkwardly to lead up, in the immemorial way, to that same old anecdote—the one Sir Dinadan told me that time I got into trouble with Sir Sagramore and was challenged by him on account of it." (*CY*, 24–25, 49–50, 109–10.)

But who is this automaton, this bit-player who is both almost nowhere and yet everywhere, this occasional walk-on who is persistently the shaper of many destinies? Why, as his title indicates, he is the "the humorist," though hardly this by virtue of seeing experience genially or practicing a steadfast congeniality in his relations with the world. Rather, he is the "humorist" whom Robert Burton defines and G. S. Weaver's *Lectures* present more sketchily. Like the narrator of the *Anatomy of Melancholy*, if he itches he needs must scratch—which is to say that when the fit is upon him he must weary audiences with the same tired prank, the same round of wearying anecdotes, and do so as the result of irresistible impulse, an all-controlling pathology of brain or bloodstream. In short, Sir Dinadan the Humorist is the prototypical Enhumored Self, funny because he is fated, condemned, forever manipulated by his own identity to be the clown of circumstance. And in this role, I believe, Mark Twain intends him to function as Hank Morgan's shadow or specter self. The parallels are decisive. As Sir Dinadan ties beer mugs to unoffending dogs, so Hank would saddle the Arthurians with social and cultural changes which are ill-suited to Camelot. As Sir Dinadan, beguiled by joking, reaches back thirteen centuries to find in the hoariest language the one joke that has been most continuously popular, so the Yankee, entranced by providing a New Deal, looks ahead thirteen centuries for the utopia which even then was very far from being utopian—which as Edward Bellamy had demonstrated in 1888 was more nearly a phenomenon of words than of facts. The Humorist and the Boss are twins, twinned by a single compulsive obsession. The "humorousness" of the one attests to the enhumoring of the other. Hence it is fitting that the one's death at the hands of the other should directly prefigure the other's destruction at the hands of his creator. As Hank standing on the threshold of a Brave New World yet pauses to hang Sir Dinadan the humorist, so it goes with Mark Twain, poised in the entryway of an initiation story. He pauses to survey his initiation motif, and finds that initiations run absurdly against the grain of reality as he knows it. Thereupon he adds to Sir Dinadan's repertoire a fine example of the sick joke. He suppresses the book and brings down its putative author-hero through the bloodlettings and electrocutions on the Sand Belt.

The way is long and torturous in Mark Twain's race to nowhere. But even when he kills the Tortoise, Achilles still loses. And yet, victim of a sick joke, enhumored Achilles might also be said to have the joke's last word. The carnage on the Sand Belt everywhere anticipates those blood-drenched, plague-ridden scenes that occur in the earlier work of Kurt Vonnegut, particularly in *Cat's Cradle,* where "'stacks of the dead [are] so deep and wide that a bulldozer actually stalled trying to shove them to a common grave.'" Moreover, in his manic glee at the prospect before him, the Yankee not only enjoys the same fit of giggles that will overcome Vonnegut's humanitarian-turned-madman; he comes close to expressing Dr. Philip Castle's largesse: Clarence, my "'son, someday this will all be yours.'"[23]

As a sick joke by Woody Allen launched the Yankee's adventures in never-never land, so closure (in the real world) comes with a distinct foretaste of Vonnegut's zany sickness. Sir Dinadan the Humorist would have loved it.


## III: In Between

Well, my book is written—let it go. But if it were only to write over again there wouldn't be so many things left out. They burn in me; & they keep multiplying and multiplying; but now they can't ever be said. And besides they would require a library—& a pen warmed up in hell.
              —Mark Twain to Howells after finishing *Yankee*

Rising, streetcar, four hours in the office or the factory, meal, streetcar, four hours of work, meal, sleep, and Monday Tuesday Wednesday Thursday Friday and Saturday according to the same rhythm—this path is followed most of the time. But one day the "why" arises and everything begins in weariness tinged with amazement.

—Camus, *The Myth of Sisyphus*

But what did the humorist Mark Twain think?

If by the later 1880s the eminent and wealthy author Samuel L. Clemens had long since banished from his mind G. S. Weaver's analysis of the humors and Weaver's stress upon this-worldliness, about another, not wholly unrelated matter the writer Mark Twain could hardly have been unmindful. Almost certainly he had to see connections between his current project and the one he had written a decade earlier in 1875. *Connecticut Yankee* may be the most bookish and "made up" of Mark Twain's works, "Old Times on the Mississippi" the most autobiographical and "private." But for all that, they tell point-for-point exactly the same story.

When the boy at Hannibal hoped for a "glorious future" on the River, he was never once fantasizing about life in some remote, wholly imagined, never-never world. But though the Mississippi had long been his near neighbor in space and time, River-life presented itself to him in such a way that it evoked images of "fires glaring bravely," of "fancy topped chimneys" and "ornamental railings," of smoke that came "rolling and tumbling out of the chimneys," of "crews posed picturesquely . . . on the forecastle." ("OT," 65.) (Note well that smoke: how it dissipates into soft, gentle movement: who could ever smell it? whose eyes could ever be reddened by the coal dust?) Accordingly, the first step in his education lay in adjusting vocabulary to a more comprehensive or down-to-the-waterline view of River experience. Hearing from Horace Bixby that the Mississippi is a sequence of "points" and landmarks, the cub does not somehow acquire magical access to what the Mississippi calls itself. Bixby's "three mile point" and "clump of china berry trees" are no less the impositions of human language than the brave fires and picturesque crews had been. Nor does the consensus among all pilots to call it "twelve mile point" have any bearing on the situation; obviously it was the consensus of Hannibal which turned the steamboat into a lyric poem afloat. What changes, however, is that words are being used to designate useful relationships in space and time, and to acknowledge the mobility and sheer panoramic complexity of River-life. The difference is between deducing the "temperament" of the Mississippi from one scene full of poetic details, seen twice daily for ten minutes and seen only between the northern and southern bends above and below Hannibal, and of breaking out of this narrow, restrictive scene into as many details as possible before trying to specify what the "temperament" of the River is like.

So, in short order (perhaps, indeed, the timing is just a shade too brisk) rhapsodizing about the River gives way to knowing River-life empirically. Halfway into Paper IV, the Mississippi is likened to a book, and the narrator proceeds to develop two ways of reading the text, portraying the differences between them as "before" and "after," but also shaping the differences into the familiar, initiatory pattern of "something gained" vs. "something lost." What has been gained occupies two long sentences, and results in the rather flat generalization that language now functions as the means of "compassing the safe piloting of a steamboat." By contrast, the theme of loss is set forth in a long paragraph-and-a-half of some of the showiest, gaudiest, most spectacular prose Mark Twain ever wrote. Depending upon one's tastes, one may feel the weight of cliché as River "turned to blood" is succeeded by River "glowed like fire" and River "shone like silver"—or be caught up by the genuine lyric grace which occurs when movements of the River are reproduced as "boiling, tumbling rings that were as many tinted as an opal." ("OT," 92–93.) (Note well that flow: who could ever really be endangered by the boiling; whose life could ever really be threatened by the rings of opal?) But whichever the reaction, the passage has clearly subverted its own message. Nothing is really lost. The speaker's vision of the River is every bit as grand and flamboyant as it had been back at Hannibal. And if nothing has been lost, neither is anything really gained. Nothing has changed. The moment of initiation is duplicitous.

From this duplicity, it becomes possible to grasp the doubling that goes on constantly in "Old Times." Looking back, we are ready for the fine joke that was planted in Paper I. Since Town seen from the standpoint of River displays exactly the same flurry of high drama that is evident when River is viewed from the perspective of Town, Town and River are not two different places; it is one misleading place, called by two different names. Looking ahead, we understand why daydreams in the boring village are replicated as the shenanigans and derring-do of steamboat pilothouses. Youth and age, expert and novice, are not two different conditions in the narrative; it is one and the same condition, denominated in two different ways. And so, finally, with the twin processes staying-at-home (which would kill you with sloth) and going-to-the River (which assures you no gentler or more dignified death). They attest to how the real world lures you in with the promise of a narrative of education and entraps you in a narrative of power, which shapes individual lives regardless and leaves you with only the knowledge of a complete moral and social futility. As in *Yankee*, then, reality is lodged in one place—until Mark Twain sees it is no damned good and, with a flourish, blows it up. When in the early 1880s, the adventures of "Old Times" were rounded off, he chose from among what must have been a great welter of possible endings the exploding boilers of the *Pennsylvania*, bodies strewn across and along the River, and a seemingly oblivious George Ealer, indifferent to the carnage around him as he maniacally reassembles his flute and chess set. The ending does not merely prefigure the battle of the Sand Belt; in terms of mood and mayhem it seems a direct rehearsal.

The snapper is identical; only the tone differs. Obviously there is no occasion for a pen dipped in hell at the end of "Old Times" (the narrator's comments on the death of Henry Clemens are casual to the point of being almost insensitive), any more than such an extreme gesture would be called for by "Jumping Frog" or the twin tales of Jim and Jacob. These texts enjoy being tongue-in-cheek and deflationary. They take pure delight from repeating Ishmael's ungrammatical, half-jocular question "Who ain't a slave?"—and from responding, with equal lack of grammar and at least twice the jocularity, *nobody ain't, for everybody is*. The pen warmed up in hell cannot therefore come in consequence of Mark Twain's jokes. It derives, rather, from the existential questions that increasingly provoked his amazement, as Mark Twain retold the jokes. Why? he had to ask himself, why, when I open the doors on reality do I discern not simply want of progress, but find any change (even the most neutral forms of process) inconceivable? And why therefore, he had to ask, why when I deplore it as the Great Lie in the fictions of others does the timeless, changeless pattern of *sub specie aeternitatis* settle on my fictions in the form of the Great, the Only, the One Irremediable Truth?

We are told that without consciousness, Sisyphus could never have raised his question tinged with amazement: the question of why "Monday Tuesday Wednesday Thursday Friday" (no commas among them) are, every one, parts of one amorphous, undifferentiated and unparticled blob of experience. Yet the burden of consciousness is what Sisyphus had to assume "to be forever happy." It will not do to withhold the same mixed blessing from Mark Twain. In spite of the frequent tendency to treat him as a writer divided against himself, his practice is actually that of everywhere totalizing experience; he unifies life endlessly and relentlessly, and the unifications often seem destructive and terrible. Summing up, we see that his poetics consist of some primal force that brings unlikenesses or opposites together into dark twinships; of one twin's habitually succumbing to (or disappearing into) the wiles of his dark brother (so that Huck disappears into Tom, the fate of Hank into fated Sir Dinadan, the humorist); of the steady decline of distinctively human values into heartless, witless nature; of the fixed race to nowhere; of an abiding faith in literary realism, together with the dead certainty that reality brings down and lays waste every good and decent impulse; and underlying all, the invariable conjunction between many beginnings and the one immutable and enhumored outcome.[24]

But if these suggest the marks of a repetitive-compulsive personality, they likewise display the same tick-tock regularity that made Petroleum V. Nasby's stage performances so hilarious. Without them, Mark Twain might have been no less funny, but he would have been funny in a lesser way. Moreover, the poetics bespeak a pertinacity of theme, and a set of persistent attitudes toward the theme. There was the pleasure of developing it, the frustration of presently discovering that it developed in and by its own momentum, the rage (tinged with amazement) that came with the realization that the theme could never be altered. These may have been the measure of Mark Twain's anguish. But they also guaranteed the supreme moments of his art. Lacking a sense of being enslaved by one subject, his imagination could never possibly have been liberated to mark, remark, and mark down the complex richness of the River-trilogy and its aftermath.

## NOTES

1. *AHF,* 15.

2. "OT," 91.

3. See "The Turning Point of My Life" and "The Turning Point of My Life: First Version," both in *What Is Man?*, ed. Paul Baender (Berkeley: University of California Press, 1973), 455–64, 521–26. Readers who will be skeptical of the causal patterns I apply to Sir Dinadan, the Humorist, at the end of this essay, and apply again to the Extraordinary Italian Twins in the essay on *Pudd'nhead Wilson* should take a look at these pieces by Mark Twain to discover what can be done with the logic of causality in the hands of a master.

4. Alan Gribben, "Mark Twain, Phrenology and the 'Temperaments': A Study of Pseudoscientific Influence," *American Quarterly* 24 (March 1972), 45–68.

5. Two texts are involved in what follows: George Sumner Weaver, *Lectures on Mental Science According to the Philosophy of Phrenology* (New York: Fowlers and Wells, 1852) and *Mark Twain's Notebooks & Journals, Volume I*, ed. Anderson, Frank, Sanderson (Berkeley: University of California Press, 1975). Where materials are copied out into the notebook, references are to *NB*. Where they appear only in Weaver, references are to *Lectures.*

6. Arthur Wrobel, ed., *Pseudoscience and Society in Nineteenth Century America* (Lexington: University Press of Kentucky, 1987). See especially Professor Wrobel's "Afterword," 223 ff. and the comments on phrenology of Robert H. Collyer in the chapter "Technology of the Soul," 31–32.

7. *Pseudoscience,* 230–31.

8. Preface to *Adventures of Tom Sawyer,* and see David R. Sewell, *Mark Twain's Languages* (Berkeley: University of California Press, 1987), esp. Chapter I.

9. The influence of Lecky on Mark Twain is developed at length by Walter Blair in *Mark Twain and Huck Finn*. But the seminal account of Samuel Clemens's later encounters with science is of course Sherwood Cummings, *Mark Twain and Science: The Adventures of a Mind* (Baton Rouge: Louisiana State University Press, 1989).

10. *A Connecticut Yankee in King Arthur's Court*, ed. Allison R. Ensor, The Norton Critical Edition (New York: Norton, 1982), 10. All references to *CY* are from this edition.

11. *Mark Twain's Satires and Burlesques*, ed. Franklin R. Rogers (Berkeley: University of California Press, 1967), 55–86; 80, 78.

12. Quoted from *Mark Twain's Notebooks and Journals* in *CY*, 291.

13. Erich Auerbach, *Mimesis* (Garden City, N.Y.: Doubleday Anchor Books, 1957), 119.

14. Reprinted in Becker, *Documents of Modern Literary Realism*, 133–35.

15. Edward Bellamy, *Looking Backward*, The Signet Edition (New York: New American Library, 1960), 204–05, 211. Bellamy's theme is insistent. The portrayal of ministers, historians, lecturers, the prototype "radio," shared dining and even the pedagogical role of talkative Dr. Leete all make clear how proper forms of communication (getting word adjusted to thing) are central to the salvation of New Boston. As a picture of Utopia *Looking Backward* is marred by many significant omissions: where, for example, are the smoke stacks necessary to all those factories busily grinding out all those commodities? But as an account of the use and misuse of language, the book still has interest and value; it remains a seminal text in any account of American Literary Realism.

16. Bellamy, he said, had "made the accepted Heaven paltry by inventing a better one on earth"; *Looking Backward*, he said, was the "latest and best of all the Bibles." See *Selected Mark Twain–Howells Letters*, 291.

17. In *Mark Twain and Southwestern Humor* (257), Kenneth Lynn invokes Thorstein Veblen, paralleling Veblen's "technological hero" with the expertise and "know how" of Horace Bixby. This particular coupling strikes me as misleading, since as I have argued in the essay on comedy Bixby, as a confirmed and self-seeking show-off, is often a good bit less than pure "engineer." But in a necessarily shadowy manner (since the grounds for the parallel do not yet exist) and also in part ironically (since this is Mark Twain, and Mark Twain knows how it will all turn out) it might be argued that the first forty chapters of *CY* gradually supplant *The Theory of the Leisure Class* with the spirit of *The Engineers and the Price System*. The values and attitudes of Chapter 40 are very Veblenesque. And if we are skeptical, this is probably less a matter of Mark Twain's tone than of our having lost touch with certain aspects of late Victorian optimism and the way they culminated in Veblen's social analysis. For general confirmation, see Louis Budd's *Mark Twain, Social Philosopher* (Bloomington: Indiana University Press, 1962), especially 130–44; Veblen, *The Theory of the Leisure Class* (1899; New York: The Modern Library, 1948), and Wesley Mitchell, *What Veblen Taught* (New York: Viking, 1947).

18. Consider James Cox on the Yankee's excesses:

He prances and struts through every conceivable burlesque, flaunting himself before the stunned Arthurian world into which he bursts, until he becomes the real buffoon of his own performance. More mechanical than any of the gadgets in which he specializes, he grinds laboriously through his "acts," his only means of attracting attention being to run faster and faster, to do bigger and bigger things, until the mechanism of his character flies apart. And fly apart it finally does. (*Fate of Humor,* 91.)

Here, the strong verbs do not simply describe a character in a story; the character seems to prance and strut quite independently of his creator's imagination. And while, to be sure, Mark Twain's complicity is presently specified, Professor Cox can never wholly drop the idea that author has "turn[ed] his narrative over to Morgan," so that it is Morgan who really "operates the machinery of the novel." It is a curious reversal of emphasis from the conclusion of Professor Cox's chapter on *Huckleberry Finn,* where Huck's actual behavior very nearly recedes from sight, to be subsumed under Mark Twain's hatred of the tyranny of conscience and his determination to maintain, at all costs, a humorous tone.

The pro's and con's of Hank's character are neatly summarized by Everett Carter in "The Meaning of *A Connecticut Yankee,*" *American Literature* 50 (Summer 1978), 418–40. Quite rightly, within the terms of his argument, Professor Carter ends up pro-Hank.

19. *Mark Twain's Autobiography,* ed. Paine, I, 146–47. Paul Baender has argued that Mark Twain invented Macfarlane as another of the "philosophical outsiders" through whom Mark Twain's late pessimism might be expressed. Though I find this view entirely persuasive, it should be observed that the melancholy of "Macfarlane" is of a kind with what Sam Clemens could express as early as 1855. See Baender, "Alias Macfarlane," *American Literature* 38 (May 1966), 187–97. "Macfarlane" is also presented in Professor Baender's edition of *What is Man?* (Berkeley: University of California Press, 1974), 76–79.

20. This same point is made very neatly, though for the sake of a different emphasis, by David Ketterer in "Epoch—Eclipse and Apocalypse: Special 'Effects' in *A Connecticut Yankee,*" *PMLA* 88 (Spring 1973), 1104–14.

21. Though the idiom is distinctively Mark Twain's it will bear noting that connections are established between *CY* and the methods (and hence attitudes) of two of the great negative utopias of modernism. Of *Heart of Darkness,* Jeffrey Meyers has written that Conrad carefully sets up antitheses—black/white; European/African; civilized/primitive; ancient/modern, etc.—only to show that each member of the pair is as corrupting as the other and that both "deny the idea of progress which had been a dominant idea in European thought for the past four hundred years." The flat denial of all value is likewise the key to *Brave New World,* worked out through Huxley's juxtaposi-

tion of the "insane life" of modern technology and the "hardly less queer and abnormal" primitivism of an American Indian culture. What was needed, Huxley later conceded, was an "ego" that could somehow "mediate between the 'superego' and the 'id.'" But Huxley in 1932 was no better able to supply a vital middle ground than was Conrad—or than Mark Twain had been in 1888 when displaying the twin defects of the identical twins "romance" and "realism." See Meyers, *Joseph Conrad: A Biography* (New York: Harper and Row, 1991), 191–92, and Huxley's preface to the Bantam Classics Edition (New York: Bantam, 1946), vii–ix.

22. He thus shares honors with Morgan le Fay (Chapter 16) and Marco (Chapter 31). They make for an interesting trio: the one all jokes, the second all willfulness, the third relentlessly stubborn. As a group they exemplify a theory of humors in a strange and perverse way, for all are thoroughly enhumored. And perhaps it could be argued that although each seems to enter and then quickly disappear from the narrative, their here-and-gone roles do not disguise the fact that all three dog the Boss's foosteps and determine his outcome (she by sharing her name with him; Marcos by being the one figure in the book whom neither Yankee logic nor Yankee magic can much affect; Dinadan by telling the joke that, after many twists and turns in the roadway, becomes the sick joke that does the Yankee in).

23. *Cat's Cradle* (New York: Dell, 1963), 134–35.

24. Dividing Mark Twain has been a critical preoccupation from Henry Nash Smith, who presented him in terms of "vernacular" and "conventional" perspectives which he was unable to reconcile; through Susan Gillman, who, expanding beyond Smith, sees Mark Twain as a veritable bevy of splits and bifurcations; to Gregg Camfield, who, rejecting Smith, yet finds Mark Twain lost in a maze, where sentimental responses remained incompatible with his taste for empiricism.

But my point from the beginning has, to use the currently fashionable term, emphasized Mark Twain as "overdetermined": the writer of one story, with one pattern of narrative-development and one conclusion (or where the work remains fragmentary, one foreseeable conclusion). If his pen name suggests two, Mark Twain was perhaps the Great Unifier of nineteenth-century American literature. For better or worse, his poetics seem grounded in the world-view of Philip Traum. Life and the fictions which reflect life are machines, permitting neither variations nor departure from their preestablished course.

See Smith, *Development of a Writer,* especially Chapters 1 and 2; Gillman, *Dark Twins,* anywhere!; Camfield, *Sentimental Twain,* where controlling terms are set up early and pursued (to my sense rather humorlessly) through much of Mark Twain's work.

# PART II
# THE RIVER TRILOGY

# Tom Sawyer:
# An Essay on Romantic Folly

[Mrs. Judge Thatcher]: Now I know you'll tell me.
   The names of the first two disciples were——

[Tom]: DAVID AND GOLIATH!

[Narrator]: Let us draw the curtain of charity over the
   rest of the scene.
                                        —End of Chapter 4[1]

A reader I know has not always appreciated the way the chapter ends. He remembers reading it first as a child, no doubt envious of Tom Sawyer's triumph,
yet irked by the thought that had he behaved so there would have been no
curtain of charity. Lightning bolts from Heaven—or a cloakroom paddling—no
longer seemed called for when, as a salaried student of literary texts, my reader
returned to the passage after some years. Now it was the art of the ending
which troubled him. Why not conclude with the capitalized punch line? This
turning of a climax into a stage direction seemed all too typical of the many
other occasions in the *Adventures of Tom Sawyer* where a chatty narrator spoils
showing with telling. The mannerism was at least faintly reminiscent of one of
the literary offenses of Fenimore Cooper.

   With the lapse of more time, though, my reader professes himself satisfied.
He thinks he understands who drops the curtain, and why; and he is aware that
unless this happens on the very last page, the curtains that fall in narrative
must presently rise again. He finds in the total action (the fall *and* rise) the key
to a theme in which Mark Twain, a committed writer of realism, uses the aesthetics of literary romanticism in order to develop a romantic tall tale and a
romanticized tall-tale hero—matters of which the writer could not possibly approve. As for its art, therefore, the end of the chapter now strikes him as both
highly deliberate and fairly bristling with the possibilities for a fine paradox. If

the curtain falls to shut out and hence protect, it also envelopes as it descends, and so from the standpoint of strict realism it must have the counter effect of walling in and entrapping.

I

O Lady! We receive but what we give
And in our life alone does Nature live:
Ours is her wedding garment, ours her shroud!
—Coleridge, "Dejection: An Ode"

Seeking to cure warts in Chapter 9, Tom and Huck go to the cemetery, where they find instead some very real blemishes on the good order of village society. One by one these uglinesses accumulate, as if in a carefully choreographed procession. There is young Dr. Robinson, nighttime criminal who, by day, goes about masked as a respected authority figure. There is Injun Joe, a villain, but one whose villainies are underlain and in some measure extenuated by the color prejudices of a slaveholding community. There is Muff Potter, his need for constant oblivion itself a wry commentary on the quality of life in St. Petersburg. And crouched in the bushes all the while are the two small boys who observe this spectacle and the bloody murder in which it culminates. Clearly the scene resonates with potential seriousness. One thinks of Young Goodman Brown's disillusioning visit to the dark forest, or of Wellingborough Redburn discovering a mother and her starving children in the midst of what a moment before had seemed serene Liverpool.

And one sees readily enough why Mark Twain requires the scene. During the long Friday-to-Monday weekend set forth in the eight preceding chapters, St. Petersburg had turned entirely too much into a "tranquil world" where, without a cloud anywhere, the "sun beamed down like a benediction." (*ATS*, 46, 57.) A darker, more nocturnal side to village life is needed if the narrative is not to succumb to early blandness and become mere child's play for an audience of children. But having deepened his material and quickened the tempo, Mark Twain has no intention of letting the seriousness get out of hand. A part of the reader's enjoyment for the next several pages lies in watching him work very hard both to have his horror, yet to keep in abeyance any really sinister implications. His strategy consists of a series of beautifully timed risings and fallings of a curtain.

First, at just the point of the murder and while the moon is hidden by clouds, the boys are taken out of the scene. Down the hill they run, genuinely and properly terrified, yet never so fearful that they are unable to make artistic capital of their experience. At once, Tom devises in his head a solemn blood oath. Next, he is shown to write out the pact with a piece of "red keel" and in the scrambled syntax and large, round, childish scrawl that is reproduced graphically in Chapter 10. (ATS, 99–100.) Finally, after many pricks and the squeezing of two, perhaps four thumbs, he and Huck are able to sign the document in blood. The effect is to use "blood" as a means of curtaining off bloodshed: not exactly to conceal the gory remains of Dr. Robinson, but to discharge the tensions of the murder scene into what the narrator calls a "return of the boys' spirit of adventure." (ATS, 102.) Through Tom's invention and most especially through the narrator's reproduction of Tom's penmanship, an incident that began as play, then turned deadly serious, has been restored once more to the pattern of a harmless game.

Meanwhile, the busy narrator is staging other exits. Muff, easily convinced of his guilt, stumbles haplessly out of the graveyard; with a last look around to assure himself that the planted evidence is all in place, Joe departs; and the premises are left to the dead—but also to one other, so-called living presence. For the last two paragraphs of Chapter 9 the moon, which all along has been moved in and out of the scene, is given a dominant role:

> Two or three minutes later the murdered man, the blanketed corpse, the lidless coffin and the open grave were under no inspection but the moon's.
> The stillness was complete again, too. (ATS, 97.)

It seems arty-craftsy at first glance, another needless and this time pointlessly lyrical way of concluding the chapter. Perhaps, though, the shift to this new perspective is necessary in order for the narrative to continue moving along in a particular direction.

Dead men tell no tales; and neither obviously can (or will) Mark Twain's moon. There is no surveillance, then. Those left behind to inspect are actually not inspecting anything at all. In effect a curtain has dropped, so that the scene must now lie there all dormant and inert, awaiting the return of the kind of interpreting consciousness which can stir the details back to significance and purpose again. The appearance in Chapter 11 of observers who break the spell becomes the last step of a total (and surprisingly complex) episode.

Taking half-holiday for the purpose, the townspeople restore interpretation by doing with the scene precisely what human life is so uniquely well fitted to do with objective reality. They look outward in wonder and horror; they chatter away about "out there" with ooh's and ah's and sundry other exclamations; they invoke if not the aid at least the presence of some Higher Power ("'His hand is here,'" intones the minister). (ATS, 103.) Above all, they yearn to assemble, evaluate, resolve, and understand the mystifying spectacle before them. And by all this furious cogitation there is produced a drama of crime and punishment which is of course patently absurd. It violates not simply those facts to which narrator, readers, and a handful of characters are privy; much more to the point, it flies in the face of the shared values and the common memories that ought to be the marks of a functioning community. How can St. Petersburg so blot out its own past that Muff Potter, hitherto the mildest, least offensive man in town, is now adjudged a murderer? How is it possible for yesterday, when Injun Joe was the well-known scourge of the village, to become today when he is suddenly made a party to detection and arraignment? Such questions will not be brushed aside by the narrator's observation that "the public are not slow in the matter of sifting evidence or arriving at a verdict," for the truth is that no evidence has been sifted. (*ATS,* 105.) The fuller explanation, I think, lies in Mark Twain's conception of the Romantic sensibility at work. Indeed, though the parallel would bewilder them (and Mark Twain might be surprised by the specificity of reference) the elders of St. Petersburg have spent Tuesday afternoon acting out verb-by-all-encompassing-verb the various powers which Coleridge had associated with the Romantic imagination in the thirteenth chapter of the *Biographia Literaria:*

> It dissolves, diffuses, dissipates, in order to re-create: or where this process is rendered impossible, yet still at all events it struggles to idealize and to unify. It is essentially *vital,* even as all objects (*as* objects) are essentially fixed and dead.[2]

Often praised as a theory of poetry, and sometimes maligned for being philosophic nonsense, this formulation is probably best read and understood as an attempt to define and describe an action.[3] The action involves lifting a curtain through consciousness. The two sentences thus focus upon the dynamics of the human mind, as mind responds to external circumstances, yet so spills outward to absorb and revitalize the external world that (as Coleridge implies) instead of taking from (or partaking of) the real, mind itself may be said to bring all meaningful reality into existence. At bottom, then, the formulation is concerned with language, the medium through which acts of consciousness must be expressed. In fact, the point of the argument would hardly be altered if the term "language" were substituted for imagination and the equation read imagination = consciousness = language. We would then have the familiar romantic notion of lifting a curtain on reality through words. The sentences would serve as commentary upon how it is via language that human life gains access to the real world, and they would assert the power of language to transform the chaos without into that well-ordered cosmos, which is the object of every human desire.

Reflections of this lofty sort do seem most applicable to meditative poetry or the philosophic insight. On the other hand, like the categories of Kant (or Freud's id, ego and superego), Coleridge's phenomenology of mind is represented as a universal principle. There is the strong implication that, in some sense or to some degree, we are all "poets" of reality. Hence simpler, humbler examples ought not be excluded just because they are simple and humble. And not only does the enterprise at St. Petersburg fit the pattern—that is, manifest the same process of comprehending reality from within and comprehending it through the gift of language; those who engage in the undertaking are motivated by every bit the same moral earnestness that is implicit in the *Biographia*. All of Coleridge's verbs are present in what the villagers bring to pass, most particularly the two last ones. For if we ask why, knowing Muff and knowing Joe, the villagers choose to act in defiance of what they know, the answer must come from their wish to "idealize" and "unify" experience. By reversing roles— calling the first "criminal," naming the other "friend of the prosecution"—the townspeople are able to have the satisfactions of justice without risk. There will be no difficulties about carting Muff Potter off to jail, whereas accusing and jailing Injun Joe would present an altogether more formidable prospect. (We note how even the professional detective from St. Louis will, a bit later in the book, find looking for clues to Joe's whereabouts more prudent than confronting Joe directly.) Moreover, the full force of Dr. Robinson's iniquity has been modified. Though obliquely acknowledging that he robbed graves, the villagers yet make Robinson the victim of an addled drunk rather than the crony and employer of one "who had sold his soul to Satan." (*ATS*, 106.) Dissolving and dissipating in order to re-create life are not just pastimes, matters of sport or of self-indulgence in the village. St. Petersburg has utilized the best means available of keeping itself a "tranquil world" where "the sun beamed down like a benediction."

I hope to have demonstrated Mark Twain at the top of his humorous, happy-go-lucky form. He dramatizes circumstances which, in balancing out the sunlit atmosphere of *Sawyer,* seem on the verge of engulfing the sunlight entirely. Twice, however, the threat is averted through the secular magic of the romantic imagination. As the play of the boys turns ugly reality back into an adventure story, so when the same play is reenacted by the adults of the village it restores to the community the look of civic and moral tidiness. The suggestion is of a resiliency of mind—a triumphant comic spirit—which can bring to terms even the worst encroachments from the world "out there." And if at the end of so much lowering and raising of curtains, one still detects a last, somewhat disturbing ambiguity, it too has been neatly accommodated.

The joke is on poor Muff. For much of the remainder of the summer he will be curtained off from booze and forgetfulness at the St. Petersburg jail. As a matter of fact, the curtain threatened to come tumbling down on him still more literally, since without the intervention of cooler heads he might well have been blindfolded and lynched on the spot. But by whom is the joke contrived? Where life is ruled by the romantic imagination, supreme authority must lie with the most imaginative. And pariah though he is officially, Injun Joe has displayed a considerable talent for manipulating the world that rejects him. Within the space of ten or twelve pages he fits into his plots, where they are constrained to play the roles he selects for them, Dr. Robinson, Muff, Tom and Huck and the townspeople generally. If he walks freely and contemptuously out of the scene, it is because he shares with Mark Twain's narrator the knowledge of when to conceal behind a curtain and when to lift the curtain for purposes of revelation. Though his status is already in the process of being challenged, Joe for the moment is endowed with the richest, most fertile imagination in all of St. Petersburg. He is nothing less than the Romantic Artist supreme.


## II

> "They have no memory."
> —Melville, "Benito Cereno"

On the face of it St. Petersburg is no country for the mischievous young. Stiff-necked and priggish, the village takes it for gospel that "children should be seen and not heard," and acts on the principle that "to spare the rod is to spoil the child." Accordingly, its officially sanctioned heroes from the younger set are Sid Sawyer and the marvelously named Willie Mufferson, that loving offspring who no doubt lisps her name as well as adores his "muffer." In such an environment the fate of Tom Sawyer promises something far worse than an occasional thrashing at home or during school hours. A likelier destiny for Tom at the beginning of his long hot summer is that outside home and school he will more often than not remain completely unnoticed.

But then, in certain fundamental respects, life in St. Petersburg is not well suited to people of any age. The town is boring: time hangs heavily in a place where none save the slaves, a renegade physician, and two grave robbers seem to work for a living.[4] Hence the townspeople are bored: as desperately as Muff Potter, and without his access to immediate relief, they hunger for some form (any form) of gratification that will spare them from the tedium of their days. On a Sunday morning in Chapter 4, this gratification arises out of an unexpected quarter. Distracted from "showing off" for one another, the elders of the village watch with awe while the principal show-off among them finagles a Bible, ingratiates himself with visiting dignitaries, and is thrust center-stage for a final triumph. Suddenly it has become evident that the best entertainment in town will never be provided by the likes of Willie Mufferson or Sid.

It is, consequently, the elders themselves who drop on Tom Sawyer the curtain that brings Chapter 4 to a close. If the words originate with the narrator, the pronoun "us" ("let us draw the curtain") is neither an editorial device nor a sly wink between narrator and reader. It bespeaks the choric and collective action of *them*. What vox populi will do forty-eight hours later on Dr. Robinson's behalf is now anticipated in a collective response to Tom. About to see him discomfited and humiliated, the townspeople will not allow their new source of enjoyment to slip back into disgrace and anonymity. They decline what they see by shifting from an act of perception to an imaginative reconstruction of the perceived. Lowering their curtain on Tom, they embrace him in a gesture of forgiveness. But the result of the embrace is to emplot Tom. The villagers do not so much re-create him as give him licence to act out a narrative—play a fictive role—which comes naturally to him, gives them pleasure, and which, therefore, they wish him to keep playing and acting out perpetually.

Re-creation is unnecessary because, as a prerequisite to being curtained by the town, Tom has already had to define the nature of the prized role. He does this by demonstrating at Sunday school that he shares with Injun Joe the strange power to control life through the use of a manipulative vocabulary. The effect would have been very different if either of these figures were to wilt or be rendered speechless under the cross-examination to which both are subjected. As it is, however, DAVID AND GOLIATH! serves Tom in the same way that words will presently serve Joe's purpose when he uses them to deceive first Muff and then the village as a whole. The utterance is the mark of a superior imagination, able to work its will on a world which sets great store by the magic of language. The curtain that encloses Tom thus falls in preparation for immediately rising again. When it goes up, Tom (like Joe) has been set perfectly free. He can now do, or say, or both do-and-say any outrageous thing he pleases; and his audience, by virtue of both beholding yet not really beholding what is done and said, will invariably love him. Embraced and emplotted, Tom is likewise empowered.

From this moment of liberation come the meaning, the shape and development, of much of the long hot summer in *Sawyer*. To claim, as some have, an initiation story for Tom's adventures is not wholly wrong.[5] What needs to be emphasized, though, is how the initiation occurs early in the narrative rather than being earned gradually and coming toward the close, in the manner of most Bildungsromans. After Chapter 4 Tom has been singled out for full membership in the community of adult values. (Not irrelevantly, his triumph is juxtaposed with the sermon in Chapter 5, which is based on the hope, as romantic as it is millennial, that "a little child should lead them.") (*ATS*, 68.) An interlude follows when he drops out of the adult eye, either because his antics take place at school or because the adults are focusing instead on the events in the graveyard. But the relationship is reestablished with the episode of "playing dead" which runs from Chapters 13 to 19. And now any lingering doubts about who is the authority-figure in the book are removed. Only half way along Tom's initiation is confirmed—and complete.

In fairness, it is not brought off without a few strained and awkward moments. For granted that "playing dead" fulfills Tom's wish that he "might die *temporarily*" (*ATS*, 87), the prank also exacts of St. Petersburg the trouble and anxiety of looking for three long days for three drowned bodies, and hence it imposes on the townspeople the very real grief they experience during the funeral service in Chapter 17. So charged is the rhetoric of this occasion that to watch the boys, as from the standpoint of the church gallery they look down on the stricken adults below, is to find the spirit of play has at least been compromised. It is a complex question as to where, or with whom, the reader's allegiances now belong. And framing the particular dilemma is the business of Tom's eavesdropping on Aunt Polly's anguish without revealing to her that he is still alive, and of his turning fact to dream vision until her credulous old head is stuffed with the notion that she has communed with angels and "speerits." All in all, these are three touchy episodes in the book. In each one a quality that, in a slightly different context, the narrator calls Tom's "vicious vanity" (*ATS*, 146) stirs and squirms and threatens to erupt into the foreground. One is hardly surprised to learn from students of the manuscript that Mark Twain was of several minds about how to continue.[6] Should he have Sid steal the "scroll" that Tom will leave behind, thus more-or-less exonerating Tom, but shifting the emphasis of the story to what would undoubtedly have been the harshness of Sid's punishment? Or should he have Tom leave the scroll and then run away for good, thus losing the thread of the story entirely?

The method he ultimately chooses seems, at first look, something of a cheat. As though a dream were being portrayed, the narrative jumps, skips, falls silent—and so manages to blur the singing of Old Hundred at noon on Sunday directly into Monday morning when Tom is acclaimed "hero of the hour." But of course the true function of the lacunae is to express what really did happen in between times. Once again, the elders of St. Petersburg terminated an action by drawing their curtain across it. With vexing questions from "out there" safely transported into the town's consciousness, action can resume as the curtain ascends on an idealized hero. The role of narration at the end of Chapter 17 thus reverses the part played by narrative language at the close of Chapter 4. Where "let us" spoke *for* St. Petersburg, the careful placing of "sold" in quotation marks ("as the 'sold' congregation trooped out") serves as the narrator's slightly sardonic commentary *about* St. Petersburg. (*ATS,* 141.) With a single exception, the townspeople have no thought of being "sold" or diddled. In their imaginative vision—the only view that counts for anything—they have been royally entertained. Exiting the church, they choose to look not backward, but ahead—and also upward to the source of their entertainment.

Exactly what they are seeing is neatly reemphasized by the only skeptic among them. "'I don't say it wasn't a fine joke, Tom,'" says Aunt Polly at breakfast on Monday, her verb-tense indicating that it *is* possible for at least one person in St. Petersbrug to remember the past, and to perceive it accurately. The key term then recurs a few hours later when, having learned from Sally Harper the full truth about Tom's tale of the scroll, Aunt Polly sees how the joke was on her specifically. And now "joke" bristles with the ambiguities of "laughter" and the pain of being laughed at:

> "Oh, child you never think. You never think of anything but your own selfishness. You could think to come all the way over here from Jackson's Island in the night to laugh at our troubles and you could think to fool me with a lie about a dream; but you couldn't ever think to pity us and save us from sorrow." (*ATS,* 143, 150.)

But, as good exceptions are wont to do, this one tests the rule, leaves it intact, and provides a basis for playing the best joke of all. It is not for nothing that in our first glimpse of her Aunt Polly was adorned with spectacles through which "she seldom or never looked." The same eyewear remains securely in place when she approaches Tom's jacket pocket at the close of Chapter 18. Even if nothing were there, she is prepared to suspend disbelief willingly: "'It's a good lie—it's a good lie—I won't let it grieve me.'" (*ATS,* 39, 152.) The fact that it is there, however, endows "scroll" with a full set of holy and scriptural connotations. Like the rest of the village, the old lady has had a religious visitation; the name of her scrolling angel is that of the figure who arose Lazarus-like from the dead (let us not be unmindful that he did so on the third day), and was not once rebuked for the cruel deception he practiced. It is, needless to say, Thomas Sawyer.

Small wonder, then, that of Tom's five principal feats in *Sawyer,* two (winning a Bible, attending his own funeral) take place inside the village church, while a third (prophesying for Aunt Polly) stresses religious terminology and raises Biblical echoes, and the two others (rescue from the cave, finding buried treasure) either begin as churchly activities or result in celebrations that lead back to the church. The setting clarifies in a last crucial way the reciprocal relationship which binds a gifted romantic magician to his ever-so-willing-and-subservient audience. To the town, Tom supplies fresh reasons for belief in the Christian promise of "ask and it shall be given." Again and again he shows that it is but necessary to speak the word, and all can marvel as an acquiescent world confers on him the sacred text, or delivers him from death and the dark underground, or yields up from its most secret depths the fortune in gold which leaves him rich and famous. And to Tom, in turn, St. Petersburg supplies the full measure of notoriety he craves, but also something more profound than just notoriety. The boy who seemed threatened by nonentity at the outset of his long hot summer has, after the passage of only a few weeks, emerged as a figure to be reckoned with in the following ways. He is repeatedly hailed as "hero of the hour." His picture and an accompanying feature story have twice appeared in the local newspaper. It is said of him by one village elder that "Tom should be admitted to the National Military Academy and afterward trained in the best law school in the country." And yet other adults—"pretty grave, unromantic men, some of them"—are emulating his behavior as they too go searching for buried gold. (*ATS*, 233.)

Clearly, such accolades go well beyond the conventions of an initiation story. On two occasions while the book developed, Mark Twain apparently entertained the idea of introducing a mysterious influence on Tom's behavior. Once, as an aftermath to the fist fight with Alfred Temple in Chapter 3, a figure would "emerge" from the darkness and begin to pursue Tom "stealthily"; next, anxieties concerning the trial of Muff were to be complicated (or perhaps allayed) by the appearance in Tom's life of "an old back country farmer named Ezra Ward, who had been a school mate of Aunt Polly."[7] But the interventions proved unnecessary because as the book turned out the repository of mystery is Tom himself. The truth is that he claims and is granted an air of the fabulous and transcendent; he walks through the village as larger than life-sized, endowed with a status bordering on the supernatural. In a parallel that always excites him he is transformed into a village Aladdin: the Aladdin of St. Petersburg, replete with "lamp" and genies. Or provided that we understand how the term cuts two ways, he might well be regarded as an early example of Mark Twain's Mysterious Stranger.

### III

[I]f we "stand back" from *Tom Sawyer* we can see a youth with no father or mother emerging with a maiden from a labyrinthine cave, leaving a bat-eating demon imprisoned behind him.
—Northrop Frye[8]

As surely as though the word were used, a curtain is drawn when, acting officially for St. Petersburg, the eminent Judge Thatcher sheathes the entrance to McDougal's Cave with a thick plate of "boiler-iron." Moreover it is set in place with the town's usual impetuousness, so that after a fortnight when it goes back up again the curtain discloses the corpse of Injun Joe, who was inadvertently walled up (walled off) inside the cave. And now ensues the familiar pattern of the book. Having dissipated unpleasantness through the simple expedient of banishing it from sight behind a curtain, the town raises the curtain in order to gaze with rapt wonder on the handiwork which it creates. The miraculous transubstantiation of Joe is completed, as to the roles it had assigned him earlier St. Petersburg adds all the various other parts it had kept in reserve for Tom Sawyer. In less time than it takes one to tell it, the half-breed is re-created as a hero, a legend, a saint—and preeminently an artist. His transition from fact into the realm of the aesthetic is confirmed when we are told that "Joe's cup" will henceforth supersede "Aladdin's Palace" as the principal showpiece of the cave's interior. (*ATS,* 221.)

But this time, for virtually the first time in the narrative, the process of make-believe does not go unchallenged. With a certain toe-tapping asperity the hitherto indulgent narrator breaks in to admonish curtain-lowering/curtain-raising St. Petersburg. He attributes to a blurred and faulty vision—what are sarcastically called the town's "permanently impaired and leaky waterworks"—the kind of perception which would aggrandize one who is "believed to have killed five citizens of the village." (*ATS,* 221.) Yet even as he professes outrage at their scaling up, the narrator himself seems to be engaged in a technique of excessive and quite pointless scaling down. Through a considerable accumulation of detail, he takes us directly inside McDougal's Cave during the fortnight's interval. That is, he is at pains to investigate everything that happened between the moment when the curtain descended on Joe and the moment when it was unlocked and removed. And the circumstances he presents are frankly preposterous.

For in terms of both the necessity for it and the manner of it, the death of Injun Joe is surpassing strange to the point of being downright kooky. It seems incredible, to begin with, that having long used the cave as a favorite hiding place, Joe would either not know about or at least be impelled to look for and discover the second, the alternate exit that conducts Tom and Becky to safety. Our sense of plausibility is not exactly heightened when we learn presently, through the actions of Tom and Huck, that the treasure buried by Joe lies only a "few paces" from this other exit. (*ATS,* 224.) Nor will it do to suppose that, small though it is, the opening would be accessible only to children. Twice it is carefully established that the other exit overlooks the River and the skiffmen below. All Joe would have needed to do is thrust out his head (surely no larger than an adolescent's body) and call for help.

But what he fails to do is as of nothing when compared to how Joe does behave during his time of immolation. From the wanderings of Becky and Tom, we know that the interior of McDougal's Cave is damp and clammy, withal as waterlogged as any underground passage in Poe. In the space of a single paragraph from Chapter 31, the children descend from "a little stream" to "a bewitching waterfall" to a "subterranean lake." The pains of lumbago or even of death by drowning might be conceivable in such an atmosphere—but hardly even the discomforts of a dry mouth, much less death by thirst. Nevertheless dread of thirst obsesses Joe, and it is the dread which kills him. Hour after long hour he affixes himself in the sealed doorway, husbanding each "precious drop of water." With escape to the rear and a veritable gulf flowing on every side, he dares not move from the single spot where water is. All he can do, or will do, is stand rooted there, medleying the *drip, drip, drip* around him with the *thump, thump, thump* which he causes, as with the futility of the hopeless (and knowing it to be futile), he hammers away at the iron door with his bowie knife. (*ATS*, 209–10, 221.)

Perhaps the aim is to create pathos: to remind us (as Joe alleged in the graveyard) that all his life the half-breed has been closed out of respectable society by the unwarranted stigma of race. If so, the actual effect is to cross very quickly the thin line which separates the pathetic from the farcical. Following him behind a curtain, we find the once clever and resourceful scourge of St. Petersburg turned into a buffoon, as addled and ineffectual of mind as he is physically fixated. The joke is on Joe. He perfectly exemplifies Bergson's principle of the "mechanical encrusted on to the living."[9] Laughter at the plight of the petrified or the enhumored man can be our only legitimate response.

But how does the laughter function? Why, having coupled true-Joe (crafty, dangerous, criminal) with the town's new image of "Joe" (legendary, saintly) does the narrator offer yet a third version in which the death of Joe is rendered an absurdity? "[I did it] in the interest of art; it never happened," says Mark Twain in one of those relatively rare moments in the *Autobiography* when he looked backward in some detail upon his earlier work.[10] So, what was the point to the art . . . what could fun-loving Mark Twain have been up to at the time? The answer, I suggest, comes with averting our eyes from Joe—clearly, he will not stir if we look away—and backtracking through the book to other incidents that took place behind a drawn curtain.

As befits the gravity of the situation, Muff Potter's trial is handled with an unusual degree of narrative realism. During fully four-fifths of Chapter 23 a kind of camera eye (or stenographic notebook) hovers over the proceedings, recording each and every particular, not excepting verbatim exchanges between the prosecuting attorney and several witnesses. All of which makes especially conspicuous the shift in narrative manner that occurs at just the point where Muff is exonerated. Though the words are Tom's, and though they are said to mesmerize his audience, the fact remains that the most significant of the words are not spoken by Tom. A hiatus, filled in only by summary, separates the beginning of his faltering (and duly recorded) testimony from the end of the chapter. It is as if a stage direction had enveloped the hero, not really enhancing what he does, but rather curtaining him from view at what, by rights, should have been one of Tom's grandest moments.

Of course the need for narrative-economy might be conjectured. There would be little point in repeating circumstances that had already been fully dramatized. On the other hand fear of redundancy is not much evidenced by *Sawyer*: consider, as contrast, how the preliminaries to Tom's funeral are first acted out and then directly retold by Tom with no loss of impact. And in any case a wish to economize will hardly account for what seems the true failure of imagination that takes place in Chapter 32. Here, after church bells peal and jubilant voices add to the din of "pans and horns," we are brought for an explanation to the figure of Tom, lying on a couch, from where he

> told the history of the wonderful adventure, putting in many striking additions to adorn it withal, and closed with a description of how he left Becky and went on an exploring expedition; how he followed two avenues as far as his kite-line would reach; how he followed a third to the fullest stretch of the kite-line, and was about to turn back when he glimpsed a far-off speck that looked like daylight. . . . And if it had only happened to be night he would not have seen that speck of daylight and would not have explored that passage anymore! He told how he went back for Becky and broke the good news. . . . He described how he labored with her and convinced her; . . . how he pushed his way out of the hole and then helped her out; how they sat there and cried for gladness; how some men came along in a skiff and Tom hailed them and told them their situation and their famished condition; how the men didn't believe the wild tale at first, "because," said they, "you are five miles down below the valley the cave is in" . . . (*ATS*, 217–18.)

But—complains the reader—not only are the "many striking additions" left unspecified; we do not even get a first-hand view of the essential facts. Why not dramatize this episode, so that coming out of the dangerous place is worked up with the same suspense, high drama and vividness, the same air of mystery and struggle, the same immediacy and great wealth of concrete descriptions that going in had occasioned? Why take another big achievement of Tom's and more than half spoil it by reducing it to a passage of inert and rather clumsy exposition? Above all, why do to Tom the ultimate indignity of quoting directly from two anonymous skiffmen, while Tom's own words recede into the voice (the mouth) of the summarizing narrator and hence, except for the fiat of attribution, cannot really be said to belong to Tom at all? The indirectness of the presentation complements the lacunae of the scene in the courtroom; and I believe that both together contribute a last, vitally important dimension to the portrayal of Tom Sawyer.

In effect three Toms cohabit the book. There is Tom of the indulgent, happy-go-lucky narrator. He is charming, gregarious, endlessly inventive Tom, best at home in the world of other adolescents, where he usually wins, but can occasionally sustain a healthy loss or two. There is the town's Tom, thrust by a combination of his design and the villagers' credulity into playing a preternatural or even supernatural role. And in consequence of the role, there emerges Tom as seen by the narrator of toe-tapping asperity: Tom-behind-a-curtain.

Placed there, he is, to be sure, set free to do anything he likes, and to do it superbly well. It grows increasingly evident, however, that the "anything" he performs so splendidly is a matter of the one, identical thing which as if by rote he must enact and reenact over and over endlessly. Let Tom's magic be "socialized"—let it be grounded in reality or presumed to affect the circumstances and outcome of some actual situation—and the toe-tapping narrator sees to it that the result is a curious diminishing of Tom's stature, an odd displacement of his heroic role. Either narration refuses to look at him directly, or it cloaks what he does in a flat and lifeless expository style which leaves both Tom and his readers at one remove from the actual experience. Thus a specter in his path turns up to dog Tom, after all. Tom-behind-a-curtain shares the fate of Injun Joe-in-the-cave. Though it seemed the means of his liberation, the falling curtain only serves to envelop Tom in a terrible confinement, to which the captivity of Joe stands in ironic parallel. By the curtain before him, Tom, no less than Joe, is forever cut off from meaningful contacts with the real world outside. Together with Joe, he has been turned into an automaton—a trick-playing machine.

If by "standing back" we discern a pattern of "romance" in *Sawyer,* the next step might be to swing in close in order to observe how the pattern is that of low-brow romance. What Professor Frye calls the "refrigerated deathlessness"[11] of the comic strip provides by far the most telling analogy for Tom Sawyer's behavior. As we do *not* see Tom emerge visually from the cave, and do *not* hear him bring to pass the exoneration of poor Muff, we ought to be reminded of the comic strip physician who during forty years of an impeccable practice has never once lost a patient because in all that time he has never had a real patient to lose. Like those of the indefatigable Dr. Rex Morgan, Tom's marvelous endowments consist of plucking a stunt-for-the-day from a single bag of tricks, then being thrust back into nothingness again, until it is time for today's white rabbit to be replaced with tomorrow's variation. The joke, which has made the rounds in *Tom Sawyer,* is therefore ultimately on Tom. But the vanishing act that expresses the joke is not of course meant to trivialize him exclusively.

Before any characters have been brought inside, Mark Twain devotes a long paragraph to an extraordinarily full description of the interior of McDougal's Cave. Long corridors are said to open into other chasms and declivities and to form a maze that "go[es] nowhere." At the entrance it is possible to "look out upon the green valley shining in the sun"; and a bit later we are told how the walls of this antechamber are adorned with pictures and scrawlings which bear "rather overly descriptive names, such as 'The Drawing Room,' 'The Cathedral,' 'Aladdin's Palace,' and so on." Further down, however, the direction of "labyrinth underneath labyrinth" is away from light and fresh air—and also away from knowledge and certainty, since "no man 'knew' the cave. That was an impossible thing." (*ATS,* 196, 209.) The same atmosphere is then intensified after the introduction of Tom and Becky by the narrator's many references to "murky aisles," flickering and uncertain light patterns, vague and apparently unsourced echoes. And as echoes abound within, so the structure of the place comes alive with a host of literary echoes. To read Mark Twain's account is to find it resonating with overtones of the cave in Emerson's essay "Illusions," Ahab's descent into the Hotel de Cluny in *Moby-Dick,* the cave of both Ms. Quested and Mrs. Moore which Forster would presently dramatize in *Passage to India.* Behind them all, furthermore, and shaping the significance of each, stands the primal cave of Western literature. It is the "den" of Socrates, set forth in Book VII of *The Republic,* wherein the inhabitants, hemmed round by ignorance and apathy, see self-generated shadows on the wall which they mistake for the realities of experience.

Situated physically on the outskirts of town, McDougal's Cave functions metaphysically—metaphorically—to define the nature of culture inside the community. St. Petersburg is a society of cave-dwellers. With humor (which is not always quite good humor) in his eye and at least some subliminal recollection of traditional philosophy on his mind, Mark Twain has shown us the townspeople as one and all they unite to lift themselves and each other out of reality and to draw their own and one another's identities back into the caverns of selfhood. Thereupon, the factual basis for human relationships vanishes, to be supplanted by fantasies that "go nowhere," by chimeras of mind that point downward and away from knowledge and certainty—in sum, by ornamentations of the real that are as farfetched and "overly descriptive" as the graffiti on the walls of McDougal's Cave. Entering the cave, then, Tom goes to complete the final stage of his initiation into the world of the American village. As before, during the episode of playing dead, he is out of view for the obligatory three days and three nights of the Gospels. When he reappears this time, however, there is no further talk of his becoming a runaway; indeed, he will spend the rest of the book using his "robber gang" as an enticement to keep Huck easy and comfortable at the Widow Douglas's. And though always a prankster and one much traveled in the future, he will depart next time as the sedate, well-dressed young gentleman, nicely tailored to the adage that you can take the boy out of St. Petersburg, but never the pomposities and myopic insensitivities of St. Petersburg out of the boy. Hence if he vanishes from sight at the point of reemerging from the cave, this is the case because, fully at home now among the rest of the cartoon figures in the village, he is no longer in any need of coming back dramatically.

The joke is on all of them. Faithful (as Nick Carraway would say) to the Platonic conception of themselves, they touch life with what Nick would call "the Midas touch"—and turn characters into caricatures. They are a gallery of the enhumored: *the* minister, *the* schoolmaster, *the* maiden aunt, *the* villain, *the* bad little boy who is simultaneously rendered by the good show he puts on into *the* good little boy: figures stripped of all individuality, of all humanness (of any sense of community) by their preference for the self-made image over facts, their romantic commitment to words before world. To say, as some have, that play subsumes darkness in *Sawyer* is to develop only half the truth;[12] in turn, play as reckless as it is foolhardy, becomes the basis for an overwhelming, all-enveloping darkness. The laughter which bubbles up at the burghers of St. Petersburg is in mockery of their happy, futile, pretentious, thoroughly trapped helplessness.[13] They have reversed Rousseau's formulation, in the sense that they are born in chains, and everywhere we are confronted with the absurdity of their attempts to set themselves free. But the laughter that arises from scorn also anticipates Mark Twain's one almost successful attempt to write a completely comic ending.

## IV

ROMANTIC: "I see that you are looking at a grasshopper there which you have found in the grass and I suppose you intend to describe it. Now don't waste your time and sin against culture in that way. I've got a grasshopper here which . . . is made up of wire and cardboard, very prettily painted in a conventional tint, and it's perfectly indestructible. . . . You may say it's artificial. Well, it is artificial; but then it's ideal too; and what you want to do is cultivate the ideal. You'll find the books full of my kind of grasshopper, and scarcely a trace of yours in any of them."

REALIST: I hope the time is coming when not only the artist, but the common, average man will have the courage . . . to reject the ideal grasshopper . . . because it is not "simple, natural, and honest," because it is not like a real grasshopper.

—William Dean Howells[14]

The uncertainties he felt about his work-in-progress are revealed by Mark Twain in several letters he wrote to Howells during the summer and fall of 1875. Was it, he wondered, a book for children? Or, having been "only written for adults" would the book find favor with an adult audience?[15] Influenced apparently by Howells's responses to the manuscript, he eventually chose to call the work an "entertainment [for] boys and girls," thus giving tacit consent to the generations of publishers' blurbs which have found in *Sawyer* "nostalgia," an "idyll," a "light-hearted excursion . . . into a dream-like world of summertime and hooky, pranks and punishments."[16] Fundamentally, though, Mark Twain knew better. He had to recognize that fantasizing St. Petersburg and the twin destinies of Tom and Joe were his means of developing two opposed responses to experience—responses that remain in implicit conflict throughout, but that are brought face-to-face in a resolving action which occurs toward the close of the narrative. (Significantly it comes *near* the end, though not quite *at* the end.) And it is not to the credit of Howells that he seems to have missed the point of the resolution. If "Coleridge" and "romantic excesses" provide convenient labels for the attitudes that destroy in *Sawyer*, the attitude that proves socially useful and morally redemptive invites being called "Howells" or "Howells's theory of literary realism."

In Chapter 28 as Injun Joe sets off on the expedition that will result in his complete metamorphosis in McDougal's Cave, the half-breed has already undergone a profound change. Back in the graveyard he could justify his violence by appealing to reality. He had a grudge to settle, a legitimate anger at Dr. Robinson, "'who drove me away . . . when I come to ask for something to eat . . . and had me jailed as a vagrant.'" (*ATS*, 218.) Perhaps, in fact, the power he then exerted over the whole town lay in his ability to see through the shams and hypocrisies that were the hallmarks of all of life in St. Petersburg. In any case, and despite the horrors he is about to perpetrate, he might for once have been dignified as *Indian* Joe, even (if you will) as Native American Joe. But now, as he goes along, Joe has become just one more fantasizing villager. The Widow Douglas has done him no harm. He has never even encountered her directly. She exists merely as his invention, an arranged grasshopper inside the head of

Joe, tricked out in the "conventional tints" of racial prejudice and other decorations of Joe's overwrought imagination. Seeking to avenge himself on her, Joe has dropped a curtain and forsaken all claims to living in the real world. It probably does not push a point to say that he has set in motion the transition which leads him from angry outcast, to "hero" of his own melodrama, to the walled-in, curtained-off state of being just nothing at all.

Suppose, as at the graveyard, Tom Sawyer were hidden in the bushes to hear Joe's narrative of violation and disfigurement. No doubt Tom would have acted; no doubt, after his fashion, he would have acted suitably and successfully. It is the law of life in *Sawyer* that Tom must never fail. In the process of acting, however, he would have taken the Widow Douglas inside his head, retouched her with a piece of red keel and assorted other embellishments, diverted attention away from the real needs of her real crisis as he made her the substance of his fiction. Thereby, before her rescue, the Widow would have been jeopardized still further—and this perhaps is one good reason why Tom must disappear from the episode.

A still better reason is furnished by the figure who *is* there to overhear. Though the news would astound him, this is a figure created to see straight through the gush of Howells's first speaker—and hence (without at all comprehending what the words themselves signified) through the full implications of Coleridge's fine verbs. Crouched in the bushes, Huck knows for a fact that the scene which gathers around him can no more be dissolved or dissipated or intellectualized into a drama of mind than it is susceptible to being idealized out of existence. The objects from out there do not remain "fixed" and "dead" until stirred to life by Huck's imagination or quickened by his vocabulary. Rather they burst in upon Huck with all the force and unloveliness of a plague of grasshoppers, perched in coarse grass, spitting venomous tobacco juice. Huck's perceptions thus begin with resistant reality, and are akin to those of the second speaker in Howells's *Criticism and Fiction*. But, as the second speaker went on to observe, it requires an act of courage to see things this way.

Acting courageously, Huck brings more to pass than the rescue of the Widow. There is no fanfare this time. Huck takes no pleasure from being involved; notably, he *is* involved only because he can recall the past: "then he remembered that the Widow Douglas had been kind to him more than once." (*ATS*, 198.) And no derring-do occurs, for Huck's first step is to invoke the aid of those stronger and more capable than he is. But neither is there any attempt—or any need—to gloss over the situation. Accordingly, Huck has redeemed the language of Mark Twain's narrative; perhaps it is not too much to say that, for Mark Twain, he has rehabilitated the methods of prose fiction generally. As he saves the Widow, so he spares the book from becoming a dead-end of dropped curtains, mechanized and half-visible "heroes," awkward and often inopportune omissions. One supposes that his full emergence at the end reflects Mark Twain's conscious need for a subject richer and more meaningful than the romantic follies of St. Petersburg. At the very least, Huck has proved himself worthy of reappearing in a very different sequel. But before the sequel can begin, Mark Twain must finish up the work-in-hand by writing one last episode.

Like much else in *Sawyer*, the Widow Douglas's ice-cream social in Chapters 33 and 34 is a simple occasion, fraught with many underlying ironies. Ostensibly Tom Sawyer's "initiation" party, it is this for the already thoroughly initiated Tom only by virtue of the fact that he can drop plump into the middle of it his last and showiest triumph: a bag filled with $12,000 in gold pieces. Actually, the initiation is for Huck. From having been careful to avoid the drunkard's son—even Tom "did not care to have Huck's company in public places" (*ATS*, 229)—St. Petersburg will now gladly let him in, always provided it can recast him in the town's image of respectability. And Huck tries to have no part of the process. His initial impulse to escape through the nearest window is followed, during the next several months, by repeated attempts to get back to the "unkempt, uncombed" days when he was "free and happy." (*ATS*, 230.) The party thus serves as one more point of departure in Huck's journey toward remaining a realistic, self-knowing identity.

Yet it begins on a certain disquieting note. Confronted by two mud-spattered boys, who have just come out of the cave, the Widow Douglas takes both into a bedchamber where two fresh suits of clothing have been laid out. "'They'll fit both of you,'" she remarks. (*ATS*, 232.) Morally and psychologically, it is easy enough to sever Huck and Tom: to locate each at the two opposed and highly paradoxical ends of a continuum. Where the first raises a curtain on reality, sacrifices the self to the greater good of society, and thereby commences to become a character—the second will have no part of life beyond the protective veil, clings fiercely to the ego, and by the prickings and promptings of self is reduced to the status of caricature, as mechanically enhumored as he is predictable. The paradoxes, however, are underlain by still another irony. Physically Tom and Huck seem indistinguishable. Reality has seen to it that they might very well be mistaken for twins. And so the question arises can Eng and Chang, Jim Blake and Jacob Blivens, Tom and Huck, ever truly be divided? As in the real world of Mt. Airy, North Carolina, we are told that Eng (though apparently in perfect health) died within a few hours of Chang's demise, can Mark Twain's Siamese twins live independently, one without the other? With this fundamental question, predicated upon the meanings of proximity and distance, the sequel must soon be engaged.

## NOTES

1. *The Adventures of Tom Sawyer,* ed. John C. Gerber, Paul Baender, and Terry Firkins, 65. All references are to this edition, hereafter referred to as *ATS*. (The stage directions have of course been added, though the highly dramatic scene invites them.)

2. *Coleridge: Selected Poetry and Prose,* ed. Elisabeth Schneider (New York: Holt, Rinehart and Winston, 1962), 268.

3. The "pro" and "con" extremes are well demonstrated by I. A. Richards, *Coleridge on Imagination* (London: Rutledge and K. Paul, 1950), and Norman Fruman, *Coleridge, The Damaged Archangel* (New York: G. Braziller, 1971). Though this is neither his emphasis nor intention, Professsor Fruman's clear preference for Wordsworth causes him to approach Coleridge with something akin to a realist's skepticism. In some purely hypothetical world where he read them both, Mark Twain would, I think, find much more to admire in Fruman's estimate than in that of Richards.

In *Mark Twain: The Fate of Humor,* James Cox (248) distinguishes sharply between the uses of the imagination in *ATS* and Coleridge's theoretical account. "[T]he imagination," Cox writes, "is shorn of the religious, romantic, and transcendental meanings with which Coleridge invested it; in Mark Twain's world of boyhood, the imagination represents the capacity for mimicry, impersonation, make-believe, and play." What this seems to me to miss is the relationship between "play" or "make-believe" and religious fervor in St. Petersburg. No longer much interested in God (their church services are more nearly social and perfunctory than not), the villagers must fall back upon themselves and their imaginations as the sole sources of value, order, stability—indeed, reality. Again, however, I stress that Mark Twain is mocking not S. T. Colerdige, but "Coleridge"—the embodiment or synecdoche for a particular point of view and not the specific author of a specific passage in a specific book.

4. Here, and at other places in this essay, I am indebted to the reading of *ATS* in Judith Fetterly's "The Sanctioned Rebel," *Studies in the Novel* 3 (1971), 293–304.

5. The precise terms (or organization) of an initiation story are set forth by Walter Blair in "On the Structure of *Tom Sawyer,*" *Modern Philology* 37 (August 1939), 77–88, and, in a yet more specific way, by Hamlin Hill in "The Composition and Structure of *Tom Sawyer,*" *American Literature* 32 (January 1961), 379. I would agree with both that an initiation motif is central to the book, though I have less faith than either in Mark Twain's serious use of initiatory rites.

6. The matter has been explored most fully by Professor Hill in "The Composition and Structure of *Tom Sawyer.*" There is a particularly interesting analysis of the whole episode in James L. Johnson's *Mark Twain and the Limits of Power,* 64–66.

7. I am indebted to Professor Baender's account of "Alterations in Manuscript," *ATS,* 573, 587. I have also consulted his *Adventures of Tom Sawyer: Facsimile of the*

*Author's Holograph Manuscript* (Frederick, Md.: University Publications of America, 1982).

8. Frye, *Anatomy of Criticism,* 190.

9. "Laughter," in Corrigan, *Comedy,* 477.

10. *Mark Twain's Autobiography,* ed. Albert Bigelow Paine (New York: Harper, 1924) I, 105.

11. Frye, *Anatomy of Criticism,* 186.

12. For example Cox, *Fate of Humor,* 139, and Fetterly, "Sanctioned Rebel," 298.

13. A community devoted to the theory and practice of "bad faith" is what Forrest Robinson calls them. Of course he is right, and I have learned much from his reading of the *Adventures of Tom Sawyer.* My only reservations would be that Professor Robinson fails fully to explain the "bad faith" in this book, as he goes on to explain it perhaps a bit too narrowly in *Huckleberry Finn*—and that he too much implicates narrator/Mark Twain in actions involving "bad faith." Mark Twain is never as much taken in by the "charm" and well-meaning follies of his characters as Professor Robinson seems to suppose. There is that voice of toe-tapping asperity.

In my view the citizens of St. Petersburg clearly anticipate the grotesques and deformities who will one day reappear in Sherwood Anderson's *Winesburg, Ohio* (1919)—though they do so with a difference. The people of Winesburg are waiting for a Voice (not necessarily God's, but that of some transcendent force) that will provide them with order, stability, a sense of purpose, a direction and identity. They are turned into distortions by their longing for this Voice, and its persistent failure to speak. By contrast, the populace of St. Petersburg feels no such need. Each one trusts himself/herself, just as Emersonian romanticism said each one should. And they are undone—rendered into distortions—by the force of their romantic egos. The difference is between the death of romanticism on the one hand, the beginnings of modernism on the other—and somewhere in between, literary realism with *its* failure to resolve the problems of "truth" and "significance" through an appeal to "reality."

14. Becker, *Documents of Modern Literary Realism,* 134.

15. *Selected Mark Twain–Howells Letters,* 48.

16. Mark Twain's description reads: "So endeth the chronicle. It being strictly a history of a boy it must stop here," 236. The blurb is from the Signet Edition (New York: New American Library, 1960), edited by the distinguished critic George P. Elliot, but it is of a kind with the standard view which appears on other book jackets and covers.

# Huckleberry Finn:
# An Essay on the Dilemmas of Realism

I ain't everybody, and I can't stand *it*.
      —Huck to Tom in *ATS*[1]

In St. Petersburg, it is as though a curtain ascends to reveal him. Partly because of his recent heroism—primarily, one suspects, because of the half-interest he owns in a $12,000 fortune—the onetime drunkard's son and village outcast is suddenly the object of every eye and mouth in town. Though the voice is Huck's, it is how Huck is seen by *them* (how vox populi reacts to Huck) which is the source of a recurring dramatic pattern.

At the *mansion* Miss Watson would make Huck a penitent. She tells him of Heaven and Hell, of the rigors of the moral life, and about all the benefits of being prayerful.

In the *cave* Tom Sawyer would turn him into a highway robber. Tom defines ransoming and thievery, and locates Huck inside a scene where such other anomalies as booty, victims, and ambuscades are also the order of the day.

In the *law office,* Judge Thatcher, apparently envisioning his future as well as his present situation, speaks to Huck of interest rates, investments, and the rules for commercial success.

In a *slave's cabin,* responding to the reward of a shiny counterfeit quarter, Jim prophesies Huck's life story. He foretells two courtships, two wives, the influence of good and bad angels, and death by hanging.

In a *shack,* located across the River from St. Petersburg in the Illinois wilderness, Pap would transform Huck into a murderer; he calls him "angel of death," chases him round and round the room, and will not be dissuaded by the plea that "it's only Huck."[2] This last event is decisive, in the sense of becoming the immediate cause for Huck to run away. And it differs from any of the others, in the sense that the content of the particular fantasy can be traced back to a drunkard's psychosis. In terms of how it functions, however, Pap's reconstruction of Huck has been prepared for by the rest and it comes as a climax to the general effect which the others had created.

The aim has been to put Huck inside the mind of every segment of village society. All are represented: adult/adolescent; town/country; high/low; rich/poor; owner/slave; relative/friend/stranger. Yet even as a curtain rises to tell him who he is, it also descends, in the form of the tellers' words, to cloak Huck in the assorted roles which they have chosen for him. The boy who at the end of *Tom Sawyer* had declined to be "everybody" is, after a few weeks' association with his new admirers, in grave danger of becoming just that. And the folly—perhaps it is the direfulness—of his situation is underscored by a figure in the narrative whose presence must never be forgotten. This is the implied author, mentioned by name in the second sentence, and present thereafter to select for emphasis and coherence each of the individual episodes that Huck relates. By assembling as he does, "Mr. Mark Twain" manages to suggest the fragmentation of a personality so severe that it points toward the ultimate extinction of Huck. Were he truly to attempt all the parts which they are so eager to impose on him, Huck would be simultaneously praying in his closet and robbing on the highway; investing his money wisely while giving it to Pap; attending school yet reverting to illiteracy; living as a child even as he is being prepared for romance and weddings, for murder and execution. The features he turns outward to greet the world would be those of saint, parricide, adolescent boy, business executive, bridegroom, and felon.[3]

With this as his predicament, Huck's departure from St. Petersburg may be viewed in a fuller light. Though all these matters obviously help to motivate him, more is involved in his going than multiplication tables, games without discernible point, adult fussiness, or even the undoubted dangers of life with Pap. Basically Huck is struggling to retain an identity: to preserve his sense of selfhood. Though he would hardly put it in these terms, he is intent upon remaining somebody, in the face of the fragmented and thoroughly muddled everybody which everybody else wants him to be. Or we perhaps come closer to how he might have thought about the problem when we say that Huck aims to become nobody. He seeks the curtain of anonymity—the state of perfect nonbeing—which will put him at a safe distance from the busybodies who would turn him into everybody. The point is that, either way, his flight has literary antecedents. For Huck runs away as the traditional victim in a realistic fiction.

The intention of realistic literature is not simply to reproduce, with great and graphic detail, aspects of what is called "the real world." Were this all, the practice of realistic art would scarcely differ from the manifestoes set forth in the preface to the *Lyrical Ballads* or developed by Emerson in the closing paragraphs of "The American Scholar" and "Self Reliance." Rather, the historical moment for an Age of Realism comes in consequence of the realist's profound reaction against the ethics and psychology of romanticism. It is largely an issue about consciousness, and about the vocabulary through which acts of consciousness are expressed. It involves a different way of telling what happens when the world "out there" passes into the aware human mind in order to be interpreted and integrated through language.

For the romantic, the results of such a passage are likely to be "value," "beauty," "insight," "truth"; the conversion of chaos into the all-illuminating symbol; in short, the closest approximations one can hope to make toward the moral and spiritual reordering of dreary, messy reality. And the result is also an exercise in power. "You think me a child of circumstance," writes Emerson in a famous passage from "The Transcendentalist." But he quickly goes on to demonstrate how inadequate this conception is, when it is measured against the full force of the romantic imagination:

> I make my circumstance. Let any thought or motive of mine be different from what they are, the difference will transform my condition and economy. I—this thought which is called I—is the mold into which the world is poured like melted wax. The mold is invisible, but the world betrays the shape of the mold. You call it the power of circumstance, but it is the power of me.[4]

As in Coleridge's *Biographia* (though with somewhat greater attention to the specifics of the drama) the inner life of mind takes precedence over merely objective facts. What began as a resistant "other" is drawn inward to be touched by "thought" and "motive," and then reemerges on the far side in the form of the pliant and subservient "other."

Circumstance, however, includes other people and the whole complex of human relationships. And the realistic writer, shifting from philosophical to social matters, must take a more guarded view of transforming the world into words and ideas. What the realist perceives is that while scenarios-in-the-mind do seem to provide our only legitimate access to objective reality, still they likewise run the risk of turning other human beings and the social scene into the characters and narratives—the pawns, tools, lackeys, wax-effigies, made-up creations—of the scenarist. Thus it is that another realistic novel, also published in America during the 1880s, turns out to shed unexpected light on *Huckleberry Finn*. The book is concerned to show the encroachment of formative circumstance upon a young American woman. Both literally and figuratively she is taken in—imported into the heads of various companions, who reproduce her in a series of pictorial images, the total effect of which is to leave her misrepresented, betrayed and humiliated, ground (all in spite of her own wishes) into the "very mill of the conventional."[5] The differences between Isabel Archer and Huck Finn could scarcely be more vast. The malign art of an Osmond and Madame Merle, like the benevolent retouchings of Ralph Touchett, achieve a lavishness and complexity which are not even to be dreamt of among the clumsier artists of St. Petersburg. All the same, the underlying processes of converting personal identity into artifact are identical. Huck and Isabel share the fate of life in a romanticizing world where the extreme gestures of consciousness no longer serve to clarify or enrich experience, but have instead turned off mean and selfish, as manipulative as they are life-denying.

But realism, because it strives to be truthful about actions of mind, admits to much overlap between the categories of victim and victimizer. If the genitive of Henry James's title signifies Isabel as the subject of portraiture (their portraits are *of* her), it points equally to the fact of possession (Isabel is the owner *of* portraits, not all of them very good or wise or lifelike, which she creates of herself and others). And of course it is just so in the real world of the explicit author, Mark Twain. Fleeing from the fabrications of St. Petersburg, Huck displays a marked (perhaps it is even a surprising) talent for some fabricating of his own.

At the *cabin,* and with the example of Tom Sawyer firmly in mind, Huck concocts an elaborate murder scene. If playing dead is his insurance against being pursued, the strategy likewise figures in new plans he has for a future role. Before the idea occurred to him, Huck had contemplated a long journey overland or "camp[ing] in one place for good" about "fifty mile" downriver. Now, "death" sets him free to linger near home as a combination voyeur and sneak thief. "I can stop anywhere I want to," Huck thinks. "And then I can paddle over to town, nights, and slink around and pick up things I want. Jackson's Island's the place." (*AHF,* 32, 38, 41.)

Meeting Jim on the *island* is a source of great jubilation. Very soon, however, his words and inflections unmistakably those of Tom Sawyer, Huck takes the part of Mr. Interlocutor, and (relentless as Tom; pompous as Judge Thatcher) he harries Jim on the topics of "speculation" and "wealth" through nearly three pages, which are the only truly dull pages in the book. Word games at Jim's expense clearly anticipate Huck's trick with the rattlesnake, just as *in the book we now have** they shape those early days on the raft when, rising to some gam-

---

* It will bear emphasizing here that, together with the last half of Chapter 12, what we now read as Chapters 13 and 14 were not parts of the 1876 manuscript, but were added by Mark Twain in the summer of 1883, just before the book was published. That is, the adventure of the *Walter Scott* and its aftermath in which Huck and Jim discuss kings and language, though they come early

bit of Huck's (was Solomon wise? do the French speak French?) Jim argues and wins, and leaves Huck sulking about the impossibility of "learning a nigger to argue." (*AHF,* 98.)

Common sense would dictate a new name and address when Huck visits *Mrs. Judith Loftus.* But the change into a woman's apparel and the botched disguise of first Sarah, then Mary Williams must surely be thought of as embellishments by the implied author, whose business is to be funny. And in order to keep the joke plausible, "Mr. Mark Twain" must once again stress the dual nature of Huck's character. There is sober, no-nonsense, essentially humorless Huck who comes straight off the last pages of *Tom Sawyer.* Underlying him, there is a puckish Huck whose delight in tricks and disguises reflects the sheer love of performing, of taking in others.

On the *River,* near what is presumably the town of Cairo, the two sides coalesce into a fascinating problem of rhetorical emphasis. "The words wouldn't come" as Huck ponders the question of what to do with Jim. Yet language flows so readily once he has launched his tale of smallpox and early bereavement that one is left to wonder whether the tale is told for Jim's benefit, or if Jim is simply an excuse for the telling of the ingenious tale. As detail gives way to ever-more-marvelous detail, it is perhaps noteworthy that the inventions of Huck exceed his reflections about Jim in a ratio of approximately two-to-one.

In 1884 Mark Twain saw fit to connect this episode to the spirit of *Tom Sawyer.* "Readers who have met Huck Finn before (in 'Tom Sawyer')," he wrote in *Century Magazine,* "will not be surprised to note that whenever Huck is caught in a close place and is obliged to explain, the truth gets well crippled before he gets through." But, as Walter Blair drily observes, this is decidedly not a reader's recollection, since "actually, Huck did not show this skill in *Tom Sawyer.*"[6] And that the ambiguity of the episode troubled Mark Twain when he wrote the passage eight years earlier in 1876 is evidenced by the way all the voices of *Huckleberry Finn* now fall silent. Having progressed so promisingly through the summer of 1876, the manuscript breaks off after only a few more pages. Although Victor Doyno has demonstrated that the break came after Huck found a temporary home with the Grangerfords, rather than with the smash-up of the raft as had previously been supposed, the fact remains that Mark Twain seems to feel growing uncertainty about his new project. He confesses to Howells that he likes it "only tolerably well"; with a touch of exasperation he adds that he may possibly "pigeonhole or burn" it.[7]

I conjecture that the reasons for his frustration become apparent if we

---

in the book, were actually inserted after the manuscript was completed. I shall turn in section V of this essay to the possible significance of these last-minute additions.

slightly recast an event that occurred back in St. Petersburg at the very height of Huck's disillusionment. Let us suppose that as the game wound down that Saturday afternoon, Huck had observed that there were neither jewels nor A-rabs to be seen—and then added, *Tom, they were only little children, and we oughtn't to treat them so. Human beings can be awful cruel to one another.* This would amount to sound realistic evaluation. The children are indisputably there as jewels and A-rabs are not. In all likelihood they have been frightened and bewildered as Tom's robber gang broke up their picnic and chased them up the hollow. Finally, the sensitivity to their plight is expressed in terms that will seem very moving and appealing to us when Huck speaks them later.[8] But the impossibility of the scene is obvious. Coming this early in the narrative— and arising out of this particular context—the words would brand Huck a spoilsport and, what is worse, a party to the Sunday school crowd of Sid Sawyer and Willie Mufferson.

We thus arrive at what is at once a general awkwardness of realistic litera- ture and Mark Twain's specific dilemma. The problem needs to be expressed paradoxically. In a fiction—a made-up construct, a world wrought from the fertile imagination and words which the imagination devises—the realist chal- lenges on the grounds of its moral and social dubiousness the fine art of human fiction-making. But for such a procedure to be effective, the fiction which re- bukes fiction-makers must somehow itself be kept lively and interesting as a fiction. Otherwise, the whole business soon degenerates into tedious, heavy- handed copybook maxims, of the "Know Thyself" variety. Otherwise, no mat- ter how outrageous or downright destructive their craftsmanship may be, those who re-create the world in their imaginations will seem aesthetically and mor- ally superior to the mere dullards upon whom the re-creations are inflicted.

This is an issue confronted more or less explicitly by all writers of the real- istic novel. And through the first 400 manuscript pages of his new narrative Mark Twain has not yet got hold of a way to resolve the paradox satisfactorily. Fresh from a book which documented the folly of turning reality into a game (of privileging words over world), he is now preoccupied with inverting the process. But when the game has been abandoned, the players rejected, what is left to write about except dreary, ugly, often unfunny reality? With the best will in the world, therefore, Mark Twain has shifted an always uneasy allegiance away from Tom Sawyer, only to find that Tom's features often displace Huck's, so that he is writing the adventures of Tom Sawyer all over again. Before the new book can be resumed, he will need to find a way not simply of making the games-people-play seem more corrupt (though that is part of it); he must turn some people's resistance to play into a more dramatic and genuinely moving experience.

## II

Ransom'd? What's that?
>                  —Ben Rogers to Tom in *AHF,* 10

What's a feud?
>                  —Huck to Buck Grangerford in *AHF,* 146

Nearly eight years later the completed *Huckleberry Finn* is prefaced by two comments from the explicit author. The first consists of Mark Twain's warning to "persons":

> Persons attempting to find a motive in this narrativee will be prosecuted; persons attempting to find a moral in it will be banished; persons attempting to find a plot in it will be shot.[9]

Criticism and reader-responses generally would suggest that very few persons have ever been heedful. So difficult is it to reconcile the warning with what we feel as the art—the organized fury—of the book, the presumption has to be that Mark Twain was winking when he made it.

If the first statement warns "persons" away, the second is an invitation to "readers." They are invited in to observe the various dialects of the old southwest that Mark Twain has assembled:

> the Missouri negro dialect; the extremest form of the South-Western dialect; the ordinary "Pike-County" dialect; and four modified varieties of this last. The shadings have not been done in a haphazard fashion, or by guess work; but painstakingly and with the trustworthy guidance and support of personal familiarity with these several forms of speech.
>
> I make this explanation for the reason that without it many readers would suppose that all these characters were trying to talk alike and not succeeding.[10]

This time the statement has received a good deal of respectful attention. Although actual demonstration does not typically go much beyond showing that Jim's speech is different from Huck's and (most of the time; as we have seen, not always) Huck does not sound like Tom, the assumption has been that in specifying many speech patterns Mark Twain points to the variety of the book and also writes one more chapter in his career-long love affair with vernacular language. Perhaps, though, one wink begets another. An alternative view of language discovers that, despite doing their utmost not to reveal it, most of the characters do succeed in talking exactly alike. They sound the same because they use words in exactly the same way to encompass a single shared end. In the unity created by their clacking tongues lie the motive and moral and (above all) the multitude of plots which kept the narrative going after, in 1876, it had seemed to come close to floundering.[11]

*Words, words, words.* Widely separated in space and time, the answers to two questions perfectly illustrate *how* language is used along the River.

(1) "I don't know," says Tom to Ben Rogers. (*AHF,* 10.) But his disclaimer notwithstanding, it is of course wholly untrue that Tom has no idea what "ransom" means. He possesses the liveliest sense of its significance in books and oral traditions where "they do it." All Tom himself cannot do is pin the term down to anything that happens—or ever will happen—in his own actual experience. Ransoming is as much a foreign importation into St. Petersburg as are "jewels" and "A-rabs," Miss Watson's "Heaven" and "Hell," or Pap's "Angel of Death." No matter, though. By saying it impressively Tom can generate experience out of "ransom." If the word is of no value to him in designating or interpreting or evaluating reality, he can fetch from the sound and the bookish definition a series of games that will give considerable pleasure to his followers. Tom is as always the primitive magician: not so much of the kind that turn the world into words; rather, one who speaks the word and thereby successfully re-creates the world anew.

(2) "Why where was you raised?" snaps Buck to Huck thirteen chapters later, responding with no hesitation whatsoever. Buck is able to deal with "feud" more intimately than Tom with "ransom" because the historical circumstances of feuding do, after all, surround him daily and hourly in the real world. Yet like Tom, Buck is unprepared to make the real world elucidate the term. He cannot say precisely when the feud began ("It started thirty years ago, or som'ers along there"). He cannot motivate it ("land I reckon maybe—I don't know"). Nor finally can he say who shot first ("laws, how do *I* know? It was so long ago"), or why the slaughter continues. For a Huck who has been fired on (if not exactly shot at) and is intent on getting his bearings in reality, Buck can do no better than another, later exemplar of abstractness and redundancy: A feud is a feud is a feud . . . is a feud. (*AHF,* 146.)

The transition from "ransom" to "feud" underscores two important points about *Huckleberry Finn.* The first is that, throughout the book, points of departure and destinations are not so much two different places as one place called by two different names. Back there and right here (then and now) are linked by the fact that a new arrival finds in progress the same pattern of activities which were going on when the traveler set out. The reenactment, however, is likely to take a darker, bleaker turn than the original, which is a second crucial fact about the narrative.

Unless we fret for the little children, Tom's miracle with ransom did no real harm. Indeed, if this were all to be heard from Tom in the book, his agile tongue might actually be thought of as socially useful in the sense of creating a pastime for bored adolescents. By contrast, Buck's act of transubstantiation is his death warrant. When Huck finds him a few days later, mutilated and dying in the shallows of the River, Buck is of course the victim of "feud," a word he can neither define nor explain. More to the point, however, he is victimized by a momentum that takes over when words are uprooted from things so that flesh-and-blood turns out to be only what flesh-and-blood is called. Had he been named Smith, Jones, Finn or Clemens, Buck might well have died peacefully in bed as a wise old patriarch. As it is he dies, simply and solely, because at an unfortunate point in space and time he bears the unfortunate appellation "Grangerford."[12]

*Words on the Mississippi.* Between them, the specific actions of frivolous Tom and self-destructive Buck Grangerford encapsulate the meaning of Huck's down River journey. Basically, it is an expedition into noise. The power to portray visually, so often attributed to Huck, is most apparent when he is showing us landscapes and River scenes, the interiors of rooms, or crowd behavior. With respect to close-ups he relies much less on the visible shapes and textures of experience. Who can describe Boggs of Bricksville, when aside from his "red face" Boggs remains only a silhouette? Or how distinguish King from Duke except to say that one is seventy and bald, the other hirsute and much younger? These are figures meant to be heard rather than seen. Their open mouths reveal them. And each is all mouth, clamorously in search of a willing ear to listen.

But noise bespeaks chaos, whereas sounds on the River are nothing if not organized. Hence the better way of defining the journey is to call it an expedition into *kitsch,* and into the reification of *kitsch.* Without always intending to do so—or at least being conscious of his intentions—Huck inscribes in the text he writes the shrill texts, the strident and overstuffed art-forms which are produced by culture. But, like the interiors of The House Beautiful in *Life on the Mississippi,* the forms have become so rigidified, so stylized and replicative, that culture may properly be styled a production of them. It is a paradox of surpassing strangeness that Huck travels through an ill-mannered world which is everywhere stifled and warped and deadened by mannerisms.

(1) Grangerfords. At the Grangerfords he reads from a sheaf of poems with one subject. He looks at several drawings with variations of the same caption. Among the furnishings in the parlor, he lingers over two chipped, plaster-of-Paris statuettes. Calling the statuettes "parrots," he defines the key characteristic of his hosts and their neighbors, which is a mindless obsession with parroting the single words Shepherdson/Grangerford. When a Shepherdson and a Grangerford do presently try to communicate as human beings, life might have

been enriched by a wedding in the parlor. But "art" is dominant; and the prospective marriage of Sophia and Harney only results in a blood-letting, a long day's mutilation in which the fantasies and captions of Emmeline's art are released into the light of everyday.

(2) Bricksville. Not only does Boggs come unaccompanied by distinguishing physical qualities; he rides up to Bricksville with a conspicuous lack of any discernible motives. Though a long-standing quarrel must be presumed, all we know—all Huck can tell with certainty—is that Boggs's mouth flies open, and out rolls "everything he could lay his tongue to." (*AHF*, 184.) In the scene before us, then, it is as if the old man were pronouncing some obscure ceremony, as pointless as it is terrible. Mocking Christian liturgy, Boggs "speaks the word only"—and loudly. And incantatory language rises up to become his executioner.

While Boggs lies dying, suffocated beneath the Word on his chest, the foreground is suddenly occupied by one of the most amazing figures in the book. Confined to three words—" 'Boggs,' " " 'Bang' " "again 'Bang' "; the plosives seem to ricochet off his lips like bullets—he is nonetheless a model of expressiveness as his "crooked handled cane marked the places on the ground where Boggs stood and where Sherburn stood." Whatever the nature of his ordinary relations with the community, this figure clearly functions now in the role of priest and bardic poet. Through his stylized gestures, the murder is heightened into ritual-art, and immortalized ("the people . . . said he done it perfect; said it was exactly the way it all happened"). At the end he is rewarded like a poet-performer of the oral tradition ("as much as a dozen people got out their bottles and treated him.") (*AHF*, 187–88.) It might even be alleged that through his dumb show he purifies the language of the tribe, since in consequence of his actions the fury of a lynch mob is unleashed.

So, what spares Colonel Sherburn from the mob's anger? Not a weapon; even if they were loaded with buckshot, he has but two bullets. Nor, despite attempts of recent criticism to treat it seriously, can safety lie in Sherburn's speech to the mob. Examined closely, this harangue dissolves into a tissue of clichés, meanderings, and self-contradictions; the suspicion grows that it is here for Huck to repeat word-for-empty-word not because much sense is made by Sherburn, but precisely because it is not. Thus deliverance must derive from the same force which wrought the murder in the first place. Victim (who bespoke his death), assassin (who killed ten or fifteen minutes before he said he would\*\*) join the performer with the crooked cane as aspects of a single com-

---

\*\* " 'I'm tired of this,' " says Sherburn on page 184, " 'but I'll endure it till one o'clock. Till one, mind and no longer. If you open your mouth against me only once, after that time, you can't travel

posite character. They are ironically akin to the legendary "jar" of Wallace Stevens, in that, taking "dominion everywhere," each imposes structure, artistic order, even a certain sort of ceremoniousness (rigid and shapely as a brick) upon what would otherwise be the most sprawling and slovenly village in the narrative. But they are likewise artists of the ugly. All have assumed autonomy in a world where semiotic flourishes—the extravagances of word and deed, of signs and symbols—have displaced any respect or need (or wish) for the objective truth of things.[13] (We will want to notice, since no one else does, Boggs's 16-year-old daughter, cowering alone and frightened in one corner of almost all this sequence.)

(3) King and Duke. Moved along by the inexorable logic of repetition and degradation, the raft acquires just south of the Grangerfords and keeps on board until just north of the Phelps plantation the two artists without peer in Huck's presentation. Wordsmiths (actors and jour printers) by trade, this pair can at a moment's notice use their stocks-in-trade to be rechristened King, Duke, pirate, Romeo and Juliet, Edmund Kean, Wilks—or whatever else the particular occasion warrants. There seems virtually no end to the literary forms which disappear into their fertile vocabularies; within the space of thirty or forty pages, sermon, drama, bill of sale, funeral service, eulogy, and book of etiquette are all specified. And with each disappearance some rich tradition dies. History is reduced to burlesque, religion to rant, art to a nonsensical jumble of misquotations, any act of communication to the utterance of a well-wrought diddle. Why, on the lips of these two even wordlessness serves as a trick, as witness the furious mouthings and "goo-goos" of the Duke-become-deaf mute at the Wilks plantation.

Yet the real horror of the King and Duke lies not in what they do, which is frequently entertaining, or even in the fact that, chameleon-like, they have no proper names and seem long since to have lost all touch with who they really are, which is absurd. Horror derives from another of those curious twinnings in the book, this time a complicity that binds tricksters to the tricked. As they "swarm" and "mill" (to use Huck's favorite verbs for crowd behavior), it grows evident that the citizens of the Mississippi Valley yearn to be taken in. They thrive on the spectacle, even when they half suspect it has been enacted at their expense. They are enthralled by a bogus and florid style, even knowing that the language is meant to demean and insult them. And when in rare moments

---

so far but I will find you.'" But "about fifteen minutes" until one Boggs reappears, and "after about five or ten minutes later" (that is, at ten or five minutes *before* one) Sherburn takes aim. In the well-organized hubbub, it is easy to forget that Sherburn's mastery of Boggs and Bricksville rests upon his being the master of verbal deceit, which is to say a liar.

the awful truth does come bursting in, the gentry's best revenge consists of inflicting their embarrassment upon other members of the gentry class. "'We are sold—mighty badly sold,'" says a Bricksville gentleman following the first performance of "The Royal Nonesuch":

> 'But we don't want to be the laughing-stock of this whole town, I reckon, and never hear the last of this thing as long as we live. *No*. What we want is to go out of here quiet, and talk this show up, and sell the *rest* of the town! Then we'll all be in the same boat.' (*AHF,* 197.)

Among the villages and at the small plantation houses, the self-styled good people of the Valley are powerless to resist their confidence-men guests. What needs to be added, however, is that nowhere have they so much lost their identities as revealed that, together with the predators, they have no authentic identities to lose.

To watch them drift and succumb is to perceive that one of the shrewdest commentaries ever written on *Huckleberry Finn* appears in an essay published seven years after the book, and entitled "Fenimore Cooper's Literary Offenses." Mark Twain's purpose in the essay is not just to assail Cooper's badness as a writer; the aim is also to explain the badness on the grounds of a failure of vision. Cooper's problem was that he would not, probably could not, *see* the real world. Reality became bearable to him only if it could be looked at as through "a glass eye darkly."[14] Consequently, Cooper could not *say* the world either. In what he wrote, either ordinary, familiar human experiences never appear at all; or an attempt is made to reproduce them, but, imagined rather than observed, they come in the form of the rhetorical excesses that Mark Twain cites in the closing paragraphs of his essay. These include Cooper's euphemisms and malapropisms, his half-words and circumlocutions, his fondness for a style that is at once outsized and outrageous—that can do any and everything except record the truth.

And however merely ridiculous in Cooper, the situation parallels what has happened all too literally in the Mississippi Valley. Unable to endure the sight of themselves as real people engaged in commonplace activities in lifelike settings, the citizens of the Valley have sought to scale their lives upward through the verbal enhancement of experience. They are afoot with a vision of their own significance. But existence in a world of fictions means both manipulating reality and being manipulated by superior fiction-makers as they, in turn, set out to manipulate the real. There is no end to the wilderness of mirrors, or to the human deformities which are reflected therein. Cooper's literary offenses have turned into the pretenses of a sick culture.

*Of Parrots and a Book.* The situation of Huck is strikingly akin to that of Jim

Baker in "The Blue Jay Yarn." He has fled dehumanizing voices with the same fervor that caused Baker to shut out the spectacle of corrupt humanity. But as flight brought Baker to the mindless and inane chatter of blue jays, so by the same principle of repetition Huck is delivered to other voices and other ruses which are but the duplicates of those he sought to leave behind. Small wonder, then, that having begun with parrots, his visitations draw to a close with the presentation of a book.

"Lay your hand on the book and swear it," insists Joanna Wilks. She wants testamentary evidence for the days and ways of Alphonso in London. Given the kitchen setting, a collection of recipes would have served the purpose. Better choices might have been an edition of Bullfinch, a copy of *Quentin Durward*, or one of the Leatherstocking tales. The Bible or a hymnal seem distinct possibilities. But with an eye on the world through which Huck has passed, the implied author lets Joanna challenge him with the one true repository of all human wisdom.

And with a backward glance at the same world, the recipient rises to the challenge. "I see," says Huck, "it warn't nothing but a dictionary, so I laid my hand on it and said it." (*AHF,* 224.)

## III

> To live means to participate in dialogue:
> to ask questions, to heed, to respond, to agree and so forth.
> —Mikhail Bakhtin[15]

> It was awful thoughts and awful words.
> —Huck to himself, 271

Words seem worthless—worse than worthless. Springing so passionately from the human minds that devise them, bouncing with such easy alacrity off the human lips that frame them, they loop back to express the subject, never outward to secure valuable, meaningful subject-to-object relationships. In terminology furnished by Mikhail Bakhtin, words in Huck's experience are the instruments of confirmed monologists, who would take reality into their heads and vocabularies, bring to bear their private authority upon the real, deal with "out there" as if it were merely a collection of their wills and whims and wishes. Consequently the dictionary, with its stress upon definition and usage, is a book without virtue, one ideally well suited to sanctify the fraudulent verbal construct.

But has Huck Finn, who acts out this knowledge, earned an insight which is worthy (in various ways) of Rousseau and Wittgenstein, of Lacan and Bakhtin? He is a refugee from fictions, yet chiefly the ones that threatened to dissipate his personality by taking him for their subject. Safely removed from these extravagances he has often seemed as lively of wit, and hence nimble of vocabulary, as any other fiction-maker. With regard to Joanna's book the complicated fact is that he belittles the dictionary only as the result of having first drawn liberally upon its resources to construct his fantasy of "Alphonso" consorting at church with "King William." Granted his purpose is always more serious than Tom Sawyer's, his motives immensely less self-serving than those of the King and Duke, is there anything in the text inscribed by Huck which grants him the moral authority to rebuke a text-making world?

*Things on the Mississippi.* The first truly grave crisis of conscience in the narrative occurs in Chapter 15, well before the raft reaches Cairo. With it, there enters into the book a dramatic counterpoint, the first fully realized corrective to fiction-making. Fresh from triumphs with "speculation" and a rattlesnake and (in the book we now have) perhaps a good bit nettled by the failure to bring off "Solomon" and the "French language," Huck sets out to persuade Jim that their long night in the fog was passed only inside Jim's dream. It is a story brilliantly executed, and credulously received—until Jim does something not hitherto attempted by any other of the St. Petersburg cast of characters. He does not, in the first instance, call into question what someone says happened, or what is alleged to be out there. He asserts what did happen, by drawing upon out there for verification:

> Jim looked at the [leaves and rubbish and smashed oar] and then looked at me and back at the trash again. He had got the dream so fixed in his head that he couldn't seem to shake it loose and get the facts back into its place again right away. But when he did get the thing straightened around he looked at me steady without ever smiling, and says:
> "What do dey stan' for. I's gwyne to tell you." (*AHF,* 105.)

The shift in emphasis here is considerable. For the first time we are not merely hearing from a voice as it complains about how words distort reality. Rather, this voice speaks out of a concern to locate the place and the contents of the real. The speaker argues that the things they name stand prior to the naming words, and that the power of things ought therefore to take precedence over word-magic. A formulation of *as in, so out* (with all the gratifications, but also the dissatisfactions which it can evoke) has thus given way to the argument *as out, so it should be within.*

No doubt it is appropriate that the new and proper ordering should first be explicitly enunciated by Jim. This confirms the close ties between the man and the underlying rhythms of reality, a connection which Huck had noted earlier on Jackson's Island when he spoke of how Jim "knowed all the signs. He said he knowed everything." (*AHF*, 59.) Also, of course, it helps to pull Jim out of the blackface routines of fortune-telling and hairballs that had been imposed upon him in the slaveholding community. Nevertheless, the beneficiary of the insight is Huck. Inside his head as he listens a curtain of stereotypes lifts, and abruptly, as never previously, Huck comes face to face with the concrete, specifiable fact of his traveling companion:

> It made me feel so mean I could almost kissed his foot. . . . It was fifteen minutes before I could work myself up to humble myself to a nigger; but I done it, and I warn't ever sorry for it afterward, neither. (*AHF*, 105.)

The trouble with verbal stunts is that they maximize human differences. They are monologic enterprises, in which the self speaks, while the other has utility only as audience or as subject-matter or as a source of entertainment. Tricks of language thus turn life into a drama of actor/acted upon: I-it. But listening to Jim's dialogue with leaves and the broken oar, Huck takes a first tentative step toward the dismantling of self which Bakhtin regards as crucial to the "dialogic imagination." Huck sees Jim's needs, heeds them, learns from them, apologizes to them, because he recognizes that they mirror needs of his own. In a moment which prefigures what will happen in Chapter 31, he has glimpsed behind the differences which are created by language the human likeness: a kinship of I-You.

*Quiet on the Mississippi.* Near the beginning, while the raft was somewhere north of St. Louis, Huck reflected on the wonder and also the sense of community which can come from participating in the real world. "It was kind of solemn drifting down the big, still river," he thinks, "laying on our backs looking up at the stars, and we didn't ever feel like talking loud, and it warn't often that we laughed—only a kind of low chuckle." (*AHF*, 78.) Almost at once, though, this moment of serenity is lost. Let their mouths but open, and Jim and Huck are soon as divided by the words they speak as, in Huck's anecdote, speakers of French are divided from the speakers of English. The truth is that bickering and hard feelings accompany them virtually every mile of the way downriver, until the reconciliation in Chapter 15. And then, as we have seen, Huck is thrust back into the game by the ambiguous action he performs off Cairo in the next chapter, and Mark Twain (as if suspecting that low chuckles alone were not enough to sustain the story) soon abandons his manuscript.

Yet it is extraordinary how the sounds of silence can again become palpable and meaningful in the noisy story Mark Twain resumes. Between the hysteria of feuding and the violent exchanges at Bricksville, Jim and Huck enter upon that tranquil period when (as Huck thinks) "the days and nights . . . slid along

so quiet and smooth" and "it was lovely to live on a raft." Now the only dis-
tractions come from a distance, in the form of "jumbled up voices" whose
thoughts and contents are no longer distinguishable. And on the raft all mean
strutting and fretting cease, subdued either to idle chatter or to the collaborative act (one is tempted to call it the practice of "negative capability") in which,
largely unmindful of themselves as egos, two speakers concentrate on "the sky
up there, all speckled with stars" and engage in lively, unresolved debates about
"whether they was made or just happened." From having started out with no
destination in view, the travelers seem carried along by the raft to an entirely
new order of being. Their relationship does not, however, rest upon the familiar romantic notion of two merging into one; it is not the drama of $1 \times 1$ (to
use a title of e. e. cummings's) or of Emerson's "me" accepting and then assimi-
lating the "not me." Instead, it is made rich and vital by the way the two members are different and know it, but can yet be joined as two together by the
respect each has learned for the values and attitudes—the integrity and sepa-
rateness—of the other. Huck and Jim have turned an aggressive monologism,
where someone speaks and someone else is merely expected to listen, into the
interplay of dialogue. Clearly, therefore, both have traveled not beyond any
need for the dictionary, but beyond the usage of the dictionary as it has been
exercised elsewhere on the River.[16]

But they have not of course passed beyond the power of conventional usage
to reach out and affect their lives. For along the banks the voices are like Sirens
of the Mississippi, never truly silent, only biding their time to entrap and cling
in one particular way. *Eeny—meeney—miney—mo,* says Mrs. Judith Loftus, in
concert with Miss Watson and an assortment of slave traders and bounty hunt-
ers. Come join us in a feud we're putting on, say the Grangerfords, and let our
household slaves attend to your needs in between times. "Fact is," says the
King, "I reckon we'd come to consider him *our* nigger." (*AHF,* 272.) Suddenly
we understand that it is not romantic flamboyance alone which medleys the
voices of the River. They are cued as well by a point of view, a shared impulse,
a single consuming subject. All aspire to the body-and-soul ownership of other
persons, just as at the plantation houses the masters possess body-and-soul the
human chattel out back. Slavery is their Master Plot. Born of the Word—propa-
gated, defined, defended, advertised, sanctified, spoken monologically through
words—slavery is itself the word (the concept) that flows outward to engender
the other masquerades and impersonations of a plot-loving culture. Slavery
provides them with the leisure to conspire; it images back to them the end of
the game, the sheer exercise of personal power, which each aspires to.[17]

Thus "slavery" leaps from the mouth of the populace to end the tranquility
on the raft. And by the sound and the sense of the dictionary definition of

"slavery" Huck is drawn inexorably to his encounter with the real world in Chapter 31.

*Chapter 31.* It is fully three-fifths dramatic monologue, a matter of Huck's thinking or speaking aloud to himself. Mark Twain called the chapter the triumph of a "sound heart" over the "deformed conscience" of River society. Others have found in it the high point of a novel which is a great language experiment.[18] What remains is to put the three points together. Then we see that the heart triumphs because for three incredible, breathtaking pages the monologist, Huck, experiments with language in its various usages—and learns how to use words greatly or with dialogic force.

(1) "The words wouldn't come" when, torn between loyalty to Jim and doing his civic duty, Huck tries to pray. As was the case near Cairo, Jim here exists as an idea, one presence among many competing presences (Tom, Miss Watson, society, God) speaking chorically inside Huck's head. And the enormity of sorting out the idea, of getting the emphasis right, of shutting off the chorus renders Huck mute—as was the case off Cairo.

(2) Words come to mind readily enough, though, as Huck next picks up the stub of a pencil and writes to Miss Watson:

> . . . your runaway nigger Jim is down here two mile below Pikesville, and Mr. Phelps has got him and will give him up for the reward if you send. (*AHF,* 269.)

Now Jim is Huck's subject matter: the topic of a lucid and orderly commercial transaction which would make Judge Thatcher proud. But the addition of a complimentary close, the same one that will actually appear later in the book, makes clear the fictive and monologic nature of what is written. With the flourish of "Yours truly" Huck would have added his own small contribution to the Supreme Fiction of American history. He would be truly theirs, a part of their monologue or collective fantasy, just as in the throes of creativity be belonged to his audience, far more than to Jim, off Cairo.

(3) An aesthetic for literary realism (and not coincidentally a basis for human dialogues) was stated succinctly and with great force by George Orwell in a famous and memorable essay entitled "Politics and the English Language." "What is above all needed," Orwell wrote,

> is to let the meaning choose the word, and not the other way around. In prose, the worst thing you can do with words is to surrender to them. When you think of a common object, you think wordlessly, and then, if you want to describe a thing you have been visualizing, you hunt around until you find the exact words that seem to fit it.[19]

Philosophically, epistemologically, it is very difficult to take this view seriously, as Orwell's warmest admirers have been quick to admit.[20] There seems scant evidence that out there furnishes the vocabulary which distinguishes "card" from "apple" ("bear" from "bath," "poison" from "privy") or any of these from "blobs of matter" and "it's." But if realism is naive, what might the alternatives be? As *1984* demonstrates, the counter-presumption that language defines life can result in the loss of all sense of personal or historical continuity. Because someone says so, today's truths collapse into the void from whence they will emerge tomorrow in the guise of falsehoods. Through the fiat of thought and word, the personal identity which a moment ago seemed so fixed and stable is already being erased into a set of radically new features. The alternatives to *as out, so in* are not just Newspeak and Big Brother; more fundamentally, they are the withdrawal from reality—the surrender of world to words; the formulation *as in, so out*—by which Newspeak is created and the tyranny of Big Brother made possible.***

Reentering Chapter 31 for the third and last time, Jim comes neither as an idea in the mind nor subject matter on paper. He enters as memory, an occasion for Huck to review the whole history of their downriver journey. Memory, however, quickens into the tangible, the immediate. Huck's present-tense verbs are insistent: "I see him" and again "I see him." As surely as if he stood there physically, Jim arises from mind and from letters-on-paper to become objective meaning, in need of being interpreted, forcing a response. And what dead leaves and a broken oar once did for him, Jim does for Huck. First, Huck finds the need to communicate irresistible: "But somehow I couldn't seem to strike no places to harden me against him, but only the other kind." Then, shaped by the fact, chosen because they adapt to and are verified by the fact which preceded them, the words come forth in a natural, spontaneous rush:

> I was a trembling, because I'd got to decide, forever, betwixt two things, and I knowed it. I studied a minute, sort of holding my breath, and then says to myself "All right, then, I'll go to hell." . . . (*AHF,* 270–71.)

***

\*\*\* Consider O'Brien, explaining how the world works to Winston Smith toward the close of *1984:*

> You believe that reality is something objective, external, existing in its own right. . . . But I tell you, Winston, that reality is not external. Reality exists in the human mind and nowhere else. (228.)

We might call it "O'Brien's disease," an affliction of the modern totalitarian state—and a set of symptoms which Mark Twain remarkably anticipates in *Tom Sawyer,* in *Connecticut Yankee,* and in the proto-totalitarian tyrannies of *Huckleberry Finn.* It is a cure for the disease—a capacity for responding and speaking each to each dialogically, rather than through private conceptions of one another—that Huck and Jim move toward in Chapter 15, make more secure in Chapter 19, and seem to have obtained completely in Chapter 31.

*Somebody.* In the ninth book of the *Odyssey* it seems sheer bravado for Odysseus to give his true name and address to the Cyclops. How foolish, we want to think, when the disguise of "Nobody" (the linguistic trick of non-being) had served him so well. On the other hand, perhaps Odysseus had no real choice in the matter. Departing as "Nobody," he would ironically have left the place as just one more Cyclops—who being all body are from the standpoint of mind and soul, from the perspective of being truly and fully human, just nobodies at all.

Since they travel light, the companions on the raft obviously carry along none of the complex burdens of the epic hero. They left St. Petersburg as nobodies, in preference to being the everybodies of everybody which, whether it was psychic or literal (socially cultivated or legally sanctioned), was the role that a life of servitude had thrust on each one. Who will doubt, though, that the reciprocal, dialogic relationship between two presences in Chapter 31 endows both with mind and soul, fleshes caricature out to character, and thereby turns nobody and everybody into two full-fledged, fully entitled somebodies?

*Next on the Mississippi.* But of course somebody does not bring the book to a close. As a matter of fact, the voice of somebody is scarcely even allowed to finish the chapter.

## IV

TOM: What? Why Jim is ——.
HUCK: . . . don't forget to remember that you don't know nothing about him, and I don't know nothing about him.
HUCK (*of Jim*): he couldn't see no sense in the most of it, but he allowed we was white folks and knowed better than him, so he was satisfied. . . .
AUTHOR (*in Chapter the Last*): Yours truly . . . (*AHF,* 284, 309, 362.)

The troubling last fifth of *Huckleberry Finn* presents a sick joke that is planned and staged from inside a tall tale. The joke and the tale are intimately connected, as effect to cause. Yet the voices which narrate them proceed out of two very different sources. A reader's task is to determine which source is which, and to distinguish one from the other even while maintaining their close causal relationship.

*The sick joke.* It comes to pass as a result of the medleying of several voices.

*Tom Sawyer* is Master of the joke. The word he might have said was "free." By carefully suppressing it, Tom creates an ordeal in which Jim is bitten by rats and spiders, fed a stone pie that smashes his teeth, hounded like an animal across the swamps, and returned at last to be cuffed, cursed, and otherwise humiliated by the adults at the Silas Phelps plantation. Tom thus demonstrates that, for all his youthful exuberance, he hates life unless it can be executed as a game. And he shows that a world of play may be plucked as readily from the magic of words left unspoken as from the ones which are, though once the game is underway the spoken word is soon reinvested with all its talismanic force:

TOM: Gimme a caseknife.

HUCK: He had his own, but I handed him mine. He flung it down. . . .

TOM: Gimme a *caseknife.*

HUCK: I didn't know what to do—but then I thought. I scratched around amongst old tools, and got a pick-axe and give it to him, and he took it and never said a word.

He was always just that particular. Full of principle.

(*AHF,* 307.)

*Huck Finn* is Accessory in the joke and eventually a co-Conspirator. By remembering to forget, he not only lays aside the promise he spoke to his readers at the end of Chapter 15: "I didn't do him no more mean tricks"; what is more to the point, he is so little able to "see Jim before [him] all the time" that he must "harden" his heart with a veritable chorus of "we's" as he joins Tom in Chapter 37 for the preparation of the witch's pie. Huck is thus made to demonstrate that in the hysteria of play it is possible both to humor Tom Sawyer by converting case knives to pick axes—and to emulate Tom's world-view by transmuting I-you back into the baser drama of I-it. Huck also exemplifies the fact that although the text he inscribes often seems to involve total recall, he himself has one of the shortest memories in all of literature.

*Jim* is a thrice-over Victim of the joke. Subjected to all manner of physical abuse, he is likewise brought face-to-face with his deepest anxiety, which as he had explained in Chapter 15 is the dread of being played with gratuitously. The chief indignity that comes to him, however, lies in the way he contributes to the game by sinking, without question or complaint, into the role of a minstrel burr head. Like that of Huck, the character of Jim is flattened out by the joke to the point of becoming oblivious even to itself. Professing satisfaction, he is made to demonstrate only that he ought to be suffering because of the joke, not that he necessarily is.

But Tom, Huck, and Jim are but figments of an imagination which was introduced by name in the second sentence, and remained thereafter to select and organize the episodes of the book.[21] And say what one will about "Mr. Mark Twain's" handiwork in the last ten chapters—say it turns character to caricature, goes on far too long, is cruel to the point of perversity—still the handiwork is funny. The heart may need hardening, but it would be dead indeed not to laugh at the sheer manic determination underlying Tom's ingenuity; at the confusions of Aunt Sally and the total bewilderment of moony old Uncle Silas; at brains spilling down Huck's forehead; at the sideshow of rats, thefts, assorted vermin, and alarm bells in the night; perhaps even at the absurdity of Jim's situation, greatly enhanced by the way Jim is kept more bemused than truly bothered. It is as though having turned off the laughter-machine in Chapter 31, Mark Twain (the explicit author, now) winds up his toys, turns the sound back on full blast, settles back mellowly, and (anticipating Philip Traum) says look at the enhumored fools and be entertained.

Or this is the case anyhow, unless (unlike the characters who never listen to her monologue), one finds merit in Old Sister Hotchkiss's contention that the world is haunted: that there are "sperits" in it. Then it might be demonstrated that the explicit author, Mark Twain, creates the voices of the joke in response to another voice which he had already heard.

*The tall tale.* If motivated by nostalgia we were to take a plane to Hannibal on the west or Missouri bank of the Mississippi River, we would find much memorabilia of St. Petersburg. There would be a plain, wooden house or two; at least one ancient burying ground; the bluffs honeycombed by caves south of town; the low-lying wharf area; and off in the distance the Illinois shoreline. But though all these might remind us of St. Petersburg, none would of course actually be St. Petersburg. Since the village and its people take substance only inside the imagination of Mark Twain, we could no more find the real place than hope to be conducted to a nearby cemetery, where we might linger at the tombs of Thomas Sawyer, Miss Watson, and Judge Thatcher, or the mounds of Huck Finn and Jim, the latter carefully segregated and with no surname given.

Nevertheless, with respect to one matter, our quest for the actual past might be fulfilled. The River would be there still, still called the Mississippi. And some peripheral changes notwithstanding, we could pause on the Hannibal wharf and watch the River moving along, flowing steadily from North to South just as it once flowed past Hannibal, rechristened St. Petersburg. Except that if this were our perception, it would be wholly different from the perception of the River which is encouraged in the narrative.

No premise of the book could be clearer, or more insistent. Names and faces change during the descent of the Mississippi. They change, however, to become reassembled as one group of characters, performing one set of highly stylized actions against the background of what amounts to one continuous setting. Thus, as from "ransom-to-feud" and the refrain "nigger, nigger" be-speak the frozen features of life on the River, so the respective rages of Pap Finn, Colonel Grangerford, Boggs and Sherburn are but the manifestations of a single emotion, while Miss Watson's pieties reappear in Emmeline's art and on the platitudinous lips of Mary Jane Wilks, and the chicaneries of the Duke and King look back to the simpler pastimes of Tom Sawyer at St. Petersburg, but are, in turn, reenacted word-for-word, deed-for-deed as the grossest cruel-ties in Tom's sick joke on Jim. The effect is everywhere a sense of déjà vu on the Mississippi. Looking and listening, we have invariably been there before. The only significant exception comes from those moments when Huck and Jim are carried by the River to the point of saying farewell to all that. Were it not for this brief interlude, the flow of the Mississippi would be better described as merely the illusion of flowing.

So, consider. By his own estimate, Huck travels eleven hundred miles from North to South. Along the way, on either riverbank, he floats past countless doors (hundreds of them, no doubt, even in 1845) where he might have paused to knock. And in the end the River delivers him to the one doorway (of all those hundreds) where Tom Sawyer is expected, so that Huck can be greeted as Tom and renamed Tom, and where (ceasing to speak with the voice of some-body) he falls at once under the spell of Tom's inflections and attitudes. It is preposterous—a coincidence so blatant (a "stretcher" stretched so far) as to seem unworthy of any novel, much less one that purports to present life real-istically. But as the blunt, matter-of-fact, take-it-for-granted tone indicates, the situation is also unassailably true. And tone, I believe, is of the essence. We are made to see that the roles finally assumed by Huck and Jim are not parcelled out to either in Tom Sawyer's imagination. At its most boorish, its steamy, fe-brile and overheated worst, the imagination of Tom could never have devised such a conclusion. Rather, the roles are the work of the one presence in the book which strictly speaking no one makes up. The River is indisputably, in-arguably of the real world. And the River on which Huck and Jim appear to move has all along caused them to move in place. It has subverted "away" and "toward," with all the connotative richness both terms acquire in the narrative, into the actual stasis of standing stock still.

Nor is this all. "'Goodness alive, AUNT POLLY,'" (*AHF,* 357) cries Tom to the figure in the doorway. And stepping through, she sets in motion a series of restitutions that are of a kind with the staples of traditional comedy. Huck, scurrying under the bed as "Tom," can now reemerge as Huck. Tom, lying on the bed as "Sid," can resume being Tom. The confusions of Aunt Sally and Uncle Silas are laid to rest, or if not quite resolved at least made productive of a "prayer meeting sermon" that "give [Uncle Silas] a rattling ruputation, because the oldest man in the world wouldn't a understood it." (*AHF,* 358.) Even Jim's freedom is officially confirmed, and while no mule is mentioned Tom bestows on him "forty dollars" and the promise of being "waltzed into town with a torchlight parade and brass band." (*AHF,* 360.) Then all are united in carnival, an endless round of self-congratulation and good will.

*But after such knowledge, what forgiveness?* More than Aunt Polly, blindly "looking over her spectacles," crosses the threshold of the Phelps plantation. What is brought downriver and deposited on the doorstep is the atmosphere of blind, fatuous, slaveholding, tale-telling, joke-playing St. Petersburg, that town of many monologues. It is as though no one had ever left home. The River has caused Huck and Jim to travel and travel, and come at last to a destination which differs from their point of departure only by the accident of being called by a new and different name.

*The Real World.* A precedent, almost certainly known to him, exists for Mark Twain's conception of the real world as an outrageous tall tale. One of the most peculiar features of *Candide* lies in the way no one is ever able to die and disappear. Again and again, Candide takes leave of acquaintances who seem bloodied and battered corpses, only to encounter each one of them later, strangely revivified and often preparing for a reenactment of the same ordeal. It is as if the book must practice a strict economy of characters, in order to demonstrate the eternal recurrence of violence and violation that lies at the core of human experience. The detachment of Voltaire, however, allows for a certain tentative adjustment to this ordering of things. Candide's last words are, "we must cultivate our garden."[22] But the addition of one more speaking voice to the concluding chapter of *Huckleberry Finn* makes it clear that no such reconciliation was available to Mark Twain.

If "yours truly" at the beginning (or end) of "Chapter the Last" represents Huck's farewell to his readers, in another, profounder way it is also an utterance which comes to us straight from the explicit author. Mark Twain has acquiesced to the curious bent of his imagination. He has said a mocking "yours truly" to the direction in which his narratives take him, the end to which he is always transported by any narrative he writes. Moreover, I believe that having said it, he proceeds to backtrack through the narrative so that the spirit and the object of acquiescence can be better integrated into the total book.[23]

## V

And the Lord said, Behold, the people is one, and they have all one language; and this they begin to do: and now nothing will be restrained from them, which they have imagined to do. Go to, let us go down, and there confound their language, that they may not understand one another's speech. So the Lord scattered them abroad from thence upon the face of all the earth. . . . Therefore is the name of it called Babel; because the Lord did there confound the language of all the earth: and from thence did the Lord scatter them abroad upon the face of all the earth.

—Genesis 11:5–9

. . . I'd noticed that Providence always did put the right words in my mouth, if I left it alone.

—Huck as Chapter 32 begins

From the researches of Walter Blair (confirmed in 1991 by Victor Doyno) we know that sometime during the summer of 1883, his project finished at last and soon to be delivered to the publisher, Mark Twain undertook extensive additions to the book. These consist of the last half of Chapter 12 and all of Chapters 13 and 14. Professor Blair has also shown that a bit later Mark Twain was urged to make a major cut from the manuscript:

> when he finished *Huckleberry Finn* and sent it to the publisher, the latter suggested that he shorten the text by omitting [Chapter 16, the episode that casts Huck as eavesdropper among the talkative crew of a large trading raft.] The author accepted the suggestion: no illustrations were prepared for this episode, and it never appeared in the novel during his lifetime.[24]

In terms of the Blair analysis, then, we find Mark Twain in the interesting situation of prolonging with one hand while with the other he substantially foreshortened his manuscript. Exactly what went on in his mind as he revised is beyond ascertaining. Yet I find it suggestive that he seems never to have contemplated dropping any of the material which he had added most recently.

Although Walter Blair (and Bernard DeVoto whom he quotes) seems to me wrong in supposing that the additions simply prepare for the introduction of the King and the Duke, I would agree that, looking back from the standpoint of the end of the book, the new sequence does also look ahead. It anticipates two terms that will increasingly fascinate Mark Twain as his deterministic philosophy turns darker and more systematically cheerless toward the end of the 1890s. The terms are "circumstance" and "temperament."[25] By "circumstance" Mark Twain means any of the infinite, sundry events that arise from the objective world to engage or to involve or to confront—perhaps the best generic term is "to waylay"—the self. The Rubicon, the American Civil War, the completed Garden of Eden are all examples of circumstance. (Since all come to pass as the result of a strict necessity, it will bear noting that none can be truly "circumstantial" in the dictionary sense of the term.) "Temperament" is a "servant to the Magician of Circumstance," in that qualities of temperament shape what any given "set of circumstances may and shall compel the [self] to do." (The verbs are instructive; again, nothing is left to chance, since "temperament is born with the self and remains unchangeable.") Thus Caesar's built-in courage caused him to meet the challenge of the Rubicon by crossing it. The temperament of General Grant required him to say, "I will fight it out on this line if it takes all summer," whereas temperament of another sort—that of Mark Twain, for instance—would not have been required to say it, and "sixteen temperaments like mine couldn't have made me do it." Finally, the tragedy at Eden derived from the fact that Adam and Eve had temperaments like butter, and hence were readily molded by temptation. Human history would have turned out differently, if only "Martin Luther and Joan of Arc" had been our first parents.[26]

"Circumstance" and "temperament," then, are the twins provocation and response. Linked by necessity—each can be only what it is—the twins share a Siamese configuration. Making all due allowances for shifting attitudes, it seems possible to say that the terms served Mark Twain very much as "luck" and "pluck" function for writers in the tradition of comedy. At all events, out of the terms, which are of course never used, he assembled the last-written episodes of *Huckleberry Finn*—mingled the terms freely, but also separated them in such a way that it is possible to distinguish between here the preponderance of circumstance, there the special influence of temperament.

(1) *Circumstance* and Temperament. Aside from its rather contrived name, the derelict steamboat in Chapter 12 neatly illustrates circumstance. It looms up out of the fog and darkness, fairly demanding responses from two surprised observers. For Jim, a fugitive dreaming of safety at Cairo, the wish understandably enough is to pass on by: "'I doan wan to go fool'n lang er no wrack. We's doin' blame' well, en we better let blame well alone, as de good book says. Like as not dey's a watchman on dat wrack.'" But Huck will have none of it. With Tom Sawyer suddenly on his mind, he recognizes that a failure to explore and rummage would amount to dishonoring Tom's memory. Board it he must; board it they do. Whereupon circumstance becomes unexpectedly complicated. (*AHF*, 80.)

For Jim was right. The derelict is inhabited, not by a watchman but by three river thugs who have delayed their departure on a skiff (the only means of egress from the sinking steamboat) while two of them plot to murder the third. Even as Huck overhears, Jim hisses to him the frightening news that their raft has drifted away. Ingenuity is called for; and weighing survival against scruples, Huck and Jim readily—without hesitation—"borrow" the skiff. Like Caesar on the near bank of the Rubicon, they have confronted circumstance, and passed safely (if perhaps not quite nobly) over to the other side.

Except that circumstance has a long reach. Secure on the raft, Huck falls to thinking of the three thugs they left to drown. In a discarded page of manuscript, his memory is especially pricked by the sudden intrusion into his consciousness of an image of the Widow Douglas.[27] So, when the fog lifts, he seeks out a real watchman, concocts a story, entices with a half-promised reward, and leaves it to the watchman to perform a rescue—and presumably make an arrest. It is all in vain, however. In his last glimpse of her, the wreck is floundering at the waterline. And if not actively callous, Huck's response at least takes the form of a highly visible shrug. He has done his best to make amends, and he reckons "if they could stand it, [he] could." The movement has thus been from a will to play, to momentary concern for the unwitting victims of playfulness, to an acceptance of the inevitable when the play goes sour. (AHF, 91.)

(2) Circumstance and *Temperament*. As it turns out, the *Walter Scott* was ideally well named. It housed a library, so that together with "seegars," "trinkets," and other truck the thugs had filled the skiff with a collection of stolen books. And now, somewhat improbably given his earlier responses to bookishness, Huck becomes a reader. Chapter 14 shows him "having a general good time . . . reading to Jim about kings and dukes and earls and such." (AHF, 93.) Though Jim listens with equanimity, the image of a half-informed white boy sharing tales of authority and subjection with his black, illiterate, round-eyed pupil will hardly be lost on us. Still, things go smoothly until the subject of King Solomon is broached.

What Huck knows about Solomon comes out of the Book, or from the Widow Douglas's reading of the Book. ("'Well, but he was the wisest man, anyway . . . the Widow told me so.'") Accordingly, he is unprepared for Jim's indignant response to a set of circumstances which he himself takes for granted:

> Now I want to ast you . . . what use is half a chile? I wouldn't give a dern for a million un um.

Least of all is he ready for the vehemence with which Jim attacks Solomon's morality:

> You take a man dat's got on'y one er two chillen: is dat man gwyne to be waseful o' chillen? No, he ain't; he can't 'ford to. *He* know how to value 'em. But you take a man dat's got 'bout five million chillen runnin' roun' de house, en it's diffunt. *He* as soon chop a chile in two as a cat. Dey's plenty mo'.

With only the Book and hearsay to fall back on, Huck turns off snappish as

Buck Grangerford ("'But I tell you, you don't get the point'") and he seeks accommodation by "let[ting] Solomon slide." (*AHF*, 94, 95–96, 96.) But the time for easy compromise has passed. Already divided by the words that conceptualize experience, Jim and Huck plunge recklessly on to a fateful encounter with their opposed conceptions of what words (any words) are meant to accomplish.

Jim, hearing of it for the first time, finds it intolerable to suppose that others should speak differently from himself:

"Why Huck doan de French people talk de same as we does?"

Very simply, his view is that all men, being men, need the bond of a common tongue if they are ever to communicate meaningfully or make themselves understood by one another. And granted that there are undeniable differences in human behavior, still these are the results of training and environment, rather than of language. Solomon's error, for example, came from "de way Sollermon was raised"; presumably the same thing could be alleged in extenuation of the murderous plottings of the thugs on the *Walter Scott*—or of Tom's use of "ransom." For intelligibility is the value by which Jim sets the greatest, the utmost store. Unless the man happened to be white, he would (as he says) "'take en bust over de haid'" any man who called him "'*Polly-voo-franzy.*'" (*AHF*, 97.)

Huck knows better. In his superior fashion he understands that men are created to be different and, what is more, that the differences are often defined by their use of many tongues:

"No, Jim you couldn't understand a word they said, not one."

He has, furthermore, a nice ear for distinguishing calling from saying:

"Shucks [*Polly-voo*] ain't calling you anything. It's only saying, do you know how to talk French?"

And this time, in his impatience, he draws the connection that links adventures to "dialogue." As "out there" defeated his attempts to secure a rescue, so by Jim's intransigence Huck is left equally balked and baffled. His only recourse is to stop "wasting words"—

you can't learn a nigger to argue. So I quit. (*AHF*, 97–98)

Suppose this busy, carefully orchestrated interlude belonged to the work-in-progress of 1876. Alternatively, suppose Mark Twain had added it directly after he resumed writing three years later. Either way, I believe, we would have good reason to think of it as contributing importantly to an initiation story. Taking advantage of a highly traditional kinship—the association between flowing

River and flowing Time—Mark Twain would have shown us what amounts to an episode in Time Now, one of the funniest in the book (Mark Twain would presently add parts of it to his stage repertoire), yet from the standpoint of developing character-relationships one of the bleakest and most frustrating. But up ahead lies possibility, the potentiality for change, the promise of Time Then. And despite many zigzags and digressions, Huck and Jim would be seen to move from Now to Then. As all unwittingly they work through to their aesthetic of realism, they come to sense that anterior to the words they speak and controlling the words as the only test of their adequacy, there is the stated order of actual, familiar, physical experience: of each other. Their movement forward would thus be shaped by a shared realization that unless the language they use has been attuned to this order, it can produce nothing except the tales and jokes—the clichés, fantasies, connivings, stereotypes—that fragment human life all down the River and that, for a long while, divide each traveler from himself and both from one another. Traveling along, Huck would lay aside the complacency and condescension he practiced in Chapters 12–13. Through listening to Jim's pawky stubbornness, he could be initiated (they would be initiated!) into the virtues of being good companions who see and say realistically and therefore can live side-by-side realistically. From a negative occasion, fraught with hostilities but also underlain by latent good will, they would push along to a positive outcome in Chapters 18–19. Moreover, Huck's willingness to risk hell, once the noisy intrusions of Duke and King subside in Chapter 31, would have had as its aim the determination to return to and maintain this outcome at whatever the cost.

Read in conjunction with the way the book ends, or as an afterthought to the ending, the interlude takes on very different implications. Criticism has duly noted that as a chunk of property, Jim has a vested (a temperamental) interest in believing that all men speak the same language. This would attest to his humanity, as opposed to leaving him a "thing" or an "object." And note has been taken of how as a slave-father whose children can be severed from him through the flourish of a pen on a bill-of-sale, Jim has good reasons for being wary of the wisdom of Solomon.[28] But of course these remain naive hopes only. The honors of logic and rightness—of cultural sophistication and historical accuracy and (if it matters) of theological truth—belong with Huck. And in making him right, Mark Twain crafts into Huck's mouth the sad truth of why the best moments on the raft must be transitory and *Huckleberry Finn* can never conclude as a narrative of initiation. We live, Huck shows, amidst ravages of the ruined Tower. Reality which might have made us all speakers of "English" or all speakers of "French" has instead, quite like Solomon the Wise, elected to divide "French"-talk from "English"-talk and hence array "French" against "English." The result is that while we polyglot humans are rarely silent, neither in the prodigality of sounds we make do we possess a true facility for communicating each to each. Or to work the irony of our enhumored lives the other way around and get the emphasis right: all of us are condemned to sound exactly alike since compartmentalized from one another and from our most familiar experiences by the words we create, each sooner or later but replicates the personal fiction in the one universalized process of fiction-making.

As Huck all unknowingly defines one aspect of the human predicament, simultaneously he discloses his own place within the confines of that unhappy circumstance. Often, when least appealing, the twin of Tom Sawyer, Huck is likewise an interesting case of twinned (perhaps it is tripled) temperamental impulses. There is his compassion, which reflects Sam Clemens's early wish that all aspects of experience might be drawn together in "love." Inimical to the compassion, however, are the two hallmarks of temperament which a more knowing Mark Twain soon distinguished as taking dominion everywhere. They are the will to play, and a stolid indifference to consequences when the play turns off harmful. In the episode of the *Walter Scott,* the three are combined hierarchically, with play and indifference easily being more assertive than the sensitivity that glimmers once across the page and is soon forgotten. To say that six chapters later this triad is still present in Huck in no way detracts from the tranquility and air of good fellowship that accompany his chats with Jim on the raft. To say, moreover, that the triad is functioning still in Chapter 31 does not diminish Huck's moral struggle, or devalue the choice he makes; least of all does it imply that he did not mean what he said, or was fickle and capricious in the saying of his "'terrible words.'" It is simply a matter of asserting, with Mark Twain, that temperament (like humor) is inborn and unalterable—and that all one can change is the "Magician of Circumstance." Alone with Jim, alone with memories of Jim, Huck can feel the irresistible tug of his natural compassion. When, by contrast, he is reunited with Tom, there once more is the even stronger lure of play; and if the play victimizes, there, as always, is the dependable response "'if he could stand it, I could.'" In Mark Twain's hands the incident of the *Walter Scott* (which is very funny, though a shade thoughtless) and the incidents of Chapter 31 (where fun is all but drowned out by Huck's sense of commitment) point equally to one end. As they now stand in the book both are but the chronicles of a sick joke foretold. And the effect is the same if, honoring the order of composition, we restore the *Walter Scott* to the end of the narrative; it then looks back to explain the joke, and to make Chapter 31 a prelude to the joke.

There is no help for it. Circumstance, in the form of the curse of Babel, dogs them every inch of the way. Temperament, which at times seemed about to lift the curse and to repair the Tower, turns out to be merely the tool of circumstance. Mark Twain has revised the traditional kinship of Time and the River into a far more ominous portrayal. Time Present is observed to flow out of Time Past in the form of endless reenactment and repetition. Time thus stands still. The River thus stands still. As for Huck and Jim, with Pluck they will go and go—the half-formed white boy; the Black man made shambling and inarticulate by years of toil—often seeming to gain new freedom from the tall tales of the world and the jokes which the tales beget. Luck, however, is the true determinant of their journey. And luck will make certain that the travelers remain affixed in the world where only the tales and the jokes have significance. At the last the relationship between Jim and Huck is approximately that of three thugs on the *Walter Scott*. It is that of Tom Sawyer to the word "ransom," of Tom to a plaything of his mechanized by Tom's will to play into "Nigger Jim." But what is saddest of all—or, rather, since neither of them seems in the least sorry about it—what is funniest of all is that, appearances notwithstanding, they have really stood in this relationship all along.

There is no help for it, though there is clarification for what cannot be helped. And so one turns finally to Bakhtin at his bleakest. "Monologue pretends to be the ultimate word," he writes in *Problems of Dostoevski's Poetics*. But its effect "closes down the represented world and represented people." From this insight Bakhtin passes on to the richer possibilities of dialogue. Passing on, however, is inconceivable in the fiction of Mark Twain. So well does Bakhtin's comment fit the waterlocked ending of the book that it might well be said to come in definition and summation of the "problems of the poetics" in *Huckleberry Finn*.[29]

## VI

> And there were many in the sky
> Who laughed at this thing.
> —Stephen Crane

It was a good joke Mark Twain played that time at the Silas Phelps Plantation. It was bully and sick for some characters and bully and sick on others; it was bully and sick on those readers who might have expected something better. The remaining issue, if an issue exists, is whether the player could live at ease with the sickness. And perhaps there is evidence to suggest he could not.

As we have seen, a decade or so later when he looked back, Mark Twain found the high point of *Huckleberry Finn* exactly where many a well-disposed reader has located it. The climax came, he wrote, when a small boy's sensibility ran up against the conscience of society, and conscience took a beating.[30] But of course Mark Twain did not stop writing with the triumph, any more than he stopped with the triumphs of "Mark Twain" in "Carnival of Crime" or of the cub or of Hank Morgan. Nor was he able to sustain the mood of Chapter 31. Hence although Leo Marx undoubtedly speaks for much of the critical establishment (to say nothing of back-row sophomores) when he concludes that "Clemens did not intend us to read the end of *Huckleberry Finn* so solemnly,"[31] it may just be that Mark Twain comes first in the long line of critics who have disliked the way the book ends. To paraphrase Hemingway, who would have us stop reading at the point where the plot against Jim begins, Mark Twain would have quit writing there, except that his steadfast commitment to realism would not permit this closure.

For what it comes down to, I suspect, is that the sick joke which for so long has engulfed everything in sight in Mark Twain's work has now engulfed Mark Twain. He is victim of the conspiracy he seems to devise. At the conclusion of *Tom Sawyer* he could look forward to developing, in Tom's companion, a different temperament about to embark on a new set of adventures. For a while anyhow, he got the different temperament right; but he was wrong about the adventures, and so ultimately the different temperament escaped him. Now, he can only set to work on *A Connecticut Yankee in King Arthur's Court* which, however much less well we may like it, is a point-for-point re-creation of the dying fall in *Huckleberry Finn,* and which at times he seems to have regarded as his last piece of fiction. But then in the early 1890s, there came to him again the lure of the River. And as he met the challenge, we may pause once more to assess what eludes us in his gaze. The eyes were sad and remote in the early 1890s because, having looked upon dreary, grubby reality, Mark Twain found a fixity and a futility and understood that, like it or not, the sick joke was his destiny. But the eyes glittered (twinkled, I think, is never quite the right word for it) with the mirth of a successful rival. Knowing himself a genius, Mark Twain also recognized in the early 1890s that he could tell the joke just as effectively as its original Creator: with the same verve and panache, with an equal display of the wickedly witty.

## NOTES

1. *ATS,* 234.

2. *Adventures of Huckleberry Finn,* ed. Walter Blair and Victor Fischer, The Mark Twain Library (Berkeley: University of California Press, 1985). Most references are to this edition, hereafter abbreviated to *AHF.*

I have also made use, both textual and bibliographic, of *Adventures of Huckleberry*

*Finn: The Only Comprehensive Edition*, ed. Victor Doyno (New York: Random House, 1996). References will be abbreviated as *CE*.

3. If we hearken to him closely, there is no end to the ironies of repetition and intersection which the implied author will create for us. Thus, Miss Watson's tales of Heaven are but a high-brow version of Pap's vision of the "Angel of Death," while Tom's obsession with money but apes in low-brow the same preoccupation of Judge Thatcher. The effect is akin to that in *The Great Gatsby*, where, though they never meet and would have nothing to say if they did, Meyer Wolfsheim, who fixes the World Series of 1919, and Jordan Baker, who fixes the lie of a golf ball, are the "twins" who define both the theme of the book and the ethics of an age.

4. *Selections from Emerson*, ed. Stephen Whicher (New York: Harper, 1965), 195. My sense of the unexpected ways in which Emerson can illuminate Mark Twain's work has here and elsewhere been heightened by James Lyndon Johnson's fine study of *Mark Twain and the Limits of Power*.

5. From *The Notebooks of Henry James*, reprinted in *Portrait of a Lady*, ed. Robert D. Bamberg, Norton Critical Edition (New York: Norton, 1975), 626. *Portrait* precedes *AHF* by three years—which is of course not to say that Mark Twain had "discovered" parallels by reading James.

6. I am much indebted to Professor Blair's editorial note in *AHF*, note 68.19, 389.

7. *Selected Mark Twain–Howells Letters*, 75. Professor Doyno's case for a different and slightly later stopping point is worked out in *Writing Huck Finn: Mark Twain's Creative Process* (Philadelphia: University of Pennsylvania Press, 1991). See also *CE*, xi.

One further point needs to be made. In *CE* Professor Doyno presents (383–84) a sheaf or so of hitherto unpublished manuscript, detailing Huck's feelings of extreme guilt after he has lied to save Jim. The feelings and language are very close to those that will presently be attributed to Huck in Chapter 31. But I suggest that Mark Twain dropped the material from the episode-off-Cairo because he sensed that Huck was more focused on his fine lie than on Jim's welfare, and hence had not earned (was not yet entitled to) the guilt.

8. This will happen in Chapter 33 when Huck sees the Duke and King (no doubt a good bit less loveable and sweet-smelling than the children) ridden out of town tarred and feathered.

9. *AHF*, "Notice."

10. *AHF*, "Explanatory."

11. The most systematic attempt to sort out the dialects (perhaps it is too rigorous and solemn for its own good) is that of David Carkeet, "The Dialects in *Huckleberry Finn*," *American Literature* 51 (November 1960), 315–32. Less systematic and generally more appealing are the views set forth by David R. Sewell in *Mark Twain's Languages* (Berkeley: University of California Press, 1987). Although I find some of Sewell's individual readings a disappointment (and although not all his categories ring true to my ear) his basic contention seems brilliant and indispensable. Mark Twain's preoccupation

with language, he argues, "transcended its origins in public-school grammar instruction and moved toward an intuition of principles just beginning to appear in his day and fully enunciated only in ours" (1–2, 95). I would like to hope my essay on *AHF,* as well as the one on Mark Twain and books and reality, are in demonstration of this "intuition of principles."

But although it apparently remains unpublished, I find the most valuable account of language in *AHF* to be in the Ph.D. dissertation of Curt M. Rulon, also entitled "The Dialects in *Huckleberry Finn*" (University of Iowa, 1967). I have also profited from Laurence B. Holland, "A 'Raft of Trouble': Word and Deed in *Huckleberry Finn,*" *Glyph* 5 (Baltimore: Johns Hopkins University Press, 1982), 66–81.

12. According to Victor Doyno's argument, the manuscript ground to a halt in 1876 not with the wreck of the raft, but while Buck is presenting "feud" to Huck. I would like to speculate about why it stopped—and what got it going again.

As was true back in St. Petersburg, Huck is listening to words used foolishly and this time self-destructively. He is a captive of the pure romantic imagination. But to have him quarrel with Buck or to question Buck's logic would be to spoil the effect of Huck's character. The narrative must pause temporarily because Mark Twain has found no way to prevent Huck's getting the worse of it, even when he is confronted with the most patent absurdities.

But in the presentation of "feud" Mark Twain has also found his subject. When the tank fills up again in 1879–80, he can turn his attention to what I am calling "Words on the Mississippi" (to the romantic imagination run riot), with Huck still cast as passive listener and naive observer, but with outrages so extreme that we are drawn in and so increasingly blatant that Huck himself must eventually take a stand (as he does among the Wilkses and again in Chapter 31).

Enhumored Buck Grangerford huffs and puffs his way to a horrible death. Yet I think it is not too much to say that, in his sad foolishness, he likewise played a role in saving a novel from extinction.

13. In what seems to have become a definitive reading, Leo Marx observes that, for the first and only time in *AHF,* Mark Twain "places great strain on the credibility of the narrative method" when he has Huck report Colonel Sherburn's "entire speech word-for-word." Professor Marx's point is that the speech is therefore of crucial importance to the author, so significant that he must find a way of including it at any cost. See *Adventures of Huckleberry Finn,* ed. Leo Marx (New York: Bobbs-Merrill, 1967), 174–75.

But the premise about technique is simply wrong. An equally gross violation of narrative realism occurs just a few pages later when Huck is suddenly made privy to a note that the Duke writes in secret to the King:

. . . the duke, he couldn't stand it no more, so he writes on a little scrap of paper, "*obsequies,* you old fool," and folds it up and goes to goo-gooing and reaching it over people's heads to him. The king he reads it, and puts it in his pocket, and says: "I say orgies, not because it's the common term, because it ain't—obsequies bein' the common term—but because orgies is the right term. Obsequies ain't used in England no more, now—it's gone out. We say orgies, now, in England. Orgies is better. . . ." (*AHF,* 217–18.)

Huck's omniscience (and X-ray eyes!) would appear to function here exactly as his trick memory had worked earlier. In its platitudinous content Sherburn's harangue makes no more sense than the Duke's recasting of a funeral service. And Mark Twain has gone to any lengths to show the power of words—and the foolishness of both word-mongers and their hapless audiences.

14. Blair, *Selected Shorter Writings of Mark Twain,* 231.

15. Bakhtin, *Problems of Dostoevsky's Poetics,* 287.

16. *AHF,* 156–58. For the way I have structured this interlude, brief but of the utmost importance in the book, I am much indebted to Bakhtin's "Discourse in the Novel" in *The Dialogic Imagination: Four Essays,* tr. Caryl Emerson and Michael Holquist (Austin: University of Texas Press, 1981), especially 345–49.

17. Though for obvious reasons no account of *AHF* can omit references to slavery, the classic treatment now is (and I believe will continue to be for some time to come) that of Forrest Robinson's *In Bad Faith.* It is a fierce and moving account, I feel an entirely successful rejoinder to James Cox's insistence in *The Fate of Humor* that true tyranny in the book comes less from "the peculiar institution" than from the human conscience.

However the first critic to note the drama of slavery-as-supreme-fiction in the narrative was Mark Twain himself. In 1895, he wrote

In those old slave holding days the whole community was agreed to one thing—the awful sacredness of slavery. To help steal a horse or cow was a low crime, but to help a hunted slave . . . or hesitate promptly to betray him to a slave-catcher . . . was a much baser crime, and carried with it a stain, a moral smirch which nothing could wipe away. That this sentiment should exist among slave-holders is comprehensible—there were good commercial reasons for it—but that it should exist and did exist among the paupers . . . and in a passionate and uncomprehending form, is not in our remote day realizable. (Walter Blair, *Mark Twain and Huck Finn,* 144.)

In other words the whole of an "unfortunate land" was in the throes of a Supreme Fiction, mesmerized by its plot and action into telling and retelling the story in all the areas of its collective life.

18. Blair, *Mark Twain and Huck Finn,* 143. For the narrative as a "language experiment," see Smith, Cox—virtually any commentary which addresses style and characterization.

19. The excerpt appears in *Collected Essays, Journalism and Letters,* ed. Sonia Orwell and Ian Argus (London: Hammersmith, 1970), vol. 4, 168.

20. For an intelligent, sympathetic (and, as it seems to me, right-minded) critique of Orwell's views, see David Lodge's fine account in *Modes of Modern Fiction* (Ithaca: Cornell University Press, 1977), Chapter 2, Chapter 4. Though Mark Twain does not appear, I am at all times much influenced by Professor Lodge's treatment of realistic fictions, and of the dilemmas they provoke for both reader and writer.

21. This point has been brilliantly established by Jane Smiley in one of the most formidable attacks ever launched on *AHF.* Holding no "grudge" against Huck ("just a boy trying to survive"), Ms. Smiley finds Huck's creator to be "a villain," the writer of an indefensible novel (its meretriciousness can only be justified through "meretricious critical reasoning"), a racist who sought in sentimentality and banality to disguise from readers and himself the depth of his prejudices—and, of course, a man. Is Ms. Smiley wrong? Frankly, I find her views far more tenable than those of a number of the critics—ranging from T. S. Eliot to David Smith—whom she quotes. I hope that nothing I can say in extenuation will hide the fact that I find the end of the book insensitive to the point of outright cruelty. But I would like to ask when—and how often—Ms. Smiley, professor as well as fine novelist, has successfully tried in the classroom *Uncle Tom's Cabin,* her example of a good, thoughtful and socially useful narrative about slavery. See Smiley, "Say It Ain't So, Huck," *Harpers Magazine* 269 (January 1996), 61–67.

22. *Candide,* tr. Lowell Blair (New York: Bantam, 1971), 120.

23. In many recent editions "Yours truly" appears in the chapter title. *AHF* locates it on the last page (THE END, YOURS TRULY HUCK FINN) where it appeared in 1884.

24. *AHF,* 393, note 107.1–123.29. See also Blair, *Mark Twain and Huck Finn,* 346–48.

25. For the terms and Mark Twain's illustrations of them, I am drawing upon two of his late essays: "The Turning Point of My Life," which was published in *Harper's Bazaar* in 1910, and "The Turning Point in My Life: First Version," which was not published during Mark Twain's lifetime. Both are included in *What Is Man?,* ed. Paul Baender (Berkeley: University of California Press, 1973), 455–65 and 521–28. For circumstances of the writing, and of both the publication and the nonpublication, Professor Baender's bibliographical notes are indispensable. I have combined the two essays in the quotations which follow.

Readers will recognize that the terms (and similar illustrations) are also central to several of the dialogues in *What Is Man?* It is also worth noting that as long ago as 1957, E. Hudson Long applied "temperament and circumstance" to a general reading of *AHF.* But, though fruitful enough, Professor Long's use of the terms is much broader and less precise than mine. He is concerned with self vs. society and so loses the more dramatic impact which occurs when self is arrayed against some specific event: the temptation to board a sinking steamboat, or the temptation to display one's superiority when one knows a word or two of French. See Long, *Mark Twain Handbook* (New York: Hendricks House, 1957).

26. "Turning Point," 464, 526–27.

27. Blair, *Mark Twain and Huck Finn*, 348.

28. For my sense of Jim's role in the narrative, I am indebted to Harold Beaver, "Run, Nigger, Run: *Adventures of Huckleberry Finn* As a Fugitive Slave Narrative," *Journal of American Studies* 8, No. 3 (December 1974), 339–61; Chadwick Hansen, "The Character of Jim and the Ending of *Huckleberry Finn*," *Massachusetts Review* 5 (Autumn 1963), 45–66; and (most particularly) to the brilliant (and so far as I can tell, much neglected) paper of Jane Johnson Benardete, "*Huckleberry Finn* and the Nature of Fiction," *Massachusetts Review* 9 (Spring 1968), 209–26.

29. Bakhtin, *Problems of Dostoevski's Poetics*, 287, 120.

30. Blair, *Mark Twain and Huck Finn*, 143.

31. Marx, "Mr. Eliot, Mr. Trilling, and *Huckleberry Finn*," 431.

# Pudd'nhead Wilson:
# An Essay on Triumphant Reality

Pull a gray hair, and three will come to the funeral.
— Old Adage

I

*The Tragedy of Pudd'nhead Wilson* (1894) is framed by an act of creation and an act of resolution. Near the beginning, two babies are exchanged in their cribs at midnight, and the course of life in Dawson's Landing, Missouri, is, for nearly twenty-five years, diverted into wholly new channels. Near the end, two lost identities are at high noon restored to their rightful owners, and life in the village resumes what a quarter-of-a-century earlier would have been deemed its proper and predictable course. By these episodes is launched and concluded the last detailed look in published narrative that Mark Twain took at the American village on the American river, and the queerest and quirkiest book he had yet written. The same procedure also carries over into "The Man That Corrupted Hadleyburg," which was published six years later (1899–1900), and it is central to the dream visions and the mysterious-stranger manuscripts which he left unfinished and unpublished. It is well worth describing as a combination of surface clarity, with an underlying murkiness which constantly challenges, contradicts, in both the old- and new-fashioned sense of the term, deconstructs the surface.

Topside, no story could be assembled more straightforwardly than the one *TPW* tells or with greater attention to what one wants to call the minutiae of actual experience. Scenes both great and small—a courtroom confrontation, the small talk of a constable and four other local yokels on a village street corner—are made to leap off the page with a quite naturalistic precision. Human thoughts and feelings are never far from the surface, so that there is no difficulty about determining why characters behave and interact as they do. The manner of the whole is that of a simple, forthright style, abounding in the sort of objective pronouncements which are well fitted to the documentary or (as the opening paragraph of *Wilson* has it) to the setting forth of a "chronicle." From below and beyond, however, presentation constantly gives rise to false leads, red herrings, the intrusion of undoubted digressions and apparent irrelevancies. This is not simply a matter of the sudden shifts backward and forward in time that characterized *Tom Sawyer,* or of the loosely organized sequences of *Huckleberry Finn.* Throughout *Wilson* we have the impression of following a beautifully totalized narrative, until a sudden rise in the roadway discloses that the facts we are given have all the while made no sense whatsoever. The hard, driving, no-nonsense manner of the book pushes us steadily along—until we arrive at points where nonsense takes over and presentation seems to degenerate into outright chaos. An extreme, though not wholly unappealing, view declares TPW to be so cluttered with confusions and contradictions as to be "patently unreadable."[1]

And yet, though the emphasis is now far more conspicuous and trying than before, a disparity between the bold gesture in the foreground, and out of the background a sense of furtive, partially hidden presences which shape the gesture, is by no means unprecedented in Mark Twain. There is nothing in the least ambiguous about anything Simon Wheeler says. Ambiguity becomes evident only when (and if) we ponder the question of why Simon expresses himself, and apparently must express himself in so strange a way. Then simplicity turns to mystery. Again, style and tone leave us to feel that nothing really remarkable occurs with Huck's arrival at a welcoming party intended for Tom Sawyer. The fact that Huck travels as one dead has persistently provoked more critical commentary than does his resurrection with Tom's birthright. It is only by worrying and wondering about the coincidence that we find it puzzling and are drawn to the deeper logic in the book which makes such an episode inevitable. Clarity and murkiness are, in short, the abiding principles of sick humor. With its outrageous actions up-front, its hint of a secret pleasure (a covert wink, a leer, a well-concealed manipulator) behind the scenes, the sick joke thrives on just this combination of the seen and audible with the barely glimpsed and mostly silent. And it is as a sick joke, I believe, that *Wilson* needs to be read. Of overt laughter there is very little. With one or two exceptions the characters are far too preoccupied with personal crises or questions of law and lineage to laugh. A reader smiles, rather than laughs aloud, at the cynicism attributed to Pudd'nhead Wilson, and (disliking false-Tom Driscoll) is hardly disposed to join in false-Tom's raillery of Wilson. All the same, the book is rampant with the atmosphere of laughing "with" and laughing "at." Somebody is forever the object of somebody's jocularity. In line with Auden's contention, furthermore, the player of the joke has left unmistakable traces of his presence on nearly every page. The trick to discovering the oxymoronic unheard mirth (the equally oxymoronic invisible creator of the mirthful) lies in considering creation and resolution, the tie which unites the two actions into a single performative gesture, and the destination to which both actions are caused to lead us as readers—really and truly lead us.

(1) *Roxy creates.* She does so as the result of a thought that comes to her in Chapter 3, an idea more hopeful and life-affirming than the temptation to suicide which had engaged her a bit earlier. Once this thought takes hold, Roxy instantly transfers it outward into the real world by exchanging the clothes and the cribs of the two infants. But even as she acts out the idea, she also subjects the adequacy of her plan to one other test. We are told that throughout the long night she is at pains to rehearse calling Chambers "Marse Tom," and true-Tom "Chambers."[2] It is as if by naming her rearrangement of reality, and doing so repeatedly, Roxy is persuaded of its being true—or, alternatively, can persuade it to become the visible and palpable truth. She is thus actuated by the same belief in word-magic that had ensured Tom Sawyer his many triumphs. Through the sheer power of nomenclature (through what Freud calls "the omnipotence of thoughts"), she creates the world anew and makes her handiwork so real, so utterly true-to-life, that all are convinced—not excluding Roxy. After a short while, as the narrator drily observes, she forgets that the life she leads is occurring inside "a fiction created by herself." (*TPW,* 19.)[3]

Nor is it solely a question of reshaping the future for two highly malleable blobs of matter. Such is the torrential force of her eloquence that halfway through the book Roxy not only humbles and brings quivering to his knees the adult false-Tom Driscoll; when she goes on to tell him of his true parentage, false-Tom both believes her, and believes to the extent of requiring no proof, no hard documentary evidence, in support of the words she speaks. At the very beginning, furthermore, her capacity to command life is expressed in a strange, wry irony. Weighing her vitality and natural hauteur alongside the aristocratic proclivities of Dawson's Landing generally, we are reminded that by rights Roxy ought to be Roxie: Village Belle and ultimately Grand Dame of the plantation culture which produced her. She was born to dominate her distinguished yet effete surroundings with a word and a gesture. That she exists instead as a servile maidservant, raped, cowering, illiterate, and suicidal in the nursery, is due of course to the fact of her being one-sixteenth black. The figure created for Queenship is legally a slave.

It is an uncomfortable irony, and one which pricks us to be generous. As she brings to pass her transformation of reality, our initial impulse is to celebrate the triumph: to exclaim Good for you, Roxy; you've suffered in silence long enough; it is high time for the white folks to have their comeuppance. Immediately, however, ambiguities intrude. In all of Dawson's Landing there is no more ardent white supremacist than the Roxy who spurns Jasper as a "'black mudcat,'" traces her ancestry back to "'Cap'n John Smith,'" derives the keenest pleasure from her memory of having been taken in rape by a "'high bawn'" member of "'ole Virginny'" stock. (*TPW,* 8, 70, 43.) Is it therefore for love or from pride that she decides to switch, then switches the babies? Concerned to keep Chambers upriver is she not equally mindful of the status that will come to him (and accrue indirectly to herself) when he has been projected into the closed circle of the First Families of the village? And even supposing that her quest for a new structuring of things is motivated by *both* devotion and selfishness, does not it also involve a reemphasizing, profound and terrible, of the structure as it already exists? In order to speak the word that provides identity and a surname to Chambers, Roxy must likewise say the word that takes these same valuable and personal possessions away from Thomas à Beckett Driscoll. The effect of her incarnation is to impose the terror of her own situation upon— well, upon an infant, the single one of her fellow creatures who is weaker and more helpless to resist than Roxy can ever be. Taken together, false-Tom and Roxy reenact a familiar interest of Mark Twain's. False-Tom becomes another version of the Aladdin figure who so haunted Tom Sawyer's dreams. Through no personal merit he is given a lamp which, when rubbed, turns the existence of one born to servitude into the career of a rich and powerful young gentleman, with two years at Yale and a life of leisure (and criminality) in St. Louis. Roxy represents a latter-day Genie of the lamp, summoned forth by Chambers's hold on her maternal affections, but evoked as well by an overweening vanity. For in Mark Twain, as in D. H. Lawrence and Henry James, the Aladdin story, with its overtones of creating Prince Charming, shades off into the sinister implications of the story about King Midas. We are given a graphic demonstration of the penalties that accumulate when wishes are turned to objects, or ideas are objectified into new material relationships. And where the powers granted to Midas loop back in punishment only of him (turning everything to gold, he is soon in grave danger of starving to death), those vouchsafed to Roxy and False-Tom radiate outward to claim many victims and hence to have a more public effect. They reduce true-Tom Driscoll to a cringing, anonymous thing and transform False-Tom into a combination spoiled-brat and arrogant wastrel, while at the same time they give rise to twenty-three years of disorder and misrule for an entire community. Trying to resolve one crisis with thought and word-magic, Roxy has but wrought another imbroglio which, after a time, will have to be resolved in a different way by a different sort of character.

(2) *Wilson resolves.* He does so by allowing himself to be guided by facts as they preexist him in the external world. The various fingerprints, including the

two crucial sets, have lain out there since the day they were made, solid and specifiable as the plates of glass on which they were recorded, aspects of reality awaiting the intelligence that can sort them out and reassemble them into their proper order. The word used by Wilson at the moment of truth makes clear his total dependence upon objective circumstances. "What a revelation," he cries. (*TPW*, 104.) And to this illumination, as it comes rushing in upon him from without, he goes on to adapt the thoughts and the language (or spoken thoughts) that will carry him to his victory at the next day's trial.

Wilson's method of discerning truth is prefigured, in small, by an earlier incident in the book. It is pointedly set forth that when he reads aright the palm of Count Luigi Capello, the Pudd'nhead is neither magician nor even one endowed with any particular powers of prophecy. The lines, whorls, and other protuberances on Luigi's hand are intensely physical hieroglyphs, the kind of unmistakable evidence which is visible to anyone. All Wilson does is supply the rosetta stone of consciousness, which deciphers and translates into language the hand's preexistent meaning and significance. He acts on the assumption that while intelligence and words may of course lead one to a better, fuller understanding of reality and are necessary for the expression of reality, still the realness of the real may not be mediated by thought or language. Accordingly, Wilson resolves in a manner that seems totally different—indeed radically opposite—from the way Roxy creates. Where she acts out the premise that thoughts and language come first and can create the world as if for the first time, he shares (with Jim, Huck, and Hank Morgan) the sense that things come antecedent to words or ideas, that the accuracy of what one thinks or says had better be verified through a constant appeal to objective processes, and that unless this verification takes place the contents of thought and speech are likely to have no value. As always in the work of Mark Twain, Mark Twain's special version of romanticism ("*as in, so out*") has entered the lists with his special attachment to realism ("*as out, so in*"); as always, honors, the honors of having the last word anyhow, lie with the realist.

Yet there are difficulties to keeping Wilson in a tradition of strict empiricism. To begin with, one is more than a little troubled by certain aspects of his professional conduct. As early as Chapter 19, it is clearly established that from the beginning Wilson has known that the man he will defend in court could not possibly be guilty of Judge Driscoll's murder. Involvement is out of the question, since the bloody thumbprint on the murder knife does not match Count Luigi's. ("'Neither of the Twins made these marks,'" Wilson thinks to himself the first time he looks.) (*TPW*, 97.) Why, then, does he decline to tell what he knows for many weeks and until the trial is so far underway that Luigi's conviction seems inevitable? Perhaps he supposes that, lacking a true culprit, the vengeful country jury will hang Luigi anyhow. More likely, he craves the thrill and excitement, the notoriety and status that will accrue to him, if he names the true culprit at the same time he exonerates the wrongfully accused. But whichever is the case a practicing attorney has both suppressed evidence and violated the trust, not to say the interests and safety, of his client. Despite the "brilliant use of forensic logic" that has often been imputed to him, one might well want to think twice before retaining David Wilson as a defense counsel.[4]

Then, there is the no less disturbing matter of the dream vision, and of its function in establishing Wilson's reputation as an amateur detective. We are told in Chapter 20 that, weary of trying to find the true criminal who will replace Count Luigi, Wilson drinks a "glass of cold whisky" and soon falls asleep:

> He was tired now, and his brains were beginning to clog. He said he would sleep himself fresh, and then see what he could do with this riddle. He slept through a troubled and unrestful hour, then unconsciousness began to shred away, and presently he rose drowsily to a sitting posture. "Now what was that dream?" he said, trying to recall it. "What was that dream? It seemed to unravel that puz————"
>
> He landed in the middle of the floor at a bound, without finishing his sentence, and ran and turned up the light and seized his "records."
>
> "It's so! Heavens, what a revelation. And for twenty-three years no man has ever suspected it." (*TPW*, 104.)

Granted that from dreams come insights (and granted too that Mark Twain had a large, pre-Freudian respect for the dreaming mind) still the use of the dream as an instrument for detection does seem odd. All planning and forethought—all reliance upon the rational faculties to evaluate evidence and design and work through to a solution—are stripped away from the detective; he becomes an empty, passive (perhaps slightly hung over) vessel into whom a solution has merely been poured. Though his use of morphine no doubt enhances our romantic conception of Sherlock Holmes, what would we think of a Holmes who *dreamt* his solutions—of any god-like or even first-rate human intelligence blundering up out of a boozy cat nap to set things aright?

If Wilson flirts with malpractice and if his intelligence as a village gumshoe is a good bit blunted by the dream vision, the last shreds of his moral facade seem stripped away by the next-to-last of his recorded words in the book. He has got the identities straight at last, the true structure of reality all neatly laid out before himself and his audience. And in what kind of language does he express his achievement? In words which reveal that he has not in the least understood the old, inhumane system which caused the identities to be exchanged and lost in the first place. "Negro and slave," he howls in high glee at false-Tom (true-Chambers), "make upon the window the finger prints that will hang you!" (*TPW,* 112.) Surely the narrative has shown us that only the perpetuation of ancient wrongs and ancient stupidities can come of coupling the demeaning words slave and Negro. Yet here is Wilson still spouting bigotry (still peering at the world in front of him through a thick haze of stereotypes), just as of course for nearly a quarter of a century he has paid sycophantic lip service to duelling, lineage, racism, slavery, aristocratic pretentiousness, and every other piece of knavery and nonsense so beloved and honored in Dawson's Landing, Missouri.

(3) *Roxy and Wilson.* They could hardly be more different: as different, we might say, as black from white; as slavery from freedom; as owned chattel from property owner. ("Wilson had a trifle of money . . . , and he bought a small house at the extreme western verge of the town.") (*TPW,* 6.) Moreover, their actions and methods for acting could hardly be more different: as different, we might add, as illusion from reality; as night from day; as "curtain down" on the true state of things from "curtain up" on the true state of things. Nevertheless, they share the fate of being pariah figures, as well as the capacity to make things happen in the community that shuns and excludes them. And as they intertwine like variations of a single continuous process, it grows evident that for all the apparent difference, they resemble each other (no, we might want to insist, they *duplicate*) each other as the hollow is said to mimic the swell.

If as a slave Roxy must construct freedom out of a dream, still once her dream is actualized she is for a long while far freer to control reality than free and fact-loving Wilson who, having made a botch of things on his first day in town, unaccountably chooses to linger on for twenty-three years, as if (with all the wide American west before him) he were enchanted to the spot. Again, if as an outsider Wilson is given the insight which strikes blinders from the eyes of Roxy and dispels the illusions of Dawson's Landing as a whole, then, by virtue of the way he expresses the truth, he discloses that he himself is permanently blinded and (what is more) as enslaved to illusions as ever Roxy was. Of one of the figures, Mark Twain observed that:

> I never thought of [him] as a character but only as a piece of useful machinery—a button, or crank, or lever, with a useful function to perform in a machine, but with no dignity above that.[5]

The plain fact is, however, that what is said about one figure applies equally well to both. Roxy and Wilson are both "pieces of machinery," "buttons," "cranks," "levers." Snapped to the ON position one can create, while the other resolves. But operating in tandem, they move the narrative from something monstrous to the contemplation of a moral void.

Perhaps, then, a still better way of expressing their relationship is to say they present mirror- or reversed-images. In a book much about twins and twin relationships, they seem linked as identical twins. And the fact of their twinship is confirmed by one more singular coincidence in a story which thrives on many singularities.

Crouched beside the cradles on an autumn midnight in 1830, Roxy sets free a slave. In consequence, she enslaves true-Tom at once; false-Tom, as over the course of years he is enthralled and corrupted by freedom; and also herself, destined presently to be sold downriver by an ungrateful son. Standing erect at the bar of justice on an April noon in 1853, Wilson sets free a slave. As a result, he enslaves false-Tom at once; true-Tom (false-Chambers) as over the course of time this pathetic figure will find himself estranged and nameless everywhere; and likewise himself, now destined to enter fully and freely into the bondage supplied by the civic affairs and warped values of Dawson's Landing. Roxy and Wilson are twins, because starting from opposite ends of a moral and epistemological continuum they arrive at a single conclusion, and (between them) make possible the reformulation of an old and bitterly funny adage. In its original application, the adage mocks enhumored selves, struggling through consciousness for release from time and nature, finding that with each conscious act the bondage only tightens and worsens: Pull a gray hair, and three will come to the funeral. The joke is hardly more cheerful as practiced in concert by Roxy and Wilson. After they have done their collective work, the adage is revised to read: *Free a slave, and three new ones will come to the celebration.*

## II

> Surface tension. A property of liquids arising from unbalanced molecular cohesive forces at or near the surface, as a result of which the surface tends to contract and has properties resembling those of a stretched elastic membrane.
> —*American Heritage Dictionary*

Borrowed from freshman physics, the concept of surface tension seems nicely suited to elucidate any story of crime and detection. So to speak, a malefactor adds to the contained structure of things a few additional drops, which are the marks of the malefactor's crime. But though the contents of the container are thereby distended and swollen almost to the breaking point, the molecules (the criminal activities) dig in, cling to one another, will not readily be dislodged. Not until the work of the detective jars the surface can the tensions be broken. Then, under added pressure, the molecules are dissevered; the excess flows down and away from the container (it of course is an image of well-ordered society); and the container is left filled neatly to the brim, but just to the brim, as it was originally.

In *Wilson* four presences know of the formation of surface tensions. Two are characters: Roxy, from having created them in the beginning; false-Tom, from being told about them presently by Roxy. Each obviously has a vested interest in keeping the surface intact. A third is the narrator who for all the intimacy and omniscience he brings to bear as the tensions are generated seems little interested in tinkering with the surface. Tone makes it evident that he is there to observe and report, never to undo. The fourth is the reader, well aware of the distortions on the surface of life, but prevented from interfering by the very nature of narrative, which makes her/him a mere spectator. The molecules which do, in fact, dig in (and shut out) for more than twenty years seem likely to cohere in place at least forever.

Criticism of *Wilson* has argued that a Stranger comes to Dawson's Landing, gradually senses the disturbances of the place, and after a while acts to resolve the unbalanced condition of society. Unembarrassed by the fact that "after a while" runs on for nearly a quarter of a century—and unimpressed by how, during this interval, the Stranger ignores (remains impervious to) hard evidence which would hardly have eluded a child of twelve (always supposing the child was looking for, or at, anything)—criticism has sometimes elevated the Stranger from village hawkshaw to the stature and status of a moral, social, even "political" hero.[6] (So far as I am aware no one has ever called him Suffering Servant or "Christ-figure," perhaps because Mark Twain wrote the book, more probably because a renewal of interest in *Wilson* postdates the New Criticism of the 1940s and 1950s.) I propose, however, to look more closely at the breakup of tensions on the surface. In my view the time involved in their collapse is approximately nine months. Moreover, those whose presence is necessary to break the tensions are, true enough, repeatedly called Strangers, for they are recent arrivals in town. But they are not named David Wilson.

Let us begin at the point where the membrane-like surface is rent so that truth comes spilling out—and then proceed backward through the plot step-by-logical-step, raising some questions as we go and trying to supply legitimate answers:

(1) Whether or not their meaning is revealed in a dream, the fingerprints are decisive. And the meaning of their meaning comes to Wilson. But why, on this particular night, is he pondering his vast collection of fingerprints so avidly?

*Answer:* Tomorrow he will bring to a close his apparently foredoomed defense of Count Luigi Capello, charged with murder. He is looking for evidence which will clear Luigi.

(2) But why has this criminal charge been brought?

*Answer:* For three reasons. First, because Luigi was found at the scene of the crime. Second, because Luigi's knife, bearing an unidentified fingerprint, was the murder weapon. And third, and most especially, of course, because someone got killed.

(3) But why *was* Judge Driscoll murdered?

*Answer:* Though two influential interpretations of the book have conjectured that false-Tom has an appointed mission to kill his surrogate father (thereby avenging himself upon the planter-aristocracy which begot him) the evidence supplied by the language *inside* the book points in quite a different direction.[7] Through the authority of his own words it is established that false-Tom travels down from St. Louis solely to "*rob* the old skinflint"; once on the scene, he acquires a weapon to protect himself "should he make a noise, by some accident, and get caught—say in opening the safe." The authority of the narrator's language makes it clear that false-Tom is never tempted to stab a sleeping victim; quite the contrary: he drops the scabbard of Luigi's knife, arouses the Judge from sleep, and murders the Judge only when the old man cries "Help, help" and reaches out to seize false-Tom. The authority of the narrator, spelling out false-Tom's responses to the unexpected, provides the final link. At this late hour Judge Driscoll would normally be fast asleep in an upstairs bedroom. Instead, he drowses in his "private study" near the strongbox which false-Tom intends to steal, or to steal from. The Judge is killed because, having departed from his normal routine, he is where he is not supposed to be at this particular time. (*TPW,* 92–95.)

(4) But why is he up so late?

*Answer:* Because (like Wilson several weeks later) he has, tomorrow, the promise of a fateful encounter with Luigi. They are to fight a duel. Nor will it be a gentleman's duel this time, a well-bred shooting match in which the participants manage to nick a few spectators, but never each other. Since Judge Driscoll now declines to meet Luigi on "the field of honor," it will, rather, be a shoot-out—a case of kill first or be killed—on the streets of Dawson's Landing. (*TPW,* 93.) The Judge has good reason to keep an unaccustomed bedtime. Knowing he may soon be dead at the hand of Luigi, he is putting his financial affairs and other papers in order.

(5) But why, when all began so swimmingly, have relations between Judge Driscoll and Luigi degenerated to the point of necessitating violence in the streets?

The *answer* takes us backward from an embittered political campaign where the Judge and Luigi were arrayed on opposite sides, to scurrilous stories about Luigi told to the Judge by false-Tom, and thence to the first duel, fought so cavalierly between Luigi and the Judge.

(6) But why was this duel fought at all?

*Answer:* Because, having determined that false-Tom had no taste for defending the honor of the family, Judge Driscoll was forced to fight Luigi on false-Tom's behalf.

(7) But why was the honor of the family sullied?

*Answer:* Because on his (their) second night in town Luigi and Angelo were gratuitously insulted by false-Tom—whereupon, false-Tom was given a resounding kick to the seat of his pants by Luigi.

We get right answers, says Wittgenstein, only through posing the right questions. Putting what at least seem legitimate questions to the text of *Wilson* yields up a pattern of causality which seems, in turn, to produce a legitimate (this time, from backward-to-forward type) question and answer.

*Question:* Suppose they had not appeared at the end of "a flaming June day" in 1852? How otherwise would or could the mystery in the book ever have been resolved?

*Answer:* For all we can tell, the book would have spun aimlessly and endlessly in an orbit of unresolved dilemmas—unresolved because no one suspects the dilemmas exist. Having stayed resolutely in place for twenty-three years, the look of things on the surface might well have persisted intact for a thousand and twenty-three more. For: lacking their appearance that day in June, there would have been no kick to provoke a duel . . . without the duel to engender them there would have been no personal hostilities and so no embittered political campaign . . . without these antagonisms there would be no reason for a showdown tomorrow . . . without the showdown there would be nothing to keep the Judge up late straightening through his papers . . . without the unaccustomed bedtime there would be no murder . . . without the murder there would be no incriminating knife . . . without murder and knife there would be no defendant, no trial, and hence no need for defense counsel . . . and so, finally, without the need for defense counsel there would be no occasion whatsoever for Wilson to go fumbling through one moral grab bag and have the far dirtier contents of another come abruptly tumbling out before him.

Luigi and Angelo thus snap buttons to the ON position. Step by step, they are seen to set in motion, and to keep moving, a sequence of events that jars the surface and succeeds in elucidating the mystery in Dawson's Landing. But if this is what we are made to see, how explain our perception? "Step-by-step" suggests purposeful action; in a detective story the phrase will imply a recognition of the crime, together with the gradual, progressive piecing together of clues and evidence that leads to a solution. And with respect to this kind of behavior the Italian (who are also the Extraordinary) Twins do nothing at all. Once, but only once, are they drawn to a judgment that bears on the true state of affairs in the village. Meeting false-Tom for the first time, Angelo is taken by his "free and easy way," while Luigi notes something "sly and veiled" about Tom. (*TPW*, 48.) Not only are both responses predictable and perfunctory (of a kind with those of the rest of the community, which is beguiled by Tom's charm even as it often distrusts his motives); the reactions underscore the Twins' aloofness from any aspect of village life that does not concern them directly. Presumably, for example, they never so much as lay eyes on either Roxy or Chambers until the last day of Luigi's trial. How, therefore, are two supernumeraries, who never much notice anything, able to influence the lives (and, what is more, the outcomes) of major characters who desperately seek not to be observed?

*Answer:* They do it by being there. They do it as two presences who after June of 1852 (but really before then; really from the beginning of time) are present. And to grasp this possibility is, I think, to understand that for some time now (perhaps always) Luigi and Angelo—Extraordinary *before* they were Italian; the title precedes the portrayal—have been present through the fact and the force of their presences in Mark Twain's imagination.

## III

> A few years ago, there was a rage . . . for telling "Horror Jokes." For example:
> A MOTHER (*to her blind daughter*): Now, dear, shut your eyes and count to twenty.
>   Then open them, and you'll find that you can see.
> DAUGHTER (*after counting twenty*): But, Mummy, I still can't see.
> MOTHER: April Fool!
> —W. H. Auden[8]

This, in the 1880s, is the way the book ends:

(1) Two adolescent boys, both old enough to know better, one deeply enough involved to have a special sense of the inappropriateness, are speaking to a black man who wants more than anything else in the world never to be fooled.

> BOYS: Shut your eyes and count twenty. Then you can come out and be with us.

> MAN (*after counting*): But I still ain't out there Mistoe Tom and Huck honey.

HUCK AND TOM: April fool!

JIM: White folks knows best.

(2) Next, position the voice somewhere off-stage, a presence in the wings, or (better) speaking from above the proscenium arch.

> VOICE: Shut your eyes and count twenty. When you open them you will find that Utopia is twice as serene and lovely as it was the day you sailed away.
>
> HANK (*after counting, looks out at a scene of utter devastation*): But why?
>
> VOICE (*modulates from that of Merlin the Magician, into that of two literary forms called "Romance" and "Realism," into that of an allegorical figure named Human History*): April fool!
>
> HANK: "Exterminate the brutes."

In a way these endings—call them, perhaps, the outcomes of Mark Twain's maturity—do not much differ from the denouements that Mark Twain has always given to his readers. From the beginning his work has thrived upon the principle of getting nowhere, of running frantically, but always in place, of moving and moving with great energy to arrive at last (when the dust settles, the boat has been tied up) at the very spot where the process of moving began. Hence both "Jumping Frog" and the "Bluejay Yarn," their narrators forever frozen into the single posture of credulous goodwill, the mouths of their raconteurs forever opening to tell yet another version of the same basic plot. Or hence, over the longer and profounder haul, the mock-melancholy last lines of *Roughing It,* with their air of "might as well have stayed at home"—and the movement in "Old Times on the Mississippi" from the decaying little town where you would likely be killed with sloth and boredom to the corpse-littered River where you are promised no kinder or more aesthetic death. Among Mark Twain's major writings of the 1860s and 1870s, only the near-conclusion to *Adventures of Tom Sawyer* seems an exception. Here, with the displacement of a comic strip hero by the embodiment of sober common sense, a whole new direction becomes possible. Yet on the final pages of even this book, it is implied that the possibility may be more illusion than fact. Hearing, at the Widow Douglas's ice cream social, that the same garments will fit both Tom and Huck, we must wryly acknowledge the boys as twins, and recognize that one day soon they may interchange perspectives as readily as a wardrobe.

And in a way, of course, getting nowhere provides readers of Mark Twain with ample reasons to rejoice. By the theme, his work is lifted out of the onward-and-upward, getting somewhere atmosphere which makes so much of nineteenth-century fiction so unbearably solemn. As a substitute for the early world of Dickens where caricature is turned to character—but at the expense of sacrificing humor to the mawkish last lines of *David Copperfield*—Mark Twain can show us an enhumored world with no great expectation of ever being dislodged from paralysis, enhumored selves caught up, with no hint of future release, in their own foibles and private obsessions. What is more, he can make us laugh at the sheer hopeless helplessness of the spectacle. It is, as he himself well knew, one more way of distinguishing our funny man from the rest of them. Others abide—nay, insist on—our moral interpretations; thou art funny.

All the same a certain note of anxiety has entered into the endings of the 1880s. They are by no means as relaxed, as jocosely at ease with captivity, as before. And this is so, I surmise, because the habit of mind that had served him so well has now begun to call into question values which, in his fiction, and no doubt his heart of hearts as well, Mark Twain could genuinely cherish, did steadfastly believe to be truly valuable. The careers of Huck and Hank, as they approach their dark conclusions, display a number of interesting parallels. Each has been drawn out of a life-denying fiction: Huck, the world of words created by River life; Hank, the elaborate medieval Romance into which a blow on the head thrust him originally. The departure of each is hastened by his commitment to something objectively real: Huck to Jim; Hank to the plebeians who were carefully excluded from the medieval Romance, but whom Mark Twain introduces to engage Hank's conscience and to excite Hank's dream of a better world. Finally, as a result of his commitment, each is brought to realize that, no matter how ugly or disagreeable or downright painful the experience may be (no matter what degree of personal sacrifice is entailed), life among real grasshoppers is superior to the contemplation of artificial ones: Huck's decision to "go to hell" anticipates Hank's renunciation of the pleasures and privileges of being The Boss. Huck and Hank thus pass the supreme test of a rite de passage. They choose to be realists. They are fleshed out from self-centered caricatures into characters. They learn—and Mark Twain does not discourage use of the sticky word—they learn to love. Yet far from ultimately being liberated by an allegiance to reality, both are destroyed by immersion in the real. As the River, mimicking motion, affixes Huck under Tom Sawyer's influence, so by the implacable and resistant forces of history (by the reality that will not be changed) Hank is brought to his ruined Utopia and the battle of the Sand Belt.

Accordingly, a standard joke, based on the creator's sardonic sense of how things are, is increasingly in conflict with the creator's perception of how things ought to be. The world no longer stands still because in moments of high hilarity this is what Mark Twain sees, or allows one of his fantasizing and oblivious characters to see. The real world really does stand still—and in its stasis thwarts and subverts and turns back into enhumored selves those characters whom Mark Twain most admires. Nor, by any conceivable stretch of the imagination, can the sick joke any longer be dismissed as aberrant human behavior, which is justified by the laughter it causes. Rather the cruelty of the joke is deeply embedded in, lies at the dark heart of, *all* human behavior. The pitilessness that once upon a time might have been excused as somebody's good fun, as a moment of play, as (after all, it is only a story) a harmless and funny form of one-up-personship is now viewed as a symptom of cosmic pitilessness. One does not wish to say of a writer of genius that he has been confounded by his own cleverness. Yet it does not exaggerate matters to say that in the 1880s the writer's endings seem not so much to be contrived from within the text as imposed upon the narrative willy-nilly by forces from the outside. The sick joke is making up the work of art rather than being created by it, or being made up in it.

With the onset of the 1890s, then, Mark Twain needed a new way of complicating and clarifying his fictions. I think he did not need the means of explaining why reality stands stock still. That much had been given him when he appended "Yours truly" to the concluding chapter of *Huckleberry Finn* and went on to accept (by inventing them) the last episodes in *A Connecticut Yankee*. Rather the question was one of technique. He needed a fresh, more compelling—perhaps the operative word is "sly"—a slyer way of expressing the truth of what he knew. It is of course not demonstrable that the need preoccupied him when, at some point in the early 1890s, he turned to writing a new, longer fiction. The evidence suggests that he was merely fooling around. What can be demonstrated, however, is that as the fiction developed he found what he was looking for. Furthermore, though it took a while and caused him a deal of trouble, he found a method of applying the discovery.

Called "Those Extraordinary Twins" the fiction reworks an old interest. Although the immediate inspiration seems to have been somewhat different,[9] it began as an enlargement, with many similarities but also significant alterations, of the sketch called "Personal Habits of the Siamese Twins," which Mark Twain remembers having written around 1868. The physical details remain unchanged. When grotesque brothers arrive for a visit to the Missouri boondocks, they consist of the Siamese configuration: two heads, "four arms, one body, a single pair of legs." But for the provinciality of "Personal Habits" a decidedly more international flavor has been substituted. These Twin brothers were born of European nobility and as gifted musicians and visiting dignitaries they are at home everywhere, having traveled extensively throughout Europe, India, and the Orient. In keeping with their cosmopolitanism they are fluent in many languages, and differences between them tend to be intellectual and philosophic. While one reads "The Rights of Man," the other prefers "his 'Whole Duty of Man.'" When the first says "'Oh, damn the people,'" the second is observed to "shudder slightly." As befits their background, the Twins are no longer called Chang and Eng. Surnamed Capello, they bear (rather like heraldic insignia) the appellations Luigi and Angelo. Luciferian Luigi is "dark skinned" and "sinister looking." The Angelic Angelo is blonde, with a "noble" and "gentle" face. (*TPW*, 125, 128, 131.)

Given allusions so rich and emphatic, Luigi and Angelo must strike one as two characters in search of the moral imagination that will do them full justice. And moral implications are not slow in coming. To bemused Mrs. Patsy Cooper and Aunt Betsy Hale, the Twins reveal that the power to control their shared body passes back and forth between them on a weekly basis. Promptly at midnight every Saturday "'the one brother's power vanishes and the other brother takes possession, asleep or awake.'" The arrangement is not only "'beautiful, wise and just'"; it proceeds so inflexibly that clocks in "all the great cities of the world" are set and regulated by it. (*TPW*, 139.)

If this is buffoonery, it is also, and is very pointedly, a theory of getting somewhere (without the exchange, as Angelo says, "'the result would be a standstill'"); and hence it adds point to Angelo's "'infinitely wise and just.'" The truth is that these Twins perfectly exemplify romantic process in action. They conspire to define a duality, flowing perpetually and harmoniously into One. They bespeak the rhythmical alternation of two different presences into an organic wholeness, forever being lost, forever being renewed and restored. Theirs, to be sure, is the world of Dr. Pangloss: as the nose is for the spectacles, so Angelo serves to make Luigi manifest and vice versa. But it is likewise a burlesque version of the same teeter-totter, back-and-forth, up-and-down world which, a half century earlier, Emerson had evoked in support of his cosmic optimism in the essay "Compensation." "Life makes amends," Emerson rejoiced:

> every excess causes a defect; every defect an excess. Every sweet hath its sour; every evil its good. . . . For every grain of wit there is a grain of folly.[10]

To which (regardless of whether he knew this particular essay) Mark Twain would add: *every Angelo hath its Luigi; for every action of Luigi's there is the compensating act of Angelo.*

It is, however, a structure of reality no sooner advanced than abruptly withdrawn. While Angelo (a creature of many naps) drowses beside him, Luigi has a further disclosure for Mrs. Patsy Cooper. "'I am six months older than he. . . . It was ordained—it was law—it had its meaning. . . . *We are no more twins than you are.*'" (*TPW*, 141.) Three decades ago in "Personal Habits" this assertion of primogeniture had been the snapper, a signal for the curtain to go down. The last, one-sentence paragraph read: "I forgot to mention until now that one twin is fifty-one, the other fifty-three." Here, just the opposite happens. The claim to seniority causes a curtain to go up.

For now in less than half a page (fewer than a hundred words) someone named Tom Driscoll is mentioned for the first time; then come references to Judge Driscoll's household; then to a Pudd'nhead Wilson. We are seeing, in other words, literally arising from *within the text* the dilemma which Mark Twain will presently relate discursively in the two-or-three-page preface to "Those Extraordinary Twins" that accompanies—either begins or ends—all editions of *Wilson*.[11] Even while Luigi's new dispensation still echoes, along come strangers who "take things almost entirely into their own hands." Evoked (certainly anticipated) by the Twins, these figures commence "working the whole tale as a private venture of their own—a tale which they had nothing at all to do with by rights." As he writes on, therefore, Mark Twain has on his hands *two* narratives that jostle, compete, will not be reconciled. In mock wonder at the fecundity of his imagination, he contemplates first one stern measure, then another. Finally it comes to him: he must murder to create. One by one certain minor characters from "Those Extraordinary Twins" are dropped down a convenient well. Both Twins are disposed of at a stroke when the town hangs Luigi. Then occurs his general description of a truly radical excision: as Mark Twain puts it, "I pulled out the farce and left the tragedy, . . . a kind of literary Caesarian operation." (*TPW,* 119–21.)

But the logic somehow manages to go awry. Given the Caesarian analogy, and who is "pulled out" from whom, Mark Twain has not so much murdered to create as killed to *re*-create, to give fresh new life to what was there already.

## IV

"You'll find that there's more about them that's wonderful than their just being made in the image of God like the rest of his creatures. . . . "
The boy Joe began—
"Why, ma, they ain't made in the im—"
"You shut up, and wait till you're asked, Joe."
　　　　　　　　　—Aunt Patsy Cooper in *TPW,* 161.

From Plautus's *The Brothers Menaechmus* to *The Rise of Silas Lapham*—from Shakespeare's *Comedy of Errors* to Mel Brooks's *Young Frankenstein*—the dynamics of comedy have traditionally resulted in freeing a slave (which may mean deliverance from physical bondage, or from some enslaving delusion of the self) and in the restoration of a proper identity (which may have been lost to the world's wickedness, or laid aside by a temporarily forgetful self). The dynamics have been expressed through "luck" (a benevolent principle which *does* work things out willy-nilly); through "pluck" (the exercise of cunning and logic in a willed struggle to break free); or, perhaps most convincingly through an artful synthesis of the two: a drama of "pluck/luck." The dynamics move, as Northrop Frye and Walter Kerr have shown, from a potential tragedy, which is circumvented, to an atmosphere of renewal and regeneration: from (in Professor Frye's terms) "the world of the cave into the sunlight."[12]

Roxy displays the comic formulation in the proportions of PLUCK/luck. Like no one else in Dawson's Landing, she has sufficient passion to feel the slave's situation and wit enough to strike out against the indignities and injustices of slavery. Feeling and protesting, she acts. And for a single enchanted moment freedom springs up where there was none before, and a new, liberated identity is created. But then things go terribly wrong. When the moment passes, it becomes evident that in defying the cave Roxy has but succeeded in enlarging its boundaries. She has thrust back down into the dark interior the master's child, her own Chambers soon to be corrupted by freedom, and herself as sold downriver and as the "'po misable sinner dat I is!'" (*TPW*, 113.) For the one slave she frees, Roxy has given life to three new ones.

Wilson exemplifies the comic formulation in the proportions of LUCK/pluck. Shunted to the edge of the community from the hour of his arrival, he must bide his time as a nonparticipating member of society, awaiting passively and in an enforced solitude (somewhat like Scott Fitzgerald's "Grant-at-Galena" syndrome) for the summons to whatever civic role he might fulfill. Then, as though in reward for his patience and realism, a tree of knowledge flowers in the Pudd'nhead's dream vision. Responding to what has been vouchsafed to him, Wilson acts. And for a single transitory moment freedom springs up where it had been suppressed, identities are properly re-sorted, "the clock struck twelve," and all gather round to salute Wilson's "sentences [which] were golden now." (*TPW*, 113–14.) But as before, things go terribly askew. When the moment passes, the narrator reveals (as from inside a cave) the egotism and bigotry of Wilson, false-Tom Driscoll peddled downriver, true-Tom Driscoll cringing and forever homeless. For the slave he sets free, Wilson has given life to at least three new ones.

Was Mark Twain right, then, to style his work a "tragedy"? I think not—unless, that is, he was making use of Henry James's ambiguous genitive. The book is David Wilson's personal tragedy. But the book is not tragic. No matter how much skewed, the conventions of comedy remain too firmly in the foreground for that. It is simply that, over the years, these conventions have sooner or later come to play a winking, catch-us-if-you-can game with Mark Twain, always there for him to exploit, always eluding his grasp. Now he is prepared to wink back.

Chapter 5 of *Wilson* opens with seven paragraphs of summary, offering a capsule view of Dawson's Landing in the years between 1830 and June of 1852. It is evident that although many peripheral changes have occurred (the York Driscolls are dead, Roxy has gone temporarily to the River as a maid on a steamboat, false-Tom has traveled to Yale and back) nothing is fundamentally different—or ever promises to be. Then exposition breaks off; the page riffles; it is a flaming June day in 1852; and without so much as one prior, preparatory reference they are dropped into the middle of the chapter-in-progress, looking for all the world like two trespassers in a narrative "which they have nothing to do with, by rights." The most that can be said of the Twins—the term is still capitalized, not habitually but more often than not—is that they are raised from the dead (back from the gallows), and that having been split morally and then chronologically in another story they are now physically divided as well, so that the brunette is the active one, while the blond, though never out of sight (their appearances make them seem quite inseparable) has been recast as a passive observer. Very conspicuously, in other words, power no longer passes to-and-fro between them. And this imbalance is confirmed when, on his first morning in town, the blond confesses to Patsy Cooper "'My father was on the losing side.'" (*TPW*, 27.) It is an odd way of putting things, suggesting that although conceived in a single womb, the two were sired by different fathers, one of whom vanquished the other, thereby reserving power and authority to the darker offspring. But if Luigi dominates Angelo, both soon dominate the town. "'They are ours, all *ours*,'" gushes Miss Rowena Cooper just before and again just after their arrival. (*TPW*, 26, 29.) In a short while, though, we have good reason to reverse her emphasis. By Chapter 15 the Twins

> were prodigiously great . . . ; the town took them to its bosom with enthusiasm. Day after day, and night after night, they went dining and visiting from house to house, making friends, enlarging and solidifying their popularity, and charming and surprising all with their musical prodigies, and now and then heightening the effects of what they could do in other directions, out of their stock of rare and curious accomplishments. (*TPW*, 74.)

Clearly, Dawson's Landing is theirs, all theirs.

And as a matter of fact some interesting connections do link the new characters to the old setting. Dawson's Landing everywhere displays the same combination of Dark and Light which is present in the Twins' appearance—and at all times enacts the same imbalance of power to passivity which is insistently portrayed in the Twins' behavior. The community is a place where dark evil is far more energetic than the light of good; where the black consequences of human slavery are far better entrenched than the profession of enlightened freedom; where crimes (however much veiled) are far more transparently in the saddle of everyday life than the passive, open look of civic virtue. Moreover, Dawson's Landing has been this way always. Descending from a steamboat twenty-five years earlier, Angelo and Luigi—had they cared to observe it—could have found a town perfectly reflecting both their colorations and the relationship they bear to one another. Whatever may regulate clocks of the "great world," the timepieces of this village are presently, have never ceased to be, were, for example, one midnight of 1830, set to the rhythms of Luigi and Angelo Capello. The bongs resound Dark, Dark, Dark; only the echoes faintly chime Light. The irony therefore is that looking at their visitors now, the hosts see mirrored back to them the image of their own moral mixture. The joke is that, loving what they see, they betray the love affair they conduct with their own deeply ingrained and deeply buried corruption.

Thus, it is appropriate that, having initially provided a context for the matter of Dawson's Landing, the Twins should be resurrected and brought back to the book at just the point where the ways of the town have settled all too rigidly and wearily into one place. With Luigi and Angelo on the scene—but not an instant earlier, as we have observed—the villagers are jerked out of *vis inertiae* and proceed steadily toward what seems a tidy wrap-up. The ending reserved for them will combine two traditional narrative forms, and it will stress their intimacy. The forms are those of the comic and of the detective story. They are related in the sense that what can be said concerning the floor plan of the one applies with equal accuracy to both. As comedy assimilates negative occasions into positive outcomes, so without the prior existence of the crime, detective fiction would be at a loss to ring down the curtain on resolution and the restoration of justice. Shakespeare dramatized the connection, particularly in *Much Ado About Nothing,* but in various ways throughout the Romantic comedies. And it does not seem farfetched when W. H. Auden finds in the pure narrative of crime-and-detection (as opposed to "thrillers" or examples from the "hardboiled school") overtones of an ultimate or a Divine Comedy. In the detective story, as Auden explains, we enjoy the fulfilled "fantasy of being restored to the Garden of Eden, to a state of innocence where [we] may know love as love and not as the law."[13] Though Auden of course does not say so, released tensions are our reward when the surface tensions of crime break up—and life is once again filled neatly to the brim, but just to the brim.

Comedy and detective fiction are of enduring popularity because they affirm our Manichean sense that the purpose of life is to extract entrapped particles of Light out of the particles of Darkness, where Light has been temporarily misplaced. The two forms restore our faith in pluck and in luck. In the hands of Mark Twain, though, traditional perspectives first reverberate; and then, as always, they must be modified. Not only does comedy produce slavery and freedom in the ratio of three palpable facts to one momentary and empty illusion; it is just so with the derangement and degradation of the customary pattern of the detective story. True, at high noon on an April day, Roxy at last faces the enormity of the kidnapping she undertook at midnight: "'De Lord have mercy on me, po' misable sinner dat I is'" (although just a moment before she has been congratulating herself for her impunity: "Safe? She was perfectly safe. She smiled privately.") True, too, that justice is served when the town sentences false-Tom Driscoll to life imprisonment (though the servicing of greed seems more nearly in the foreground when false-Tom is immediately pardoned and sold downriver). And true, most especially, that despite their racist import the sentences of David Wilson are "golden now," and that from noon until long past nightfall he is serenaded by "roaring groups of enthusiasts" who sing and shout themselves hoarse with his praises. Yet at the edge of the frivolity, our attention is directed to the victim of crime—true-Tom Driscoll, reborn to be himself, but bereft, orphaned, alone and uninvited:

> He could neither read nor write, and his speech was the basest dialect of the negro quarter. His gait, his attitudes, his gestures, his bearing, his laugh—all were vulgar and uncouth; his manners were the manners of a slave. Money and fine clothes could not mend these defects or cover them up, they only made them more glaring and the more pathetic. The poor fellow could not endure the terrors of the white man's parlor, and felt at home nowhere but in the kitchen. The family pew was a misery to him, yet he could nevermore enter into the solacing refuge of the "nigger gallery"—that was closed to him for good and all. . . .

Nothing has been settled or bettered. When the molecules of crime break up, they reveal a new order that is but a rearrangement (and what is worse) a bleak continuation of the order that was. The world stands still—as enhumored worlds must. (*TPW,* 112–14.)

It becomes, then, not so much a matter of who pushes buttons as of whose button got pushed. If Roxy pushes and creates, with dire and destructive consequences; if Wilson pushes and resolves, with results that are no less destructive or dire, it follows that, betwinned and predestined, Roxy and Wilson constitute a single button, snapped to the ON position by the exertions of some higher power. Extraordinary force is needed. And shaping in the farce circumstances and a cast of characters which they then round off in the novel; but also mysterious and remote; ever intrusive, though profoundly indifferent to the effects of their influence; rarely judging, yet forever being judged; mostly silent, but habitually talked about; for all their foreign airs as familiar and readily at home as the world at the doorstep; and like the world at the doorstep, just indisputably (just humorously) *there*—in each of these roles, the Extraordinary Twins fill the bill nicely. Through Luigi and Angelo Capello, Mark Twain pops into place the last essential piece in his exposé of why the world works as it does. They are the total machine to which the others belong as mere auxiliary "cranks," "levers," and "buttons"—which is to say they function as Mark Twain's metaphors for triumphant reality. Exercising his rights of primogeniture, Luigi makes things happen. But it takes both Twins in concert to make the happenings coherent and to explain why they occur as they invariably do. By the out-of-balance relationship of Blond to Brunet, the primacy of darkness is asserted. The mystery of how opposites in nature and morality—crime/detection; fantasizing/empiricism; slavery/liberation; superstition/science—are always only different names for a single condition is resolved. Above all, it is demonstrated that when dark human deeds are unearthed and brought out into the light of day, the effect must be the descent upon High Noon of an all-enveloping Midnight.

## V

There are scenes in this novel where we hear Satan, off stage, snickering.
—Wright Morris of *TPW*[14]

"God hath made me to laugh, so that all that hear will laugh with me."
—Sarah in Genesis 21:6

Having questioned the book so relentlessly, I must next question the adequacy of my answers. To put it bluntly: how can my reading seem viable, anything other than a critical sophistry, when so many readers of great acumen have found in Wilson, if not the hero, at least the vital center of the narrative and have treated as more or less extraneous—sometimes an intrusion, again a downright unmentionable—anything that goes on outside the Roxy-Wilson-Driscoll plot, with which after all the story both certainly begins and certainly ends. For justification, I fall back on method, initially the method of a single scene. The last third of Chapter 11 presents usually torpid Dawson's Landing in a most unusual guise. As was the case in "Personal Habits of the Siamese Twins," The Templars and the Tipplers are hard at it. Insulting words are spoken on both sides. A fight breaks out, much encouraged by false-Tom Driscoll. Soon the meeting hall is in flames. Then the fire-boys mounted to the hall and flooded it with water enough to annihilate forty times as much fire as was there: for a village fire company does not often get a chance to show off, and so when it does get the chance it makes the most of it. Such citizens of that village as were of a thoughtful and judicious temperament did not insure against fire, they insured against the fire company. (*TPW*, 57.)

The scene is straight out of a Keystone Cops comedy, all boisterousness and undirected kinetic energy, virtually the only place in the book where we are caused to laugh purely.

Except, except. In the midst of the racket comes a well-aimed swift kick. From the moment it is executed, that kick ramifies outward, gathering momentum as it goes somewhat in the manner of a pendulum that has been magnetized, until at the farthest point of the arc (there can be no return because of the magnetic tug) the molecules of crime break up as if booted from place, and fawning David Wilson, as though rising by his bootstraps, is catapulted to a new home among the First Families of the village. Mark Twain *is* a wag.

His tactic is that of "deep structure": a ploy in narrative whereby some trivial detail mentioned only cursorily, all but brushed aside in the first instance, yet emerges from obscurity and is seen in retrospect to have launched a momentous action or to clarify themes of great importance. By way of parallels, one might recall the death of Billie the oiler in Crane's "Open Boat"; the twenty-two intrusions of Mrs. Littlejohn into the man-made sound and fury of "Spotted Horses"; the grandmother's cat in "A Good Man Is Hard to Find" (O'Connor is past mistress of the "deep structure"); perhaps even the blank, unseeing (all seeing!) eyes of Dr. T. J. Eckelburg. And Mark Twain has finessed with a skill worthy of Crane, O'Connor, Faulkner, and Fitzgerald. The kick he records is incongruous (who would have expected it of the gentlemanly Luigi?). It is inconspicuous, very nearly lost in the surrounding hubbub. It seems a gesture made and forgotten, of no real consequence. Yet, it is also like a squeak in the machine, a scarcely perceptible shifting of gears, meant to nag at consciousness until from the total arc there emerges an action as momentous as the exchange of the babies, far more decisive than Wilson's courtroom theatrics. The trick lies in trying to imagine what would have happened (never would have happened) if Luigi's kick to the seat of false-Tom's pants had not occurred.

The difference between "deep structure" and the "sub-text" is one of degree, a difference of the single detail from the total plot. There seems no logical or artistic justification for the break that takes place midway through Chapter 5. Though the effect of Mark Twain's Caesarean surgery was clearly to bring them kicking and squirming back to life ("I pulled out one of the stories [the farce] by the roots"),[15] still Angelo and Luigi must strike us as totally out of place, interlopers who disrupt the flow of the story, mysterious strangers to be sure, but with their Siamese link gone no longer strange enough to be interesting, and mysterious primarily in the sense that it is a mystery why the busy-busy author bothered to re-create them. For many readers, they remain necessary nuisances, about whom the least said (and it has been possible to ignore them entirely) the better for the rest of the book. Yet the sub-text which they create—or which Mark Twain furnishes through them—turns out at the last both to write and to explicate the text on the surface. For the trick this time is two-fold: to imagine what would have happened (never would have happened) had Angelo and Luigi not been reintroduced to Dawson's Landing; to see that even before they become manifest physically, the Dark One and his Blond Accessory have all along been shaping the book—and therefore, by legitimate extension, writing human history as well.

The idea of Mark Twain's "River Trilogy" has always been more nearly a matter of intuition than of point-for-point illustration. Obviously, in the third volume, characters change, and so too in a profoundly meaningful way does setting: south of St. Louis this time (so that, departing the village, False Tom always goes up to St. Louis), downriver, ever deeper into slave country. Yet through technique a trilogy relationship is warranted. As "Old Times on the Mississippi" served to preface *Tom Sawyer* and *Huckleberry Finn*, so *Pudd'nhead Wilson* functions as last chapter, a conclusion and summing up. The trick lies in looking back from *Wilson* to discover that it shares with the first two books the same reliance upon deep structure, sub-text, and an all-encompassing metaphor for reality.

(1) *Act One: Cave*. A dark fatality hovers over St. Petersburg. Here, we soon come to feel, are people who can never get anything straight. They will not see; and there is more to it than inept actions or the nearsighted judgment. Each citizen seems to move in a twilight zone behind his/her fallen curtain. All lapse into falsity and error, because, preferring the personal dream and the private illusion, they never make meaningful contact with objective reality. Their collective situation is beautifully expressed through the metaphor of the Cave. Though McDougal's Cave does not appear until Chapter 12, it very quickly assumes a more than ornamental value. With its labyrinths, echoes, and false lights, it becomes the traditional cave of Plato. It is the place where some go to die, but also the symbol of the living death which all enact each day.

Incarnating the limitations of one American village, the Cave comes in Chapter 33 to acquire a still larger significance. Speaking from inside the dark interior, the narrator reflects on the corpse of Injun Joe as he once pointlessly husbanded his drop of water—then raises his eyes for a look at the long sweep of human history. "That drop was falling when the Pyramids were new; when Troy fell; when the foundations of Rome were laid; when Christ was crucified; when the Conqueror created the British empire; when Columbus sailed; when the massacre at Lexington was "news." It is falling now. . . . (*ATS*, 222.)

Thought of as panegyric, the passage seems excessive to the point of absurdity. What have the Pyramids and Troy—the Crucifixion, the birth of the American republic—to do with the death of Injun Joe? The answer lies not in contrasting the big events with the "human insect," but in noting the continuity they share. Like Joe, the monuments of history have been brought into the cave to be trivialized. They are parts of one pointless process which will be "swallowed up in the thick night of oblivion," and of which the death of Joe is just one more random, nonsensical example. Though the human mind honors the monuments, it does so in the same spirit that will cause tourists to find something marvelous in "Joe's cup." All alike resonate with the same empty and meaningless sound of drip-drip-drip.

But who made the Cave, this boneyard wherein human values are trashed and dissolved into nothingness? Literally, geologically, time and nature did it. In Platonism, however, the Cave is a timeless wonder, devised by the gods as a means of distinguishing between occasional knowledge and the pervasive ignorance of most of humankind. And in terms of the drip and the long preparation for the drip, one could do worse than look for the same Creator in *Sawyer.* Although a concordance would list many religious observances in the book, only one example of the alleged intervention of God appears. In Chapter 11, as he surveys the scene in the graveyard, one of the local ministers intones "'His hand is here.'" (*ATS*, 103.) Given the drift of the chapter—its emphasis within a half-dozen pages upon the false arrest of Muff Potter, the token exoneration of Dr. Robinson, the relaunching of Tom's career, the huffing and puffing, milling and swarming, that sets Joe free for further mayhem and death-by-thirst—an inference seems in order. It is that the clergyman of St. Petersburg spoke larger, and with a more universal application, than he knew.

(2) *Act Two: Tower and River.* Words flow: from mouth to ear, speaker to listener and back again. Water flows: from point to point, departure to destination, perhaps back again, perhaps with enlarged understanding. When the flowing stops, life is left hopelessly fragmented, while at the same time and by a strange paradox, the world is contracted into one place altogether bereft of hope. Without communication each one is compartmentalized. Without movement all are affixed in a single, stagnant, unchanging and unchangeable blob of mere enhumored matter. For these conditions, deeply embedded almost

everywhere in *AHF* and so absolute at the end, the traditional Tower and Mark Twain's novel view of the unmoving River seem admirable symbols.

But by whom was the Tower razed—then raised as a barrier? Who stilled the River? If the first question is answered by the rather spiteful declaration in Genesis 11, I suggest we might find an answer to the second by considering Mark Twain's amendment of the purple prose of a well-known nineteenth-century American orator:

> When God made the world [pontificated one S. S. Prentiss] He had a large amount of surplus water which he turned loose and told to go where it pleased; it has been going where it pleased ever since. And that is the Mississippi River.

Although I have no evidence that Mark Twain either heard from or heard of S. S. Prentiss, it is clear that he shares with Prentiss (and of course countless others including the Native American shaman, the French explorers, the pieties of T. S. Eliot) a sense of the River as mystic presence, a key to the meaning of life. Hence from the undrifting drift of *Huckleberry Finn* I infer the following response. *When God made the world He had a large amount of surplus water to which He said Seem to rage and be turbulent, give off the illusion of ebb and flow. But from the standpoint of purposed and practical movement, stay still in one place forever. To the always provocative question of why Tom Sawyer must reappear at the end of a story which is not his, let the answer be that Tom never really went away.*

*And that is the meaning of the Mississippi.*[16]

(3) *Act Three: Father.* No village intellectuals appear in St. Petersburg or if we except the highly exceptional Colonel Sherburn among the villages and homesteads of *Huckleberry Finn*. But the prankish twins of "Those Extraordinary Twins" fairly bristle with intellectual insights. Only let Angelo and/or Luigi speak and soon the story is chattering away about one or another of the big issues of traditional metaphysics: Time; Origins; Purpose; Law; the nature of Reality. Like much else in the farce, this penchant for speculation helps to shape the special atmosphere of the so-called tragedy.

For while the Wilson who told a dumb joke and stayed on unloved and unappreciated for more than twenty years could hardly have written the aphorisms ascribed to his notebook and while more is heard about that from Judge Driscoll's debating society, still from the implied author (who wrote the aphorisms) and from sundry other quarters *Wilson* emits a steady stream of philosophical musings. Thus, preparing to exchange the babies, Roxy takes comfort from two analogies. "'White folks has done it,'" she reflects. And, after a solemn moment, so has God:

"He do jis' as he's a minter. He s'lect out anybody dat suit him, en put another one in his place, en make de fust one happy en leave t'other one to burn wid Satan." (*TPW,* 15.)

Then, many years later, railing against secular fatherhood, false-Tom Driscoll extends his indictment to include another Father:

"Why were niggers *and* whites made? What crime did the uncreated first nigger commit that the curse of birth was doomed for him? And why is this awful difference made between white and black?" (*TPW,* 44.)

But most crucially, with the return of the Twins, Time-Law-Purpose-Origins-Reality are compressed into the problematic grammar of a single sentence of Angelo's "'My father was on the losing side.'"

And the other one? the dark Twin's father? The Father who won? I presume Him to be the figure who made the Cave, razed and raised the Tower, stilled the River. As always in Mark Twain, the mark of His victory is that He divides to conquer, though this time He has resorted to a different tactic. He might have created the world as comedy, not necessarily making it all Light, but tempering and curbing darkness so that the Dark runs even in the race with Light. He could have made us all Black or all White, or He could have spoken a world where Black and White mingle easily and equally. But our Father is a humorist, which is to say He thrives on the sick joke at our expense. He has set White over Black socially in order to derange and polarize human experience, thereby securing the preeminence of Dark over Light morally. He has enhumored (which is to say, enslaved) us every one.

We do not know how to read Mark Twain in the 1890s. With the funny man's own lavish encouragement, we figure him sitting there in the two-or-three-page preface to "Those Extraordinary Twins," every inch the bamboozled novelist, awash in plots he cannot control, becluttered with pages of manuscript which, like the balls of yarn in an Emily Dickinson poem, ravel out of reach and beyond all possibility of order or sequence. What we fail to detect is the elaborate hoax whereby our curiosity is so piqued by the author's confusions that we will read sequentially both parts of what he wrote and, so to speak, read them at a single sitting. And the bumpkin takes us in. Read we do, even if the result is a misreading, or provokes the eminent bibliographer to declare all of it quite unreadable.

But we mistake him in the 1890s for the excellent reason that we have, in some considerable measure, mistaken him all along. No increase of critical sophistication ever seems quite to dispel the illusion that "after all, it is only old

Mark Twain," writing lyrically of slow, mild afternoons in some River setting; writing of love and play, of childish innocence and good country people, of "sound hearts" and "high intentions"; writing vernacularly about vernacular charms and vernacular wisdom; writing of "fate" and "destiny" (as James Cox assures us) but managing these matters so that they generally come around to a good-humored ending. True, the rage and the hostility must sooner or later be confronted. These, however, can be, and often are, passed off as results of the misfortunes that came to Samuel Clemens in his old age. And for a long, golden time before they happened, it was "after all just old Mark Twain, born to excite laughter in all God's creatures, and loving every minute of it."[17]

The price of the illusion, I think, is the cost we incur by underestimating Mark Twain's complex and highly conscious art. Not to put too fine a point on it, we fail to see how antics ("Good Boy/Bad Boy" where justice can never be done) are but the obverse sides both of angst ("Carnival of Crime" where justice can never be done) and of fierce anger ("The Victims" where justice can never be done). We fail to see the uncanny repetitions of his endings: how the corpses stacked for firewood in "Carnival of Crime" are of course replicated in the corpses of the later chapters of "Old Times on the Mississippi" and in the Connecticut Yankee's stacked corpses, but also reappear as the living dead made ready for burial at the close (respectively) of *Tom Sawyer, Huckleberry Finn,* and *Pudd'nhead Wilson.* We fail to grasp the relationship between artist and audience: how Mark Twain must have hated his readers for missing the point; his live audiences who came to bray and would not be instructed; himself because the eternal unfitness of things drove him time after time to the same dead end and always prevented the bildungsroman he wanted to complete. Or, to put a very fine point on it, we slide past the rare achievement of *Pudd'nhead Wilson.*

For the truth is we do the book no favors interpreting it solely within the context of Southwestern Humor or even, for that matter, as the culminating volume of a trilogy. In his ultimate account of a God without love, presiding over a world without hope, Mark Twain breaks free to a versatility and virtuosity of technique which we never much look for because, the author being "only old Mark Twain," we never much expect it. His work is allied now with the cold, hard brilliance of Stephen Crane (I think not only of "The Blue Hotel" which has been mentioned in my second essay, but likewise of "The Monster" and such poems as "God fashioned the ship of the world carefully," "A slant of sun on dull brown walls," and "The impact of a dollar upon the heart"). It prefigures the broken structures and the freakish characters of Nathanael West, John Hawkes, and Robert Coover (noting how by presence alone Luigi attests to the superiority of Darkness in human experience, I am particularly mindful of the Sheriff in Hawkes's *Beetle Leg* and of the ubiquitous, unchanging Caretaker amidst the kaleidoscopic others in Coover's "The Magic Poker"). Most especially perhaps, it anticipates the downward arc and the sudden voids of cinema noire: Polanski's "Chinatown," for example, an account of crime and detection wherein detection triumphs, innocence is reclaimed, villainy is brought to bay, and in brightly lit Chinatown (as seemingly irrelevant to the main plot as are the Italian Twins to the main plot of *TPW*) we are finally mocked (as in Wilson's courtroom at high noon in April) with an all-enveloping horror which is far deeper and darker than any we could have conceived of earlier.

And actually, after *Pudd'nhead Wilson* and its linear if not immediate successor "The Man that Corrupted Hadleyburg," Mark Twain somewhat softens his quarrel with the nature of things. In the fictions written after 1897 and published much later, he often appears to reach out in search of some form of tentative reconciliation. The result, I think, will leave him less original and much less funny than before. But the change underscores his philosophical bent. And in ways that are unexpected and of course wholly unconscious, it will couple him with Herman Melville, that other creator of true stasis in the midst of apparent motion—that other inveterate quarreler with the Father who won, whose blackest and bleakest work is also an unremitting quest for reconciliation.

## NOTES

1. See Hershel Parker, *Flawed Texts and Verbal Icons* (Evanston: Northwestern University Press, 1984), 116.

2. *Pudd'nhead Wilson and Those Extraordinary Twins*, The Norton Critical Edition, ed. Sidney E. Berger (New York: Norton, 1980), 14–15. All references are to this edition, hereafter abbreviated as *TPW.*

3. See Freud's "Animism, Magic, Omnipotence of Thoughts," *Pelican Freud Library*, vol. 13 (London: Pelican, 1950–55). As the argument develops Freud quotes as follows from Frazer's *Golden Bough:*

Men mistook the order of their ideas for the order of nature, and hence imagined that the control which they have, or seem to have, over their thoughts, permitted them to exercise a corresponding control over things." (p. 142)

Obviously, this account of primitive magic characterizes the behavior of Tom Sawyer—and what is more—of the adults (whether at St. Petersburg, the Phelps plantation, in

Camelot or Dawson's Landing, Missouri) who model their lives on Tom. It is, in other words, a classic statement of Mark Twain's sense of the Romantic Folly.

4. The phrase is from Frederick Crews's extended and largely negative review of Susan Gillman's *Dark Twins*, in *New York Review of Books* 36 (July 20, 1989), 41. Professor Crews makes it clear that any reading which fails to recognize Wilson's "heroism" is "a drastic misreading." In contrast to this view, Professor Gillman strikes me as having all the better of it, though it will bear noting that she gladly adds her own voice to the chorus of praise for Wilson. She writes: "Alone among Mark Twain's fictional detectives . . . David Wilson is genuinely adept at the procedures of detection and proof." And elsewhere she adds that Wilson's "superior intellect" and "superior visual observations" are never at fault *per se;* they are undercut, rather, by Mark Twain's uncertainty about the value of any and all methodologies. (*Dark Twins,* 86, 87–88.) The problem, I think, is that, ever sensitive to Mark Twain's ambiguities (which makes her a better reader of *TPW* than Crews), she nevertheless persistently refuses to see how the ambiguities are ultimately resolved. It is the besetting sin of *Dark Twins:* not that the book is overspecialized and partial (given Professor Gillman's bias, we can readily understand why there should be only six or seven sentences on *Huckleberry Finn* and nearly twenty-five pages on a sketch called "Wapping Alice"), but that in mistaking certainty for confusion and "elusiveness" (a favorite word), the book misses Mark Twain's ironic totalizings—hence his fun—hence, for example, the creation of vain and myopic Wilson as a figure to be laughed at.

And one thing more: to the objection that Mark Twain would not have been much interested in legal niceties, one needs only point to the prefatory "Whisper to the Reader," where (p. 1) a certain (and no doubt apocryphal) "William Hicks" is said to have used his skills as a "trained barrister" to ensure that all the legal activities in *TPW* will be seemly and accurate. Surely "William Hicks" would have whispered in Mark Twain's ear that if they came to light Pudd'nhead's actions, with respect to evidence and the proper discovery of evidence, could only lead to his disbarment—even in Missouri, and even in the 1850s.

5. *The Love Letters of Mark Twain,* ed. Dixon Wecter (New York: Harper, 1949), 291.

6. See, in particular, F. R. Leavis's account in the Grove Press edition to *TPW,* and the far better reasoned (if, as it seems to me, dead wrong) analysis of Robert Regan, *Unpromising Heroes: Mark Twain and His Characters* (Berkeley: University of California Press, 1966), 240–41.

7. Cox, *Mark Twain: The Fate of Humor,* 232; and Leslie Fiedler, "'As Free as Any Creetur . . .'" in *Mark Twain: A Collection of Critical Essays,* ed. Henry Nash Smith (Englewood Cliffs, N.J.: Prentice Hall, 1963), 135, 137–38.

8. "Notes on the Comic," *The Dyer's Hand,* 371.

9. Mark Twain tells us he first saw his new set of twins in a picture (see *TPW*, 119); later he explains that the "Italian freak," consisting of "one body, one pair of legs, two heads and four arms" had recently been "on exhibition in Philadelphia." See *Mark Twain: Life As I Find It*, ed. Charles Neider (Garden City, N.Y.: Doubleday, 1961), 323–33.

10. *Ralph Waldo Emerson*, ed. Frederic I. Carpenter (New York: American Book Co., 1934), 117.

11. Though inexpensive editions of *Pudd'nhead Wilson* do not always include the text of "Those Extraordinary Twins," the prefatory note (which makes very little sense without "Twins") is, so far as I know, invariably presented.

12. Frye, "The Argument of Comedy," *English Institute Essays*, 61.

13. Auden, "The Guilty Vicarage," in *The Dyer's Hand*, 158.

14. In the "foreword" to the Signet Edition (New York: New American Library, 1964), xii.

15. The emphasis of Mark Twain's revisions will bear repeating: "I had no further trouble. I pulled one of the stories out by the roots, and left the other one—a kind of literary Caesarean operation." Obviously the Twins survive by the fine, obstetrical process of being reborn. *TPW*, 119.

16. In *The Dramatic Unity of Huckleberry Finn* (Columbus: Ohio State University Press, 1976) pp. 8, 11, George C. Carrington locates another unifying symbol. Interpreting Huck's downriver journey as increasingly a trip into nullity, Professor Carrington finds in the spinning wheel a perfect means of expressing Huck's sense of emptiness and his dread of death and of being alone. Turning always, but in one place, giving off sound, which is always meaningless sound, the spinning wheel would seem of a kind with the looming, unseen Tower and the motionless River.

Together with much else that sheds light on Mark Twain, S. S. Prentiss's oration is included in *A Treasury of Mississippi Folklore*, ed. B. A. Botkin (New York: Bonanza Books, 1955), 264. By sheer (yet haunting) coincidence Mark Twain's "amendment" of Prentiss is presently duplicated in D. H. Lawrence's sense of the Mississippi. Seeing it for the first time as he passed through New Orleans, Lawrence found "a vast and weary river, that looks as if it had never wanted to start flowing." Quoted in Brenda Maddox's *D. H. Lawrence: Story of a Marriage* (New York: Simon and Schuster, 1994), 335.

17. Thus it is that sense can be made of Camille Paglia's well-known attack on Mark Twain at the beginning of the last chapter of *Sexual Personae*. Surely she is wrong to identify him with "Wordsworthian idylls" and "bourgeois fantasies about childhood and lower class life." Yet one deplores her wrongheadedness, which personally I find very rare, less than the stereotypes inflicted by her professors which have helped to create and confirm the image. See *Sexual Personae: Art and Decadence from Nefertiti to Emily Dickinson* (New York: Vintage, 1991), 623.

But since I do not much like to argue with Professor Paglia (whatever her extravagances, she is constantly saying useful things about literature—a rare achievement nowadays) consider the same attitude in what is undoubtedly a more chic and fastidious context:

> After a vast silence in the cab, she politely regretted the delay she had caused me and hoped she had not kept me from "something important." I admitted that I had a lecture to give at the New School within the hour, and that I would probably just make it. What was the subject of the lecture? I confessed that it was on *Huckleberry Finn*. Much laughter from Mrs. Onassis: "Do people actually give lectures on *Huckleberry Finn?*" "Alas," I said, "I do." Alfred Kazin, *A Lifetime Burning in Every Moment* (New York: Harper/Collins, 1996), 160.

# PART III
# A LAST, SPECULATIVE ESSAY

# Mark Twain and Melville: An Essay on the Metaphysics of Twinship

Every fine evening, about sunset, these two, the cook and steward, used to sit on the little shelf in the cook-house, leaning up against each other like the Siamese twins, to keep from falling off, for the shelf was very short; and there they would stay till after dark, smoking their pipes, and gossiping about the events that had happened during the day in the cabin.

> —Melville's *Redburn* (1850)

[To] me at least all twins are prodigies. . . . Are not our thumbs twins? A regular Castor and Pollax? And each of our fingers? Are not our arms, hands, legs, feet, eyes, ears, all twins; born at one birth, and as much alike as can possibly be?

> —*Redburn*

[T]he two stood together; the old miser leaning against the herb-doctor with something of that air of trustful fraternity with which, when standing, the less strong of the Siamese twins habitually leans against the other.

> —Melville's *The Confidence Man* (1857)

So, then, an elongated Siamese ligature united us. Queequeg was my own inseparable twin brother; nor could I in any way get rid of the dangerous liabilities which the hempen bond entailed.

> —Ishmael in "The Monkey Rope"

[Y]et with me, as with the colt, somewhere those [mystic] things must exist. Though in many of its aspects this visible world seems formed in love, the invisible spheres were formed in fright.

> —Ishmael in "The Whiteness of the Whale"[1]

## I: MELVILLE AND MARK TWAIN

At the end of the 1880s, Melville had for some years been a householder in East 26th Street of New York City. During the same period Mark Twain came not infrequently to New York, for both business and social purposes. (In 1886 he created a stir of interest in the metropolitan newspapers when he read excerpts from an early version of *A Connecticut Yankee in King Arthur's Court* to the Military Service Institute meeting on Governor's Island.)[2] Suppose they had met by chance, two gentleman authors, one nearing 70, the other in his early 50s, taking their constitutionals in the lower reaches of Central Park? One is intrigued by the virtual certainty that there would have been no flicker of acknowledgment, no nod or bow, on either side. One is haunted by the thought that this would be so because neither had ever so much as heard of the other.

There are good reasons why Mark Twain might have been wholly unaware of Melville, none of which bears on his personal reading habits. Mark Twain was fully knowledgeable about Melville's sometime mentor, James Fenimore Cooper; about Hawthorne, who he confessed "just tired [him] to death"; about Poe, whom he once coupled with Jane Austen as one of the two worst stylists in the English language. But the work of these figures remained in the public domain after the American Civil War, whereas by 1857 with the appearance of his novel about life on the Mississippi (oddly, this was the same year Sam Clemens began piloting on the River) Melville had pretty much completed the long, quick decline that took him from being a widely popular writer into obscurity. Though he would continue to publish, it was no longer prose fiction, and the publications were occasional, private and relatively few in number. If new admirers sprang up toward the end of his life, they were never numerous and can be best described as members of a coterie group. As the obituary notice in the *New York Post* would say in 1891, "if the truth were known even Melville's own generation has long thought him dead, so quiet have been the later years of his life."[3]

That Melville should never have heard of Mark Twain is more difficult to believe. Surely, one thinks, since it follows the same exotic itinerary that he himself had taken twelve years earlier, Melville would have been drawn to *Innocents Abroad* when that book was a best-seller of 1869. Or would not the celebrity status of its author alone have prompted Melville to read *Huckleberry Finn* in 1884? Everyone else was. All we know is that, as a prolific reader and habitual annotator of what he read, Melville left behind no reference to these or any other of Mark Twain's works. The entries "Clemens, Samuel/Mark Twain/Twain, Mark" are conspicuously absent from the indexes of both the *Melville Log* and Professor Merton Sealts's systematic account of Melville's library and reading habits.

So, they pass through and out of my fanciful scene like two ships of an aborted "gam," like the fog-enveloped up-boat crossing wakes with a fog-shrouded down-boat. And in truth even had a flicker of recognition given rise to the perfunctory nod and bow, I think we can imagine little of common interest to sustain a conversation between Melville and Mark Twain. A few qualities they do obviously share. Each turned to an exciting, adventurous and dramatic past for the stuff of his later fictions. Each was largely dependent upon this one particular source, so that when the personal experience proved unusable both, neither necessarily to his best advantage, replaced it with materials taken from books (consider *Israel Potter* and *The Prince and the Pauper*). Each looked backward from the standpoint of a mature perspective that caused him to darken and deepen past events even as he remembered them and transformed memory into narrative. Where they differ significantly is in how they expressed what they saw, took, recalled, and recast as narrative. Although much concerned with the pestilences of "that awful country" (the phrase is Huck's) just south of Cairo, Illinois, Mark Twain would hardly have conveyed his impression of the place in this brooding, syntactically dense description from Melville's *Confidence Man*.

> At Cairo, the old established firm of Fever and Ague is still settling up its unfinished business; that Creole grave-digger, Yellow Jack—his hand at the mattock and spade has not lost its cunning; while Don Saturnius Typhus taking his constitutional with Death, Calvin Edison and three undertakers, in the morass, snuffs up the mephitic breeze with zest.[4]

Nor, though much interested in how the tone and rhythms of narrative can be set by a folksy, half-jaunty/half-melancholy narrating voice, would Melville have followed "Call me Ishmael" with Mark Twain's more intimate constructions:

> You don't know about me without you have read a book by the name of *Mardi;* but that ain't no matter. That book was made by Mr. Herman Melville, and he told the truth, mainly. There was things which he stretched, but mainly he told the truth.

Perhaps, then, at some point Mark Twain did look at a book of Melville's before casting it aside as "deep" and "ponderous" and certain "to tire him to death." Perhaps, having glanced at *Huckleberry Finn*, Melville discarded and forgot the book for its lack of high seriousness. At all events, if we are honest, either-or is likely to characterize the response of most modern readers. Professionally (intellectually) we must admire both, as great, perhaps *the* great, writers of prose fiction in nineteenth-century America. But it is also a matter of cats vs. dogs, or of Scotch whiskey vs. Bourbon. True enthusiasm for the one has a way of somewhat diminishing a fully developed taste for the other.

Nevertheless, presuming they never met and would have been little impressed if they had, I wish to couple them at what turns out to be a seminal moment in the creative life of each. Sometime in the mid-1840s, Melville in all likelihood saw the Siamese twins, Chang and Eng, exhibited at the P. T. Barnum American Museum in New York City. The Museum opened in 1841–42, and within a year Chang and Eng, together with General Tom Thumb and a bevy of mermaids, were among the stellar attractions; much touted as the "original Siamese Twins," they were presumably still on display in 1846, while Melville was in and out of the City putting the finishing touches on a revised or second edition of *Typee,* and during the summer of 1847, after he had become a New Yorker and was writing about the Barnum sideshow in his spoofs of General Zachary Taylor's pants.[5] Sometime in the 1860s, Mark Twain read about the Siamese twins when, boggling the imagination (or at least exciting a certain prurience of mind), Chang and Eng were fathering twelve and ten children respectively, and their personal habits were very much in the popular press. The moments are seminal because they set free two imaginations, and released them in ways so surprisingly parallel that the imaginations become mutually clarifying and confirming. Without what Melville did with his memories from an exhibition, I believe I would have failed to grasp the full import—the gradually exfoliating demonism—that Mark Twain attached to twinship. But intertextuality is a two-way street. Without Mark Twain's many amendments of some trifling newspaper articles, my sense of the opening quotations in this essay would have been that they are little more than Melvillian window-dressing, examples of a bogus erudition that in no way forwards the development of plot or character, and that, in the case of Queequeg and Ishmael, half buries a genuinely moving relationship beneath a distracting allusion. What would have been missed is the darker contexts to which the passages belong. I would have failed to see that out of his slightly hysterical creation of doublenesses, Melville goes on to extract singletons who are every bit as fragmented and partial as the caricatures of Mark Twain. It would have gone unnoticed that the apparently seamless wholes which spring so lavishly from Melville's work are actually forever being enveloped by Mark Twain's air of division, fixity and futility.

## II: A Theory of Twinning

From the many contemporary accounts and at least one surviving picture of the Siamese twins Chang and Eng, one physical detail is often isolated for special notice. Due presumably to the diagonal, stomach-to-chest ligature that binds them, Chang seems to bend in toward Eng, or to be tucked up under Eng, the top of his head just reaching Eng's eye or ear line. There is a certain look of conspiracy about this configuration. One might sense two heads drawn together in the exchange or apparent exchange of secrets which they will not, cannot, divulge to the rest of us. Optionally, one might picture two heads yearning to communicate, but (lips and ears mysteriously sealed) prevented from doing so—or for that matter two heads with nothing whatsoever to say, yet locked together, against their respective or collective wills (possibly even desperate to pull apart), in a wry parody of communication. The conspirators, with their air of fraternal secrets, have become victims of somebody else's or something else's conspiracy. But the configuration also possesses distinct overtones of authority. Perhaps Chang leans in for succor and protection from the more upright Eng. Alternatively, by virtue of being the more physically upright, Eng perhaps is exacting a bow of obeisance from his weaker, less forceful, even less mature brother—faulty genetics in all likelihood, but stylish as metaphor. Doubtless an element of questionable taste runs through all these scenarios. Our own tenderer, or anyhow more Title-bound, age would not display the freak; would look discreetly away from his (their? its?) handicap.*

But freakish fictions must take for grist what the mills of creation require. Not only did Melville and Mark Twain look with no hint of embarrassment at the deformity; my argument is that, separately of course, yet in strange conjunction (as if they themselves were the twins) they took from the grotesque spectacle of Chang and Eng the basis for a theory of twinning as cosmic conspiracy and/or the basis for twinning as a parable of power and servitude.

## A: Turkey and Nippers; Ahab, the Whale, the Other

Everyday the clerks in "Bartleby" sit side by side, cheek to jowl and often brushing against one another, inside the confining, cubicle-like interior of a tiny office. Day after day, they are conjoined in a common endeavor, their heads bowed as one head over the collaborative task of copying legal documents. As in a Greek creation myth, they often seem (except for the voice that tells about them) the only living figures in an otherwise unpopulated world. Turkey and Nippers (no surnames are given—or real ones for that matter, since these are nicknames) thus constitute twins or doubles, linked by setting, activity, and the lack of any discernible background as tightly and completely as though the connections between them were biological. Yet on no day of any conceivable year does the possibility exist that they might ever communicate. By morning, Turkey is voluble to the point of exuberance, whereas the morning behavior

---

* Nonsense, says a voice over my shoulder. Nothing changes. We would go to any lengths to maintain their legal rights, while simultaneously exploiting them on the afternoon talk shows. Of course Mark Twain is right.

of Nippers is sullen, irritable, wholly withdrawn, and silent. By afternoon, Nippers has settled cheerfully into the office routine, while promptly at noon Turkey suddenly explodes into a manic deportment that rules out speech, conviviality, or any other form of coherent conduct. Twelve o'clock meridian thus settles athwart what might have been a team or pairing, and splits the twosome into two self-contained entities, as remote from each other as though they stood at opposite ends of the cosmos. As the lawyer who relates the circumstances observes, "their fits relieved each other, like guards. When Nippers was on, Turkey was off, and vice versa."[6] ("Bartleby," 45.)

To this lawyer (since no name appears, let us call him Mr. Anonymous, or "the man who prefers to") what unalloyed pleasure would come from putting the parts together into two disciplined and integrated personalities! If only they were to join, somewhat in the manner of the hands on Mark Twain's pocket watch. If only Turkey's morning energies could enter into Nippers and hence enliven Nippers's morning sloth; if only Nippers's afternoon decorum could somehow impinge upon Turkey and hence serve to curb and restrain Turkey's afternoon hysteria—then either way (both ways) the lawyer would have available to him two fully functioning assistants who do practical and useful chores all the time. Behind the narrator's ruminations, however, stands an implied author, shaping meanings and prodding reader-responses in very much the way of that voice which broke through the narrative surfaces of "Jumping Frog" and *Huckleberry Finn*. What the implied author shows is that, for all his smugness and air of keeping busy, the man who prefers to is not truly at home with his many preferences. In bewilderment at first, then with self-mockery, but finally in increasing desperation, Mr. Anonymous reaches out to Bartleby as if suspecting in the behavior of the stranger with one name the presence of spiritual or other-worldly values. Conversely, Bartleby may well reflect back intimations of spirituality; perhaps he is Christly: certainly he is called "the last standing column in a ruined temple" and is repeatedly described as "meek," "mild," and "forlorn."[7] Yet reflection is all he can bring to pass, since by virtue of "preferring not to" he stands entirely cut off from involvement or participation in any actual human experience.

Like Turkey and Nippers, then, Mr. Anonymous and Bartleby are in grave need of being assembled. The energy of the one promises to animate the rather repellent passivity of the other; the latter's independence and air of dedication to higher laws might well lend point and purpose to the empty, sterile existence of his employer. They need each other for the sake of being humanized. And like Nippers and Turkey, they too are separated by a yawning gulf, an uncrossable space between that sends the one to his crucifixion (with no hint of any resurrection) in the courtyard of Tombs prison and drives the other to his final, cheerless meditation about the sorrows of humanity in a world of "dead letters." ("Bartleby," 73.)

So what keeps them all apart? How is it that four caricatures—three half names (at least two of them probably bogus) and an anonymity—should be bundled into a context where being fleshed out to character or the achievement of a full identity would seem as readily managed as the putting together of two sets of natural twins? What twins them in the womb-like office, yet simultaneously exiles them into the world as so many integers, forever cut off each from each? Once again, an explanation comes from coupling the narrator's vocabulary (and insouciance) with insights which are slyly intruded by the implied author. We are told of Turkey that his activities are "inflamed," that his hair is "red and radiant" and that he is the proprietor of a face which, always of a "fine, florid hue," can in moments of intense excitement be "flamed with augmented blazonry, as if canel coal had been heaped upon anthracite." When Nippers is described, the emphasis falls upon "sallow features," the "nervous . . . irritability" he evinces, and a manner so sour and bile-like that it presently invites the word "choleric."[8] Turkey and Nippers are, in short, two enhumored selves. Judged by the terms of the classic formulation, Turkey of the red face and unruly disposition is the pure sanguine type—possessed by a sanguinity so excessive that it remains untempered by any of the other humors. It is even so with Nippers, ruled absolutely by the dark bile that courses through body and brain to dominate every aspect of his behavior. The two give a special, sardonic twist to the phrase "every man *in* his humor." Not only must each be (and be exclusively) what he is; both are fated to be forever separated. For humor is destiny; and a sanguine temperament that knows no trace of bile can no more comprehend the bilious disposition than the bilious, unmodified by sanguinity, can live on neighborly terms with one of a sanguine temperament.

And of course, though the term is nowhere specified, humor is likewise destiny for the two major figures in the story. Magnetized by Bartleby's presence and example, Mr. Anonymous may feel the lure of the Christian beatitude of loving the stranger as oneself. He may at one point declare openly, "'I am content. Others may have loftier parts; but my mission in this world, Bartleby, is to furnish you with office room for such period as you may see fit to remain.'" ("Bartleby," 56.) At bottom, however, he remains the secular "type," defined and consumed by this-worldly commitments—just as the life of the otherworldly seems so affixed and eccentric that the temple's last "upright column" can only succeed in violating all the traditional precepts of the temple itself. What is urgently called for in "Bartleby" is the influence of some new dispensation. This would involve a synthesizing force—a third or ameliorating condition—powerful enough to bend the rigid dualities and blend them into meaningful wholenesses. But no such influence is forthcoming. Without it the narrative "of Wall Street" must end where it began, an account of four partial lives, each in dire need of self-transcendence, all walled off (walled in) by the nature of things from this one unattainable outcome.

Together with several other tales of the mid-1850s,[9] "Bartleby" fine-tunes a vision of life that had engaged Melville for a decade, ever since (at the time, no doubt half-consciously) he had stumbled upon the truth of the vision in connection with Tommo's sense of the ambiguous, which-is-which? relationship between the twin groups, Happars and Typees. The vision is shaped—and I am convinced eventually shaped quite consciously—by Melville's indebtedness to the two key narratives that are contrasted and then assembled in Plato's *Symposium*. In the first, Aristophanes tells of human beings from some long ago Golden Age who were circular in structure rather than upright. They formed a circle because each was actually composed of two identities, wrought together in a perfect harmony and compatibility. But having by their happiness excited the envy of jealous gods, the circular beings were presently disassembled and split into two upright lines. Ever afterward the experience of love consists of the endless and usually unsuccessful quest by one half of the fractured circle for its original companion and counterpart. Life is a frustration of potential, but rarely to be realized, twinnings.

Aristophanes's story is soon dismissed as a mere grotesquerie. It is merely the invention of the well-known comic poet. Who would wish to take it seriously? Toward the end of the *Symposium*, however, all the details are subtly repeated, reenacted when Socrates recalls (or imagines) the narrative of Diotima. Now the upright lines are turned over on their sides and become horizontal, one lying below the other. The lower line stands for the world of sense, with all its attendant confusions and irresolutions. In the upper line is embodied the world of Spirit, resplendent with the Good, True and Beautiful in their eternal aspects. And this time the two realms, though separate as parallel lines must be, are susceptible to being reconciled. As in an act of love the adoring self reaches up to grasp the Eternal, so Eternity bends downward to receive the spiritualized, Platonized identity back into its midst. The full argument of the *Symposium* is to present the physical division of twins which is yet compensated for through the metaphysical union of a spiritual twinning.

With some special new emphases, the structure of the *Symposium* is transformed into the structure of *Moby-Dick*. Both narratives from the Socratic dialogue enter very deeply into the novel, which first explores the frustrations of being twinned (and untwinned) in the world below, and then takes for its subject the dream of a metaphysical synthesis between Lower and Upper worlds. Because of its greater scope, furthermore, *Moby-Dick* is able to do one additional thing. It has space to address explicitly questions about twinship which, three years later, could be taken for granted and hence left implicit in "Bartleby." The questions are three-fold: what force creates physical twins as a prelude to cutting them apart? what force might reassemble the riven two into a new and fresh wholeness?; in short, what action would be required to put the humpty-dumpty world of "Bartleby" back together again?

Although he has been heard and glimpsed from a distance before, Captain Ahab makes his first close-up appearance in Chapter 36 of *Moby-Dick*. We watch him mount to the quarterdeck as a wounded man who, in consequence of the wound, is also man betwinned and man bereft. In the climactic, off-stage moment when his leg was reaped off and devoured, a portion of Ahab flowed outward into the whale. The dismembered member literally became part of the whale's substance. But the flowing process is circular. Since the artificial leg he now wears is made not of the customary wood or metal but has been shaped from the bone of a sperm whale's jaw, a portion of the whale has flowed out into Ahab where it becomes part of his being. Sheer appearance thus gives the lie to Starbuck's indignant complaint that Ahab renounces his humanity by "'seeking vengeance on a dumb brute.'" (*MD*, 967.) Where Starbuck would draw categorically the line that sets human sea captain apart from mere sea creature, the tableau in Chapter 36 shows the two as twins, formed and joined organically. Man and Whale. Whale and Man. They have been merged into a physical oneness. Yet in the very moment of merger, they were instantly divided. As the white whale struck, dismembered, and then swam maddeningly away, Moby-Dick and Ahab were separated into hunted and hunter, or into the Mystery and the Detective of a Philosophical Detective Story.

What, then, is the object of the hunt—the aim of the Detective Story? I conjecture that it involves a strange wish for re-union leading to communion. Notwithstanding the view of Starbuck and a good many commentaries, the voyage of the pursuing *Pequod* is not primarily motivated by the desire to inflict bodily injury on a purely physical foe. The white whale has been totemized, if not exactly into a metaphysical presence (that is the undetermined issue of the book) at least into metaphors which are suggestive of a metaphysical presence. Moby-Dick is a "pasteboard mask," a "wall shoved near to [Ahab]," the source of intolerable mystery and inscrutability, "a symbol of that intangible malignity to which even modern Christians ascribe one half of the world." (*MD*, 967–68, 974.) By laying aside the mask, or by breaching the wall, Ahab seeks to reenact the moment when he flowed into the whale and the whale flowed into him. Then, with his adversary brought into the light of day, all resistances overcome, he believes a Sign will be given, an enlightening Voice vouchsafed, a redeeming Vision will descend, all of which will explain and, explaining, justify the riddle of the collision. Perceptive criticism has sometimes toyed with the idea that, for all his ugliness and ultimate absurdity, Ahab may yet be "right" in *Moby-Dick*.[10] Perhaps the measure of his "rightness" lies in the fact that although he projects all evil onto the whale, he never once implies that all reality and all human experience are given over to evil. Ahab is an unwilling dualist, goaded and tormented by the perception of how terrifying contrarieties (yon smiling sky vs. the cannibalism of the sea) seem merely to coexist randomly, with neither half of the pair ever accommodating or elucidating the other. Like Father Mapple, whose rigor, though not of course faith, he curiously shares, Ahab would "'burn and pluck out'" the dark underside of existence. But he would do so by comprehending evil philosophically—that is, by reforming the circle in the world below in order to circumscribe it within the closed and completed metaphysical circle, thereby unmasking its Cause in the world above. His aim is to be healed through a process of being betwinned twice over. (*MD*, 989, 845.)

The end result of his desire, however, is to make him at once the victim and the villain of a form of melodrama which I would call New England gothic. The gothic is a literature of entrapment and entombment inside some sinister interior. Peculiar to both the Puritan and the Transcendentalist sensibilities, New England gothic occurs when, despite the intensity of one's Socratic passions, one is denied access to what toward the end of *Nature* Emerson had grandly entitled the "upper air . . . of absolute Truth and Justice," and so feels thrust back willy-nilly into a chaotic swirl of "swine, spiders, snakes, madhouses, prisons, enemies"—and of course white whales.[11] Emerson himself has more than casual brushes with New England gothic, particularly in such later essays as "Fate" and "Illusions." The situation is central to Whitman's "As I Ebb'd With the Ocean of Life" (for all its Long Island setting), and to a great many of Emily Dickinson's portrayals of nature's "haunted house." In *Moby-Dick*, as later in "Bartleby," the haunted world of gothic is embodied in a drama of dividing and confining walls. What seemed the readily penetrated, almost neighborly wall of Chapter 36 has by Chapter 125 reemerged in Ahab's mind as the "'dead, blind wall, which butts all enquiring heads at last.'" At the end, in each of the three days' chase, Moby-Dick maintains distance by taking the form of a strangely mobile wall, swimming round and round to keep Ahab at bay, until the wall contracts into a final, unilateral, all-destructive rush. And, again as in "Bartleby," the enclosure, whether signifying unwelcome confinement or bespeaking unwelcome exile, is a rich place for the venting of grotesque frustrations. Inside, howling to get out; outside, clamoring with ever-increasing frenzy to get in: it makes no difference finally. Ahab as the book goes along is gradually transformed into an automaton—an example of the thoroughly enhumored self.

Frankly, he is something of an embarrassment to latter-day criticism. Rantings and ravings, even when cloaked in Shakespearean rhetoric, are still rantings and ravings—a torrent of words and antic posturings that are as noisy and wearying as they are futile, and more nearly the marks of madness or senility than of the potentially tragic hero. Not only does Ahab presently prefigure Turkey in turmoil; he comes uncomfortably close to resembling Injun Joe in the cave or Colonel Grangerford, as altogether consumed by self and quest as the others are obsessed by self and dripping water, or self and Shepherdson. With its scraggly, flowing hair and fixated eyes, the well-known lithograph of Ahab by Rockwell Kent could readily represent all these figures; all are equally susceptible to a formulation applied to the flaw of the humorous type in Ben Jonson's comedies: "All [their] thoughts force [them] back to the same subject. [They] rant with a vigor which, whatever its peculiarities, obeys a pattern. . . . For [their] stream of humor rushes like a river which, the more deeply cut, the more tedious and confining it is."[12] Understandably, critics prefer to focus on Ishmael, or cetology, or texts and hieroglyphics—on anything in the book except the book's putative hero.

Yet even at his overwrought worst, two things serve to keep Ahab from becoming quite the pre-programmed robot. One is our recollection of the mood of Chapter 36, an atmosphere which invites being expressed in the phrase, *If I was not meant to have answers from my Twins, why was I born with sufficient consciousness to ask the Twins questions?* The second is the way intimations of twinship keep pricking at Ahab from the outside to goad him along on his quest. This second subject is brilliantly executed in the *Pequod's* initial encounter with another whaling ship, a meeting that occurs before the term "gam" has been defined, yet functions as the most important single gam in the book.

Looming up as though out of nowhere, the *Albatross* comes attired all in white, its "bleached" sides and rigging "furred with hoar frost" suggestive of the ghostly, the supernatural, the whiteness of the whale. Among her masts swing members of the crew, each one endowed with the same descriptive terms will presently reappear in the portrayal of Bartleby. They are "mild," "meek," "forlorn," altogether withdrawn and silent. So, the two ships draw close, like veritable twins in mid-ocean: the *Pequod* which would know whiteness, the *Albatross* which everywhere displays the absence of all color; the other-worldly *Albatross*, the this-worldly *Pequod*; the text waiting to be read, the avid and anxious pursuer of the text's secret meaning. Little wonder that an act of communication is attempted, as Ahab picks up a speaking tube and cries out to the stranger: "'Ship ahoy! Have ye seen the White Whale?'" And now, wonder of wonders, the "strange captain" of the *Albatross* seems set to reply. He "put his trumpet to his mouth," and begins to form words. In their last guise as twins, therefore, *Albatross* and *Pequod* become linked in the circular, reciprocal pattern of Question and Answer, about to make contact.

But in anticipation of Bartleby, the captain of the *Albatross* suddenly prefers not to. Or perhaps it is a wind that springs up to drown out the stranger's words and to drive the two ships rapidly apart, each bound on its own straight-line course away from the other.[13] In any case, this is ever the way in Melville. One reaches out to embrace one's twin, and the twin slips and slides away, becomes remote and apparitional. One renounces the embrace and lo! there is the chimerical twin again, still somehow linked to one, still beckoning one on with the tantalizing promise that if only some new tack were to be taken, some fresh rapprochement devised, the glorious communion of self with Other might yet be consummated. Just as the pain lingers on long after the limb is severed, so constant failure does not make twinning any less an emotional and psychological necessity.

If the event in Chapter 52 registers Ahab's predicament and lends at least some dignity to his later frenzy, the words that come in summation of the chapter belong to Ishmael. Liberal-humanistic criticism has often been pleased to find in Ishmael's survival the marks of a redeemed or resurrected character. The argument goes that amidst a cast of caricatures—Ahab's unremitting anger, Starbuck's prudence and Christian platitudes, the unfailing jolliness (or mediocrity) of Stubb and Flask, etc. etc.—Ishmael alone is capable of change, so that having set out sympathetic to Ahab he gradually withdraws from Ahab's destructiveness into a more balanced view of experience and, most especially, into the healing human companionship that begins with Queequeg and (in a chapter like "A Squeeze of the Hands") extends outward to embrace and encircle all the members of the *Pequod*'s crew. To put the case this way, however, is to miss the full force of how and where Ishmael ends up in *Moby-Dick*. On the last pages it is not simply that he finds himself enveloped by whiteness and the great shroud of the sea, or that he is picked up by the bereft and wailing *Rachel* as another "orphan"; above all, his situation is that of one who has watched all his "dear, dear friends" sink lifelessly to the bottom of the Pacific Ocean. In effect, he is quite literally back on page one, "involuntarily pausing before coffin warehouses" and bringing up "the rear of every funeral [he] meets."

Hence, watching the *Albatross* disappear, Ishmael comments with prescience on his outcome, that of Ahab, and the outcomes of Melville's dark tales of the mid-1850s. The world turns, he reflects, and perforce individual identities turn with it, forming circles as they go. Yet unless it turns toward the world above, or turns in accord with the benevolent laws which framed it from above, the lower world can only be said to turn without progress, development, or purpose, and the physical circles remain transitory and meaningless. Left undiscovered, the invisible spheres which have shaped the spheres we know must seem "formed in fright." And if this is the case circumnavigations through the world below go nowhere. Either, like Ahab, the voyager is "midway . . . whelmed"; or in the manner of Ishmael he lives on, but survives as a more knowing Huckleberry Finn, recognizing (as of course Huck cannot; Huck can only dramatize the fact) that in a world devoid of lasting connections or stable moorings, too far west is east, so that lighting out for the territory ahead only results in passing through "barren mazes" and "numberless perils" to arrive at the same point "from whence [the traveler] started, where those [he] left behind . . . were all the time before [him]." (*MD*, 1846.)

### B: Angelo and Luigi

Although Luigi (being six months older) logically comes first in the order of creation, it is Angelo who makes creating him necessary. Consequently, we must begin with the blond one—or, rather, with the drawn-from-life sibling who made creating Angelo necessary.

By mid-morning, as Mark Twain wrote to Howells, Orion Clemens had completed and mailed off to a publisher the outline of a treatise "whose purpose was to destroy Christianity." Later that same day he lost all interest in the project, and set to work on his life story, to be entitled "The Autobiography of an Ass."[14] By the time both manuscripts were returned to him (without editorial comment) both were long forgotten, for he had, temporarily, resumed "rabid membership in the Presbyterian church." This was the typical pattern of the humorist's brother, ten years his senior. Orion was utterly destitute of staying powers, a will-o'-the-wisp in perpetual motion who could not be pinned down to any persuasion or practical undertaking for longer than it takes an eye to blink. Itemizing his career for Howells in 1879, Mark Twain could say of Orion that he "had belonged to as many as five different religious denominations"; had been an avid supporter of Tilden but also an eloquent speaker for Hayes in the national election of 1876; had practiced law (with seldom a client and never a paying one) and been a chicken farmer (who regularly gave away what few chickens survived); had attempted with little success anywhere lecturing, authorship, journalism, literary criticism, prospecting, politics, and keeping a boardinghouse in Keokuk, Iowa; and was at one point his wife's bridegroom, while being simultaneously affianced to another young woman in a nearby Illinois village.[15] Nor did Orion appear capable of pinning himself down. Through the entries in Mark Twain's *Autobiography*, we come to see him as one who daily ran the gamut from extreme optimism to the profoundest melancholy, whose impracticality was matched by a fierce personal probity (every new congregation he joined soon elected him treasurer), and whose seeming arrogance as he took up each fresh position rested upon a consuming hunger to be approved and loved.[16] In 1879, Orion had twenty more years to live. He would spend them spinning his wheels, futilely trying to square the circle of existence—until, as Mark Twain records in the *Autobiography*, he died aged seventy-two, sitting bolt upright at a table in Keokuk, pencil clutched in his hand, as if ready to write out one more of his innumerable schemes-for-the-day.[17]

Professor Franklin Rogers has observed that it took Howells's tact together with a brother's hard-won struggle for reticence to prevent Orion from being treated as the object of open mockery in Mark Twain's work.[18] One wants to add, though, that the tact and rectitude seem principally a means of deflecting attention away from the real person: of protecting the name of the innocent, so to speak. Actually, in deed as well as temperament, Orion is never far removed from the writing. Literary history, and psychological criticism, could do worse than see him as one of the prime movers *for* the writing, a figure who, many times multiplied into various names and shapes, becomes a particular influence upon one of writing's major subjects. From the beginning, on to the crowds and crowd-scenes he so loved to portray, Mark Twain habitually projected everyone of his brother's vagaries and peculiarities.

As the River narratives and Hank Morgan's Camelot amply testify, to "swarm" and "mill"—to "gape," and "gawk" and "chatter" aimlessly—express the physical side of crowd behavior. Suggestive of a certain mass sluggishness, but of apathy interspersed with sudden spurts of activity, the verbs are equally revealing of the moral and emotional ebbs and flows which are displayed by people in groups. For as drowsy much of the time as their village surroundings, Mark Twain's characters can be aroused to abrupt flights of fancy; to headlong plunges into the next new thought or plan that pops up into their collective consciousness; to impulsive behavior that has as its purpose the achievement of neither security nor stability, but seems motivated, rather, by a kind of nervous irritability which can be dangerous, and by the belief (equally full of peril) that any novel idea, no matter how outrageous or incompatible with its predecessors, is immediately the superior in value of all other ideas. Hence the creation in the early 1890s of Angelo Capello serves at a stroke the needs of a double purpose. Temperamentally, Angelo knows "all the climes of feeling, from the sunny heights of joy to the black abysses of despair." Intellectually, he is chameleon-like, always in search of some new religious belief and of the different denomination that will be worthy of his spiritual ardor. Physically, he is hypochondriacal, a collection of ever changing symptoms, whose dread of medicine is exceeded only by the relentless quest he undertakes for the next physician and next form of quackery that might cure him. ("Those Extraordinary Twins," 119, 136.) Chiefly, though, Angelo is just silly. The shared power that is imputed to him in "Those Extraordinary Twins" results in no meaningful actions—unless running for cover is a meaningful action. For the most part, he is rendered as an absurdity, petulant, querulous, ever obtuse, strutting and fretting through the alternating weeks of his own inconsequentiality. And in manifesting such qualities the blond twin perfectly incarnates the "damned fool" who was an intimate, almost everyday exasperation in Mark Twain's personal life. And he manifests equally as well the circular journeys from nothing to nowhere—nowhere to nothing—that Mark Twain had long been projecting onto the "damned human race."[19]

Both are "damned"—the living man, the imagined throngs—because despite the freedom and fecklessness they appear to exemplify, both labor under the pressure of two terrible and unforgiving compulsions. First, each is condemned to be consistently inconsistent. Secondly, therefore, even in seeming to explore all the byways to chaos, both remain affixed in and ruled by one pattern of behavior, and it the very pattern that is guaranteed (fated!) to do the greatest possible harm to themselves and others. As he ponders Orion's career, Mark Twain has to linger with a certain awe over the compulsive logic that cost his brother high political office in Nevada because on election eve Orion abruptly changed from being a partisan of the right to strong drink into a temperance addict. He has to find more at work than an inopportune moment when, several years later as the Clemens's land in Tennessee was about to be sold for vineyards, Orion spoiled the transaction by suddenly deciding that to make wine was sinful.[20] And it is just this perversity—this strange combination of excessive means to reach trivial ends, or no end at all; this air of being frenetically on the move that is actually the reenactment of one, single blunder, as baffling as it is wrong-headed—which dominates crowd-actions in Mark Twain's fiction. Why when they fear him and know him so well does the populace of St. Petersburg resist seeing the concrete evidence that might at least have sent Injun Joe fleeing for cover to the next township, and then, contrary to all reason, canonize Joe after his death into the village legend? Granted that the abuse of language is the key to self-destructiveness in *Huckleberry Finn*, why is it that everyone (predator and prey, good and bad equally) sounds just like everyone else, since everyone misuses words in one, uniform way? How can it be, when every peasant at Camelot has in some measure profited from

Hank's reforms, that the Yankee is left with a following of only fifty-three partisans (Clarence and the anonymous fifty-two young men), instead of the battalions of workers and farmers who ought to have flocked to his cause?

Obviously these matters cannot be said to beggar the imagination; Mark Twain too much loved to invent them and to keep them life-like for that. What they do defy is rational explanation. They seem the performances of enhumored selves—or, since the idiom is Mark Twain's, they are actions performed by those who are not so much human beings, endowed with mind and will, as "cranks" and "buttons" disguised in a human form. (Mark Twain will once liken Orion to a "motor.") But for the metaphors to be meaningful, someone (something) must be discerned to push the button; to turn the crank; to rev up the motor. "I never met the twin of it," Mark Twain says of his brother's personality in the *Autobiography*.[21] The fact remains, nevertheless, that not only did Mark Twain twin Orion with Angelo and with the multitude of fictional caricatures created in Orion's image; but having betwinned them, he found it necessary to couple them beneath the weight of another and far more powerful twin. Now, he was ready for dark Luigi.

The blond one shows what happens in a giddy, fickle yet strangely foredoomed world. The brunet explains why. He is the one authentic actor in the drama, the figure to whom the actions of the others, no matter how dynamic and capricious they may appear to be, come merely as reactions. Called Eng in his first avatar, he exerts authority and seniority to intoxicate right-living, befuddled Chang, just as playing the part of "Green Face" he will presently occupy the mind and space of poor, indecisive "Mark Twain" (ever of at least three contradictory opinions about any moral issue) and turn "Mark Twain" into a hardened criminal. In both instances it is as if an elder, more upright twin, bends down, all mouth, to pour temptation and dark mischief into the helpless ear of the figure below him.

But between these sketches a significant variation occurs. Neither physically described nor (apparently) brought into physical contact, Bad Boy/Good Boy no longer incarnate the brunet-blond dichotomy; they represent two moral sensibilities, driven to one cataclysmic ending by a darkness which envelops and determines the conduct of both. And it is this sense of darkness dispersed throughout experience as a generalized or universalized force which dominates Mark Twain's major fictions of the 1870s and 1880s. Looming now as force from above over shrunken impotence, the powers of darkness are made palpable as the Spirit of the River, arresting the flow of life on the Mississippi for pure devilment in "Old Times," but mingling mischief with pathos when the same stasis descends on *Huckleberry Finn*. Again, the dark one presides as the Voice of History, travestying historical processes which have prepared for (or culminated in) the ridiculous death of Injun Joe, but finding in the same travesty the unmoving-movement of history which brings Hank Morgan to his appointment with disaster and death on the Sand Belt. With the onset of the 1890s, however, Mark Twain resumes personifying darkness. And now, for the next twenty years, his work will join the mainstream of a traditional (if regionalized) form of American melodrama. I would call it the form of distinctively Southern gothic.

Perhaps the key lies in how the tenets of Calvinism were domesticated into a theory of social and cultural behavior in the American South. No doubt, behind that domestication, there is the fact and afterward the legacy of black slavery. At all events, Southern gothic persists in finding the grounds of horror and unwelcome entrapment *inside* the events of the physical world. Indeed, the Southern gothic form acts as if the more mundane and commonplace are the containers of darkness, the greater the menace is, and the more likely its eruptions into broad daylight. Thus Poe early on unifies a series of sketches around the theme of "the Devil was in it," and presently reemphasizes both preposition and object when he locates the "imp of the perverse" not in the supernatural or some never-never region where imps properly belong, but traces perversity back to the "innate and primitive principles of all human behavior." Thus in our first glimpse of him, Faulkner shows us Flem Snopes as suggestively Satanic—

> One moment the road had been empty, the next moment the man stood there . . . materialized apparently out of nothing

—while at the same time we are made to see Flem, here and elsewhere, as just one more slack-eyed, tobacco-chewing redneck, "dressed in his soiled white shirt and cheap gray trousers."[22] Or thus the underlying violence shared by humor of the old Southwest and the dark farces of Ambrose Bierce (his imagination forever affected by his Civil War experiences); the atmosphere of nightmare (that is never quite hallucinatory) in the haunted stories of Eudora Welty; or (all in spite of her somewhat arcane Catholicism) the outright diablerie that can spring forth from the characters and landscapes of Flannery O'Connor. In "Those Extraordinary Twins" Mark Twain burlesques Southern gothic. Watching while Luigi leers at Angelo or plays games with Aunt Patsy Cooper at the breakfast table, we are in the presence of the twirled mustachios and other broad gestures of the stereotypical gothic villain. Using the same characters, the fifth chapter of *Pudd'nhead Wilson* provides a more serious version of Southern gothic in motion.

After her letter from the outside world is received and read, Aunt Patsy sits "on her porch gazing out with unseeing eyes upon the shining reaches of the mighty Mississippi." (*TPW,* 25.) What can the old lady be dreaming of? one wonders; what vision is it that seems fairly to leap out at her from below the blank face of the River? In one sense, unquestionably, she is anticipating her change of fortune as the proprietress of the town's only boardinghouse. Yet the sentence is portentous, freighted with an air of meanings that extend beyond the obvious import. And given what will happen next, it seems plausible to suppose that through the mind of the most naive citizen in Dawson's Landing there has flickered a premonition of the Dark One, who will soon float down the "shining reaches," invade the village, enthrall it, cure it with a kick, and then with his blond brother in tow depart again, leaving behind a darkness and accursedness that are more total than ever before. Aunt Patsy thus functions here as she and Rowena will function a bit later in the parlor when, with rapt attention, they listen to the four-handed piano recital of Luigi and Angelo— and we recognize in the chords, major and minor, nothing less than the basic rhythm of human experience itself. (*TPW,* 30.) Like Faulkner's Will Varner seeing Flem on the roadway, she has had an inkling of the demonic emerging out of the ordinary, everyday world.

Late in life Mark Twain would claim he regretted that the Siamese configuration which he rediscovered in "Those Extraordinary Twins" had to give way to the physical separation of Angelo and Luigi in *Pudd'nhead Wilson.* Without the ligature to connect them, he felt, the twins lost all energy and individuality and "took no further interest in life. They were wholly futile and useless . . . they became mere shadows."[23] Presumably this is why he elected to dismiss them in two terse, flat sentences on the last pages of the novel:

> The twins were the heroes of romance now, and with rehabilitated reputations. But they were weary of western adventures, and straightway retired to Europe. (*TPW,* 114.)

Yet the fact is of course that except in the farce Angelo never had any real individuality to lose. Elsewhere he was less character than composite: a living, speaking, bumbling compendium of all the folly and fatuity which Mark Twain detected as actuating humankind generally. Consequently the separation of the twins and their alleged return to Europe do not mean that Angelo is stripped of a certain kind of importance or in any way disassociated from the American scene. He blends readily back into the crowd scenes from whence he stepped forth in the first place. Granted even an ounce of self-awareness, any member of any group created by Mark Twain after 1895 would have to echo the Flaubertian formulation: *Angelo, c'est moi.* What is stressed, however, is the strange reenergizing and rehabilitation of Luigi. Like Candide's acquaintances, he will not die. Hanged in the farce, deported from the novel, he is very soon brought back to the American Republic, to resume his role in a story of crime and detection. But with resumption comes difference. Where once he resolved with a kick and quietly withdrew, the Dark One now swoops down upon a crime scene with all the power and craftiness of an avenging demon. He is a many faceted presence, always at the center of things, following 1895: a jester; a mischief-maker; the lord of misrule; at times a sadist; ultimately, a self-styled savant—the enhumoring force with a thousand faces. And, above all, his sallies downward into a crime-ridden world are increasingly portrayed with trappings of the supernatural, as if the Dark Twin spoke for (or as!) the Dark Father who had been on the *winning* side.

I believe, for example, that in "The Man That Corrupted Hadleyburg," appearing in *Harper's* in December 1899, five years after the publication of *Pudd'nhead Wilson*, he alone is responsible for several decisive actions that appear to come from several different quarters. At the beginning, we see him as a practical-joker-supreme named Stephenson. Out of a "dark night" he emerges, borne along by what may be the slyness and cunning of a Simon Wheeler but what is certainly Simon's apparent lack of any specifiable motive, to galvanize the town into action with his bag full of specious coins and his nineteen handwritten notes, all postmarked from a different and "distant State." Near the end in the form of an "amateur detective gotten up as an impossible English earl,"[24] the same figure watches while Hadleyburg's sham morality is unmasked, and he completes his triumph by swindling the town collectively before bilking the richest of its nineteen prominent citizens of $40,000 in negotiable checks. But between these two appearances lie many mysteries, a veritable plethora of narrative red-herrings which prevent "Hadleyburg" from being read as a tidy, straightforward account of crime, guilt, and punishment.

For one thing there are the puzzling Richardses. Why do both episode and narrating voice persist in sheltering them, when by their snivelings and cupidity, the lifelong love affair they have conducted with their own priggishness and cowardice, the old couple are branded as among the worst and most offensive of the town's nineteen? Why does being sheltered have the ironic effect of killing them with a fear of disclosure? Or consider the Reverend Mr. Burgess. What unnamed offense (and since Richards has always known it to be groundless) what strictly invented offense cost him the favor of the community? Why has he been selected by Stephenson to adjudicate the matter of the town's "reward"? For that matter, since he has long been banished, why is he still present to perform this chore, and why, despising him, does the town tolerate him in the role of its judge? As the evidence is read and re-sorted, the conviction grows that (as the title emphasizes) it is one personage who corrupts Hadleyburg. The man destroys the town as a mark of contempt for its general hypocrisies, and the particular hypocrisy which made him an outcast. He protects the Richardses in order to send them two notes, bristling with innuendo, which will result in their death. Though variously called Stephenson, detective, earl (and perhaps Barclay Goodson) he bears, in reality, a single name, which unifies his personality. The name is Burgess—a fitting name for one who controls the destinies of his fellow burghers.

Nor does the fact that at one point Burgess and the detective are seen to confront and address each other detract from this interpretation. It signifies, instead, the excursion into pure black magic which has always been a potential of Mark Twain's imagination. A part of the magic consists of the absolute immobility of all human experience. As in Mark Twain's previous work, the words of the narrative move; but as if enchanted, the subjects and events of narrative stand stone still. Hadleyburg cannot *be* corrupted, any more than one might add green to emerald and cannot be ridded of corruption, any more than one might extract sweetness from sugar. Hadleyburg *is* corrupt, so that the two postmarks at the end of the story are but different labels for the same, continuous community of dead souls. This time, however, the reasons for stasis are given more clearly than ever before. The corporate identity of Hadleyburg has long since incurred demonic possession, a form of paralysis that comes when all belong to Satan, yet none acknowledges Satan's existence. True to the traditions of Southern gothic, the Devil now arises from the most mundane of everyday activities to collect His booty. If He doubles (triples, quadruples) himself into *now* Stephenson, *again* Burgess, *next* detective disguised as earl, *finally* earl-detective conversing with Burgess, this is so because, as an actor on the human scene, Satan hath power to assume many shapes and to conduct his business through creating the illusion of many different voices.

And it is as a structuring principle as well as thematic concern that the Dark Twin acts for Mark Twain in his later fiction. Among the unfinished manuscripts collected by Professor John Tuckey into the volume *Which Was the Dream?*, by far the longest and most interesting is a novel of nearly 400 pages entitled *Which Was It?* Begun in 1899, the year "Hadleyburg" appeared in *Harper's* Magazine, it resembles the short story, as well as *Pudd'nhead Wilson*, by interjecting a series of loose ends into a deceptively clear and unbroken narrative surface. Before our eyes, the realistic anatomy of an antebellum American village is undertaken, while simultaneously we are forever encouraged to play peek-a-boo with matters in the background that are left half-stated and underdeveloped because, apparently, they are too complex or horrible to be dealt with directly. The effect is to create too many characters, to supply a vast accumulation of incidents that often seem duplications of one another even as they remain unlinked as a group, to bury the whole beneath an atmosphere of the surreal and cluttered which seems most appropriate to nightmare. Yet despite the implications of the title and opening frame, *Which Was It?* is no nightmare, at least not a bad dream from which there will ever be any possibility of awaking. Nor does the great variety of episodes lack for transitional devices. Coherence comes with the realization that almost every individual episode might well be prefaced with the words IF ONLY.

The words are deeply embedded into events from the foreground of the book. *If only:* an old man named Andrew Harrison had not lied cravenly and needlessly . . . his grandson, Tom, had remembered to deliver a whole message instead of half of it . . . a maidservant had not removed important papers from the breakfast table to the mantel where they lay unnoticed for a long period . . . George Harrison (Andrew's son; Tom's father) had not overheard the plot of a miscreant named Jacob Bleeker to burn down the house of Squire Fairfax . . . George's uncle in far-off Memphis had died a day or two earlier. Again, the terms are central to those mysterious circumstances that keep badgering us from outside the narrative proper. *If only* the good twin Harry Osgood had survived a house fire rather than his evilly disposed brother, Alan. *If only* the inveterate meddler Sol Bailey (who means them nothing but good) could refrain from bringing disorder and sorrow into the lives of his friends and neighbors. *If only* a Mrs. Miliken had never read the book of a famous French swindler; *if only,* having launched her own scam with borrowed money, she had not been too selfish to repay her unwitting accomplice, a mulatto slave called Jasper. But there is no need to continue. Though examples could be extended almost indefinitely, what count in *Which Was It?* are the consequences of life in the subjunctive mode: of following one course of action, while ignoring or being denied access to the alternative. These consequences include robbery, embezzlement, murder, blackmail, false imprisonment, a constant process of misdeed and betrayal. Without knowing all the circumstances, or being willing to face some that he is privy to, George Harrison accurately sums up the direction of the narrative when he reflects that "all of us . . . seem consigned to a cursed world, . . . and a person's got to stand it."[25]

What, then, transforms a potential comedy of errors into melodrama and tragedy? Why does every step prove a misstep, each opportunity to clear things up with a word become a lost opportunity? What brings George Harrison to the verge of acting honorably, then draws him back with the somehow comforting thought, " 'If only I could do it. But I am not a man' "? Along the way, and not altogether consistently, Mark Twain investigates a number of the moral premises that were preoccupying him during the later 1890s. The fault, he theorizes, lies with "training," or with man's innate selfishness, or with the misspent energies of a professional do-gooder, or with the utter enslavement of humanity to conscience and the "moral sense." Dramatically, though, he provides a more unified explanation. The "what if's" and "if only's" of *Which Was It?* coalesce into an endless succession of sick jokes. After the opening pages, once he loses interest in the possibility of a dream vision, Mark Twain's rhetorical query increasingly takes the form of *what* is it?—what irresistible, inscrutable force is at work in the world that causes characters, at whatever social station or geographical locale, to plot so remorselessly in secret the undoing of those whom they publicly call friend, neighbor, or kin? And the pinnacle of sick joking is reached in a passage of some considerable power, which presumably is the last passage written for the manuscript. Here, George Harrison, having more or less inadvertently murdered Jacob Bleeker and let Squire Fairfax take the blame, has been found by the mulatto slave Jasper. Discovery gives rise to three extraordinary recognition scenes. First, Jasper discloses to George that the two of them are first cousins. Next, he thrusts George in front of a mirror, and as George cowers in fear and trembling, we watch Jasper being miraculously transfigured:

> The meek slouch of the slave was gone from him, and he stood straight, the exultation of victory burning in his eyes; and not even his rags and tatters could rob his great figure of . . . the pride of mastership and command that was rising in his heart. He *looked* the master . . . (*Dream*, 415)

Finally, it is established that ever afterward relations in the Harrison household are to be inverted. The fragment ends with Jasper seated at table, while in the background (still prattling of his "'good name,'" his lost "'spiritual values'") George scurries to bring the slave food and the satisfaction of his other whims.

In one sense, it would appear that Mark Twain has at last brought off the bold thematic stroke which he could not muster with reference to Jim, and which eluded him still more noticeably in *Pudd'nhead Wilson*. He has revealed the man of color enraged: a vigorous and virile slave as he arises in glory from the shambles—the social-cultural-spiritual-moral ruins—of white mastery. It is as if Injun Joe broke the fetters of the cave to take, in fact, as *Indian* Joe the dominion that was reserved for him in St. Petersburg's mythology; as if Jim cried *No* to Tom Sawyer, *I won't be played with by trash*; as if, instead of leaving him to shrink and cower in the "'nigger gallery'" Mark Twain had let Chambers (born free-Tom Driscoll) howl down imprecations on the heads of those who had tormented him for twenty-three years. The conclusion of *Which Was It?* thus anticipates the creation of Bigger Thomas, Joe Christmas, and Lucas Beauchamp, just as (no doubt at least half consciously; note the curious similarity of names—and the ethnic leapfrogging of the names) it looks back to the representation of George Harris in *Uncle Tom's Cabin*, and (no doubt quite inad-

vertently) it "finds" a source in the portrayal thirty years earlier of defiant Babo
in Melville's "Benito Cereno."

There is, however, no accompanying air of affirmation, no sense of old accounts settled and brought into a new balance. Far too many ambiguities enter
into the portrayal of Jasper. Power, not the redress of ancient wrongs, has always motivated him. He is carefully divided throughout between Jasper-by-day,
flogged and reviled as a former slave, and nocturnal or gothicized Jasper, freed
at nightfall to practice blackmail and other forms of obscure terror. Hence,
while Mark Twain is on familiar enough grounds when George Harrison bows
and truckles before the mirror (*Angelo, il est moi*), for the full force of the twinning which the mirror records I would summon up examples from Melville. I
see Jasper as Mark Twain's incarnation of the same dark shadow that fell
athwart each and every "If only" in "Bartleby" and left four walled-in caricatures consigned to a "black world [which each] had got to stand." Together
with Burgess, he is Mark Twain's incarnation of the same Cosmic Jester who
persuaded jovial Ishmael "to take this whole universe for a vast practical joke,"
but left doleful Ishmael to cope with the practical effects of joking at the end
of *Moby-Dick*. Most especially, Jasper embodies another version of Mark
Twain's own Great Dark, and doing so looks backward to Babo settling ineradi-
cably upon the psyche of Captain Delano, and thence backward still further to
echo the same Great Dark which another sea captain sought to banish, but
which lay in wait to madden, to annihilate, and (what is most important) *to
survive* Captain Ahab.

For, in contradistinction to the Blacks in Stowe, Wright, and Faulkner, the
second figure in Mark Twain's mirror resists strict social or political interpretation. Instead Jasper, quite like Melville's Babo, functions as a subject for philosophical criticism. The full formulation which twins him with George Harrison
is at once metaphysical, Manichean, and profoundly Melvillian. The formulation reads: *Angelo c'est moi*. But since the "what is it?" of *Which Was It?* is surely
Jasper, it follows that *tout le monde, c'est noire Luigi's*.[26]


III: THE PRACTICES OF TWINNING

The amenities are enacted by Edmund Clarence Stedman. He is the editor,
critic, and minor poet whom Mark Twain had asked, in 1887, to make a final
pre-publication check of the manuscript of *A Connecticut Yankee*. Strolling with
Samuel Clemens down Broadway a year or so later, he sees coming toward
them a venerable figure, whose identity would be known to few others. It is
Herman Melville, from whom he has recently solicited a poem, a picture, or

"other extracts" for inclusion in his forthcoming *Library of American Literature*. Naturally introductions are in order.

A bit nervous in the ensuing silence, Stedman falls back on the question that writers have asked one another since time immemorial. What are you gentlemen working on currently? Of course voluble Mark Twain replies. Ever brimming with future projects, he speaks of a recent interest in the relationship between dreams and waking. He has half a mind to work up his brother's life under the title of Autobiography of a Damned Fool. He has lately seen, or seen pictured, a pair of Italian Siamese Twins. He is inclined to think that something might be done with them.

Whereupon a chime sounds in the mind of Melville. Not only did he himself see the famous Siamese twins exhibited many years ago; his fiction has often made use of them. Both directly or indirectly they have served him as central metaphors in what, more than three decades earlier, Hawthorne had called his tireless pursuit of "providence, futurity, and everything that lies beyond human ken." So Melville moves on, past the encounter that never happened, beyond words never spoken, not stimulated to do so (for stimulus is neither given nor needed) but meditating as he often does about the curious implications of the twins Chang and Eng. Perhaps something remains to be done with them.[27]

### C: *Billy Budd: Sailor*

His pondering comes to fruition a few paragraphs into Chapter 12 of *Billy Budd: Sailor,* as the climax to several pages of background during which, with an increasing sense of futility, the narrating voice has sought to lend shape and definition to the character of John Claggart. There are, says Melville in his last written allusion to Siamese twins, two

> passions [which] irreconcilable in reason nevertheless in fact spring conjoined like Chang and Eng in one birth.

The passions which ought not to be akin, yet in the case of Claggart do somehow cling tenaciously to one another, are "envy" and "antipathy."[28]

I must confess that having pondered the assertion off and on for a good while, I find it not so much pretentious as simply false. Whoever supposed any estrangement between envy and antipathy? What can be their normal relationship if not that of unhappy cause to unfortunate effect? In *Paradise Lost*, a brooding (if, at times, misleading) resonance throughout *Billy Budd*, the first is responsible for the second, and the two, merging and operating in concert, logically beget the War in Heaven, the Fall into Hell, the Temptation, and the second Fall from Eden. To claim for these conditions a unique coexistence in John Claggart in no way enhances his mystery. Quite the contrary, uniting the two provides, and very straightforwardly, our firmest ground for understanding the master-at-arms. Claggart is envious of Billy. To put it a bit blandly for the moment, he envies Billy's contentment, or Billy's air of being perfectly at home with himself, which he finds incomprehensible. Accordingly, he hates the inscrutable thing in Billy, and acting on the hatred he sets out to turn Billy into something "scrutable" by mastering him intellectually. Whether he also means to destroy Billy physically seems to me uncertain; I suspect that once the play has begun Claggart is less concerned with any specific outcome than with the joy of trumping successfully and sustaining the game for as long as possible. But the point is that—Melville notwithstanding—the necessity for play was put in Claggart's head by covetousness begetting a deep-seated animosity toward the possessor of what is coveted. And yet. If the two passions must be accounted an irony or a joke too deep for fathoming or perhaps a mistaken stutter of Melville's, about the relevance of the rest of the formulation there can be no question. From first to last, *Billy Budd* parades before us irreconcilables in reason, conjoined like Chang and Eng in one birth. I hope to display the pattern of twinning through character, action, rhetoric, and interpretation. Ultimately, I hope to show that, against all probability, the twins of Melville's last fiction twin the twins in two of the sketches with which Mark Twain began his career a quarter of a century earlier.

*Billy Budd and John Claggart.* Despite significant differences in age and station (except on formal occasions one would not think of dignifying the one as "Budd"; one would never familiarize the other as John) they are strangely linked. They come out of the same murky and uncertain past, so that Billy, the "by-blow," can bring no information concerning his parentage, while "nothing is known of Claggart's former life," not even if he was born English. Both are physically arresting, Billy's famous "rosiness" and "delicacy of feature" leaving him not a whit more aesthetically compelling than Claggart is made by "silken jet curls," his "shapely face and head," unusual "pallor," and "air of distinction." Both are flawed, and their flaws work in parallel ways. In moments of crisis Billy is rendered mute and hence socially impotent by his stammer, though most of the time he has an innate capacity to charm and control society. And it is just so with Claggart. Though most of the time he remains socially in control through the reserve and intelligence that have brought him his post as master-at-arms, in moments of crisis his natural depravity erupts, and he becomes a danger to society. Most crucially, therefore, they can retain their roles as human characters, acting against the backdrop of a British battleship in a narrative of life at sea during a particular moment in history, while simultaneously they are elevated out of realism to serve as symbols, or archetypes, or (as it may be) caricatures. They represent, or appear to incorporate, binary opposites: good vs. evil; innocence vs. sophistication; illiteracy vs. urbane wit; the rosy sanguine temperament vs. the dark and pallid choleric. So extreme are the oppositions that coming to it straight from "Bartleby" a first-time reader of *Billy Budd* might well conclude that if only it were possible to mediate hollow with swell (assemble positive and negative) the result could be a normal, balanced, completely developed, and fully functioning personality. But although, in a bleakly ironic way, the unified self does eventuate in *Billy Budd,* the emphasis for a long while is upon reintroducing the pattern of "Bartleby," but inverting it.[29]

Far better for the foretopman and the master-at-arms if on the boundless ocean they had never met. Or having been thrust together by circumstance, how better for both if, like Turkey and Nippers, each had remained walled off from any possibility for contact or communication with the other. Better for Billy in ways that need no demonstration, though surely a point has been missed if it is not noted that the phrase "if only they hadn't" applies equally to the master-at-arms. I think we are meant to infer that once Billy registers on his consciousness, Claggart would have gone to any lengths to suppress the image. Then he might have lived on as a "respectable and discreet [officer] of minor grade," the turmoil within kept hidden, perhaps even in some measure from Claggart himself. But the soup spilled in Chapter 10 brings all his latent hostilities surging into the open. Unable to regard the event as happenstance, seeing it instead as michief and, furthermore, as a misdeed that is somehow a reflection on him, Claggart is constrained to reach out and form a circle with Billy. Nor, despite the erotic byplay in the chapter, is the circle he craves primarily a matter of erotic coupling. If homosexual rape were the intent, that could readily enough be brought off by Claggart and his cohorts in some private place. Rather, in Claggart's twisted mind, forming the circle is tantamount to an act of scientific enquiry. Convinced of a blemish on Billy's facade of innocence, he must enter more deeply into what he finds incredible, in order to investigate the innocence, to test it, to (of course) find it wanting, and to bring it down in disgrace publicly. For all the Biblical imagery that surrounds him, Claggart is less the Tempter in the Garden than an Iago-like figure, a diddler set to diddling not by money or revenge or even sexual desire, but rather by the will to know, and by the sheer, pleasurable curiosity he takes from speculating about how his diddle will turn out. He is a true exemplar of the "motiveless malignity" which Coleridge famously ascribes to Iago. (Were it possible for us to summon him off the page and say *Claggart, Claggart; why are you doing these evil things to Billy Budd?,* I think he might giggle—and answer, *Because I want to see what will happen.*)

*Actions and Reactions.* The two figures summoned through Captain Vere's cabin door have gradually passed from difference yielding to superficial resemblances to the most profound kind of kinship. After thirty pages of exposition, both are shown as the alleged victims of a cosmic joke, the Marplot that imposed a debilitating stammer on Billy corresponding exactly to the Creator "which alone is responsible" for Claggart's scorpion-like behavior. Each is, or anyhow feels himself to be, a victim of the other's joke. While he toys with Billy, playing on him here a trick and there a trick, Claggart suspects in Billy's spilling of the soup "the sly escape of a spontaneous feeling . . . more or less answering to antipathy of his own." All that separates them as they enter the cabin are intent and awareness, the one having come full of a wish to bring dark mischief to a climax, the other arriving in the expectation of praise and promotion. Watching two upright lines poised on the verge of action, a reader might well think of the implacable iceberg lying in wait and of the ship sailing blithely along toward destruction in Thomas Hardy's famous poem. All that is needed for a final, absolute convergence of the twain is for the "Spinner of the Years" to say "Now!"

As in Hardy, "Now!" gives way to the most rending form of collision, in which identities are not simply lost, but, for the moment, actually exchanged. First, Claggart's eyes "leap outward as the paralyzing lurch of the torpedo fish." Under their magnetic pull, Billy is drawn out of himself, ceases to be Billy Budd, becomes in fact the character of Claggart's fabrication. Next, however, the roles of teller and told-upon are reversed. Failing to speak to the enormity of his situation, Billy must answer in the only way he knows how. He "releases his right arm, quick as the flame from a discharged cannon at night." (*BB,* 98–99). Under the force of the blow, Claggart is drawn out of himself, ceases to be John Claggart, becomes the character of Billy's violence. (One suspects that in his last seconds of life Claggart, not knowing precisely what to expect, was as astonished by Billy's reaction as Billy was shocked by Claggart's accusation.) And now choreography is underscored through the complex architecture of Captain Vere's quarters. In small rooms, on opposite sides of the main chamber, two straight lines are separated and affixed in new positions: the horizontal line of a recumbent corpse; the vertical line of a living seaman, erect and awaiting trial. But the geometric figure that remains palpable in the main chamber is very differently constituted. There a physical circle has been formed through a process long delayed, but always inevitable, and at last consummated: the flowing into oneness of two personalities "irreconcilable in reason." It is the memory of this circle that will dominate the rest of the story. Or, better, the conclusion of *Billy Budd* is dominated by attempts—apparently successful—to circumscribe the physical circle within a larger circle, and, through circumscription, to give moral and metaphysical justification to the undoubted act, the living deed.

*Constructions and Deconstructions.* The change in presentation that comes after the blow has not been sufficiently remarked. There is no longer suspense, since Captain Vere knows the outcome from the moment the blow was struck, and knowing it, strips of all urgency or tension the somewhat perfunctory objections of his drumhead court. Nor is there any further pretense of narrative realism. Whereas Vere, an embodiment of common sense, once thought of Billy Budd as an efficient sailor with a pleasant demeanor, he now suddenly turns Billy into metaphor and allusion: "Fated boy," "Angel of God," "the divine judgment on Ananias." And although he is illiterate, Billy's handful of responses are rendered in language too stately and elegant ever to be mistaken for the real speech of any hold of any ship on any ocean: "'Captain Vere tells the truth. It is just as Captain Vere says, but it is not as the master-of-arms said. I have eaten the King's bread and I am true to the King.'" The effect of the change is a radical scaling upward of tone. In the last third of *Billy Budd,* manner becomes ceremonial, ritualistic, above all, portentous and hence laden with significance. Meaning, revelation—the closing of the circle which will explain the mysterious inner circle—seem about to leap forth from every paragraph of every page. (*BB*, 100–101, 106).

There is just one problem, as four decades of critical controversy amply demonstrate.[30] It is a problem of rhetoric and reader response. Since Melville wrote with no apparent thought of publication, did not even begin a fair copy of the voluminous pages he marked as finished several months prior to his death, there seems scant reason to distinguish the narrator's voice from that of the author, and Melville thus writes for an audience of one, namely himself.[31] Yet if no public readership is envisioned, the manuscript gives the liveliest sense of an inner audience, an "implied you" with whom Melville shares his ruminations and digressions, and to whom he presents his ending. And upon you the ending he presents imposes a heavy burden. Your situation is not unlike that of Ahab, struggling to hear the Captain of the *Albatross*. The words form, but what do the words signify? Or you are faced with the challenge set forth in Mark Twain's late title. It is up to you to ascertain, if possible, *which was it?*

Well and good if, abiding by symbolism that is obvious to the point of seeming labored, you take *Billy Budd* as an example of Christian allegory. Then you have twinned Time with Eternity. But you must also decide whether the undoubted crucifixion is a redemptive act, witnessed by congregants who murmur "'God Bless Captain Vere'" and watch Billy "ascend into the full rose of the dawn"—or whether the same Marplot that devised Claggart and gave Billy his stammer has also created a Captain Vere made mad by a moment of crisis, in which case crucifixion degenerates into mere spectacle, as needless as it is cruel, a lunatic sideshow, performed for "a congregation in hell, listening to a clergyman's announcement of his Calvinistic text." (*BB*, 122–23, 117.) Again, well and good if, concluding the religious imagery is unworkable, you secularize the text and read it as a parable about mutiny and morale during a time of war. Then you have twinned Justice with human needs. But you must also not only try to determine whether Vere is a prudent leader, or insane, or a martinet (more drawn to the Articles of War than to simple human justice), or a patriarchal figure imposing his masculine will, like rape, on the beautiful Billy (and there is ample evidence for each of these views); you risk embarrassment by finding your secular reading travestied in a newspaper account (*BB*, 132), which turns the crime (if crime there was) into a stabbing, and so garbles national identities as to make a mockery of the patriotic theme. Or, finally, well and good if focusing on the triumvirate Vere-Billy-King, you are reminded of the Father of Faith (Abraham is mentioned) and the traditional scapegoat (so, too, is Isaac), enacting a version of *Credo quia absurdum* (that profession of utmost fealty to God's laws, which has haunted the religious sensibility from Genesis to Paul to Kierkegaard) and acting it out not for immediate change but in promise of the millennium to come. Then theologically and existentially, both the metaphysical and the ethical circles are closed. But you must next cope with closure in the story: with the ballad ascribed to Billy commemorating his last hours alive. The poem not only fails to mention either King or Vere. It conceives of victimhood as brutal fact with none of the trappings of sacrifice ("'O, 'tis me, not the sentence they'll suspend.'"). It asserts the supreme reality of physical death ("'the oozy weeds around me twist'") over any dream of resurrection. Most emphatically, it submerges all values, present or prospective, into Billy's final, sardonic question ("'But arn't it all a sham?'"). (*BB*, 132–33.)

Sham, indeed. Giving with one hand what the other immediately withdraws, the narrative deconstructs itself far more ably than the most gifted deconstructionist critic could do. Not even the *Bellipotent*'s triumph over the *Athee* or Vere's reposeful death are immune. It is alleged at this high point that only the Captain of Marines, the one most reluctant to condemn him, "knew who Billy was." (*BB*, 129.) It is not, however, said what he knows. The tale seems determined to pursue its tail toward the annihilation of all meaning—a fact which shapes one possible reading, though not, I think, the only or even the best one.

*Dead Letters; Living Letters.* Trying to fathom Bartleby and the unaccountable yearnings that drew him to the scrivener, the lawyer-narrator arrived at the notion of "dead letters." Ahab also heard dead letters when he accosted the *Albatross,* just as the world he dies out of—the one where Ishmael survives as "another orphan"—remains a world without a voice. Dead letters register the object of a seeker's desire; measure the distance between what a seeker went looking for and the ambiguities he actually found. In *Billy Budd* the recipient of dead letters is the figure who devises them. Pairing Billy and Claggart as twins, dramatizing their inexorable flow into oneness, Melville is conscious of what he terms the "deadly space between." His objective is to fill in that space: not to illustrate the mystery (like foretopman and master-at-arms); not to regard the mystery as engrained into the texture of experience and beyond meaningful resolution (like the Dansker); not to be maddened by the mystery or, alternatively, to tidy up its aftereffects through an act of moral and social expediency, or (still alternatively) to accept it through a profession of faith *in extremis* (like Vere, depending upon what we make of Vere)—but rather to know, and know rationally, why good and evil coexist and why the history of the world is the record of their interpenetration. For the space to be occupied, however, the physical circle would have to be contained within the metaphysical circle. The Twin that twins the twins, brings them together and says "Now!," would have to be identified. Then, and not otherwise, might dead letters yield up the Voice (the Sign, the Revelation, the Dialogue) which could synthesize two principles "irreconcilable in reason" and synthesize them into the pattern of a harmonious, purposeful universe. And as always in Melville, the invisible spheres remain withdrawn and mute.[32]

Thus, in his final venture into Siamese twinning, Melville seems wholly to invert Mark Twain's theory of twinship. Whereas, with big hand running perpetually atop little hand, Mark Twain could readily snap into place the certain or totalized (if not always the most satisfying) conclusion, Melville so multiplies the options of interpreting the twins that *Billy Budd* appears to arrive at the blank of no-conclusion-possible. A shared interest in Chang and Eng has led to fictions where darkness must invariably prevail and a fiction where freely choosing raises the suggestion that nothing is certain except the dark absence of every certainty. They seem incomparable fictions, as, rhetorically speaking, the declarative Both are One! lies beyond meaningful comparison with the interrogatives Which is Which? or What is What?

And yet. And yet. Beneath his deep personal involvement in the quest theme, there has always lain Melville's recognition of the social costs of questing, his ironic sense of how an obsession for grasping at circles can distort the personality and make it unfit for life in the world below. It is this aspect of his creativity which caused him to turn Ahab into a monstrous, enhumored self, even as he dignified the reasons for Ahab's voyage; which allowed him to see the comic futility of four characters in "Bartleby," even as he shared the pathos of their situation as four fractured Socratic circles. And now, writing for his eyes only, he can give free rein to the social—the lea shore—bent to his imagination. If the words of *Billy Budd* die in consequence of groping for an impossible dream of Absolute Truth and Justice, what the narrator insistently calls the "realism" of the story brings the words quivering back to life again. Irreconcilable passions are eliminated, in order to restore a workable society. And resolutions are provided which are meant to satisfy both the tender hearted (who find in *Billy Budd* an example of "malice reconciled") and the tough minded (who see the story as an instance of "divine depravity").

For the tender hearted, John Claggart is obviously not to be borne by the real world. Whether the fault lies with him or with his Creator, he is a sociopath and paranoid, who should never have been born in the first place—a time bomb forever ticking away, in careful control most of the time, yet constantly threatening to explode against the good order of the human community. Billy was quite right to kill him. Sooner or later, somebody would have had to. For the tough minded, however, it is just as clear that the real world cannot long bear the presence of Billy Budd, either. Precisely because he is transcendently pure and beautiful, he constitutes a temptation and a threat—and what is far worse, like the re-arisen Christ in Dostoevski, an anomalous stranger whom society must destroy for its own protection. Already, aboard the *Rights of Man*, he has had his first brush with the closed, antagonistic group. And while in that small and liberal environment the fight apparently ended happily (we never hear directly from Red Whiskers, of course), still the cynical smiles of the oldest salts on the *Bellipotent* are not without significance. The sad truth is that the foretopman might function well enough as the animal, to which he is repeatedly likened, or as a Casper Hauser in the wilderness. But with respect to the work-a-day world of a man-of-war, he is what Claggart first calls him and then all too graphically demonstrates him to be. Billy is a "mantrap." "They were right to hang him," as Camille Paglia observes.[33] She does not add that sooner or later somebody would have had to. Nor, probably taking the point for granted, does she comment that the one socially useful action ever performed by Claggart was to drive Billy into a corner where he had to be hanged.

In 1925 in honor of his ninetieth birthday an admirer presents to Samuel L. Clemens a copy of the recently, posthumously published work mistitled *Billy Budd: Foretopman*. Well knowing that he is an irascible reader with a low threshold for boredom, the admirer adds as an enticement the fact that in this work about twins, Clemens might be amused to find the surname of his penname used repeatedly. So Mark Twain reads, and after a while not just to count the nine references to twain. Against all odds, he is rewarded with what Melville himself had once called the "shock of recognition." *I wrote this story more than sixty years ago. Mine was less ponderous and highfalutin, but it aimed to show that society can afford neither the demonic bad boy nor the equally demonic actions of the good boy. I called them Jim and Jacob. One was sent to the Legislature, where the likelihood of assassination would be greater. The other was dispatched more decisively by scattering him across four townships.*

*Strange, isn't it, how twinning two irreconcilables in reason brings both under the spell of a presence that Melville calls "Marplot of Eden," Hardy calls "The Spinner of the Years," but to whom I eventually gave the folksier name, Luigi's Father? Then the two look exactly alike. And what you have is an example of the Infernal Oneness.* ** 

### D: Strangers and Familiars

When Mark Twain began "Those Extraordinary Twins" early in the 1890s, he may, as he said, have been inspired by a display or a picture of Italian Siamese twins, who were recently exhibited in Philadelphia. Alternatively, he could have been building imaginatively upon the conception of Chang and Eng which he had developed twenty-five years earlier. Or it seems entirely possible to suppose that somewhere in his wide reading from history, philosophy, and folklore, he had encountered the Zoroastrian twins, so that Luigi and Angelo were specifically modeled upon Ahriman, who was dark, disruptive and first-born, and the younger, gentler, less forceful Ohrmad. At all events the Manichean configuration, the ur-structure of his work, has been repeated. Left to his own devices, Angelo would have settled in, scuttled for safety at the first signs of danger, married Rowena, fathered a passel of hypochondriacal children, served as a model of temperance and piety, and lived (as we say) happily, if undramatically and rather stupidly, ever afterward. Only by virtue of being linked to the dark older one does he achieve the dramatic distinction of disgrace, cowardice, a day in court, denial by Rowena, and hauled kicking and screaming to the gallows denial of life itself. It is ever the way in Mark Twain. The dark twin acts; the hapless blond merely behaves. In *Pudd'nhead Wilson* Luigi kicks—and launches several lines of behavior through which Dawson Landing's dirty linen is strewn into the open, though (such being the power of

---

** Like all agile, though elderly, memories, that of Mark Twain is better focused on the remote past than the nearer-at-hand. He might have added that, changes of gender being allowed for, he also published the same story in 1894, when if "angelic" Wilson and "demonic" Roxy do not come to violent ends, this is less a tribute to them than a commentary upon the society which is too bland and dense to recognize the dangers they pose.

Darkness even after it leaves town) by no means laundered and left clean. When Darkness is portrayed as the Spirit of the River or the Voice of History, the Dark disposes; eventually the more modest proposals of Huck and Jim on the raft or of Hank Morgan the erstwhile reformer are brought down in ruins. To resort once more to Mark Twain's own metaphor, human beings and human relationships are just "buttons," "cranks," and "levers." It requires Dark Force to snap On and Off the button.

But in the form of "Spirit of the River" or "Voice of History" where exactly does Darkness reside? What is its abode, place-of-residence, its *locus?* One is tempted to say that Darkness inheres in the physical, near-at-hand phenomena of the visible world. This view conforms to Mark Twain's use of Southern gothic and to his strict empiricism: his anticipation of William Carlos Williams's dictum of "no ideas but in things." Together with allusions to Fathers who won and lost the war, however, such fictions as "Crime in Connecticut" and "Hadleyburg" imply another possibility. When "Green Face" sweeps into the study to see straight through "Mark Twain's" apologetics, to twin and then assimilate "Mark Twain"; when Burgess, having once lived there realistically and been realistically cast out, swoops down on Hadleyburg to twin sham innocence with actual hypocrisy and to subject the quivering hypocrites to an act of demonic possession—in both instances an element of the fabulistic or the downright supernatural has been added to Mark Twain's realism. "Green Face" and Burgess's multiple identities cannot plausibly emerge from this world; they come into this world as outsiders, endowed with Powers and Prerogatives that identify them as supra-worldly or otherworldly. As in Melville and *The Symposium*, therefore, upright lines have been laid over on their sides, one running horizontally below the other. The feeling is that with a slight modification the two could be coupled into a circle. And this, I believe, is the aim of the three narratives which Mark Twain worked and reworked from 1897 until 1908, two years before his death. Though very different in length, value and influence, what we have come to know as the *Mysterious Stranger Manuscripts* can be seen as constituting Mark Twain's second trilogy. They are narratives united by a shared attempt to close the metaphysical circle—and close it, furthermore, in terms of the traditional purposes of metaphysics, which are to explain the grounds of experience and (if possible) to supply the grounds with moral justification.***

---

*** The reader needs to have up-front a clear view of the fourfold composition of the "Mysterious Stranger" manuscripts. (1) First came the earlier version of "The Chronicle of Little Satan," written between November 1897 and January 1898. It consists of the first two and a half chapters of what we now read as *The Mysterious Stranger: A Romance*, then moves very quickly to the trial

Some generalizations will help to explain my sense of a trilogy. In all three narratives, this world is populated by familiars. They are familiars in the sense of being ordinary people, living out ordinary lives in recognizable places at a certifiable time in history. And they are familiars in that they have constructed social structures, moral hierarchies, and systems of belief through which they believe they are familiar with reality and with each other—which is to say that, being members of a Mark Twain crowd, of course they understand nothing. Into their midst drops the Stranger. No matter if He comes from the world above or, as his name and lineage suggest, out of the world below; perhaps, like the Progenitor of his supernatural race, He has occupied and still inhabits both places.[34] The important point is that finding Him amongst them, in a place where nothing happens, or ever seems likely to, the familiars react to the outsider with predictable alarm, awe, resentment, discomfiture, embarrassment, etc.—though in at least a few instances with feelings of having been revitalized and transfigured. For the Stranger brings along a magic which is very different from the necromancy hitherto practiced in Mark Twain's fiction. Tom Sawyer's secular magic had been the prelude to obscure cruelties. Secular magic was Hank Morgan's means of surviving, and after a while the measure of an ego that helped to destroy him. Magic masked a latent hostility in "Carnival of Crime," and was the instrument of vengeance in "Hadleyburg." In marked contrast, the magically endowed Strangers are never indifferent to their audiences and, with respect to the particular kinships they form, never vindictive. They practice magic in order to defamiliarize the familiar: that is, to give to familiars a true sense of who they are and what they are in the cosmic scheme of things. Then, with blinders removed, an act of twinning occurs. The Stranger chooses a con-

---

and vindication of Father Peter and breaks off. (2) Next comes "Schoolhouse Hill," a six-chapter fragment, based on a still earlier notebook entry, but written in November and December of 1898, and soon broken off never to be returned to. (3) *After* "Schoolhouse Hill," Mark Twain returns to "Chronicle of Little Satan" and between May and October of 1899, and again between June and August of 1900, greatly expands the narrative by inserting before the trial and "happy madness" of Father Peter many incidents and the dialogues between Philip Traum and Theodor. The material ends finally in August of 1900, with Philip and Theodor in India (the last episode in *The Mysterious Stranger*, as we now have it, prior to the all-is-a-dream conclusion). (4) "No. 44: The Mysterious Stranger" was begun in 1902, when Mark Twain altered the first chapter of "Chronicle of Little Satan" to fit a new setting, a different time, and a fresh set of characters. I shall return in my discussion of "No. 44" to the various stages of its composition. For now, it will bear emphasizing that while there are four stages of composition, there are but three different narratives. Hence my justification for putting them together as Mark Twain's "second trilogy."

Like all students of Mark Twain, I am greatly indebted to William Gibson's edition of Mark Twain's *Mysterious Stranger Manuscripts* (Berkeley: University of California Press, 1969). I do, of course, reserve the right to disagree with Professor Gibson's specific interpretations of the material he has edited so skillfully.

fidante, and through word and actions instructs him on the best means of accommodating to the earthling's new and vastly shrunken stature. Waiting in the wings since *Huckleberry Finn*, Bakhtin's theory of dialogic fiction thus reenters the mysterious stranger manuscripts. Each is a dialogue, wherein the supernatural speaker enunciates the virtues (but also the immense difficulties) of maintaining a dialogic relationship with the real world, and tries to show his human companions that (for all their illusions about community) they remain woebegone creatures because, in Bakhtin's sense of the term, they are inveterate "monologists." So consistent is the pattern that, I shall call Act I of the three exchanges The Promise; Act II, The Promise Kept—But Unfulfilled; Act III, The Promise Fulfilled.

*The Promise.* By all odds the least of the narratives is "Schoolhouse Hill," consisting of six short chapters and apparently written during the course of six or seven weeks at the end of 1898. At the beginning, Son of Satan appears one day in the antebellum St. Petersburg schoolhouse, is rechristened Forty-four, and quickly exceeds the other scholars in mastering languages and the multiplication table. At the end, having taken up residence with an older citizen named Oliver Hotchkiss, he is busily engaged in multiplying household servants out of thin air and ordering them about in several languages. The sketch seems an aborted exercise in fooling around. Yet, somewhat mysteriously, the working notes insist upon a relationship between Forty-four and the Admirable Crichton, who since Barrie's play did not appear until 1903, Mark Twain must have been thinking of as the sixteenth-century Scottish prodigy, his gifts devoted to occult scholarship and social reforms as well as many adventures.[35] And the point to the relationship comes in a single moment of high seriousness, when a startling concession is followed by a still more extraordinary promise. "'I see,'" says Forty-four to old Hotchkiss, "'that my father's error . . . conferred [upon humanity] the passionate and eager and hungry *disposition* to do evil.'" In the next breath he continues, "'a part of the burden of evil consequences can be lifted for your race, and I will undertake it.'"[36] Nothing more is heard of the promise. One guesses it is broached and dropped because, evoked for the first time since the mid-1880s, St. Petersburg has somehow been shorn of the slavery and boredom, the "Pap's" and "Joe's" and graveyards, that make it accord with Forty-four's premise. For the pledge to be meaningful, Mark Twain must broaden beyond the cloistered schoolroom and parlor, to find a setting far richer in the human propensity to do evil.[37] Fortunately, there lies at hand awaiting revision "The Chronicle of Little Satan," which he had broken off a year earlier.

*The Promise Kept—But Unfulfilled.* After a brief flurry of pyrotechnics, Philip Traum, also called Little Satan, gets down to a more comprehensive display of his supernatural origins. Taking up a handful of dust, and working in exact emulation of the first creation story in Genesis, he shapes a little world, populates it, observes it for a while in its diligence and craziness, grows weary of his handiwork, and squashes it back to oblivion again. Although his audience—Theodor Fischer and other adolescent boys living in Eseldorf, Austria, in 1590—are properly horrified by the spectacle, it is quite evident that Philip invents nothing. His is an imitation; the world he makes is a version in miniature of the world as it really exists. From the spectacle of Philip's manikins squabbling and dying in the dirt, the boys and Mark Twain's readers need but raise their eyes to find that the same murderous bickerings have always characterized the long history of Eseldorf—and the great world beyond Eseldorf. If birth, grief, frustrated hopes, copulation, pain, and extinction form the unvarying cycle of Philip's sideshow, the nasty, brutish, and short are equally the constituents of a dungeon scene in Eseldorf, of life in a French sweatshop, of the greed and vanity of an Indian prince—and, ultimately, of the panorama of human affairs, from Cain to Napoleon, that Philip unscrolls in Chapter 7. For none of the atrocities which turn up in his expeditions and reminiscences is Little Satan ever alleged to bear responsibility. Yet for all his sardonic commentary, neither can he remain completely unmoved by the clear evidence that "'for a million years [your] race has gone on monotonously propagating itself and monotonously reperforming this dull nonsense.'"[38] Rather, Philip is bound by the promise which Forty-four made to Oliver Hotchkiss. It is as if, returning to him in the light of Forty-four, Mark Twain will have Philip redeem that pledge. He will show Little Satan lifting the "burden of evil consequences" by introducing his human double into the terms and demands of a great initiation story. No doubt the presence of the pedagogical theme was what made "Chronicle of Little Satan" so eminently publishable after Mark Twain's death, just as by its valedictory tone (and knowing better) we are encouraged to confer upon *The Mysterious Stranger: A Romance* the distinction of being Mark Twain's last written testament.

Human life, Philip tells Theodor, exists as inside a machine and is itself thoroughly mechanized. Like the toppling of the first brick in a long row of bricks, the initial response or primary event in an individual's life sets in motion the one future which, of a billion potential futures, now becomes as fixed and unalterable as rotations of the globe in space, as little susceptible to later modification as are the strictly material relations between moon and tides. Thereafter, as Philip explains, "'every man is a suffering machine and a happiness machine combined. . . . In most cases [a] man's life is about equally divided between happiness and unhappiness. Where this is not the case, unhappiness prevails—always; never the other.'" (*MSR*, 350.) Although Philip makes no attempt to elucidate the reasons behind the world he describes—indeed hedges a bit when Theodor presses him on this point—the stress he places upon sequence and necessity bears an unmistakable resemblance to the argument of philosophers in the Stoic tradition. The Stoic, too, confronts an essentially closed universe. He must acknowledge that whether because of the invincible will of the gods, the invariable properties of matter, or the inescapable limits with which Divine and Natural laws deploy their forms, he is contained by a scheme in which actions can never be freely chosen, shuffled, rearranged, or recombined. Nevertheless, he also recognizes that such a prospect can be contemplated without panic, and even with a certain equanimity. For the Stoic, as for Philip Traum who speaks the language of Stoicism, the nature of things is, in and of itself, not causally related to despair.

Despair is a circular process, originating ironically in the same source that must likewise suffer the effects of despairing. Flung into the machine from the outside (or better yet probably, evolved within the machine through its own internal operations), humanity brings along what amounts to the curse of consciousness. As creatures driven by ego, members of the human race seek to impose their will upon the intractable, to treat reality as if it were a private preserve for the fulfillment of their desires, their fictions and monologues, their refined sense of what is mine and what belongs to you. As believers in an idiocy called "the moral sense" they try to parcel out a wholly indifferent field of energy into the "good" and the "bad," the "saved" and the "damned"—the witch and the witch hunter. The pathetic fates of Nickolaus Baumann and Lisa Brandt demonstrate the results of tinkering from above with life inside the machine. But the full folly of tinkering must, of course, come from below and develop out of a specifically human experience. Attempting to imitate Philip as he offers facsimiles of the real world, the boys of the village try their hands at creating little men and horses out of dust. And "having no art for such things," they produce only deformities that "reeled and sprawled around . . . and finally fell over and lay helpless and kicking. It was a shameful thing to see." (MSR, 316.) What Nickolaus, Sieppi, and Theodor bring to pass is nothing less than the central theme—and the central outcome—of Mark Twain's recurring drama. Always and everywhere, the characters of Mark Twain have been obsessed with supplying themselves and one another with new identities, different images of the self that originate solely inside the head of the beholder. But they have no art for such things—and no capacity for violating the inviolable. The results must be that they turn one another *and themselves* into deformities that reel and sprawl helplessly and are a shameful thing to see.

*World before words, then; a grasping and full comprehension of the pressure of the experiences that impinge on us from "out there" prior to the language with which those experiences are labeled and conceptualized.* In *The Mysterious Stranger: A Romance* Mark Twain in no way abates his case against the damned human race. Yet he does soften and modify the indictment by portraying the Dark Twin as spokesman for the aesthetics and morality of realism. "'I have wrought well for the villagers,'" Philip tells Theodor at one point, "'what I am doing . . . will bear good fruit one day.'" (*MSR*, 352.) And moving from what Philip has shown to what he says, we find this neither idle boast nor an instance of Satanic duplicity. Where human kind is now constrained to weep for the failure of its many projects, Little Satan would teach it to laugh at the absurdity of the spectacle it presents. Where each one now pulls and tugs frantically in his/her own special direction, Little Satan would have all live equably together, even if this means living like cogs in a machine. And where by believing in freedom, the race now ensures a life of slavery, Little Satan would show that in an acceptance of slavery lies the key to freedom. Philip's story is not bitter or cheerless; these are the properties of the ways of the world that occasion his narrative. The story itself is told in hope, at times even with the tone of a certain exaltation.

And from the exaltation, I believe, one is justified in sensing parallels, partly ironic, yet partly serious, that link the story Philip tells to another famous rite de passage being constructed in the 1880s and 1890s. Only apprehend the real as the single reality there is, Frederic Nietzsche was saying. Only accept, as a given, the "eternal recurrence" of things, and allow between yourselves and repetition no kindly illusions. Do this, and the personal will to power is already in the process of being satisfied. To read that part of *The Mysterious Stranger: A Romance* which builds on the "Chronicle of Little Satan" is to be struck by the presence of similar perspectives. Playing with the pun in Lucifer, Mark Twain has not only transformed the Prince of Darkness into an Apostle of Light and enlightenment, not only for once created the Dark Twin as brother, teacher, good companion to a confused blond counterpart; without ever arriving at the point of exactly saying so, Mark Twain has implied that with vision clarified, the myopia of the "moral sense" struck from his human, all-too-human eyes, Theodor Fischer may one day see as the gods, because he and his kind will have put on godly knowledge of the realities they live in. Then, in its own inimitable way, Mark Twain's fiction will have twinned time with Eternity within the metaphysical circle.

There is just one problem. Mark Twain could not find a satisfactory ending for Act II. That task had to be undertaken for him posthumously by another hand. We have learned the details from John Tuckey's publication in 1963 of the bibliographic and textual study *Mark Twain and Little Satan*. As Tuckey explains, in 1916, six years after Mark Twain's death, Albert Bigelow Paine took

up the manuscript called "Chronicle of Little Satan," excised a number of passages he found offensive, created a new character called "the Astrologer" to
perform the more heinous actions of Father Adolph, wrote a handful of transitional sentences, added as a final chapter six pages of manuscript which Mark
Twain clearly intended as the conclusion for a draft entitled "No. 44: The Mysterious Stranger"—and published the book we now have in the guise of Mark
Twain's last completed narrative. Despite a certain amount of academic tut-tut-
ting, critics seem rarely disposed to quarrel with Paine's choice of the concluding episode. Edwin Fussell, writing before Tuckey, observed that the solipsism
at the end of *Stranger* is actually "a theme deeply embedded in the whole
story," while James Cox, agreeing that the emphasis upon dreaming is not unprepared for, finds in Paine's emendations the best version of *Stranger* we are
ever likely to get.[39] Yet notwithstanding Philip's surname (Traum = dream), the
reflections of the last chapter are, to my ear, diametrically at odds with the
spirit of everything that has gone before. Throughout, Philip has argued for
waking up; for confronting reality without the transforming lens of subjectivity,
and hence without the dreams and delusions which subjectivity creates. Dialogue has been both his method and the substance of his pedagogy. To find him
retreating into the monologic mind at the end is so incongruous that, were
it not for the lyric power of the passage, one guesses Chapter 11 of *Stranger*
might and should have been suspect even before Tuckey's account was published. Moreover, with respect to the integrity of Paine, the interesting question
would appear to be not what he did in his large, unauthorized way, but rather
why he had to do anything. In other words, after he had so carefully brought
the narrative along from ignorance to wisdom, what prevented Mark Twain
from finishing it himself?

I surmise the answer has much to do with the phenomenon that Melville
called "dead letters," and much to do with Mark Twain's attitude toward letters
that are dead. Philip Traum can explain without the slightest difficulty *what* the
world is. He is prepared to show with great facility *how* one should live in the
world as it is constituted. Where he flounders is in the face of the question *why*.
Why, "of a billion potential futures," should reality have been cast into the one
rigid, unvarying pattern it everywhere takes? Why and by whom was it foreordained that man must be "a suffering machine and a happiness machine," with
any imbalance falling on the side of suffering? Though language, and the correct uses of language, are deemed to solve every problem, Philip cannot say. He
cannot find (or may not ultimately be given) the words that would explain
these mysteries. As I noted earlier, when Theodor presses him for an answer,
the Stranger turns off as mute and evasive as any character in Melville, ponder-

ing the silence and remoteness of the invisible spheres. For the life of him, he cannot cross the "space between": cannot utter the last words which would twin time with Eternity.

The odd thing, of course, is that Mark Twain himself perfectly well knows the answer. He has been portraying it for years. It was the integument which, if only we troubled to look for it, bound together his trilogy of the River; it was the accusation he delivered with terrible, though private, finality in the letter he addressed to Susy Clemens following her premature death in 1896.[40] But always in the fiction the answer has been handled covertly, with indirectness and sly allusion. For Philip Traum to have satisfied Theodor by looking beyond the first falling brick would have amounted to bringing into the open the fact that God is responsible, that to twin time and Eternity is to recognize that God alone caused the brick to fall. And this in 1898 Mark Twain was unwilling to do. Possibly the face-to-face confrontation unnerved him a little. More likely, he recognized that the structure of his initiation story would come crashing down as Philip's premise of human culpability turned into the image of humanity's total helplessness. At all events refuge in Melvillian dead letters, though hardly a necessity, was a great convenience. Instead of finishing "Chronicle of Little Satan," Mark Twain would twice-over start over. He would set to work on a new narrative; and since not all that needed to be said could be said through Philip Traum, he would replace Philip's solemnities with an antic Stranger who will close the circle through the simple expedient of thumbing his nose at the circle's Creator.[41]

*The Promise Fulfilled.* The Forty-four of "Schoolhouse Hill" and Philip Traum, whose character Forty-four serves to expand, came trailing very real clouds of glory; as self-announced descendants of Satan, they easily forced a wondering world to adjust to the miracle of their presence. An altogether different pattern defines the development of the second 44. He wanders into the Austrian printshop as a combination rogue, straight off the pages of *The Unfortunate Traveller,* and forlorn waif, roaming the roadways of the world in the rags and tatters of apparent orphanhood. Since he brings no otherworldly credentials, the full mystery of the Mysterious Stranger must gradually be revealed as he works his will on immediate, close at hand experiences. Thus, having initially been reviled and humiliated by his fellow workers in the print shop, he performs his first miracle, with the creation of invisible duplicates to do the chores of the workmen on strike. Presently, he will be burned to death by a rival magician—and as promptly resurrected and made physically whole again. Even during the somewhat manic middle chapters, after a profusion of his duplicates turns the print shop into an "insane asylum," 44, having himself known suffering, can still listen with sympathy, and acquiescence, to an Emil

Schwarz, who begs to be set free of these "'bonds of flesh, this decaying, vile matter, this foul weight and clog . . . in which my spirit is imprisoned.'" As late as Chapter 16 comes a final and powerful recognition scene, when once again under sentence of death, the "strange youth" is suddenly transformed to a "core of white fire" and a pious old servant named Katrina steps forward to kiss the smitten hand.[42]

It will be observed that scrambling the narrative, a technique which began in earnest in *Pudd'nhead Wilson* now seems to have reached crisis proportions. If the adventures of 44 are funny and pathetic at times, capable in spurts of producing magnificent scenes and some genuinely interesting surrealistic touches, still the scenes can seem magnificently pointless, and the overall effect is that of an unfocused and self-indulgent author, not the least of whose indulgences are tasteless blackface routines and a generous sprinkling of anti-semitic one-liners. Though not "patently unreadable" in the final analysis, one cannot easily imagine reading "No. 44" straight through with sustained pleasure.[43] All the same, two matters keep the narrative a concept-book and not a collection of diverse episodes. One is the atmosphere, at once Poesque and Melvillian, provided from the opening page by August Feldner. What this background demonstrates is that the world 44 enters is no machine. Rather, it looms as a Haunted Castle, a confining and constricting interior, done in the manner of the House of Usher or the "Apostles" of *Pierre*, Melville's most Poe-like romance. The second source of ideas is the conduct of 44 once he enters the dark interior. Where Philip Traum, though fairly wallowing in theories about reality, never belonged to the real world, 44 must endure reality, even as he brings it to terms and makes it his plaything. Emerging from his beggar's corner to intimidate and terrorize, but also to serve, to emancipate, to dazzle luminously, above all, to cause material structures to disintegrate and reappear—playing all these parts, the Stranger increasingly seems the Good King-Incognito of legend, revealing his true identity out of a concern for the welfare of his subjects. What will 44 do next? Very soon, one concludes that it lies within his conjurer's power to extinguish the Castle. All he needs is suitable motivation.

According to Professors Tuckey and Gibson, the first eight or nine chapters of this curious, sprawling work were written in 1902–03, while the Clemenses were living in the United States. After their return to Florence, Mark Twain added fifteen or sixteen new chapters in the winter and spring of 1904, and at some point during this period wrote a sequence of six pages, numbered separately and marked "Conclusion of the book." Back in Dublin, New Hampshire, a widower now in 1905, he destroyed (he says) some 30,000 words and replaced them with Chapters 26 to 32, breaking off if not in mid-sentence at least in mid-sequence. (*MSM* 9–11, 489–92, 558–603.) In Chapter 32, madcap 44 thinks of arresting the flow of time, but concludes instead to set all the clocks in the world running backward so that without stirring an inch he and August Feldner can ponder the passage of history from now back to then. As if in the presence of a film run in reverse, they see

> yesterday's battles . . . being refought, wrong-end first; the previously killed were getting killed again; . . . and on the oceans the ships, with full-bellied sails, were speeding backward over the same water they had traversed the day before. . . . (*MSM*, 400.)

They reach the point of watching the split skull of Henry I reassemble itself (the effect being like that of the coat that puts on a man in an animated cartoon sequence or Keystone Cops routine). Thereafter, several hundred pages unbridged to an ending, the manuscript lay dormant, until perhaps thinking of publication, or for whatever reason, Mark Twain returned to write and insert one last chapter in 1908. (*MSM*, 402–12.)

Three things need to be said about Chapter 33, the first of which is that it is cued by and grows directly out of the farce in Chapter 32. Having presumably reached moment zero (the actual first moment of creation), 44 next greatly enlarges the hall of the Castle in order to present history as it moves forward. A second point, therefore, is that the procession he displays to August is superficially akin to the march of civilization that Philip had unscrolled for Theodor. But there are real differences. Whereas Philip's then-to-now was a steady succession of human folly, here no judgments are made, no aspersions cast. Wave upon wave they simply come: "skeletons of Adam's predecessors," the corpses of yesterday, Biblical figures, "kings and kings till you couldn't count them," Arthur and his knights, a woman still weeping for her child lost "five hundred thousand years ago." They are members of a vast multitude whose only "sin" was to be born; they are dancers in a vast, clacking *valse triste,* linked not by guilt or stupidity or greed or vanity; only by the misery they share, the fact that death has brought to not one of them any sense of respite or release. Then Poof!; 44 makes a gesture, and "we stood in an empty and soundless world."

The third point to be made is that Poof!, "silence" and "emptiness" are of course controlling terms in the conclusion that Mark Twain had prepared four years earlier. This six-page fragment may now be understood as a summation—a judgment—of what it means to dwell in the Haunted Castle. For whether time flows *fro* up the corridors of the Castle or flows *to* down the corridors, time is an unparticled, monolithic moment of human suffering. Accordingly, residence in the Castle is not to be borne. As Mark Twain blew up reality at the end of "Old Times on the Mississippi," as Hank Morgan laid waste all physical structures on the last pages of *Yankee,* so 44 here finds in dialogic action a substitute for the words of explanation which eluded Philip Traum. Here 44 razes the real world. In the process of doing so, furthermore, he demolishes one other thing.

Brought down in the shambles of a failed initiation story, Huck had neither the wit nor the insight to explain his situation; all he and Jim could do was continue to act as if nothing strange had happened to them. It required the services of an implied author to backtrack through the narrative and locate in Him who scattered Babel the cause of the failure. The same thing is true at the Battle of the Sand Belt. Though Hank obliterates life, the implied author must manipulate the circumstances that render obliteration necessary. And if in *Pudd'nhead Wilson*, the imbalance of Luigi and Angelo explains the morality of Dawson's Landing (to say nothing of the rest of the world), the "explanation" of Angelo and Luigi must come from characters who, though deeply involved with reality, understand nothing about reality. But 44 has neither illusions nor limitations. He shares with the author a knowledge of who is at fault and where the blame truly lies. He knows all about the Father on the winning side.

That Father might have made us all "French" or all "English," all black or all white, all creatures of consciousness or all automata, instead of creatures whose consciousness is the basis for becoming automata. Oh, as 44 sees, there is no end to what He might have done: He might have made "'good children,'" might have made them "'happy,'" might have made them free of "'biting miseries and maladies of mind and body'"; might have made them "'prize life.'" But there is likewise no end to what the Father did do:

> He preferred to make bad ones . . . cursed his children . . . invented hell . . . created man without invitation, then tries to shuffle the responsibility for man's acts upon man, instead of honorably placing it where it belongs, upon himself . . . (*MSM*, 404–05.)

If the Castle comes tumbling down, so, too, must the Architect by Whom it was planned and built. He is not responsible for a metaphysical error, as Fortyfour once told Oliver Hotchkiss: that could have been corrected. He is guilty of metaphysical persecution. Either He is the malign demon whom Descartes contemplated and discarded. Or He is the Idiot-Clown-as-sadist who in the opening chapter of "Letters From the Earth" devises a cosmos by spinning colored balloons mindlessly—and cruelly—through space. Whichever is true, He must be abolished. And in effect, by reducing His handiwork to dream, 44 enacts the murder of God.

The pronouns of the enactment gradually modulate from singular to plural. "'I am perishing.'" "'You are not you.'" "'I, your poor servant have revealed you to yourself.'" "'We are free.'" And so, no doubt unconsciously, Mark Twain

comes full circle back to the moment of his first literary triumph. Once at center-stage laughter was doubled when a mechanical man from stage-right met
his equally mechanized twin entering from stage left. Now, transformed by the
story from strangers to "brothers," a last set of twins meets center-stage to be
liberated through the dialogue they speak. Mark Twain's curtain which has so
often fallen on scenes of foolishness and cupidity only to ascend immediately
upon other scenes of cupidity and foolishness will rise no more. In a quixotic
way, and in the only way he knows how, Mark Twain has at last written a successful "initiation" story. If life inside the machine shrivels the human spirit,
while looking beyond the machine yields up only 44's portrayal of the unspeak-
able, let the rest be silence. Let time be twinned with Eternity through the creative fiat of extinguishing both. This way, the joke is that there will remain nothing to be initiated into; the snapper is that there will be none left to be initiated.
Exit August. Exit 44. Exit Angelo and Luigi and all their progeny. *Exeunt omnes.*

Or, better to say exit all, save one. For whatever psychic relief comes from
banishing in a few hours of writing-time the cosmos that God wrought in seven
days and devoted countless aeons to corrupting, Mark Twain still looks up to
find himself a participant in the unparticled, monolithic moment. The joke is
finally on him. Like another famous narrator, echoing four narrating voices inside another famous narrative of catastrophe and devastation, Mark Twain has
alone escaped to tell the story. (*Moby-Dick,* "Epilogue"; *Job* I.)


## IV: CONCLUSION: *APRIL FOOLS!*

> If you see a blind man, kick him. Why should you be kinder than God?
> —shared with me by an Egyptian student, as an instance
> of ancient Arabic wisdom.

For Melville a world which cannot be defined metaphysically is a world hopelessly divided, a world characterized by the actions of enhumored twins. *Damned
if I ever knew* could be Tommo's only legitimate response to one who asked him,
*where were you really, Tommo? were you safe or in danger? were "they" the good
ones or the bad ones?* One up-close, the other from a distance, Tommo has
watched the movements of two primitive groups—seen Happars and Typees
enact their rituals, sometimes to seemingly different patterns, more often in apparent concert. But the key to why the twinned groups behave as they do—the
key that would separate cannibalism from benevolence, would truly distinguish malevolence from friendliness—remains forever unfathomed and unfa-
thomable to him. Though the issue in *Typee* is primarily social or "anthropological" (a chapter or two from Lévi-Strauss would have greatly modified

Tommo's dilemma), the situation is electric with philosophic and epistemological questions that will soon come to dominate Melville's fictions. Tommo's response would have to be that of Captain Ahab were someone to ask, *what did you finally find out about Moby-Dick?*, and that of the lawyer-narrator in the face of the query, *what did you ultimately make of Bartleby?* And by the time *Billy Budd* was written the response has become a kind of general consensus. To the question of why characters interact as they do—why fate unites human beings in twinships, yet bans them from meaningful relationships—characters, author, readers (all alike) would have to respond: *fate and ban and this-worldly relationships are the eternal mysteries. Damned if we know what the twins signify. Damned if we ever shall.*

For Mark Twain the world is enhumored and "be-twinned" precisely because life can be known and read aright. Reality is a double, like the two-faced God whom Samuel Clemens described in his 1897 letter to the dead Susy—or, in its own way, like the *Albatross* which bent in close before backing off duplicitously in *Moby-Dick.* As if in an elaborate game of "tag," reality invites being touched, insists upon fealty to the real as the grounds for an intelligently lived and socially useful existence. Then, when one has accepted the invitation (laid hands on the real; declared the fealty; won the game) reality snaps suddenly shut, enclosing one's best hopes and aspirations in a "hell of pains . . . wanton shames and miseries." Together with the God who devised it, the real world never ceases to make overtures—and "never does a kindness."[44] And all alike are doomed to endure the trap which the real world poses. If the dark twin is six months older and strides along six feet in front of his blond counterpart, still (fixed as fate) it *is* always a matter of just six months and just six feet. Despite an appearance of freedom and superiority, the dark twin who tricks and deceives in Mark Twain's narratives is himself finally as much an automaton—as helpless to do or to be otherwise than what he is—as are the addled blond dupes of his trickery. Both move to the measures of the Father who won the war.

Others write a fiction of enhumored lives in the American nineteenth century. In Ernest Sandeen's fine reading of "*The Scarlet Letter* As Love Story," we are shown characters driven by forces beyond their control to ends they would never consciously have wished to achieve.[45] Through his Freudian analysis, John Crowley has drawn our attention to a Howells who, particularly in *A Modern Instance,* portrays human life as desperate, driven, out of all touch with rational solutions for the irrational quandaries it creates, or that are created for it. Yet there is a real sense in which Melville and Mark Twain, who never heard of each other, share an intimacy greater than Melville's with Hawthorne or Mark Twain's with Howells. Where Howells can go on to synthesize the worst and the best in Lapham and to portray Lapham redeemed, and where in "The Maypole of Merrymount" Hawthorne had already pictured the kind of cultural richness that might have come of a symbiotic relationship between the twins "barbarism" and "culture," in the fictions of Melville and Mark Twain there are no "outs" and no exceptions. Flask and the *Rosebud*, who never so much as really heard of him, end up knowing just as much about Moby-Dick as do Ahab and Ishmael, who are obsessed with the white whale. Jim ends up meaning just as much to Huck as Jim means to Tom Sawyer, for whom he exists not as a human being, but (like "ransom") as word or label, an image in Tom's mind. Thus Melville and Mark Twain conspire to present a world of fools, a world wherein the act of presentation itself is but another form of foolishness—though it is one that remains always vitally necessary.

On April 1, a steamboat called the *Fidele* (as miserably misnamed as the *Delight* in *Moby-Dick*) departs the St. Louis wharf bound for New Orleans. Although compass points and geography anticipate those in *The Adventures of Huckleberry Finn*, the ensuing journeys differ in ways more profound than a shift from the ornate interior to the raft-in-the-open-air. For the consecutiveness, what in retrospect seems the inevitability of *Huckleberry Finn, The Confidence Man* substitutes a *discordia concors*. After the opening sequence, one senses that subsequent events could readily be shuffled into a variety of different orders, without greatly affecting the development of the whole. Character relationships either form to dissolve, or form, dissolve and reappear to dissolve again, but whichever is the case remain, with respect to meaning, uncertain and inconclusive. Throughout, one has the impression of being adrift in a wilderness of mirrors, where nothing is what it appears to be, while at the same time each new reflection is, and is only, its actual self. In the end, therefore, the *Fidele* does not simply fail to reach New Orleans. Seeking to twin chimeras with reality, to find the governing principle that would provide purpose and significance to the masks and masquerades in the world below, the steamboat has at once followed a straight line to no destination, and traveled circularly to turn forever backward upon its own opacity. Quite literally, the ship of fools, outward bound on a fool's errand, has moved and moved and gotten nowhere.

Yet on the last page, in the final sentence, there is a resilient voice, promising that "something further may follow of these masquerades." Whether Melville had a sequel already in mind is not to the point, I think. What counts is that, resuming narrative after the lapse of nearly two decades, he used different characters and different settings to tell exactly the same story in *Clarel*, just as, following another fifteen years, the same story would emerge from the concatenation of still other characters and settings in *Billy Budd*. Over the years Melville must have felt increasingly victimized by great peals of hollow, mocking laughter. Exhausted and largely unread by 1857, he had to recognize that his words, like the travelers in *Mardi*, were foredoomed to travel all around a subject without ever reaching it. Still later, he had to see that to pick up the tools of his craft again was to become, like Pierre Glendinning, "'the Fool of Truth, the Fool of Virtue, the Fool of God.'" Somewhere up ahead, though, loomed what Ishmael had called "the key to it all," (*MD*, 979) the promise of some fresh and life-giving dispensation that would pair the doubles, Lower world and Upper world, into a meaningful wholeness. And Melville was compelled to pursue this synthesizing force, even if pursuit left him one more fool in a world of fools, another enhumored self caught in the coils of an enhumoring reality.

The courtroom scene in the next-to-last chapter of *Pudd'nhead Wilson* is prefaced by the April 1 entry from the so-called calendar of David Wilson:

> April 1. This is the day on which we are reminded of what we are on the other three hundred and sixty-four.

April has shaded into October eight pages later, when this entry prefaces the concluding chapter:

> October 12, the Discovery. It was wonderful to find America, but it would have been more wonderful to miss it.

Given the content of the novel, one is surely justified in relating both entries to the American scene. It is a land of fools, a land whose long history of slavery and injustice means that all would have been better off had the great land mass to the West lain forever undiscovered. But I believe the full force of the entries-in-tandem may be realized by changing a single word in the second one. It then reads:

> It was wonderful to find the world, but it would have been more wonderful to miss it.

Ours is the one world we have been vouchsafed, and perhaps we should be grateful for having known it. Yet if life has nothing fairer to show us than the Witch-at-midnight and the Fool-at-high noon, than both Tom Driscolls driven to the same bitter corner, than the false-dawn of comedy underscoring a palpable midnight of farce and tragedy, how better for us to have missed the experience. At the close of his trilogy of the Mississippi, Mark Twain has come face to face with the bitter insight of Sophocles's chorus: "Never to have been born would be best for man."

And now, from the depths of the bitterness, comes a "snapper." Suddenly we recognize that as the book portrays him, poor Wilson could no more have uttered these comments on his own than (say) Ahab and Ishmael might have collaborated in a chorus of "There's a wideness in God's mercy." Sycophant, shyster, detective-as-dullard ("crank," "button," "lever") the Pudd'nhead is merely a ventriloquist's dummy for the fixed and irreversible roles of Luigi and Angelo Capello. But Luigi and Angelo are, in turn, also front men, bespeaking the ways of God who sundered Dark from Light to ensure the invariable triumph of Darkness. And behind them all stands Mark Twain, devising a Chinese box of speakers because he, too, is a mechanical toy, through whom the black universal determinism is made manifest. Wisdom, from whatever mouth it seems to proceed, is but a joke on the unwary, a parodying of what it means to be wise.

No doubt, over the years, he often felt much laughed *at*. An unwilling chronicler of caricatures, he was himself, as he came to acknowledge, the ultimate caricature: "God's fool." But if the comic resolution lay beyond him, there were the jester's cap and bells which could, in some measure, assuage the failure and the frustration. What did he do next, one wonders, when having assured Susy Clemens in a sentence that God could never hurt him again, Samuel Clemens looked up from the page to find that his moment of anguish was interminable? How did he react when, after destroying reality repeatedly in narrative, he laid aside his pen to find there on the wall the old clock, still ticking furiously away, big hand astride little hand, so that it registered both movement and sameness? One fancies he laughed. (In fact, one has hard evidence: in 1909, he created a Satan who would make a direct frontal assault on God in Heaven, and wrote in "Letters From the Earth" the opening sallies of one of the funniest, most acerbic fictions he ever undertook.)[46] Let us honor the funniness of his vision of moral and social futility by joining to laugh *with* him.

## NOTES

1. References to *Redburn* and *Moby-Dick* are from *The Library of America*, ed. G. Thomas Tanselle (New York: Literary Classics of the United States, 1983), 96, 294, 1135, 1000. All subsequent references to *Moby-Dick* (hereafter *MD*) are from this volume. Reference to *The Confidence Man* is to the Norton Critical Edition, ed. Hershel Parker (New York: Norton, 1971), 93. Melville also alludes to Siamese twins in *Israel Potter, Clarel,* and (as we shall see) in *Billy Budd.*

2. See *CY*, 293–96.

3. In *The Melville Log,* ed. Jay Leyda (New York: Harcourt Brace, 1951), II, 836.

4. *Confidence Man,* 112.

5. Chang and Eng were involved with Barnum well after their retirement. In

1869, they suspended procreation briefly and toured England under Barnum's sponsorship. The gimmick was that they were in search of a surgeon who might divide them. It *was* a gimmick of Barnum's. Yet one wonders whether fifteen years later Mark Twain, who never saw Chang and Eng (but was always highly aware of Barnum's showmanship) remembered the projected "surgery" when he wrote *Pudd'nhead Wilson.* See, for much interesting and amusing information, Neil Harris, *Humbug: The Art of P. T. Barnum* (Boston: Little, Brown), 1973.

6. "Bartleby, the Scrivener," in *Great Short Works of Herman Melville,* ed. Warner Berthoff (New York: Harper & Row, 1969), 39–74. All references to "Bartleby" are from this edition.

7. "Bartleby," 45–46, 61. Explication has frequently stressed the Christly role of Bartleby. See, e.g., the history of interpretation from Richard Chase, *Herman Melville* (New York: Macmillan, 1949), 144–49, through John Seelye, *The Ironic Diagram* (Evanston: Northwestern University Press, 1970), 104–05. Seelye, it seems to me, is correct in stressing that Bartleby is both "Christly" and "repellent." One wonders why, until Camille Paglia (of whom more later), no one seems to have found exactly this same combination of qualities in Billy Budd (of whom more later).

8. "Bartleby," 41–45. So far as I am aware, little attempt has been made to discuss Melville in the context of the humors—not even in Edward Rosenberry's fine account of *Melville and the Comic Spirit* (Cambridge: Harvard University Press, 1955). It will therefore bear noting that Melville could have come to the theory of humorous behavior in any of several books he was reading in the late 1840s or early 1850s: Bayle's *Dictionary;* Chambers's *Universal Dictionary of Arts and Sciences;* or of course the *Anatomy of Melancholy* itself. Needless to say, any of these would have offered a fuller, richer version than the one which Sam Clemens was reading five or six years later.

9. A very similar theme is developed in "The Piazza," the diptych "Paradise of Bachelors and Tartarus of Maids," "Cock-A-Doodle-Doo," and most especially in the concluding episode of "Benito Cereno," where differences in national, theological, moral, and historical perspectives are (still more fundamentally) the differences between two enhumored selves: sanguine Delano; melancholy Cereno, each psychically and emotionally unable to be other than what he is, each forever beyond meaningful interchange with the other.

10. The view is treated seriously, though in the end perhaps a bit ambiguously, in the best single book yet written on *Moby-Dick:* Paul Brodtkorb, Jr., *Ishmael's White World* (New Haven: Yale University Press, 1965), 66–82.

11. *Nature* in Whicher, *Selections,* 53, 56.

12. John J. Enck, *Jonson and the Comic Truth* (Madison: University of Wisconsin Press, 1966), 49 and Chapter 3.

The difference between Chapter 36 and Chapter 119 ("The Candles") measures the enhumoring of Ahab. He is shown to descend from a caricature yearning to become a character into a howling, raging madman who has turned into a caricature of himself. No doubt, Melville means Ahab to be Lear in Chapter 119; my sense is that he has merely made him noisy.

13. *MD*, 1045–47. Not insignificantly, the gam with the *Albatross* comes directly after the portrayal of the "Spirit Spout"; it also gives rise to the definition of "gam," which is carefully constructed in the next chapter. All emphasis, in other words, is upon abortive or aborted meetings: encounters which promise to take place, and either do not or result in frustration.

14. *Mark Twain–Howells Letters*, 147–48.

15. *Mark Twain–Howells Letters*, 123–29.

16. *Mark Twain's Autobiography*, II, 268–75, 317–25.

17. *Mark Twain's Autobiography*, II, 331–32.

18. In Franklin Rogers, ed., *Mark Twain's Satires and Burlesques* (Berkeley: University of California Press, 1967), 167–68.

19. There is an excellent discussion of the relations between Angelo and Orion Clemens in Frederick Anderson's introduction to the facsimile edition of *Pudd'nhead Wilson and Those Extraordinary Twins* (San Francisco: Chandler, 1968).

20. *Autobiography*, II, 318, 321.

21. *Autobiography*, II, 268.

22. *The Hamlet* (New York: Vintage, 1958), 22.

23. *Mark Twain: Life As I Find It*, ed. Charles Neider (Garden City, N.Y.: Doubleday, 1961), 232–33.

24. "The Man that Corrupted Hadleyburg," in Blair, *Selected Shorter Writings*, 280.

25. *Which Was It?* in *Which Was the Dream?*, ed. John S. Tuckey (Berkeley: University of California Press, 1967), 266. All references are from this edition, hereafter called *Dream*.

26. I confess to qualms about what I have written. Perhaps my reservations can be clarified through three examples, leading on to a rather clumsy generalization. The examples: Jasper is insistently "the mulatto." The figure who enters so oppressively into Delano's consciousness is, notoriously, "the negro." Through seemingly pointless circumlocutions, "miscegenation" is associated with the act of banishment in "Hadleyburg." (Thus we are told that Goodson falls into disrepute because after her death, the town "found out, or thought it had found out, that [the girl he intended to marry] carried a spoonful of negro blood in her veins," 262. But since the true—or fully dramatized—outcast is Burgess, one is left to wonder if this is an indirect way to saying that Hadleyburg had concluded, rightly or wrongly, that *he* carried a spoonful of negro blood in *his* veins.)

Now the generalization. I believe a book remains to be written on—to use the awkward term—"negritude" in both Melville and Mark Twain. Such a book would surely couple Jim and Pip as potential saviours of their white companions. But it would need to take into account Mark Twain's fondness for minstrel routines, and to explain the curious juxtaposition of "negroes," "sullenly," and "revenge" in the first epigram to Melville's "Bell Tower." Finally, in all candor, it would be compelled to show how both writers at times identify skin pigment with evil, demonic possession—in sum, with Satanic or Manichean darkness, or with the Dark Wing of the allegory in Plato's *Republic*.

With respect to Mark Twain, the book would surely not need to make him as overtly racist as he becomes in Guy Cardwell's *The Man Who Was Mark Twain: Images and Ideologies* (New Haven, 1991); but it would probably be less determinedly multicultural than *Was Huck Black?* I fancy the book would be a trouble to write—and a trouble to read. Nevertheless, it is needed.

27. With respect to the facts: Stedman's connections with *Yankee* are recorded in The Norton Critical Edition, 297–99; with Melville in the *Melville Log*, II, 804–05; Hawthorne's famous observation is taken from *Melville Log*, II, 529.

With respect to the fiction: it contains one lie and one damned lie. The lie is that Mark Twain did not see (or see pictured) the Italian twins until early in the 1890s. The damned lie bears on the uneasiness I have attributed to E. C. Stedman. From the tone of his letter about *Yankee* and of his solicitations to Melville, it is clear that he would have felt no anxiety. He would have regarded himself as the most important figure on the premises.

28. *Billy Budd, Sailor*, ed. Harrison Hayford and Merton M. Sealts, Jr. (Chicago: University of Chicago Press, 1962), 77. All subsequent references to *BB* are from this edition.

29. References to Billy's appearance and background are concentrated on 50–53; the strikingly similar presentation of the physical and historical Claggart is presented on 64–66. Billy's stammer is introduced on 53; the "scorpion" analogy, accompanied by the point that the "creator alone" seems responsible for the scorpion's strike (and hence by extension for Claggart's behavior), is on 78. Though at all points description and backgrounds seem parallel, and the parallels have been duly noted, the possibility of Billy and Claggart as "twins" seems to have received no critical attention.

30. The history of explicating *Billy Budd* makes for a fascinating subject. First, there are the extremes, well represented in E. L. Grant Watson, "Melville's Testament of Acceptance," *New England Quarterly* 6 (June 1933), 319–27, and Lawrance Thompson, *Melville's Quarrel With God* (Princeton, 1952), 355–416. Of equal interest is a shift in focus that separates *Twentieth Century Interpretations*, ed. Howard P. Vincent (1971) from a second collection of essays, *Critical Essays on Melville's Billy Budd, Sailor*, ed. Robert Milder, published two decades later in 1989. Whereas the most interesting critiques in the former (those of Auden, Camus, Montale, etc.) stress Billy and Claggart, the best essays in the second (those of Charles Reich, Joyce Adler, Barbara Johnson, Brook Thomas) are socially-politically-"linguistically" oriented, and can scarcely wait to get to the subject of Captain Vere. In their anxiety to deconstruct the narrative or to translate it into some one or another of the postmodern critical disciplines, recent critics seem to forget that Vere exists and has meaning solely by virtue of his being the observer

of Billy and Claggart. They are extremely sophisticated essays; but this does not obviate the fact that they are talking more at what Melville wrote than about it. The significant exception would be a fine essay by Paul Brodtkorb, Jr., "The Definitive *Billy Budd*," to which I shall return.

31. According to Sealts and Hayford, Melville appended "end of book" to the ms. on April 19, 1891. He died in September of that year. (*BB*, 11–12.)

32. As was the case with *Moby-Dick*, I find the shrewdest reading of *Billy Budd* to be offered by Paul Brodtkorb, Jr., in "The Definitive *Billy Budd*: 'But Aren't It All Sham?'" *PMLA* 82 (1976), 602–12. "What the story records," says Professor Brodtkorb, "is Melville's last and dogged making up his mind (as he once prematurely told Hawthorne he had 'pretty much done') to be annihilated."

33. Camille Paglia, *Sexual Personae*, 594.

34. Actually Mark Twain's cosmology is of more than passing interest. In "Letters from the Earth" (written in 1899; not published until 1962) Satan has not been cast out of Heaven, in the manner of *Paradise Lost*. Together with Michael and Gabriel, he functions as the third member of an often bewildered Grand Council, sitting at God's Right Hand. Though sometimes banished for his sharp tongue, he is a Visitor on Earth, and his Letters (sent home) are addressed to Heaven. He thus has less in common with Milton than with *Job*, where Satan goes "to and fro in the earth" and reports back to the Lord. I am indebted to Elaine Pagels, *The Origin of Satan* (New York: Random House, 1995), for useful distinctions between demonology in the Old Testament (upon which Mark Twain appears to draw) and the New.

35. Mark Twain refers to "the Admirable Crichton" twice in his notes for "Schoolhouse Hill." See *Mysterious Stranger Manuscripts*, 428, 435. Interestingly enough, when Barrie used the same figure three years later, he did so in a perfectly executed (and perfectly snobbish) Edwardian comedy of manners.

36. *Mark Twain's Mysterious Stranger Manuscripts*, ed. William M. Gibson (Berkeley: University of California Press, 1969), 217. Except where noted, all references are to materials in this volume, hereafter *MSM*.

37. In 1897 Mark Twain set down a series of notebook jottings which he entitled "Villagers of 1840–3." Though the ugliness of Hannibal (or as it is called "St. P.") sometimes breaks through, the surprising thing is the degree to which the village is now seen as simple and idyllic, a place where purity and prudence are very much in the foreground. Clearly this conception is the stumbling block of "School House Hill." Mark Twain is no longer prepared to confine the "damned human race" to the actors and activities of a single Missouri village, partly perhaps because of nostalgia, but more especially, one suspects, because he needs for his subject the whole sweep of human history. It is this totalized picture which the other two parts of the trilogy will supply in great detail. "Villagers" was published for the first time in Walter Blair's collection *Mark Twain's Hannibal, Huck and Tom* (Berkeley: University of California Press, 1969), 24–36.

38. *The Mysterious Stranger* in Blair, *Selected Shorter Writings of Mark Twain*, 371. Although Professor Blair omits the subtitle, all references are to *MSR*.

39. Cox, *The Fate of Humor*, 270, 272. It should be emphasized, however, that not all the scholarly community has been so content with Paine's meddling. Thus in his introduction to *MSM*, William Gibson pronounces the publication of 1916 a "fraud," and goes on to hope that someday another "writer will imagine a new, wholly satisfying ending to 'The Chronicle of Young Satan' . . . or perhaps be able to condense, rework and strengthen 'No. 44' and end it with [the] last chapter in its proper place." (62.)

Admiring his honesty, one nevertheless finds Professor Gibson's hope a trifle ridiculous. What could one more reconstruction bring to pass except a further muddying of Mark Twain's intentions—a "new" retelling that would be as much facsimile as what Paine cobbled together? The best way of dealing with the material, as I am trying to show, lies in granting each text its own integrity, and then reading all three serially, as if they were conjoined as parts of a trilogy.

40. Titled "In My Bitterness" by John Tuckey the letter was first published by Professor Tuckey in *Mark Twain's Fables of Man*, 131–32. It reads "You are out of His reach forever; and I too; He can never hurt me any more."

41. James Cox also notes how Philip backs off from attacking God directly, and offers (as one explanation) the problem of accommodating the attack to Mark Twain's initiation story. See *Fate of Humor*, 281.

42. *MSM*, 369, 308–09. Though the interpretation of any character-relationship is risky in "No. 44," I hazard the following conjecture: Emil Schwarz is established as the dream-self or double of August Feldner. Thus when 44 releases Emil from the bonds of flesh, he is satisfying an unconscious desire of August himself—a wish that will be fulfilled explicitly in the conclusion of the narrative.

43. The most sustained attempt to do so is that of Sholom J. Kahn, *Mark Twain's Mysterious Stranger: A Study of the Manuscript Texts* (Columbia and London: University of Missouri Press, 1978), 91–190.

44. "In My Bitterness," 131.

45. In *PMLA* 77 (1962), 425–35. For Howells on enhumored lives, see John W. Crowley, *The Black Heart's Truth: The Early Career of William Dean Howells* (Chapel Hill: University of North Carolina Press, 1985.)

46. Critics were entertained when "Letters from the Earth" was finally published in 1962, though the common complaint was that in a more-or-less secular age Mark Twain's tirades against God had somewhat lost their bite. But, to quote Robert Coover, "the universe is closing in on us again." And I hope it will betray a prejudice if I suggest that the Christian Right could profit from reading Mark Twain's Satan on the analysis of Old Testament brutalities—or on the topic of God, Godly knowledge, and the hookworm. Coover's phrase is from "Seven Exemplary Fictions" in *Pricksongs and Descants*, 78; "Letters from the Earth" are in Paul Baender's edition of *What is Man?*, 401–54.

# Selected Bibliography

## BOOKS

Anderson, Frederick, ed. Introduction to Facsimile Edition of *Pudd'nhead Wilson and Those Extraordinary Twins*. San Francisco: Chandler, 1968.

—— et al., eds. *Mark Twain's Notebooks and Journals*, Vols. I–III. Berkeley: University of California Press, 1975, 1979.

——, William M. Gibson, and Henry Nash Smith, eds. *Selected Mark Twain–Howells Letters, 1872–1910*. Cambridge: Harvard University Press, 1967.

Auden, W. H. *The Dyer's Hand*. New York: Random House, 1948.

——. *The Enchafed Flood*. London: Faber and Faber, 1951.

——. *Secondary Worlds: Essays*. New York: Random House, 1968.

Auerbach, Erich. *Mimesis*. Garden City, N.Y.: Doubleday, 1957.

Baender, Paul, ed. *Adventures of Tom Sawyer. Facsimilie of the Author's Holograph Manuscript*. Frederick, Md.: University Publications of America, 1982.

Baetzhold, Howard G. *Mark Twain and John Bull, the British Connection*. Bloomington: Indiana University Press, 1970.

Bakhtin, Mikhail. *Problems of Dostoevski's Poetics*, tr. Caryl Emerson. Minneapolis: University of Minnesota Press, 1987.

——. *The Dialogic Imagination*, tr. and ed. Caryl Emerson and Michael Holquist. Austin: University of Texas Press, 1981.

——. *A Bakhtin Reader*. Ed. Pam Morris. London and New York: E. Arnold, 1994.

Becker, George. *Documents of Modern Literary Realism*. Princeton: Princeton University Press, 1963.

Bellamy, Edward. *Looking Backward*. New York: New American Library, 1960.

Bellamy, Gladys Carmen. *Mark Twain As a Literary Artist*. Norman: University of Oklahoma Press, 1950.

Bentley, Eric. *The Life of Drama*. New York: Atheneum, 1964.

Berthoff, Warner. *The Example of Melville*. Princeton: Princeton University Press, 1962.

——, ed. *Great Short Works of Herman Melville*. New York: Harper and Row, 1969.

Blair, Walter. *Mark Twain and Huck Finn*. Berkeley: University of California Press, 1962.

——, ed. *Selected Shorter Writings of Mark Twain*. Boston: Houghton Mifflin, 1962.

——, ed. *Mark Twain's Hannibal, Huck and Tom*. Berkeley: University of California Press, 1969.

——, ed. *Native American Humor*. San Francisco: Chandler, 1960.

———, ed. *Huck Finn and Tom Sawyer Among the Indians and Other Unfinished Stories.* Berkeley: University of California Press, 1969.

Blues, Thomas. *Mark Twain and the Community.* Lexington: University Press of Kentucky, 1970.

Bobb, Earl Victor. *Education, the Protagonist, and the Nature of Knowledge in Melville and Mark Twain.* Ph.D. diss., University of Oregon, 1977.

Botkin, B. A., ed. *A Treasury of Mississippi Folklore.* New York: Bonanza, 1955.

Branch, Edgar. *Literary Apprenticeship of Mark Twain.* New York: Russell and Russell, 1966.

Brodtkorb, Paul, Jr. *Ishmael's White World.* New Haven: Yale University Press, 1965.

Brooks, Van Wyck. *Ordeal of Mark Twain.* New York: Dutton, 1933.

Brown, Peter. *Augustine of Hippo.* Berkeley: University of California Press, 1969.

Budd, Louis J. *Mark Twain, Social Philosopher.* Bloomington: Indiana University Press, 1962.

Cady, Edwin, and Louis J. Budd, eds. *On Mark Twain: The Best from American Literature.* Durham: Duke University Press, 1987.

Camfield, Gregg. *Sentimental Twain, Samuel Clemens in the Maze of Moral Philosophy.* Philadelphia: University of Pennsylvania Press, 1994.

Camus, Albert. *Myth of Sisyphus and Other Essays,* tr. Justin O'Brien. New York: Vintage Books, 1955.

Cardwell, Guy. *The Man Who Was Mark Twain: Images and Ideologies.* New Haven: Yale University Press, 1991.

Caron, James E., and E. Thomas Inge, eds. *Sut Luvingood's Nat'ral Born Yarnspinner: Essays on George Washington Harris.* Tuscaloosa: University of Alabama Press, 1996.

Carrington, George. *The Dramatic Unity of Huckleberry Finn.* Columbus: Ohio State University Press, 1976.

Cassill, Kay. *Twins: Nature's Amazing Mystery.* New York: Atheneum, 1982.

Chase, Richard. *The American Novel and Its Tradition.* New York: Doubleday, 1957.

———. *Herman Melville.* New York: Macmilllan, 1949.

Clemens, Samuel L. *The Adventures of Huckleberry Finn,* ed. Walter Blair and Victor Fischer. Berkeley: University of California Press, 1985.

———. *The Adventures of Tom Sawyer,* ed. John C. Gerber, Paul Baender, and Terry Firkins. Berkeley: University of California Press, 1980.

———. *A Connecticut Yankee in King Arthur's Court,* ed. Allison R. Ensor. Norton Critical Editions. New York: Norton, 1982.

———. *Letters from the Earth [and New Uncensored Writings by Mark Twain],* ed. Bernard DeVoto. Greenwich, Conn.: Fawcett, Crest, 1962.

———. *Life on the Mississippi.* The Signet Edition. New York: New American Library, 1961.

——. *Mysterious Stranger Manuscripts,* ed. William Gibson. Berkeley: University of California Press, 1969.

——. *Pudd'nhead Wilson and Those Extraordinary Twins,* ed. Sidney E. Berger. Norton Critical Edition. New York: Norton, 1980.

——. *Roughing It.* The Signet Edition. New York: New American Library, 1962.

——. *Mark Twain's Satires and Burlesques,* ed. Franklin R. Rogers. Berkeley: University of California Press, 1967.

——. *What Is Man? and Other Philosophical Writings,* ed. Paul Baender. Berkeley: University of California Press, 1973.

——. *Which Was the Dream? and Other Symbolic Writings,* ed. John S. Tuckey. Berkeley: University of California Press, 1967.

Coleridge, S. T. *Selected Poetry and Prose,* ed. Elisabeth Schneider. New York: Holt, Rinehart and Winston, 1962.

Corrigan, Robert, ed. *Comedy: Meaning and Form.* San Francisco: Chandler, 1965.

Cox, James. *Mark Twain: The Fate of Humor.* Princeton: Princeton University Press, 1966.

Crowley, John W. *The Black Heart's Truth: The Early Career of William Dean Howells.* Chapel Hill: University of North Carolina Press, 1985.

Cummings, Sherwood. *Mark Twain and Science: The Adventures of a Mind.* Baton Rouge: Louisiana State University Press, 1989.

DeVoto, Bernard. *Mark Twain at Work.* Cambridge: Harvard University Press, 1942.

——. *Mark Twain in Eruption.* New York: Harper, 1940.

Doyno, Victor A. *Writing Huck Finn: Mark Twain's Creative Process.* Philadelphia: University of Pennsylvania Press, 1991.

——, ed. *Adventures of Huckleberry Finn: The Only Comprehensive Edition.* New York: Random House, 1996.

Dryden, Edgar. *Melville's Thematics of Form.* Baltimore: Johns Hopkins University Press, 1981.

Emerson, Ralph Waldo. *Selections,* ed. Stephen E. Whicher. New York: Harper, 1965.

Enck, John J. *Jonson and the Comic Truth.* Madison: University of Wisconsin Press, 1966.

Faulkner, William. *Go Down Moses.* New York: The Modern Library, 1942.

——. *The Hamlet.* New York: Vintage Books, 1958.

Fiedler, Leslie. *Love and Death in the American Novel.* Cleveland: Dell, 1966.

Fishkin, Shelley Fisher. *Was Huck Black? Mark Twain and African American Voices.* New York and London: Oxford University Press, 1993.

Florence, Don. *Persona and Humor in Mark Twain's Early Writings.* Columbia: University of Missouri Press, 1995.

Franklin, H. Bruce. *Prison Life in America.* New York: Oxford University Press, 1989.

——. *The Victim as Criminal and Artist.* New York: Oxford University Press, 1978.

———. "Mark Twain and Science Fiction." In *Future Perfect: American Science Fiction of the Nineteenth Century.* New York: Oxford University Press, 1966.

Freud, Sigmund. *Jokes and Their Relation to the Unconscious,* tr. James Strachey. New York: Norton, 1960.

———. *Pelican Freud Library.* London: Pelican, 1955–60.

Fromm, Erich. *Escape from Freedom.* New York: Farrar and Rinehart, 1941.

Fruman, Norman. *Coleridge, The Damaged Archangel.* New York: G. Braziller, 1971.

Frye, Northrop. *Anatomy of Criticism.* Princeton: Princeton University Press, 1957.

———. "The Argument of Comedy." *English Institute Essays.* New York: Columbia University Press, 1949.

Gay, Peter. *Reading Freud: Explorations and Entertainments.* New Haven: Yale University Press, 1990.

Geismar, Maxwell. *Mark Twain: An American Prophet.* Boston: Houghton Mifflin, 1970.

Gerber, John C. "The Relation Between Point of View and Style in the Works of Mark Twain." *English Institute Essays.* New York: Columbia University Press, 1958.

Gillman, Susan. *Dark Twins: Imposture and Identity in Mark Twain's America.* Chicago: University of Chicago Press, 1989.

———, and Forrest G. Robinson, eds. *Mark Twain's* Pudd'nhead Wilson: *Race, Conflict, and Culture.* Durham: Duke University Press, 1990.

Gribben, Alan. *Mark Twain's Library.* Boston: G. K. Hall, 1980.

Hardwick, Elizabeth. *Bartleby in Manhattan and Other Essays.* New York: Random House, 1983.

Hauck, Richard B. *A Cheerful Nihilism: Confidence and the Absurd in American Humorous Fiction.* Bloomington: Indiana University Press, 1971.

Higgins, Brian, ed. *Critical Essays on Moby-Dick.* New York: G. K. Hall, 1992.

Hill, Hamlin. *Mark Twain: God's Fool.* New York: Harper, 1973.

Hoffman, Andrew, *Twain's Worlds; Twain's Heroes.* Philadelphia: University of Pennsylvania Press, 1988.

Hook, Sidney, ed. *Determinism and Freedom in the Age of Modern Science.* New York: Dell, 1958.

Howells, William Dean. *My Mark Twain.* New York: Harper, 1911.

———. *The Rise of Silas Lapham,* ed. Don L. Cook. Norton Critical Edition. New York: Norton, 1982.

Huxley, Aldous. *Brave New World.* New York: Bantam, 1946.

James, Henry. *The Portrait of a Lady,* ed. Robert Bamberg. Norton Critical Edition. New York: Norton, 1975.

Johnson, Edgar. *Charles Dickens: His Tragedy and Triumph.* London: V. Gollancz, 1952.

Johnson, James Lyndon. *Mark Twain and the Limits of Power: Emerson's God in Ruins.* Knoxville: University of Tennessee Press, 1982.

Jonas, Hans. *The Gnostic Religion.* Boston: Beacon Press, 1958.

Kahn, Sholom J. *Mark Twain's Mysterious Stranger: A Study of the Manuscript Texts.* Columbia, Mo.: University of Missouri Press, 1978.

Kaplan, Justin. *Mr. Clemens and Mark Twain.* New York: Simon and Schuster, 1966.

Karcher, Carolyn. *Shadow Over the Promised Land: Slavery, Race and Violence in Melville's America.* Baton Rouge: Louisiana State University Press, 1980.

Ker, N. P., ed. *Morte d'Arthur.* New York and London: Oxford University Press, 1976.

Kerr, Walter. *Tragedy and Comedy.* New York: Simon and Schuster, 1967.

Kiely, Robert. *Reverse Tradition.* Cambridge: Harvard University Press, 1993.

Kraus, Sidney, ed. *Essays on Determinism in American Literature.* Kent: Kent State University Press, 1964.

Langer, Susanne. *Feeling and Forms.* New York: Scribners, 1953.

Leonard, James S., and Thadius M. Davis, eds. *Satire or Evasion? Black Perspectives on Huckleberry Finn.* Durham: Duke University Press, 1992.

Levine, Lawrence. *Black Culture and Black Consciousness: Afro-American Folk Thought from Slavery to Freedom.* New York: Oxford University Press, 1977.

Leyda, Jay, ed. *The Melville Log.* New York: Harcourt Brace, 1951.

Lodge, David. *Modes of Modern Fiction.* Ithaca: Cornell University Press, 1977.

Long, E. Hudson. *Mark Twain Handbook.* New York: Hendricks House, 1957.

Lynn Kenneth S. *Mark Twain and Southwestern Humor.* Boston: Little, Brown, 1959.

Melville, Herman. *Moby-Dick,* ed. G. Thomas Tanselle. New York: Literary Classics of the United States, 1983.

———. *Billy Budd, Sailor,* ed. Harrison Hayford and Merton Sealts. Chicago: University of Chicago Press, 1962.

———. *The Confidence Man,* ed. Hershel Parker. Norton Critical Edition. New York: Norton, 1971.

Michelson, Bruce. *Mark Twain on the Loose: The Comic Writer and the American Self.* Amherst: University of Massachusetts Press, 1994.

Milder, Robert, ed. *Critical Essays on Melville's Billy Budd, Sailor.* Boston: G. K. Hall, 1989.

Miller, J. Hillis. "Three Problems of Fictional Form: First-Person Narration in *David Copperfield* and *Huckleberry Finn,*" in *Experience in the Novel: Selected Papers from the English Institute.* New York: Columbia University Press, 1968, pp. 35–60.

———. *The Disappearance of God.* Cambridge: Harvard University Press, 1963.

Mitchell, Wesley. *What Veblen Taught.* New York: Viking, 1947.

Molière. *Tartuffe,* tr. Richard Wilbur. New York: Harcourt, Brace & World, 1965.

Morreal, John, ed. *The Philosophy of Laughter and Humor.* Albany: State University of New York Press, 1987.

Morris, Wright, ed. *The Tragedy of Pudd'nhead Wilson.* The Signet Edition. New York: New American Library, 1964.

Neider, Charles, ed. *Mark Twain: Life as I Find It.* Garden City, N.Y.: Doubleday, 1961.

Orwell, George. *1984*. New York: Harcourt Brace, 1948.

———. *Collected Essays, Journalism and Letters*, ed. Sonia Orwell and Ian Argus. London: Hammersmith, 1970.

Pagels, Elaine. *The Origin of Satan*. New York: Random House, 1995.

Paglia, Camille. *Sexual Personae: Art and Decadence from Nefertiti to Emily Dickinson*. New York: Vintage, 1991.

Paine, Albert Bigelow. *Mark Twain: A Biography*. New York: Harper, 1912.

———, ed. *Mark Twain's Autobiography*. New York: Harper, 1924.

———, ed. *Mark Twain Notebook*. New York: Harper, 1936.

Parker, Hershel. *Reading Billy Budd*. Evanston: Northwestern University Press, 1990.

———. *Flawed Texts and Verbal Icons*. Evanston: Northwestern University Press, 1984.

Plato. *Great Dialogues*. New York: Mentor, 1956.

Pommer, Henry. *Milton and Melville*. Pittsburgh: Pittsburgh University Press, 1950.

Regan, Robert. *Unpromising Heroes: Mark Twain and His Characters*. Berkeley: University of California Press, 1966.

Richards, I. A. *Coleridge On Imagination*. London: Rutledge and K. Paul, 1950.

Robinson, Forrest G. *In Bad Faith: The Dynamics of Deception in Mark Twain's America*. Cambridge: Harvard University Press, 1988.

Rogers, Franklin. *Mark Twain's Burlesque Patterns*. Dallas: Southern Methodist University Press, 1960.

Rulon, Curt M. "The Dialects in *Huckleberry Finn*." Ph.D. diss. University of Iowa, 1967.

Sattlemeyer, Robert, and J. Donald Crowley, eds. *One Hundred Years of Huckleberry Finn*. Columbia: University of Missouri Press, 1985.

Sealts, Merton. *Melville: A Checklist of Books Owned and Borrowed*. Madison: University of Wisconsin Press, 1966.

———. *Melville's Reading*. Columbia, S.C.: University of South Carolina Press, 1988.

Seelye, John. *The Ironic Diagram*. Evanston: Northwestern University Press, 1970.

Sewell, David. *Mark Twain's Languages*. Berkeley: University of California Press, 1987.

Sloane, David E. E. *Mark Twain as a Literary Comedian*. Baton Rouge: Louisiana State University Press, 1979.

Smith, Henry Nash. *Mark Twain: The Development of a Writer*. Cambridge: Harvard University Press, 1962.

———. *Mark Twain's Fable of Progress: Political and Economic Ideas in a Connecticut Yankee*. New Brunswick: Rutgers University Press, 1964.

Stevenson, Robert Louis. "Strange Case of Dr. Jekyll and Mr. Hyde." *Complete Short Stories of Robert Louis Stevenson*, ed. Charles Neider. Garden City, N.Y.: Doubleday, 1969.

Stone, Albert E. *The Innocent Eye: Childhood in Mark Twain*. New Haven: Yale University Press, 1961.

Sutcliff, Rosemary. *The Sword and Circle: King Arthur and the Knights of the Round Table.* New York: Dutton, 1981.

Sypher, Wiley, ed. *An Essay on Comedy.* Baltimore: Johns Hopkins University Press, 1956.

Tave, Stuart. *The Amiable Humorist: A Study in Comic Theory and Criticism.* Chicago: University of Chicago Press, 1960.

Tuckey, John S., ed. *Mark Twain's Fables of Man.* Berkeley: University of California Press, 1972.

——. *Mark Twain and Little Satan.* West Lafayette: Purdue Studies, 1963.

——. *Mark Twain's Mysterious Stranger and the Critics.* Belmont, Calif.: Wadsworth, 1968.

Vanderbilt, Kermit. *The Achievement of William Dean Howells.* Princeton: Princeton University Press, 1968.

Veblen, Thorstein. *The Theory of the Leisure Class.* The Modern Library. New York, 1948.

Vincent, Howard P., ed. *Bartleby the Scrivener, A Symposium.* Kent: Kent University Press, 1971.

——, ed. *Twentieth Century Interpretations of Billy Budd.* Englewood Cliffs, N.J.: Prentice-Hall, 1971.

Voltaire. *Candide,* tr. Lowell Bair. New York: Bantam, 1961.

Weaver, George Sumner. *Lectures on Mental Science According to the Philosophy of Phrenology.* New York: Fowlers and Wells, 1852. (Photocopy)

Wecter, Dixon, ed. *Love Letters of Mark Twain.* New York: Harper, 1949.

——. *Sam Clemens of Hannibal.* Boston: Houghton Mifflin, 1952.

Wiggins, Robert. *Mark Twain, Jackleg Novelist.* Seattle: University of Washington Press, 1964.

Wilson, Edmund. *Patriotic Gore.* New York: Oxford University Press, 1960.

Wonham, Henry. *Mark Twain and the Art of the Tall Tale.* New York: Oxford University Press, 1993.

Wood, Michael. *In Search of the Dark Ages.* New York: Facts on File, 1987.

Woodward, C. Vann. *Strange Career of Jim Crow.* New York: Oxford University Press, 1960.

Wrobel, Arthur, ed. *Pseudoscience and Society in Nineteenth Century America.* Lexington: University Press of Kentucky, 1987.

## ARTICLES

(Many of the most stimulating recent articles on both Mark Twain and Melville have been written for the collections and symposia, listed under "Books.")

Baender, Paul. "Alias Macfarlane: A Revision of Mark Twain Biography." *American Literature* 38 (May 1966), 187–97.

——. "'The Jumping Frog' As a Comedian's First Virtue." *Philological Quarterly* 40 (February 1963), 120–29.

Banta, Martha. "Escape and Entry in *Huckleberry Finn*," *Modern Fiction Studies* 14 (Spring 1968), 79–91.

Beaver, Harold. "Run, Nigger, Run: *Adventures of Huckleberry Finn* As a Fugitive Slave Narrative." *Journal of American Studies* 8, No. 3 (December 1974), 339–61.

Benardete, Jane Johnson. "*Huckleberry Finn* and the Nature of Fiction." *Massachusetts Review* 9 (Spring 1968), 209–26.

Blair, Walter. "On the Structure of *Tom Sawyer*." *Modern Philology* 37 (August 1939), 75–88.

Brodtkorb, Paul. "The Definitive *Billy Budd*: 'But Arn't It All Sham?'" *PMLA* 82 (1976), 602–12.

Brodwin, Stanley. "Mark Twain's Masks of Satan: The Final Phase." *American Literature* 45 (May 1973), 206–27.

——. "Blackness and the Edenic Myth in Mark Twain's *Pudd'nhead Wilson*." *Texas Studies in Literature and Language* 15 (1973–74), 167–76.

Carkeet, David. "The Dialects in *Huckleberry Finn*." *American Literature* 51 (November 1960), 315–32.

Carter, Everett. "The Meaning of *A Connecticut Yankee*." *American Literature* 50 (1978), 418–40.

Cummings, Sherwood. "Mark Twain's Acceptance of Science." *Centennial Review* 6 (1962), 245–61.

——. "Mark Twain's Theory of Realism: or the Science of Piloting." *Studies in American Humor* 2 (1976), 209–21.

——. "*What Is Man?*: The Scientific Sources." In *Essays on Determinism in American Literature*, ed. Sidney Kraus. Kent: Kent State University Press, 1964.

Duncan, Jeffrey L. "The Empirical and the Ideal in Mark Twain." *PMLA* 95 (1980), 201–12.

Ellison, Ralph. "Change the Joke and Slip the Yoke." *Partisan Review* 25 (1958), 212–22.

Fetterly, Judith. "The Sanctioned Rebel." *Studies in the Novel* 3 (1971), 293–304.

——. "Disenchantment: Tom Sawyer in *Huckleberry Finn*." *PMLA* 87 (January 1972), 69–74.

——. "Yankee Showman and Reformer: The Character of Hank Morgan." *Texas Studies in Literature and Language* 14 (Winter 1973), 667–79.

Fussell, Edwin S. "The Structural Problem of *The Mysterious Stranger*." *Studies in Philology* 49 (1952), 95–104.

Gerber, John C. "*Pudd'nhead Wilson* as Fabulation." *Studies in American Humor* 2 (1975), 21–31.

Green, Timothy. "The Comic Theory of W. H. Auden." *Renascence* 39 (Winter 1977), 86–95.

Gribben, Alan. "Mark Twain, Phrenology and the 'Temperaments': A Study of Pseudo-scientific Influence." *American Quarterly* 24 (March 1972), 45–68.

Hansen, Arlen J. "Entropy and Transformation: Two Types of American Humor." *American Scholar* 43 (Summer 1974), 405–21.

Hansen, Chadwick. "The Character of Jim and the Ending of *Huckleberry Finn*." *Massachusetts Review* 5 (Autumn 1963), 45–66.

———. "The Once and Future Boss." *Nineteenth Century Fiction* 28 (1973), 62–73.

Hays, John Q. "Mark Twain's Rebellion Against God: Origins." *Southwestern American Literature* 3 (1973), 27–38.

Hill, Hamlin. "The Composition and Structure of *Tom Sawyer*." *American Literature* 32 (January 1961), 379–92.

Hoffman, Michael J. "Huck's Ironic Circle." *Georgia Review* 23 (Fall 1969), 307–22.

Jehlen, Myra. "The Ties that Bind: Race and Sex in *Pudd'nhead Wilson*." *American Literary History* 2 (1990), 39–95.

Kallen, Horace. "The Aesthetic Principle in Comedy." *American Journal of Psychology* 22 (April 1911), 137–57.

Ketterer, David. "Epoch—Eclipse and Apocalypse: Special 'Effects' in *A Connecticut Yankee*." *PMLA* 88 (October 1973), 1104–14.

Lehmann, Benjamin. "Comedy and Laughter." *University of California English Studies* 10 (1954), 81–101.

Marx, Leo. "Mr. Eliot, Mr. Trilling, and *Huckleberry Finn*." *American Scholar* 4 (Autumn 1953), 423–40.

Parsons, Coleman. "The Background of The Mysterious Stranger." *American Literature* 32 (March 1960), 55–79.

Pearce, Roy Harvey. "Huck Finn in his History." *Etudes Anglaises* 24 (1971), 283–91.

Schmidt, Paul. "The Deadpan on Simon Wheeler." *Southwest Review* 41 (Summer 1956), 270–77.

Schmitz, Neil. "The Paradox of Liberation in *Huckleberry Finn*." *Texas Studies in Literature and Language* 13 (1971), 125–36.

———. "Twain, *Huckleberry Finn*, and the Reconstruction." *American Studies* 12 (Spring 1971), 59–67.

Smiley, Jane. "Say It Ain't So, Huck: Second Thoughts on Mark Twain's 'Masterpiece.'" *Harper's* 269 (January 1996), 61–67.

Tanner, Tony. "The Lost America—the Despair of Henry Adams and Mark Twain." *Modern Age* 5 (Summer 1961), 299–310.

Waggoner, Hyatt. "Science in the Thought of Mark Twain." *American Literature* 8 (1937), 357–70.

Wexman, Virginia. "The Role of Structure in *Tom Sawyer* and *Huckleberry Finn*." *American Literary Realism* 6 (Winter 1973), 1–11.

Wigger, Anne P. "The Composition of Mark Twain's *Pudd'nhead Wilson and Those Extraordinary Twins*." *Modern Philology* 8 (November 1957), 93–102.

Wilson, James D. "Huck Finn: From Abstraction to Humanity." *Southern Review* 10 (1974), 80–94.

———. "'The Monumental Sarcasm of the Ages': Science and Pseudoscience in the Thought of Mark Twain." *South Atlantic Bulletin* 40 (1975), 72–82.

# Index